# WOMEN AND RIGHT-WING MOVEMENTS
## *Indian Experiences*

Edited by

TANIKA SARKAR

URVASHI BUTALIA

**Zed Books Ltd**
London and New Jersey
1995

*Women and Right-Wing Movements:*
*Indian Experiences*
was first published in South Asia by Kali for Women,
B 1/8 Hauz Khas, New Delhi 110 016, India

and in the rest of the world

by

**Zed Books Limited**
**7 Cynthia Street**
**London N1 9JF**
**U.K.**

ISBN 1-85649-289-3 hb
ISBN 1-85649-290-0 pb

*Cover designed by Andrew Corbett*

Typeset by Shruti Designs, New Delhi 110085 and
printed at Pauls Press, E 44/11 Okhla Phase II, New Delhi 110020

A catalogue record for this book is available
from the British Library

US CIP data is available from the Library of
Congress

# Contents

Introductory Remarks
  TANIKA SARKAR AND URVASHI BUTALIA                          1

'Where Women are Worshipped, there the Gods Rejoice':
  The Mirage of the Ancestress of the Hindu Woman
  KUMKUM ROY                                                10

Surat, Savarkar and Draupadi: Legitimising
  Rape as a Political Weapon
  PURSHOTTAM AGARWAL                                         29

Muslims and Hindus, Men and Women:
  Communal Stereotypes and the Partition of India
  URVASHI BUTALIA                                            58

Communalising Gender, Engendering Community:
  Women, Legal Discourse and the Saffron Agenda
  RATNA KAPUR AND BRENDA COSSMAN                             82

The Frying Pan or the Fire ? Endangered Identities,
  Gendered Institutions and Women's Survival
  VASANTH KANNABIRAN AND KALPANA KANNABIRAN                 121

Redefining the Agenda of the Women's Movement
  within a Secular Framework
  FLAVIA AGNES                                              136

Feminism Inverted: The Gendered Imagery
  and Real Women of Hindu Nationalism
  AMRITA BASU                                               158

Heroic Women, Mother Goddesses:
  Family and Organisation in Hindutva Politics
    TANIKA SARKAR                                              181

Hindu Nationalism and the Construction of Woman:
The Shiv Sena Organises Women in Bombay
    SIKATA BANERJEE                                            216

The Woman Shiv Sainik and her Sister Swayamsevika
    TEESTA SETALVAD                                            233

Women, Hindutva and the Politics of Caste in Tamil Nadu
    V GEETHA AND  T V JAYANTHI                                 245

Resisting Women
    ZAKIA PATHAK  AND  SASWATI SENGUPTA                        270

Report of the Women's Delegation to Bhopal,
  Ahmedabad and Surat
    AIDWA/CWDS/MDS/NFIW                                        299

Interviews with Women
    S ANITHA, MANISHA, VASUDHA, KAVITHA                        325

## Dedication

*For CV Subbarao, friend and guide,
with love and remembrance*

# Introductory Remarks

## TANIKA SARKAR and URVASHI BUTALIA

### I

On 6 December, 1992, self-styled Hindutva militants demolished a historical mosque and unleashed a storm of violence against the besieged community of Indian Muslims. The forces of the Indian state reacted to the carnage with partisan fervour, withdrawing even a semblance of protection from the victims. Compared to the current international scale of ethnic violence, and given the fact that Indian governments have more often than not shielded and furthered violence by groups with social power — high castes, landlords, capitalists and men — the events of 6 December do not seem to constitute a very important turning point. Nonetheless, their significance was crucial and overwhelming for the subcontinent as a whole: Indian developments will inevitably set off reactions in Pakistan and Bangladesh, our communalism and fundamentalism being precisely mirrored over there and vice versa. We remain, on these occasions, the same subcontinent after all.

The significance lay in the fact that the political formation that organised the Hindutva movement explicitly claimed that the act of demolition was a move to transform the Indian polity as a whole. The proclamation of a Hindu nation that was, they hoped, going to replace the secular self designation of the Indian state, was a precursor of far reaching changes. A serious study of the political writings of the Sangh combine unambiguously points

to designs for a majoritarian, authoritarian and markedly milita-
ristic state order that is, in its fundamentals, incompatible with
democracy or social justice.

Those were very dark days that followed. The Indian left, at
least for that moment, seemed virtually paralysed and incapable
of calling up a dynamic or adequate counterpoint to the mass
forces of the right. Communal violence swept over even left-
ruled Calcutta, a city that had forgotten what such conflict was
for the last 28 years. It seemed that tiny, ad hoc groups of secular
individuals, not necessarily politically experienced or active earlier, would have to   step into the role of combatants. And,
suddenly, far too many of them seemed far too interested in
deconstructing the theory and practice of Indian secularism, in
describing its political nature not in terms that demanded a more
authentic and honest application but in terms of self distancing
from secularism itself. The virulence of their anti-secular critiques occasionally matched the anger of the right and, surprisingly, sometimes the grounds of criticism were disconcertingly
similar: that secularism was an alien notion that had entered
India through colonial mediation and was a sign of the continued cultural domination of the West, that it was intrinsically
contemptuous of religion — this was indeed an astonishing
charge to fling at a group that had been unquestioningly horrified by the demolition of a place of worship. The allegation that
secularism had systematically denigrated religion managed to
obscure the basic and simple truth that the secular agenda is
nothing more than the demand that the religious faith of all
Indians should be equally respected — as indeed, the right of not
having any faith should be — and that this can only be ensured if
the state does not affiliate itself to a particular denomination. It is
a sad truth that we need to remind even ourselves that all
violence against persons and sacred places of any religious persuasion in this country had always been the work of people
belonging to the other religion and never of secularists.

We were also told that secularism, and not religious conflict,
had produced the worst violence of this century, that fascism
and the world wars have been secular conflicts. There were few
indeed to point out that conflicts are not characterised according
to the beliefs of people involved in them — secular or otherwise
— but according to the issues that are at stake. Two religiously

inclined combatants do not create a religious conflict unless they are fighting over religious differences. By the same logic, when irreligious people (even though fascists cannot really be called that) enter a conflict, it cannot be branded as a secular conflict unless the cause of fight involves the issue of secularism. Nor are non-religious issues secular per se, for the opposite of the sacred is not secular but mundane, profane. Elementary exercises in logic, we know — but necessary because the cream of the Indian intelligentsia seemed to abdicate that logic and to use the demolition of the mosque as a stick to beat the secularists with, rather than turning it against the Sangh 'combine' (the Baratiya Janata Party, the Rashtriya Swayam Sevak Sangh, and the Vishwa Hindu Parishad — BJP, RSS,VHP).

The left and secular women's organisations, as well as civil liberties groups, were a resource of unforgettable strength and hope in those days. No paralysis of will or action, no sudden upsurge of intellectually fashionable and politically convenient self doubt there, but a suspension of their normal schedule of activities and concerns, and all hands to the firefighting activity. The total strength they have built up among women in slums, factory belts or rural organisations was mobilised entirely and sustainedly to hold back the forces of the right from their bases.

Without that history of hope and faith we probably would not have had the courage to explore the theme of women and the Hindu right. Because, for the first time in our history, have so many women participated so prominently on the side of the right. Radha Kumar has written about the anguish that feminists experienced when they came face-to-face with women marching in support of widow immolation.[1] The editors of this volume have remarked elsewhere on the enlarged dimensions of that problem in the course of the Hindutva movement.[2] Politically and methodologically this assertive participation of women in right wing campaigns, pulled many of our assumptions into a state of crisis for we have always seen women as victims of violence rather than its perpetrators and we have always perceived their public, political activity and interest as a positive, liberating force. The strident words of hate uttered by a *sanyasin* (technically woman renouncer) that have led to so many deaths, the presence of thousands of *karsevikas* ( a term drawn from the Sikh religion to denote people who do manual work as part of service to their religion. Here, in a curious inversion, it was used for the destroyers of the mosque) from distant parts who came to witness and celebrate the demolition of an old mosque seemed to cruelly mock our convictions, our tools of analysis.

We need to understand what we are faced with. For we do have before us a large-scale movement among women of the right who bring with them an informed consent and agency, a militant activism. If they are imbued with false consciousness then that is something that includes their men as well and if they are complicit with a movement that will ultimately constrain themselves as women, then history is replete with examples of women's movements that foreground issues other than or even antithetical to women's interests. Feminist convictions are not given or inherent in women, after all.

That, then, was not what we set out to prove or disprove. We needed to identify the social bases of the women's contingent, the domestic ideology and gender notions as well as the larger social interests with which they have been moblised, the changing forms of their mobilisation and activism over time and space, the directions into which such activism was going to lead both in terms of gender politics and the politics of the Hindu right in general. We had a great problem here, because even after the growth of the Hindutva movement the politics of the right in India have not received focused attention or analysis. We have had, in recent years, a growing interest in theorising the community as a concept in political and cultural theory and we have had writings on the purely discursive aspects of communal literature or audio-visual propaganda. However, since these are not anchored in a concrete understanding of the history and politics of the right as a palpable, historical, force, they have not clarified our notions of a specific and vital political formation. Nor would identifying the caste/class base and interests of this formation, a necessary but, after all, a relatively simple task, exhaust the historical function and political purpose of the movement.

Since the study of the Indian right has not really got off the ground so far, and the study of its women's component is practically non-existent, we could not follow clear, known paths of enquiry. We decided, therefore, to tackle the more circumscribed, bounded phenomenon of the gender ideology and women's activism within the Hindu right as well as to see what this right has done to women of another community. In the absence of a formed body of serious, scholarly literature, we decided to have something like a montage — reports on violence after the December 6 events, critical self evaluation of secular women's understanding of communalism, histories of women's experience in past carnages, cultural resources and historical referrents in the right's gender ideology, present patterns of activism and gender thinking among the women leaders of the right. Hopefully, a multifaceted probing and multiple forms of information gathering and analysis will constitute a coherent picture of a partial but vital dimension of rightwing policies and intentions.

This book has been unforgivably long in the making. We would have been really glad if the time lag had made its concerns dated and irrelevant by now. And, indeed, in a way, the urgency of the threat seems to have receded. The agenda of social justice, however problematically and imperfectly conveyed by the politics of lower caste groups, has overshadowed the communal imperatives, especially after the elections in Andhra Pradesh and Karnataka. The democratic system, again with all its many distortions in our country, has managed to give a new turn to political concerns — so much so that even the BJP has moved over to a rhetoric of economic problems, shelving Ram for the time being. The unfolding logic of structural adjustments is already making evident the unbearable strains that the near subsistence economy of very large numbers of very poor Indians confronts when the commands and interests of the World Bank and the IMF are internalised by their own government. The right, among all Indian political groups, is least prepared to tackle such issues or even to think coherently about them. In a sense, this precious reprieve is best made use of by trying to comprehend more systematically the developments we have seen in the last few years.

Yet, unfortunately, our exercise remains more than a retrospective. The right is infinitely stronger than it was five years ago. Unless we are very careful, its critique of secularism will enter into the vitals of what are, so far, non or anti right forces. Our sense of the Sangh 'combine' is that immediate political power is less of a long term concern with it than a fundamental, thoroughgoing political and cultural transformation of its upper caste/ middle class base that would combine a communalistic interpretation of Hinduism and tradition with the energies of a compradore consumerist bourgeoisie that is deeply committed to the commodities produced by the West. It is this project of hegemonising its own base in every particular that creates the space for the relevance of its women.

## II

In compiling the papers for this volume we have tried to cover a broad range of issues. The processes through which identities are constructed are complex and cannot necessarily be contained within a single framework. Appropriating the past selectively in order to create an almost unitary, convenient and ahistorical identity for women has been a project of the revivalists and Kumkum Roy shows, through a detailed examination of the Rg Veda and some later Vedic literature (including the principal Brahmanas and the Upanishads) as well as the Manusmriti, how the representations constructed in this staple are used by the revivalists. Purshottam Agarwal makes a related argument when he looks at rape as a recurring metaphor — and reality — in communal violence. He critiques the secular intelligentsia for seeking to explain the phenomenon of commualism only in terms of religion and what he calls 'the socio-economic causes of anger and frustration.' Instead, he suggests (and this is a premise that is echoed by many writers in this volume) that communalism needs to be understood as essentially a political project, which uses religion as a racial denominator of the political community. Thus, for him, to the participants in communal violence, every riot is actually a battle in the unfinished war not between two religious communities, but between two racially defined na-tions. In this context then, normally reprehensible acts such as rape, are legitimised and given ideological sanction.

The partition of India, and the communal violence that accom-panied it, provides a most immediate referent in recent violence against the Muslim community in India today. Perhaps the most emotive issue that communalists have been able to manipulate into their agenda of aggression, revenge and retribution for past wrongs, was the mass rape and abduction of women during, and following on, the partition. Urvashi Butalia's paper looks at how this issue was used — in two parallel discourses, that of the RSS mouthpiece the *Organiser*, and that of the Legislative Assembly — to construct the identity of the Muslim man, the Hindu man, the Muslim woman and by implication, the Hindu woman, and how the woman's body and her sexuality became the field on which the entire discussion took place.

A matter of considerable concern to women's groups has been the rise of militant women within specific right wing Hindu political formations. In Bombay, the Shiv Sena has been able to mobilise large numbers of women actively and, Sikata Banerjee and Teesta Setalvad argue, more successfully than women's groups. They have managed to create a sense of community, — a point also noted by Flavia Agnes — to provide solutions to immediate problems and, have created a social niche for women that challenges notions of female emancipation that feminists have held dear. Looked at from another angle, this appropriation is also indicative of the success of the autonomous women's movements which have mobilised successfully on these issues, whose potential the Hindu right has been quick to seize.

There are, nonetheless, important differences between the two: while the women's movement challenges notions of women's domination within the family and society, the ideology of Hindutva places women squarely within the home and propagates a patriarchal model. What has this appropriation of issues, tactics, strategies on the part of the Hindu right meant for the women's movement and how have women's groups responded to it ? This is a question that Flavia Agnes addresses from an insider's perspective. For many years an activist in the women's movement, Agnes critiques the majoritarian biases within the movement itself and argues that the rise of Hindu militancy, and the mobilisation of women by the Hindu right, has forced women's groups to examine these biases, leading to more reflection and considered responses.

The involvement of women in the Hindutva movement, however, need not necessarily be seen as the success of mobilisation on a range of issues. Amrita Basu's analysis of the 'real' women of Hindutva shows how for women leaders such as Uma Bharati, Vijayeraje Scindia and Sadhvi Rithambara, the opportunity offered by the Ram Janmabhoomi agitation has helped to advance their personal and political agendas. The kind of space communal parties have created has also been diverse enough to accommodate the varied gendered imagery and actual roles of women. Basu describes forms of women's activism for which parallels can be found in right wing racist movements in Germany and France, and her examination of the rise of a militant female leadership among Hindu women raises the question of whether this has been enabling for the women in question or merely expedient.

What kind of logic is there, then, in women's militant leadership ? The position occupied by women leaders seems partially to serve their own purposes and also those of the party they belong to. The anti-Mandal agitation that gripped sections of youth in north India in 1990, more particularly Delhi, also saw the emergence of militancy among younger women, particularly college students who feared the loss of job opportunities. Taking the diary of a young student at the time, Zakia Pathak and Saswati Sengupta look at the appropriation of the goddess Durga and the Durga myth by the right wing. What, they ask, is the nature of female militancy, and how 'true' or deceptive are the promises that political movements of the right and left make for the emancipation of women.

While this may be one aspect, it is also true that the strategies of the Hindu right are diverse and wideranging. Ratna Kapur and Brenda Cossman argue that the legal discourse, and more particularly the concepts of secularism and equality have become sites of contested meanings as the Hindu right has sought actively to redefine these meanings, an attempt which is part of a broader struggle for ideological harmony waged by the forces of Hindutva. They stress the importance of reappropriating this ground and placing the women's movement's visions of secularism and equality at centre stage in the popular consciousness, but ensuring that these visions remain democratic.

A series of reports produced by civil liberties and women's groups on different communal riots were a timely and important reminder of the negative impact of communalism for all women and of the fact that, while one may see a new militancy, women still are victims of such violence in very specific ways. The report of the delegation of four women's organisations to Surat, Ahmedabad, Bhopal and Bombay gives an understanding of women's own perception of communal violence and its impact on their lives. It also looks at official measures for relief and rehabilitation and tries to assess their effectiveness in meeting the specific needs of women. The report marks how, in situations of communal strife, women of both communities are vulnerable, those of minority communities being more so.

While the presence of women within the Hindu right is disturbing, it is necessary that we examine what this political presence has to offer to women. It is with this in mind that some of the essayists in this volume have interviewed women who are in positions of relative importance within right wing parties. Amrita Basu's interviews are supplemented by the more detailed ones carried out by a group of young college students involved in anti communal work.

For many years the rise of the Hindu right, and the phenomenon of communalism, has seemed to be a north-India based one. V Geetha and TV Jayanthi show how the BJP and other parties of the Hindu right have begun to make systematic inroads in the south as well. Multiple strategies are used by the Sangh combine to two specific purposes: firstly, to persuade women to see themselves as legitimate, equal and valued participants in public and even political demonstrations of Hindu fervour and faith, and secondly, the careful erasure of boundaries between home and the world, private and public spaces, religion and politics through ceremonial enactments of familiar household rituals transforms and reinscribes the public Hindu cause as a deeply felt and experienced private wrong that every woman, irrespective of her caste and community origins, will willingly nurse in her heart. This is a timely reminder to us that we need to be more vigilant than ever and to devise ever newer strategies to counter this well organised move to a majoritarian, intolerant, patriarchal society.

## Notes

1. Radha Kumar, *The History of Doing: An Illustrated Account of Movements for Women's Rights and Feminism in India, 1800-1990*, Delhi, Kali, 1993.
2. Tanika Sarkar, 'The Crucible that Moulds,' *The Pioneer*, 23 December 1992; 'The Woman as Communal Subject: Rashtra Sevika Samiti and Ramjanmabhoomi Movement,' in *Economic and Political Weekly*, 31 August, 1991 and others; Urvashi Butalia, ' Community, State and Women's Agency: Some Questions on the Partition of India,' in *Economic and Political Weekly*, 24 April 1993; 'Women Bear the Brunt of Post-Riot Traumas,' *The Pioneer*, 23 December, 1992 and others.

# 'Where Women are Worshipped, there the Gods Rejoice'
## The Mirage of the Ancestress of the Hindu Woman

KUMKUM ROY

## I

The curious visibility accorded to women in colonial and post-colonial discourse as well as in the praxis of political parties has been the subject of investigation and analysis over the past decade or so. What has emerged is, broadly, an understanding that the concern with constructing and reconstructing women stems from a variety of agendas which are not necessarily women-centred, as a result of which women's identities are constituted through processes which are complex and by no means bounded within the framework of a single logic.

The identity of the Hindu woman in particular has been foregrounded in the context of the new, strident wave of Hindutva apparently sweeping through north India at present. Defining the Hindu woman, who has attained and been accorded a re-markable, literal visibility, thus acquires a certain urgency.

Focusing on this particular form of womanhood rests implic-itly (and occasionally explicitly) on a number of assumptions — that Hindu women are different from non-Hindu women, that they are different from Hindu men, and that they are a homoge-neous category. In other words, possible differences along caste/class/regional lines are glossed over, a specific gendered under-standing is centralised, and a communal identity is sharpened, if not created. There is thus a tendency to universalise and generalise on the one hand, and to differentiate on the other, to sustain an

impression of sameness and uniqueness at two mutually reinforcing levels.

Although (or perhaps because) the image of the Hindu woman
is located within the context of the present, it has been endowed
with an impressive past, to which at least lip service continues to
be paid rather consistently. This past is constituted, basically,
from two elements, one defined as the Vedic age, and the second
associated with the *Manusmrti*.

The focus on these two areas of the past is by no means
accidental. The *Vedas* are the earliest textual sources available in
India, and are, by definition, sacred and by extension sacrosanct.
The *Manusmrti*, on the other hand, is amongst the most well-
known prescriptive texts of early India. Hence, appropriating
ideas actually or even purportedly contained within such textual
traditions is probably inevitable in any enterprise which seeks to
claim respectable antiquity.

Yet, this appropriation is not necessarily unproblematic. It
involves glossing over differences (and difficulties) at a number
of levels. Chronologies, for instance, are often left deliberately
vague, so that historical developments/variations do not disturb
the process of mythification. While dating early Indian texts
remains an acutely controversial matter, any debate or discussion on this issue is avoided. The only concession to historical
processes or events is the recognition conferred on invasions, the
incursions of 'foreigners' which are invoked to justify almost any
and every restriction imposed on women and to account for
what is perceived as a steady decline in the status of women
from a condition of near-idyllic bliss. Alternatively, problems
are seen to originate within and because of non-Hindu traditions, such as Buddhism, and, to a lesser extent, Jainism. Such
perspectives, popularised and simplified by the votaries of
Hindutva, are, however, not new. Most of them can be traced
back to Altekar's work, *The Position of Women in Hindu Civilisation*
(Ist edition 1938).

What emerges in terms of historical explanation is then, very
often, a causal link between patriarchal institutions and the
threat of the outsider/other. Thus, there is an implicit and even
explicit understanding that patriarchal tendencies are basically a
response to external threats or challenges. Hence, Hindu society
is logically absolved of any inherently oppressive characteristics.

Besides, an agenda for action is offered — if Hindu women remove any outside influence and/or collaborate with their men in such an endeavour, they will automatically be freed from the bonds of patriarchal restraints. Externalising the problem also provides for a certain respite from confrontations within what is defined as Hindu society, as such confrontations can then be viewed as irrelevant and counter-productive. I would suggest that while such an understanding may have initially been projected by masculinist, patriarchal, authority figures, it evidently strikes a chord among women as well. It provides an escape for those opposed to patriarchal oppression, who are spared the discomfort and unease of confronting an enemy who is close in more senses than one. Instead, they can attack an alien, outside force with undiluted vigour and with little or no sense of guilt. That the agenda is clearly persuasive is evident from the mobilisation and active participation of women in the activities of the Sangh *Parivar* (family) before, during, and after the destruction of the Babri Masjid.

At another level, somewhat less obviously, an attempt is made to stretch historical boundaries to fit the contemporary situation. We have thus references to 'Vedic India'. Apart from the fact that the notion of the nation state is absent in early India, Vedic literature is focused on specific geographical areas. Early Vedic compositions, for instance, are related to the region drained by the Indus and its tributaries, that is, the north western part of the sub-continent, while later Vedic texts reveal a more easterly orientation, around the mid-Gangetic valley. The *Manusmrti* (II.17-22), likewise, possibly pertains to India north of the Vindhyas. What needs to be remembered is that other parts of the sub-continent contained settled populations during the periods ascribed to the composition/compilation of these texts (*c* 1500-60 B.C. in the case of Vedic literature and *c* 2nd century B.C. 2nd century A.D. in the case of the *Manusmrti*). These peoples may have evolved precepts and practices that need not necessarily have conformed to the texts which are foregrounded. Thus, defining the past in terms of 'Vedic India' for instance, obliterates the pasts of non-Vedic peoples and, in fact, contains an implicit denial of the need to investigate into the existence and beliefs of such peoples. We are left with a unified (and uniform) past whose intrinsic homogeneity was or could be violated only by extraneous interventions.

As is obvious, this construction of the past can be questioned at a variety of levels. However, I will confine myself to examining certain themes commonly perceived as central to the identity of the Hindu woman. These include the extent to which men and women are viewed or constructed as similar/dissimilar, the extent to which the category of 'woman' is constructed as homogeneous, the basis for differentiation and/or homogenisation, and the justifications offered for the impositions of patriarchal norms. I will explore these questions drawing on evidence available from Vedic literature and the *Manusmrti*.

Defining Vedic literature in itself is somewhat problematic. Do we mean the four *Vedas* — the *Rg, Yajur, Atharva,* and *Sama Veda,* of which the *Rg Veda* is commonly regarded as the earliest, or do we also include later Vedic literature, the *Bhrahmanas,* the *Upanisads,* and what are knows as the *Vedangas* or the limbs of the *Vedas*? The problem is not simply one of fewer or more texts, but is partly chronological and geographical, as mentioned earlier, and, equally, if not more important, one of content. The four *Vedas* consist of hymns and chants meant to be used on ritual occasions. The texts themselves are not prescriptive. The problem is further confounded by the fact that all later prescriptive texts begin with an almost standard formulaic invocation of the *Vedas* as either one or the ultimate authority for the subsequent injunctions for example, *Manusmrti* (II.6). However, searching for Vedic parallels for latter-day prescriptions is somewhat futile and leads to far-fetched and imaginative reconstructions. As a last resort it is suggested that Vedic parallels are probably to be found in texts, or extant works reworked and reinterpreted beyond recognition thus receive a rather dubious authoritative status. And once one enters the domain of the 'may have beens' contestation and critiquing become well-nigh impossible. I will not even attempt this but restrict myself instead to the *Rg Veda* and a sample of later Vedic literature, including the principal *Brahmanas* and *Upanisads.*

The *Manusmrti* is fortunately more tangible as a text. It is, however, very different from Vedic texts in terms of language, style, and content. It is amongst the earliest works composed entirely in the popular *anustubh* metre (also commonly used in the epics), a metre which lends itself to easy recitation, memorisation, and composition. It is likely that this facilitated widesperead dissemination of its message. Besides, its focus is explicitly broad — in fact, virtually the entire gamut of human existence is brought within the purview of prescription and prohibition. While such an understanding may have been implicit in Vedic literature, the latter is primarily concerned with the sacrificial ritual within which the complexities of the social and cosmic order are worked out through a range of symbols. There is thus an underlying difference in perspective and purpose

## II

As school-going children, most of us learnt that there were women seers in the Vedic age. This was (and was meant to be) reassuring, especially for those of us who were first or second generation women with access to public education, as we could locate ourselves within a heritage stretching back to hoary antiquity. It was only much later that some of us realised that the token women seers were not enough.

The *Rg Veda* consists of over a thousand hymns — of which, those attributed partly or wholly to women seers do not number more than twelve or fifteen, that is, approximately one per cent. The representation of women seers is thus obviously marginal. If this is an indication of the access women had to the construction of prestigious, sacral traditions, it is not particularly inspiring. As important, while we do have references to women philosophers such as Gargi, women rarely figure as students or teachers in formal situations of transmitting learning. In other words, such women were probably interlopers rather than participants in routine scholarly activities.

An attempt was made to systematise this situation in the *Manusmrti* (II.67), where women were denied access to the *upanayana* or initiation which marked the beginning of access to sacred learning. This was reinforced by suggesting substitutes for women, marriage was portrayed as equivalent to the initiation of the male, serving the husband was equated with the period o. studentship, and the performance of household duties was identified with the worship of the sacred fire (*Manusmrti* II.67). The acceptance of such prescriptions would have meant that any non-domestic activity was viewed as unwomanly or unwifely.

What is often forgotten, however, in our focus on the Hindu woman, is that there were women scholars within other contemporary traditions such as Buddhism, whose existence is well-attested in inscriptions from sites such as Sanchi. Within the brahmanical tradition, nevertheless, women's ability to define and transmit prestigious learning was by and large denied. In other words, the very composition and preservation of the traditions which are claimed as precursors of present-day Hindutva were processes which were structured in terms of gender.

It is not surprising then, that one of the major strands worked into and through such traditions is that of gendered difference. This is not something which is taken for granted or assumed. Rather, it is carefully developed through a number of strategies which are mutually reinforcing.

The concern with structuring and delimiting understandings of procreation constitutes, in a sense, the core of such strategies. The form in which this concern is represented, in both early texts and in well-known contemporary interpretations of the theme is at least partly spiritual — legitimate procreation is *the* means of acquiring sons, who in turn ensure the welfare of the patrilineage both in this world and in the next. This perspective is evidently useful in that it obviates the need for further exploration and questioning. Although one can either believe or disbelieve in the efficacy of sons for salvation, the latter course is obviously slightly more risky, both here and hereafter.

Equating sons with saviours also glosses over the fact that it was part of a complex strategy for defining procreative relations and goals. It is important to remember, for instance, that procreation or women's procreative abilities were not valorised per se, but in a context within which women were expected, by definition, to have little or no control. This was typified by the ideals of the marriage hymn of the *Rg Veda* (X.85.44-45) where a prayer was offered to ensure that the bride would be the mother of sons. In other words, the production of sons was located within a specific socio-sexual context, a specific kind of marriage.

The ingredients of heterosexual intercourse within such a situation are worked out in other texts, including a section of the *Brhadaranyaka Upanisad* (VI.4). This defines intercourse in terms of dominance and subordination, with provisions for cajoling, coercing, and even forcing the woman to submit if necessary.

While compelling women to submit to sexual, and by extension procreative relations was thus opened up and recognised as a legitimate possibility, procreation itself was constructed as a process which was not simply, or even primarily, physical. Most of us are familiar with traditions of prayers and/or sacrifices as a means of obtaining offspring. Such devices were probably a response to the uncertainties surrounding childbirth. However, the specific form in which they were encoded within the sacral tradition meant that such ritual occasions were concerted into situations for enacting and underscoring an understanding of procreative relations as asymmetrical. This was in part ensured through the presence of the male priesthood which directed the proceedings and invoked divine assistance, and by the fact that such rituals could be commissioned by the male sacrificer of the *yajamana*. While the wife of the sacrificer was expected to participate in the process, her role was defined in terms of instrumentality rather than control or equal partnership (e.g., *satapatha Brahmana* III.8.2.5). Occasionally, moreover, certain kinds of knowledge were defined as generative (e.g. *Brhadaranyaka Upanisad*, V.13.1). Given that women found it rather difficult to gain access to such empowering lore, they would have been perceived as particularly disadvantaged and hence dependent vis-a-vis learned men.

At another level, the tradition distinguishes between physical and spiritual births, the latter being most characteristically typified by the *upanayana* or the initiation, recommended for boys or men belonging to the three higher *varnas*. In this context, the boy was reborn from the priest-teacher, the brahmana (e.g., *Satapatha Brahmana* XI.5.4.12) and this spiritual birth was frequently exalted as superior to the production of the 'mere' physical body (e.g., *Manusmrti* II. 146-148). Besides, it marked out the initiate as one who was eligible to study the sacred traditions, thus opening up possibilities of further empowerment.

The definitions of procreation thus offered and sanctified envisage a distancing of the process from physicality — children are/ can be obtained not merely through heterosexual intercourse, but through sacrifices, rituals, prayers, knowledge. Besides, the ideal birth is spiritual rather than physical. The physical/ spiritual dichotomy, moreover does not operate within a vacuum, but is equated implicitly and explicitly with what are defined as feminine and masculine roles — women are confined to the mundane, whereas men participate in both realms. What is more, their access to the ritual/spiritual sphere then justifies their control over the 'lesser' more worldly activities as well. In other words, areas of human existence are distinguished not simply to differentiate them but to relate them, one to another, in terms of hierarchy and power.

Despite the energy expended on disembodying the notion of procreation it evidently remained problematic. This was probably because the role of women in the process, no matter how carefully structured or devalued, could not be entirely denied. While unilateral assertions of the superiority of the sperm vis-a-vis the womb (e.g., *Satapatha Brahmana* VI.3.1.70) offered a possible resolution, ova being fortunately unknown and hence non-existent, there were limits to this strategy.

The problem and its somewhat uneasy resolution crop up time and again in later brahmanical texts, including the *Manusmriti*. Here (*Manusmrti* IX.33 ff), the womb is equated with the field, in which men sow seed, offspring being determined by the nature of the latter, with the former conceived as a passive, supportive receptacle. The field, moreover, is ideally owned by a man, and, by extension, the produce of the field is his. What complicated this neat analogy was the possibility that the owner of the seed and the owner of the field need not have necessarily been identical. This was countered by warning men off one another's fields/wives.

It is also likely that the woman/field may have at least occasionally proved somewhat intractable. Hence, the ideal bride/procreative instrument had to be carefully selected following criteria which explicitly or implicitly ensured her subordination. For instance, men were expected to marry women or girls who were far younger than them (*Manusmrti* 9.94), with a difference of sixteen or eighteen years being recommended. Besides, while the bride was ideally to be chosen from the same *varna* as the man, marriage with low-status women was also permitted for high status men (*Manusmrti* III.4,13). The insistence on exogamy (*Manusmrti* II.5) meant that the bride would have had no prior kinship ties with the family into which she was incorporated — as such, her position would have been insecure, to say the least.

Besides, the provision for excluding women from families which did not conform to ritual norms, or where patriliny was not important, effectively restricted *Sastric* recognition to households which fell in line (*Manusmrti* III.9,10). What emerges then is that in both the Vedic traditions and the *Manusmrti*, the relationship between men and women was structured in terms of inequality, even though specific elements of the relationship were emphasised to a greater or lesser degree in different contexts.

The relationship of men and women to material resources was also somewhat similarly ordered. In the *Rg Veda*, where wealth is conceived of primarily in terms of cattle, it is men rather than women who pray for the ownership or acquisition of wealth. Where, occasionally, such prayers are attributed to women (e.g., *Rg Veda* V.61.5), the circumstances define this as exceptional. As important are the references to gifting women, along with goods such as horses, chariots, etc., and the bride, who is considered as the gift of the gods to the bridegroom (*Rg Veda* X.85.40). In other words, women tend to be assimilated to material resources, whereas men, by and large, are differentiated from and in control of such goods. This is not to suggest that all men could stake identical claims to such resources. Nevertheless, the difference envisaged between men and women, was as sharp, if not sharper, than that envisaged between and among men belonging to different social categories.

Later Vedic traditions underscored the value of the gift of the daughter through legends, including that of Sukanya (literally the good daughter) who was given by her father to placate the angry sage Cyavana (*Satapatha Bhrahmana* IV.1.5.7). Besides, rituals were manipulated to ensure that women were deprived of *Virya* or valour and this was then extended to deny them an inheritance (*daya*) selfhood (*atman, Satapatha Brahmana* IV.4.2.13). Thus women were defined as powerless within prestigious, sacral contexts, and this definition was explicated in rather concrete terms.

Women were also implicitly excluded from participating in a variety of material transactions which were acquiring significance — from the giving and receiving of *daksina* and *dana* on most ritual occasions, and from giving and receiving tribute or taxes and from directly offering and demanding hospitality. Apart from their tangible content, such exchanges symbolised extra-domestic bonds which were being forged amongst men. Once again, such bonds were not necessarily reciprocal — some, such as religious gifts or tributes for instance, were clearly expected to flow towards dominant social groups. At the same time, the ability to participate in these exchanges, even as subordinate donors, would have demarcated participants from those who were not considered worthy of incorporation within such networks.

Most of the preoccupations of the early and later Vedic traditions are formulated as more or less universalistic prescriptions in the *Manusmrti*. This is apparent in the privileging of forms of marriage which rested on the gifting of the daughter (*Manusmrti* III.27 ff) and in the recognition of women as a kind of property (*Manusmrti* VIII. 149). Besides, while women were granted access to some forms of property or possessions including *stridhana*, literally women's wealth, which probably included jewellery, utensils, clothes, etc., the relations of kinswomen and kinsmen to property were constructed asymmetrically (e.g., *Manusmrti* IX. 119). The extent of the difference envisaged becomes obvious if one compares the means of acquiring wealth legitimately open to men and women. The former were granted access to inheritance, profit, purchase, the fruits of victory, interest on loans, gifts (*Manusmrti* X. 115) whereas the latter were restricted to receiving gifts from their kinsfolk during marriage (*Manusmrti* IX.194) and were not allowed to accumulate wealth without the permission of their husbands (*Manusmrti* IX.199).

There was thus an attempt to convert the edging out of women from control over procreative and productive activities into a somewhat routine process. This was accompanied by a rather dramatic conceptualisation of the gendered nature of political processes, especially within the Vedic tradition. Here, myths and rituals raised and attempted to resolve questions of the distribution of power.

Perhaps the most remarkable of such myths are those of Indra and Usas. As in well-known, Indra was ranked among the principal deities especially in the early Vedic tradition. What is more, his heroic attributes, including valour, virility, generosity, were considered typical of ideal male leader or rulers, and rituals frequently identified Indra with those who claimed to be his human counterparts. Usas's attributes are also striking—she was conceived of as endowed with strength, wisdom and wealth (*Rg Veda* III.61.1) However, the similarities between Indra and Usas end there. What we find instead are myths of battles between the two, which inevitably end in the defeat of the latter (e.g., *Rg Veda* II.15.6) Besides, Usas, unlike Indra, has no recognised imitators in the human situation. The contrast is underscored by the fact that *rajni*, the feminine form of the term *rajan* (masculine, commonly translated as king), is virtually never applied to the wives of rulers — they are either referred to as *patni* (wife) or *mahisi*, literally the she-buffalo, a symbol of benevolent fecundity. The perpetuation of the values embedded in such myths and rituals would have ensured that any attempt by women to exercise direct control over political processes would have been construed as illegitimate. Nevertheless, the threat remained, and the need to guard against women in general, and royal women in particular is reiterated in the *Manusmrti* (e.g., *Manusmrti* VII.153, 217).

It is obvious that gendered relations in a number of connected domains were framed within notions of sacrality, which were expected to render them inviolable. Hence, it is not surprising that access to the sacred was also gendered. This is especially evident if one examines the Vedic sacrifice. The ritual itself centred around gods rather than goddesses, as is evident from the fact that the latter are invoked rather infrequently.

Interaction with the gods, was, moreover, a function of the priesthood and the *yajamana*, the man who commisioned the sacrifice. Both were by definition male. The term yajamana, as may be expected, has no feminine equivalent. While his wife was required to participate in rituals, there were provisions for maintaining ritual continuity in her absence (*Altareya Brahmana* VII.32.8) or for obtaining another wife (*Manusmrti* V. 1680). One searches in vain for provisions enabling the wife to continue with the sacrifice on the death of the *yajamana*. Clearly, while the presence of both was essential for the sacrifice, its implications were different for men and women. To talk in terms of the 'rights' of women to participate in Vedic rituals, is then, somewhat simplistic.

What is possibly more likely is that women's participation in such rituals was required because this was one means of ensuring that they got the message — the message that women were instrumental but not in control of procreation, that they were ideally possessions rather than owners and that their subordination was divinely ordained. Occasionally, the message was represented rather vividly, as for instance, in the *asvamedha*, where the ewe to be sacrificed for the goddess *Sarasvati* was placed under the more prestigious sacrificial horse meant for the god *Prajapti*, to ensure that women would be subservient to men and follow them (*Satapatha Brahmana* XIII.2.2.4).

In this situation, the much-quoted statement from the *Manusmrti* (III.56) characterising the worship of women as a means of pleasing the gods, appears somewhat paradoxical. Apart from pleasing the gods, it has frequently been interpreted as pleasant indication of the status accorded to women. After all, what more can women want? What is often overlooked in this entire enterprise of elevating womanhood is the context within which the statement is located, and the forms of worship enjoined, the former explicitly domestic, a domesticity overlaid with patriarchal values. The forms of worship include giving women ornaments, clothes, and food on festive occasions (*Manusmrti* III.59). Any claims to similarity with the worship offered to the gods is at best superficial and at worst fraudulent. The latter possibility is strengthened if one considers the subsequent statement (*Manusmrti* III.61), that no children are born if the woman is not attractive to her husband. Thus, the accessories of worship would in effect enable the woman to comply with her designated function as a procreative instrument — they would hardly be an acknowledgement of her power, which is what is often implied in the worship and invocation of gods and goddesses.

It is evident, then, that the elements of our traditions which are foregrounded by exponents of Hindutva constitute men and women differently.

### III

The differences between women and men are, however, not the only ones of significance — as important are the bases on which women are differentiated from one another. These differences are systematically elaborated in the *Manusmrti*, but figure in the early and later Vedic traditions as well. At one level, the differences envisaged among women seem to correspond with those among men. Yet, given the gendered context outlined earlier, this similarity is, as we shall see, apparent rather than real. What is more, while the categories conceived of as important for women are embedded within the familial context, men's identities are located both within this as well as within extra-familial situations.

Perhaps the most central and common identity envisaged for women was wifehood. In fact, the nature of wifehood was elaborated at length. As we have seen, the ideal process for becoming a wife involved a certain denial of a woman's personhood, implicit in the notion of *Kanyadana*. Besides, the wife was increasingly defined as the *bharya* (she who has to be borne, e.g., *Brhadaranyaka Upanisad* III.4.1) and less frequently as the *jaya* (the procreative woman) or the *Patni* (the feminine equivalent of the term *pati* or husband).

The contents of wifehood are developed systematically in the *Manusmriti*. The wife was expected to be thrifty, and do her housework cheerfully (*Manusmrti* V.149), to obey her husband in life and death even if he was devoid of qualities (*Manusmrti* V.151,154), and observe celibacy after his death (*Manusmrti* V.160). While wives were to be 'protected' and were ideally to be imbued with the belief that this was for their own good, such protection was explicitly recognised as valuable for the man, for his selfhood, his offspring, family, and dharma (*Manusmrti* IX.6-12). Disobedient women were threatened with dire consequences in both the present and subsequent births (*Manusmrti* V.164), with the husband being granted the right to beat them, as well as other domestic personnel (*Manusmrti* VIII.299). This could be backed up by state support, as is evident from the provision permitting the ruler to throw a recalcitrant woman to the dogs (*Manusmrti* VIII.371). As opposed to this, the destitute widow who had been devoted to her husband, but lacked the support of her kinsfolk, could expect succour from the ruler (*Manusmrti* VIII.28).

Somewhat less central was the notion of motherhood. Vedic religious practices and beliefs, were, as is generally recognised, patriarchal. Thus, the notion of the goddess as mother was marginal in the early Vedic tradition, and presents a contrast with the almost stereotypical invocation of gods as fathers. Also, later Vedic sacrifices provided for the worship of the *pitrs*, the patrilineal ancestors, who were thus deified and routinely remembered in the monthly (*Satapatha Brahmana* II.4.2.12) and later daily ritual (*Manusmrti* III.70). In this context, the occasional glorification of motherhood as superior to fatherhood (*Manusmrti* II.145) remains just that — an occasional, token concession which is not developed into an even essentialist perspective on motherhood as natural or empowering.

If the existence of wives and mothers was accorded a certain strictly qualified recognition, daughters and sisters were perceived as almost irrelevant. While the gifting of daughters has been referred to earlier, their identity crisis is perhaps most tellingly reflected in a prayer ascribed to Ghosa (one of the legendary woman seers). She appeals to the gods as a son to the father, thus denying her sexual being in order to transcend (or probably transgress) the limits of accepted sacral norms (*Rg Veda* X. 39.6). Her attempt is explicable in view of the routine references to strengthening the father-son bond through ritual such as the daily fire sacrifice or *agnihotra* (e.g., *Satapatha Brahmana* II.3.4.41).

Sisters are, if anything even more marginalised. While some goddesses are occasionally conceived of as sisters (e.g.,*Usas, Rg Veda* 1.123.5) neither men nor women invoke them as such. As opposed to this, men at least occasionally aspire to brotherhood with the gods (*Rg Veda* II.1.9.).

Women who could not be fitted within the farmework of the ideal patriarchal kinship structure were, not surprisingly, condemned. This is evident from the list of women who (among others) were considered polluting, and whose gifts of food could not be accepted. These include the *ganika* and the *pumscali* (courtesans or prostitutes, *Manusmrti* IV. 219-220) as well as the woman who was without a husband or a son (*Manusmrti* IV.213). Such condemnations would have reinforced the notion that women could receive social recognition only when they submitted to subordinate identities locating them within the patriarchal family.

Efforts were also made, especially in the *Manusmrti*, to deal with the intersections of *varna* and gender hierarchies. A number of strategies were adopted to cope with such situations. On the one hand, sexual relations between high-status men and low status women were considered particularly polluting, a high status man who married a *sudra* woman being considered equivalent to her (*Manusmrti* III.15). At the same time, *varna* differences among men were reinforced by permitting high status men access to low status women (*Manusmrti* VIII.362, III.13), whereas low status men gaining access to high status women were punished much more severely for both adultery and rape (*Manusmrti* VIII. 364, 365), which were, in any case, defined as violating or defiling another man's property/woman rather than as an act involving the woman herself. The access to *varna* identities which was thus conceded to women, was mediated through their relationships to men, and was not necessarily empowering. While the status of the wife of a *brahmana* and the wife of a *sudra* was by no means identical, each was, nonetheless, vulnerable, although in different ways. The former would have been the focus of 'protection' to ensure an impeccable identity for progeny, while the latter, construed as relatively 'free' or available, would have had to cope with the attentions of both high and low status men.

What is evident then is a tendency to conflate the categories of woman and wife, reflected, for instance, in the usage of the term *stri*. While wifehood was centralised as a dominant, if not the sole, identity available to women, it was also constituted in terms of dependence.

The marginalisation of non-wifely kinswomen and the denial of non-kin identities to women, which complemented the focus on wifehood, further narrowed down the options legitimately open to them. The absence, or at least the paucity, of such options would have made it increasingly difficult for women to function in extra-domestic contexts. Within the domestic realm too, the only option which was valorised was one of cheerful subordination. It is this, almost unitary identity which is constructed for women which probably renders this aspect of the tradition particularly appealing to revivalists. It can be projected as the basis for a common, communal identity. It can also reaffirm faith in the validity of the patriarchal enterprise, by containing and channeling womanhood along 'appropriate' lines. What is also deliberately or otherwise overlooked in the process of appropriating purportedly traditional values is that alternatives, not recognised (for understandable reasons) within the *sastric* tradition, evidently existed. Converting a single tradition into *the tradition* ignores the complexities of our past. Besides, there is the larger question of the possibility, or more important, the validity of attempting to re-enact the past either partially or even totally.

## IV

The problems inherent in such attempts to appropriate the past are probably nowhere as evident as in the case of justifications offered for a gendered societal order. The traditions we have examined are virtually unanimous in recognising that a certain degree of structuring is required in order to contain and control what is implicitly or explicitly understood to be the nature of women.

What exactly are the elements which constitute this problematic nature? To start with, there is the question of intellectual inferiority — an undisciplined mind and a slightly woolly brain. This assessment of womankind is incidentally, attributed to Indra (*Rg Veda* VIII.33.17). The implications of this are worked out much later in the *Maunusmrti*, which discusses the possibility of interrogating women witnesses during legal disputes. In the ultimate analysis, we are told that the evidence proferred by even a number of pure women should not be accepted, owing to the instability of their intellect (*stribiddhi asthiratvat, Manusmrti* VIII.77). Small wonder then, that kings are cautioned against confiding in women, those eternal betrayers of secrets (*Manusmrti* VII.150).

As if inferiority were not enough, women are, by nature, hostile towards those who know better. In fact, exorcising the hostility of the wife, in particular, is a constant theme. The marriage hymn in the *Rg Veda*, for instance, includes a prayer to ensure that the bride will not be of fearsome eye, or a destroyer of her husband (*Rg Veda* X.85.44, *aghoracaksu, apatighni*). Besides, chants were employed in marriage rituals to ensure that the bride did not destroy her husband, offspring, cattle or the household (*Sankhayana Grhya Sutra* I.18.3). The bride was also subjected to tests to determine her 'true' nature (*Apastamba Grhya Sutra* III.3.16) and rituals were recommended to ensure that the wife did not retort (*Aitareya Brahmana* III.12.12,13).

While the inherent dishonesty, hatred and bad conduct of women are taken for granted in the *Manusmrti* (IX 17), the mechanisms for coping with them are somewhat different. These include threats directed towards women who actually manifested any kind of defiance. For instance, the much-cited verse placing women as dependents, under the 'protection' of their father, husband, and son, is followed by a warning that any attempt to break away from such control results in disgrace for both families (*Manusmrti* V.148,149). Besides, the wife who spoke unpleasantly could be abandoned immediately (*Manusmrti* IX.81), hostile wives could be superseded (*Manusmrti* IX.79) and women who were hostile towards their husbands or embryos (possibly those who underwent abortions) those who wandered or drank spirituous liquor, or associated with heretical sects, were denied funeral rites (*Manusmrti* V. 90).

The threat posed by women is also frequently defined in terms of their sexuality, coping with and controlling which becomes a central concern, especially within the later Vedic traditions and the *Manusmrti*. This was, at one level, linked with the concern with structuring procreation, noted earlier, and is reflected in the annual *varunaprghasa* where the sacrificer's wife was publicly asked whether she had any lovers. If she admitted to their existence, Varuna would punish them. If she had lovers but did not declare this, her guilt would fall on her kinsfolk (*Satapatha Brahmana* II.5.2.20). Thus, wives, but not husbands, could be subjected to routine interrogations regarding their sexual relations.

The notion of women's potential promiscuity, inherent in the formulation of such rituals, is explicated more consistently in the *Manusmrti*, where women's insatiable sexuality (*Manusmrti* IX.14), and its disruptive consequences, are elaborated at length. Thus, even mothers, sisters, or daughters can pose a threat to a man (*Manusmrti* II.215).

This is then extended to the notion of women as polluting. Such an understanding is evident in the later Vedic tradition, where certain kinds of sacral knowledge, for example, could not be imparted in the presence of women, *sudras*, dogs, or crows (*Satapatha Brahmana* XIV.1.1.31), this being considered synonymous with mingling light with darkness and truth with falsehood. Besides, celibacy was enjoined as a routine prerequisite for sacrifices — the avoidance of women being grouped with the avoidance of meat, and not telling lies (*Apastamba Srauta Sutra* XXII.3.16). In this context, menstruating women were regarded as especially polluting (*Brjadaranyaka Upanisad* VI.4.13, *Manusmrti* V.84).

It is obvious that the nature of women, thus constructed, and the specific norms envisaged for women, feed into one another, reinforcing a more or less consistent logical structure of gender relations. Current reappropriations of such constructions by votaries of Hindutva, however, do not explicitly recognise this connection. Thus, the specific understanding of women's nature, which provides the underpinnings for much else, is not denied, but, to an extent obscured. This may be partly owing to a certain reluctance to make explicit notions of sexuality, which are viewed as somewhat indecent, especially in the context of what is purportedly a 'high' tradition. What is substituted instead are explanations or justifications for gendered norms in terms of external threats. These are conceived in terms of alternative belief systems, such as Buddhism, or in terms of foreign invasions. Gender stratification is then perceived as a response to such aggressions. And of course, the fact that Muslims/Islam have been systematically depicted as posing a threat at both levels, results in a logical extension whereby an anti-patriarchal agenda can be converted and diverted into a communal, specifically anti-Muslim campaign.

At another level, the fact that the underlying assumptions of what is identified as the 'Hindu' tradition remain beyond question implies that these can be drawn upon as and when required. These constitute, as it were, an unspecified reserve of patriarchal values.

What we find then is a combination of not necessarily mutually consistent logics. On the one hand, we have the argument of antiquity, whereby everything old and 'Hindu' is automatically sanctified. On the other hand, anything which appears blatantly discriminatory by present standards (as for instance the denial of the initiation or *upanayana* to women in the *Manusmrti*) is explained away in terms of external factors. Besides, as we have seen, the appropriation of the past is selective. What is more, the criteria underlying choices are implicit rather than explicit. This means that the grounds for selection can be shifted almost imperceptibly from one occasion to another, and issues can be blurred.

The strategy of splitting Hindu women's past into the good, which ought to be imitated, and the bad, the creation of the 'other', goes into the making of an ahistorical understanding of women's current situations. In apparently offering a plausible agenda for action, moreover, it prevents the raising and resolution of more searching questions about our pasts and our futures.

Note: I have used the following texts for this essay:

Agashe, R ed., 1977 *Aitareya Brahmana*, Part II, 3rd edition, Poona.

—— 1979 *Aitasreya Brahmana* Part 1, 3rd edition, Poona

Garbe, R ed., *Apastamba srauta sutra* 1882 Vol 1, Calcutta.

—— 1885 *Apastamba srauta sutra*. Vol II, Calcutta.

—— 1902 *Apastamba srauta sutra* Vol III, Calcutta.

Jha, G ed., 1932. *Manu-Smrti*. Vol I, Calcutta.

—— 1939 *Manu-Smrti* Vol II, Calcutta.

Max Muller, F (9ed) 1965, *The Hymns of the Rg Veda*, Varanasi (1877).

Sastri, AC ed., 1928, *The Apastamba Grhya sutra, Banaras.*

Sehgal, S R. ed., 1960, *Sankhayana Grhya sutram*, Delhi.

Vasu, S C ed and tr., 1933, *The Brihadarnyaka Upanisad*, Allahabad.

Weber, A ed., 1964, *The Satapatha Brahmana, Varanasi.*

# Savarkar, Surat and Draupadi
*Legitimising Rape as a Political Weapon*

## PURSHOTTAM AGARWAL

> Sexually awakened women affirmed and recognised
> as such would mean the complete collapse of the
> authoritarian ideology.
>
> *Reich*[1]

I did not see them myself. Instead, I was told by a
volunteer that 'Pakistan Zindabad' was engraved on the
foreheads and on the hands and breasts of a number of
women. God knows how many of them had such names
tattooed on them.

But, a large number of Muslim girls were also brought
on whose hands miscreants had tattooed even the dates
of their crimes and their names. A girl who had fled
from Patiala showed me her hands, which she had burnt
with some acid in order that she could efface the stigma
of infamy that the ruffian had carved on them for ever . . . .

It's true that when Hindus caught hold of Muslim girls,
they, partly with a view to taking revenge upon them,
partly due to anger and partly with the intention of
demonstrating they were Hindu, felt the necessity of
tattooing different parts of their bodies. When these girls
were taken off to Pakistan, Muslim girls who had their
hands tattooed by mujahids, also came back. However,

as regards their crime, the warm-hearted people of Punjab have tried to excel one another. Girls who were found in Delhi were brought to us with the mark of 'Om' engraved on their hands. At the same time we also came across those victims on whose private parts were tattooed the names of rapists and whose breasts were stamped with the marks of savagery these rapists had indulged in.[2]

# I

The events that took place in Surat in December 1992 and January 1993, as well as in Bombay in January 1993, were undoubtedly horrendous but were not, by any means, unprecedented. Violence in general, and sexual violence in particular, has always been an integral part of any authoritarian world view. Such world views cannot allow themselves to admit to women's sexual agency or its logical implication, that women are capable of exercising control over their bodies and minds. This is something that threatens the very semiotics of the fascist political construct, of which Hindu/Muslim/Sikh communalism is only an Indian variant.

Societies whose social values derive sanctity from and whose discourse of power is rooted in women's complete subjugation to men, tend to turn women into autonomous and inanimate symbols or carriers of social honour, often even into embodiments of the sovereignity of the state.[3]

Woman thus becomes a name which the contestants of power attribute to a complex strategic situation and her sexuality becomes an arena of this very contest. This underlying symbolism of women's sexuality becomes explicit in a moment of crisis. In a secular variant of patriarchal nationalism this symbolism operates as an attitude: communal fascist ideology, on the other hand, makes it its leitmotif. Thus the rhetoric about the piety of the family and the dignity of 'our' women only complements the aggressiveness such ideologies direct against the women of the 'Other'. Indeed, they present themselves as protectors of the dignity of women precisely because they treat it (not them) with an impersonal contempt.

## II

Rape, even in an individual context, is not just a matter of sexual lust. Sometimes consciously, sometimes unconsciously, it is an affirmation of women as objects of pleasure and an underlining of the power of men. In a collective context, rape becomes an explicitly political act and in the context of an organised aggression, it becomes a spectacular ritual, a ritual of victory — the defilement of the autonomous symbol of honour of the enemy community.

Initial reports from Surat (after December 1992) spoke of the videotaping of mass rapes of women. Fortunately, these remained unconfirmed. What is important to remember, however, is that this does not contradict the fact of rape being transformed from an act of lust in an individual context into a performance in a collective context, for what was confirmed was that the mass rape of Muslim women was performed under the glare of floodlights.[4]

What is distressing is that there is a tendency on the part of the middle-classes and intelligentsia to underplay or even rationalise such acts. Many observers of Surat noted that 'feelings of guilt, shame and embarrassment' about what took place on the day of the pogrom are quite rare among people. In retrospect, for many Hindus, the killing of Muslims seems to have been rationalised by suggesting that this was a 'proper' punishment for a minority, which has stepped out of line. The massacre can thus be explained as a ritual of purification in order to pacify divine wrath.[5]

The real question that needs to be posed in this context, however, is how things have come to such a pass that the normal condemnation of acts such as wanton killing, destruction and mass rape has come to be replaced by an unashamed approval. Obviously, this is a complex question which can be approached from various angles. But it is curious how little attention has been paid to the making of the 'communal mind-set' in both its active and supportive variants. All too often communalism as a phenomenon is sought to be explained only in the context of religion and the socio-economic causes of anger and frustration. Given this, it is not surprising that the suggested remedy then becomes either broad democratic mobilisation on socio-economic

issues, with confrontation with the political context of communalism being given a very low priority, if any at all; or there are
attempts to convince people of the need to be either religiously
tolerant or rationally intolerant of religion. What is usually forgotten is that communalism is essentially a political project,
which uses religion not in any ephemeral or spiritual sense, but
as a racial denominator of the political community. By its own
admission, the primary agenda of communalism is to transform
the traditional, religious identity into a modern political one. In
this sense, the communalist project is as non-religious as any
other project of nation-building; the real conflict thus is not
between religious fanaticism on the one hand and the secular
world-view on the other. It is actually between two notions of
nationalism itself — authoritarian and democratic.

The misplaced contextualisation of communalism solely within
religious intolerance and socio-economic collision leads most
liberal commentators to see a communal riot as just a riot, while
to the participants or to the abettors, every riot is actually a battle
in the unfinished war not between two religious communities,
but between two racially defined nations. It is with this perspective of nations-at-war that communalism appropriates collective
memory and constructs falsified historical narrative in order to
justify its present political practice. It also constructs parallel
notions of morality: the morality of war is different from the one
that prevails in normal times!

This self-image of the community at war is a crucial component of the complex process of the construction of the communal
mind-set. Surat, the principal mercantile town of southern Gujarat,
with its horrible tales of decimation and marginalisation of Muslims, the performance of rape as a spectacle, the direct participation of middle class men and women in banditry and vandalism,
has sprung up to symbolise the essential internalisation of this
war morality. However, such morality is not a sudden thing,
generated overnight, nor are only the so-called more rabid and
degenerate of the communal ideologies solely responsible for
it. Historian Sudhir Chandra, writing from post-riot Surat,
observes :

> Events in Surat, thus, reflect a disturbing approximation
> between the manifestation of communal violence and

the enunciations of the relatively less rabid ideologies of Hinduism. Hindu communal violence in Surat seems to have made another alarming contribution to the escalation of communalism. It broke a crucial psychological barrier that had hitherto divided the physical perpetrators of communal violence from those who verbally justified or even abetted it.[6]

The 'less rabid ideologue' referred to in Sudhir Chandra's article is Swami Chinmayanand, 'whose lecture on the Gita has won him an impressive following among the urban literati'.[7] Sudhir Chandra is surprised to find Chinmayanand saying belligerently, 'let the goverment make the Muslims understand that they will have to make the sacrifice.' It is interesting that we find it less easy to accept a Chinmayanand talking in this vein, whereas it seems natural when Uma Bharati or Vinay Katyar adopt such sentiments. What is important is to remember that talk of death and destruction is integral to the communal fascist world view and is not dependent upon how more or less rabid individual ideologues are. This is all the more true in relation to the 'crucial psychological barrier' that divides the physical perpetrators from those who verbally justify or abet violence. What we do not realise is that by making only the Vinay Katyars, Rithambharas and Uma Bharatis scapegoats for all the degeneration and destructiveness of communal politics we are simply playing into the hands of the fascists. By doing this we miss the continuity that exists between a Savarkar, a Chinmaynand, a Vinay Katyar and a rapist on the street.

Even more disturbing than Sudhir Chandra's surprise is the hurt and disappointment of leading scholar and playwright G P Deshpande who commented on the state of the Indian polity and culture post-Ayodhya thus:

If you look up a book by Savarkar on 'Hindutva', written in 1923 and any speech by Vinay Katyar in recent times you will discover a world separating them. Not many secular thinkers are even aware of this. In other words, secular discourse has stagnated for various reasons and on the other hand, the Hindu discourse has degenerated. These things have gone on parallelly. And you cannot blame the one without blaming the other. You cannot

simply condemn the degeneration of the Hindu discourse without taking adequate notice of the stagnation
of the secular discourse.[8]

He further writes:

Under pop-Hinduism what is now being created is the
Book, one Lord, one priestly class and the notions of *'kufr'*
and *'kafir'* (Arabic words), believers and non-believers,
etc. This has happened over the last 30 or 40 years
essentially. Earlier, even in the late nineteenth century
'Hinduism' was not trying to turn itself into an organised
religion. And that is why the logic of numbers acquires a
certain potency now. This logic of numbers was not
important in the nineteenth century.[9]

G P Deshpande contrasts the current pop-Hinduism with
what he calls the neo-Hinduism of the nineteenth and early
twentieth centuries. Yet, much more striking than the contrasts
are the continuities between neo and pop-Hinduisms and it is
surprising that a scholar of his calibre should not remark on
these. We will come to detailed treatment of Savarkar later. Here
it is important to remember that the process of making Hinduism an organised religion on the lines of Semitism with one book,
one Lord and only one valid interpretation of the Divine Revela-
tion actually started with Dayanand Saraswati and the Arya
Samaj. His *Satyarth Prakash* is so vehement in introducing the
notions of 'Vedic' and 'Avedic' in an ethical sense that even
books by Kalidas and Tulsidas are proscribed for a model Arya
household simply because they go against Dayanand's interpretation of Vedic texts[10]. So far as the potency of the logic of
numbers is concerned let it not be forgotten that the recent
Meenakshipuram conversions provide such a powerful handle
to contemporary Hindutva forces precisely because they had the
potential of rekindling memories of the historical conversion
and reconversion conflicts of the late nineteenth and early twentieth centuries. The role of the Census and the resultant significance of numerical strength as a powerful tool for winning
favours with the colonial power is also well known. The bitter
exchange between Arya Samajis and Muslims of Punjab in the
last decade of the nineteenth century and the riots that followed,

as also the murder of Arya Samaj leader Swami Shradhanand can both be located within the potency of numbers. In fact, since the last quarter of the nineteenth century, the numerically defined strength, assurance and anxiety of the 'community' has been a significant component of the communal consciousness. The significance of numbers operated in such a way that 'both communities lived in fear and both saw themselves as persecuted minorities.'[11]

It is even more worrying when Savarkar is cited as someone who symbolises the sober and not so degenerate discourse of Hindu communalism. In fact, the elements of continuity between the neo and pop- Hinduisms are best summed up in the political praxis of the degenerates of the Vinay Katyar type. It is Savarkar, who ought to be credited with trying to make such degenerateness theoretically tangible and morally acceptable.

These are indeed harsh words to use for someone who is revered not only by his followers, but even by his critics. The liberal secular intelligentsia hold Savarkar in such high regard that when the present writer mentioned in the course of a seminar that Savarkar had criticised Shivaji because he (Shivaji) had 'a perverse notion of virtue in respecting the chastity of even the Muslim women' he was challenged by the Hindutvawallahs to physically present the relevant texts and was condescendingly told by the leading liberals that perhaps he had read a bad translation of Savarkar!

In this paper I would therefore like to examine and analyse the links and continuities between the practice of degenerate Hindutva and the precepts of Savarkar in the specific context of the symbolism of the female body.

### III

The semiotics of sexuality in the Hindu-Muslim relationship is a relatively unexplored area. Nonetheless, it is a very powerful element in defining the mutual responses and psychological barriers, so much so that the bardic legend of Padmini and Alauddin, for example, has acquired the status of historically authentic event not only in what is called popular perception but also among the articulate middle class intelligentsia. The transformation of a legend into a historical event gives a fair indication of the historical perspective which is imposed upon scattered pieces of experience. Alauddin, apart from being an archetype of the ruthless aggressor, also becomes an epitome of a furiously libidinous Muslim.

Indeed, what is important in understanding the cultural significance of a legend or a myth is not its historical basis. Rather than look at how closely legends approximate to actual historical happenings, we need to look for the matrix of anxieties, fears and attitudes reflected in the construction and cultural acceptance of a particular legend or a myth. This is true especially in the context of Indian society where the oral tradition has been a most potent and reliable medium of preserving and transmitting collective memories and anxieties. Therefore, for the purpose of interpreting the making of the communal mind-set, what is more important is not whether Padmini was the real cause of Alauddin's aggression on Chittor. Instead, it is the fact that a whole community has *chosen* to *preserve* and *believe* that this was so that deserves more serious attention on our part. As Sudhir Kakar remarks: 'The spell of the story has always exercised a special potency in the oral based Indian tradition and Indians have characteristically sought expression of central and collective meanings through narrative design.'[12]

Such expressions of central and collective meanings in turn go into the making of deeper layers of consciousness. The significance of the legend in the cultural sense becomes more important than its meaning in a positivist sense for the myth or legend to become an acceptable explanation for experience in the natural as well as in the cultural realm. Such explanations penetrate very deep into consciousness where they then serve as the bases for internalising cultural stereotypes and political prejudices, so much so that while studying possession by evil spirits Sudhir Kakar arrives at the startling conclusion that:

> The fact that fifteen out of twenty eight patients were possessed by a Muslim spirit indicates the extent of this projection in the sense that the Muslim seems to be the symbolic representation of the alien in the Hindu unconscious. Possession by a Muslim *bhuta* reflects the patient's desperate efforts to convince himself and others that his hungers for forbidden foods, tumultous sexuality and

uncontrollable rage belong to the Muslim destroyer of taboos and are farthest away from his 'good' Hindu self.[13]

In such a situation the oral tradition contributes tremendously in shaping attitudes, and legends come to be loaded with contemporary political significance to such an extent that they make their contribution to the creation of popular historical narrative, and the anxieties and fears generated penetrate even the unconscious. The task of creating a democratic, dialogic discourse is thus rendered extremely difficult, especially when there are forces who have a stake not only in perpetuating such fears and anxieties, but also in creating their contemporary versions. It is indeed sad that one of the reasons for the inadequacy of the secular discourse is precisely this — that the problematic of sexuality has actually been an area of darkness where secular discourse is concerned. As historian Bhagwan Josh rightly observes:

> A survey of the history of relations between Hindu and Muslim elites over the centuries points towards a dark area of experience located in the primordial realm of sexuality. Perhaps it was this experience which had given the relationship a psychological structure which tied the contradictory responses in a frame of unity. Perhaps it required something more than the common purpose of attaining *swaraj* to dismantle the conditioning of this character mould. The common goal was not sufficient to make a dent in diffusing the web of this experience and the lines of psychological force and hegemonic effects emanating from its stereotyped versions. The general matrix of inferiority activated by these stereotypes reproduced a structured psychological behaviour in everyday life.[14]

What Bhagwan Josh calls the general matrix of inferiority is sustained by the construction of two antithetical stereotypes. On the one hand, there is the stereotypical image of the Muslim as a voluptuously lustful rapist, which is sought to be confirmed by citing passages from the Koran. This serves the purpose of the Muslim 'community' with the followers of Islam as a religion. On the other, the self-image of a passive, docile, hopelessly virtuous, nay impotent, Hindu inevitably complements the image of a lustful Muslim. Right from nineteenth century Hindu cultural discourse to the bloodthirsty rhetoric of contemporary degenerate communalism, these images and their attendant assumptions continue. In fact, the 'effeminateness' of the Hindu self-image is a major problem even for a person like Vivekananda who, disgusted with Hindu passivity, blames it on 'devotion to such figures as Radha, which has made the whole nation effeminate.'[15] This is not to say that nineteenth century Hindu cultural discourse has a linear relationship with the contemporary Hindu communal discourse but the commonality of concerns regarding effeminateness is nonetheless striking. Yet another interesting aspect of such stereotypes of the 'Self' and the 'Other' is that these are most pronounced in a typical Hindu conceptualisation of the relationship with the Muslims. Why this is so, is outside the purview of the present argument but it obviously re-emphasises the need for a critical survey of Hindu-Muslim relations over the last thousand years. It also brings to the fore the crucial subliminal link of approximation between the Hindu cultural discourse and popular perceptions of the Hindu self and the Muslim 'Other'. There is a symbolic relationship between the two in which the Hindu cultural discourse has rarely tried to interrogate popular notions in a self-conscious way. By contrast, the Hindu communal discourse has quite expectedly only tried hard to further reiterate such notions and castigate Hindus for their perverse notions of virtue and impotence.

In all patriarchal world-views, more than anything else, it is the woman who symbolises the honour of family and community. Exclusive control of her sexuality by the legitimate 'owner' is the practical aspect of the notion of honour. That is why it is expected that an ideal woman should end her life, which is incidental anyway, if her chastity has been defiled. While this holds true in the context of honour, where the community is concerned, an ideal woman is expected to offer herself for the supreme sacrifice even if there is merely a probability of defilement. Urvashi Butalia has shown how such sacrifices become a spectacle and celebration in collective memory.[16] By the same logic, in struggles between different communities (for communities read men) woman is metamorphosed into a metaphor of both sacredness and humiliation. And the virility of the community comes to hinge upon defending one's honour and humiliating the 'Other' through the agency of the sexuality of woman. Duryodhana could think of no better way than ordering the public disrobing of Draupadi to decisively emphasise the humiliating and final defeat of the Pandavas in the game of dice, and the Pandavas could not protest for the simple reason that Duryodhana, even in his reprehensible act, was justified in terms of the moral paradigm of patriarchy which was binding upon the Pandavas.

## IV

In spite of the symbolism of the female body, rape is a morally abhorrent act to all traditional world-views.At the very least, it is also a matter of great embarrassment. Even if there is a recognition of the fact of rape or an implicit approval of it (especially under 'not-so-normal' circumstances) any rationalisation, even theorisation, of the *necessity* of rape is something unimaginable. The matrix of complex human values and perceptions creates a kind of grey area in this regard. Even a rapist would try to put the blame on the victim herself. It is simplistic to dismiss this as mere hypocrisy. Rather it reflects a much needed sense of moral inadequacy, which in its philosophically abstract form, works both on the conduct and incentive for the achievement of perfect moral behaviour. In fact, this works as a powerful antidote to the sense of moral self-righteousness and a departure from the intrinsic questioning of any notion or construct of the self or the community.

What happens if the sense of moral inadequacy or self doubt is eliminated ? What happens when a nation or a construct refuses to submit itself to any kind of self-doubt and actually seeks to reverse the very connotation of moral and immoral ? What happens when a political discourse consciously seeks to contextualise rape exclusively in the problematic of the contest between two communities or nations, thus transforming it into a morally defendable act, in fact into a much needed political strategy?

The political discourse and historical narrative of Savarkar give a horrifying answer to these questions.

## V

In this context, it is both interesting and natural that Savarkar has been presented as symbol of the sophisticated discourse of Hindutva. It is natural because of all the ideologues of Hindu communalism, Savarkar occupies a unique place of high esteem in the minds of ordinary people as well as among the intelligentsia. He is known as an undaunted fighter against British imperialism, as someone who had to suffer long prison terms; a man modern in his outlook, one who wholeheartedly supported industrialisation and strongly opposed the practice of untouchability. More importantly, he is credited with interpreting the 1857 uprising from a nationalist perspective. He is also the first person to quite consciously undertake the project of constructing the political categories of Hindutva and Hinduness, as quite distinct from the traditional religious term Hinduism. While outlining the essentials of Hindutva, Savarkar is unambiguous in emphasising that 'Hindutva is different from Hinduism.' He makes it abundantly clear in the following way:

> Hindutva is not identical with what is vaguely indicated by the term Hinduism. By an 'ism' is generally meant a theory or a code more or less based on spiritual or religious dogma or system. But when we attempt to investigate into the essential siginficance of Hindutva we do not primarily — and certainly not mainly — concern ourselves with any particular theocratic or religious dogma or creed. Had not linguistic usage stood in our way then 'Hinduness' would have certainly been a better word than Hinduism as a near parallel to Hindutva. Hindutva embraces all the departments of thought and activity of the whole being of our Hindu role.[17]

In religious discourse the community is defined in terms of a shared creed or dogma. In the political discourse of communalism, the community is defined primarily as a race. Religion, instead of being a defining criterion, is transformed into a fetish owned by an already defined community. Savarkar was by no means the first to attempt a racial reconstruction of the traditional religious community. But he was undoubtedly the most articulate. It was in his discourse that attempts to theoretically construct a Hindu political community which shared the same racial bonds and historical memories came into shape.

It is also interesting to see Savarkar presented as the symbol of the sophisticated Hindutva discourse, particularly as it is his political discourse and historical narrative that unambiguously seeks to do away with the possibility of religiously defined morality acting as a constraint on political praxis. In all fairness, Savarkar can be credited with constructing an amoral political discourse. The essay 'Hindutva', which is contrasted with the speeches of Vinay Katyar, has all the roots of the kind of degeneration Vinay Katyar and his ilk have come to symbolise. 'Hindutva' can actually be described as a watershed in the ocean of Savarkar's thought. Before it was published, Savarkar's historical narrative had duly taken note of the Hindu-Muslim antagonism in medieval India; nonetheless, he continued to speak of the need for peaceful co-existence, even for cooperation. But since 'Hindutva', a very different version of history can be seen evolving in Savarkar's writings and speeches, which culminates in his magnum opus, *The Six Glorious Epochs of Indian History* (completed in 1963). As the English translator of this book (which was originally written in Marathi) S T Godbole, remarks, 'Vir Savarkar's book is a commentary — not a history in its academic sense — on the significant events and periods of our national life taking a broad survey of growth and survival of our Hindu race.'[18] The book is not only a historical commentary but it is also one that can be said to draw some moral lessons for the entire Hindu nation. Explaining the purpose of this exercise, Savarkar states:

> On reading such titles of chapters as 'Alexander's Invasion of India', 'Saka Aggression on India', foreign as well as native readers are generally misled into a belief that the whole of India was overrun either by Alexander or by the Huns, and the country lost its independence. Under this delusion, many of the enemies of India and her so-called well-wishers have raised such objections and propounded such theories, as to mean that the whole life of the Indian nation — i.e. the Hindu nation, has passed under in foreign salvery. It is to bring to light and refute this foolish and wicked charge and to show that it is due to either unintentional ignorance or wilful malice

that such theories are ever propounded that this book
has been purposely written."[19]

It is not only for the purpose of refuting this delusion, but also
that of explaining the causes of defeats of the Hindu nation that
Savarkar tries to reinterpret the events and their causes. Underlying these exercises are some basic assumptions which bring
into sharp focus the fact that Savarkar is striving to put scattered
collective memories and various events into a historical perspective. This is obviously a common device in all historical narratives, but is usually used in a dialectical way. The perspective of
the historian is considered logical only insofar as it has a demon-
strable factuality and tenable approach to the interpretation of
objective evidence. In Savarkar's case, this is hardly so. In fact,
the real significance of the book becomes comprehensible only
when the text is read in relation to Savarkar's political praxis.
Actually, in this commentary on history, the present does not
flow from the past. Instead, it grows entirely from his purpose
which is to achieve a justification of his present political stance.

The political perspective of Savarkar dangerously approximates the popular notions of the impotent Hindu 'Self' and the
libidinous sexually dissipated Muslim 'Other'. Characteristically,
instead of trying to interpret or interrogate such notions, the
narrative only seeks to corroborate and perpetuate them. Thus,
the inquiry into the past is not inspired here by a need for
broadening its frontiers, rather it is a desire to exploit people's
sentiments that is the driving force and this goal is attained
through the elevation of these sentiments themselves to the
status of historical perspective. What Wilhelm Reich calls 'political mysticism' is operating at its best or worst here, depending
upon how you see it.

Some features of this perspective are quite discernible. The
most striking one among them is the attempt to replace God with
nation as a crucial referrent for moral decisions. The anxiety of
making the notion of the Hindu race free of religious dogma is
crucial because by this the attempt to marginalise and even
eliminate the moral aspects of religious dogma are brought into
shape. The nation replaces God or the divine head as the ultimate source of morality. This replacement is most important for
the communal fascist world-view as we shall see presently in the

specific context of sexuality. The construction of an internal enemy who can be blamed for the humiliations and defeats of the nation is yet another crucial aspect of this perspective. In addition, there is an attempt to make the belief in the Vedic Hindu religion the prime determining factor of patriotism and loyalty to the nation.

## VI

As pointed out earlier, the attempt here is to draw lessons for the present. Where Savarkar's writings are concerned, the proper lessons were drawn so well that admirers and followers could establish unmistakable links between discourses of the past and the present. As Savarkar's hagiographer Dhananjaya Keer remarks,

> He said that Pakistan's inhuman and barbarous acts such as kidnapping and raping Indian women would not be stopped unless Pakistan was given tit for tat. Two years earlier Savarkar had expressed his opinion that the liberal policy adopted by Shivaji in case of Muslim women was wrong as this cultured and human treatment could not evoke in those fanatics the same feelings about Hindu women. They should have been given tit for tat, he observed frankly, so that they might have realised the horrors of those brutalities.[20]

This 'nationalist' approach towards rape is by no means an aberration. It is typical of the communal fascist world-view to propose the humiliation of the women of the 'Other' as retribution or a pre-emptive measure — in order to defend the honour of 'our' women.

Moreover, this is also a nationalistically moral method to achieve ethnic cleansing, a practice which we are witnessing in epidemic proportions in Bosnia today and an articulate theorisation of which was provided by the exponent of the so-called 'more sober' Hindu communal discourse, Savarkar. Such a theorisation of rape did not suddenly appear in *The Six Glorious Epochs*. The truth is rather different as Bhagwan Josh underlines, when he cites the following passages from a speech of Savarkar's delivered in 1938. 'It was a special feature of V D  Savarkar's speeches that he combined the problem of molestation of Hindu women with the denunciation of Congress, Gandhi and non-violence.'[21]

Thus the denunciation of non-violence and impotence along with the perversion of virtue reflected in Shivaji's having been decent towards Muslim women are closely interlinked. If this contextualisation of the sexuality of women is a symbol of degeneration, then the fact is that the historical narrative of Savarkar is both a product and a progenitor of the degenerate communal discourse.

Apart from the obsession with the semiotics of sexuality, the other feature of communal discourse is the construction of an internal enemy. According to *The Six Glorious Epochs*, in pre-Muslim India, the Buddhists fitted the bill for this status of internal enemy. In Savarkar's view therefore, 'So long as Samrat Ashok called himself a follower of the Vedic religion, that means till about 200 B.C., the north western frontier guards of Mauryan Empire remained well-equipped and invincible. But as soon as Ashoka adopted Buddhism, this security of the Empire fell to pieces.'[22»]

With characteristic sophistry Savarkar pays handsome tributes to Lord Buddha himself. But so far as his followers are concerned, they come in for the most vicious and incisive attacks. An entire subsection of chapter III is entitled 'Hereditary Disloyalty of the Buddhists'. Naturally, the decline of Buddhism in India has been attributed to 'the extreme hatred, which the Vedic Hindus felt towards the Buddhists for their high treason.'[23] The complex history of the persecution of the Buddhists has been explained thus:

> Pushyametra and his generals were forced, by the exigency of the time, when the war was actually going on, to hang the Indian Buddhists who were guilty of seditious acts and to pull down the monasteries which had become the centres of sedition. It was a just punishment for high treason and for joining hands with the enemy, in order that Indian independence and the empire might be protected. It was no religious persecution.[24]

As a natural corollary to the logic of the construction of an internal enemy, the disloyalty of the Buddhists is hereditary while the treachery of Vedic Hindus was only 'individual and exceptional.'

Such an interpretation of the Vedic-Buddhist relationship is actually nothing but an attempt to historically prove Savarkar's discourse. That is, a change of religion is tantamount to a change of nationality and only a Hindu (not necessarily a follower of Vedic dogma, but nonetheless one who believes in its cultural primacy and political hegemony) can be a real patriot. Both these themes were theoretically propounded in *Hindutva* and only sought to be demonstrated or substantiated in *The Six Glorious Epochs*. Of course, the impact of the present political concerns is far more direct in *The Six Glorious Epochs*. The tirade against the hereditary disloyalty of the Buddhists has a clear-cut connection with the challenge posed by the neo-Buddhism of Ambedkar. Having described Ambedkar as 'a man burning with hatred against Hinduism,'[25] Savarkar goes on,

> Those of the untouchables who are still under the delusion that the Buddhists gave no quarter to untouchability and so extol that sect, should do well to remember that the Chandals, the Mahars and other untouchables were far more miserable under the violently non-violent Buddhists than under the Vedic people who accepted the principle of Ahimsa with its limitations. The Buddhists, once again I should like to repeat, aggravated and not mitigated 'untouchability'. They should examine the validity of this statement in the light of the undisputed evidence cited here and then alone should they choose whatever is beneficial to them[26]

However, it is with the introduction of the Muslim as a character in the narrative that Savarkar comes into his element. The discussion of 'The Epic Hindu-Muslim war' is followed by a quotation from Will Durant which describes 'the Mohammadan Conquest of India' as 'the bloodiest in History'. Savarkar makes a clear distinction between other invaders and the Muslims:

> for the Greek, Saka, Huna and other invaders, who came pouring in down the plains of the Punjab, had political domination of this country as their sole objective. Barring this political aim their raids had never been occa-

sioned by any cultural or religious hatred. On the other hand, these new Islamic enemies not only aspired to crush the Hindu political power and establish in its place Muslim sovereignity over the whole of India, but they also had, seething in their brains another fierce religious ambition, not heretofore dreamt of by any of the old enemies of India. Intoxicated by this religious ambition, which was many times more diabolic than their political one, these millions of Muslim invaders from all over Asia fell over India century after century with all the ferocity at their command to destroy the Hindu religion which was the lifeblood of the nation.[27]

It is typical of the Hindu communal discourse that while other racial groups are not defined in religious terms, the various ethnic groups owing allegiance to Islam are transformed into a single race, that is, Muslim. This is essential in order to historically validate the construction of the Muslim as the principal enemy of the Hindu nation today. It is this validation which transforms what we call the riot into a battle in the communal mind-set. Then, there is an attempt to historically prove the validity of the image of the Muslim, the rapist. In his typical way, Savarkar carefully constructs this image not in abstraction, but in the form of a story or a narrative, which approximates both with the popular method of preserving and transmitting memories and the impressions contained therein. The Muslim, ergo the rapist, figures not merely in the Indian context, but also in the context of Portugal and Spain where 'womenfolk too, were abducted and violently defiled'.[28]   In the Indian context the theme of Muslim aggressors and their violent defilement of Hindu women is used repeatedly, such that it renders 'the perverted conception of virtues' one of the causes of the defeat and humiliation of the Hindu nation. To this, Savarkar devotes one full chapter. As pointed out earlier, the problematic of the perversion of virtues is not articulated in abstract theorisation, but is carefully transmitted through narrative. This gives rise to a kind of psychological vulnerability on the part of the reader making him/her want to share Savarkar's irritation at the 'perverted conceptions of virtue'. This again coincides with the typical upper caste Hindu self-perception according to which Hindus have been tolerant and virtuous all along and have actually suffered because of this. This makes it possible to justify even the ruthless persecution of the Buddhists at the hands of the Hindu king Pushyamitra as a just punishment for their hereditary disloyalty to the fatherland and not see it as religious persecution at all.

Savarkar opens his discussion of the perverted conception of virtue in his characteristic style:

> Besides the silly superstitions of the Hindus about caste-system, the various bans on exchange of food and drink, redemption of the outcastes and others of which we have already written fully, and which had done tremendously more harm than the two-pronged religio-political Muslim offensive had done, another suicidal morbidity had completely possessed the Hindu mind for a long time. This morbidity paralysed their own offensive and counter-offensive might. Far greater than the Muslims could ever attempt were the defeats inflicted on themselves by these morbid, virtuous Hindus! If a comparatively mild term is to be used for this infatuation, this mental imbalance of the Hindus, which caused disastrous losses for themselves, we have to call it a perverted sense of Hindu virtue.[29]

After philosophising about the qualification and relativeness of virtues, Savarkar laments that,

> Having only learnt by rote the maxim to give food to the hungry and water to the thirsty is a virtue, the Hindus went on giving milk to the vile poisonous cobras and vipers. Even while the Muslim demons were demolishing Hindu temples and breaking to pieces their holiest of idols like Somnath, they never wreaked their vengeance upon those wicked Muslims, even when they had golden opportunities to do so, nor did they ever take out a single brick from the walls of Mosques, because their religious teachers and priests preached the virtue of not inflicting pain on the offenders.[30]

Here an interesting process is at work. First, the self-image of

a tolerant Hindu is arbitrarily constituted and then, it is contrasted with the ferociously intolerant 'Other' and the tolerant
Hindu is invited to become equally ferocious. The difference
between traditional religious notions of virtue and the 'modern
nationalist' discourse on it is clear.

To Savarkar, apart from religious tolerance, the other perverted
virtue is the misplaced chivalry to enemy womenfolk.[31] It is not just
a matter of hurt sentiments or pride, but of calculated moralisation
and deliberation as far as Savarkar is concerned. He builds up his
case first as a logical culmination of the story told thus far and
second, as a sociological explanation. According to him,

> One side-issue of the Muslim religious aggression, which
> caused a continuous drain on the numerical superiority
> of the Hindus was the diabolic Muslim faith that it was a
> religious duty of every Muslim to kidnap and force into
> their own religion non-Muslim women. This incited their
> sensuality and lust for carnage and, while it enormously
> increased their number, it affected the Hindu population
> in an inverse proportion. To hesitate to acknowledge
> this hard fact under the guise of politeness is simply a
> puerile self-deception. This abduction of thousands and
> millions of Hindu women by the Muslims is not such a
> trifling thing as to be dispensed with by calling it reli-
> gious fanaticism or simply by conniving at it. Even if it
> were a madness, there was a method in it! And the
> method in this Muslim madness was so horrible that,
> with the mistaken Hindu neglect of this so-called reli-
> gious fanaticism, the Hindu nation came to have a per-
> petual bleeding sore. For, as a matter of fact, the religious
> fanaticism of the Muslims was not madness at all; it was
> an effective method of increasing the Muslim population
> with special regard to the unavoidable laws of nature.
>
> The same law of nature is instinctively obeyed by the
> animal world. If in the cattle-herds, the number of oxen
> grows in excess of the cows, the herds do not grow
> numerically in a rapid manner. But on the other hand,
> the number of animals in the herds, with the excess of
> cows over the oxen, grows in mathematical progression.
> The same is true of man, for at the core man is essentially

an animal. Even in the pre-historic times, the so-called wild tribes of the forest-dwellers knew this law quite well. The African wild tribes of today kill only the males from amongst their enemies, whenever there are tribal wars, but not the females, who are eventually distributed by the victor tribes amongst themselves.[32]

As we have noted above, in this peculiar sociology of sexuality, woman is only a medium, one whose role is to produce progeny for the community, apart from being a symbol of honour. Both these functions of women are linked by a total disregard for woman's individual self. In Savarkar's interpretation the core of the millenium-long Hindu-Muslim war is precisely this function of woman as a medium and symbol. The interpretation at one level refers to the past and at another, more siginficant level, to the present as well. The tirade continues:

> With this same shameless religious fanaticism, the aggressive Muslims of those times considered it their highly religious duty to carry away forcibly the women of the enemy side, as if they were commonplace property, to ravish them, to pollute them, and to distribute them to all and sundry, from the Sultan to the common soldier and to absorb them completely in their fold. This was considered a noble act which increased their number.

Because of the carefully constructed narrative and its dialectical relationship with popular stereotypes and subconscious prejudices, the past tense used here actually unfolds itself in present tense in the minds of a receptive audience and becomes both a framework of reference to their present perceptions and a moral rationalisation for their present practices. As if to break the last vestiges of the moral hesitation, Savarkar explains in some detail that 'Muslim women too played their devilish part in the molestation and harassment of the Hindu women.' He goes on to say:

> The Muslim women never feared retribution or punishment at the hands of any Hindu for their heinous crime. They had a perverted idea of women's chivalry ...

> Muslim women were sure that even in the thick of battles and in the confusion wrought just after that, neither the

victor Hindu chiefs, nor any of their common soldiers nor even any civilian would ever touch their hair.

Savarkar poses the moot question:

> Suppose, if from the earliest Muslim invasion of India the Hindu also, whenever they were victors in the battle-field, had decided to *pay the Muslim fair sex in the same coin* or punished them in some other ways! That is, by conversion even with force and then with this horrible apprehension in their heart they would have desisted from their evil designs against any Hindu lady. (emphasis added)

Savarkar is extremely sorry that

> But haunted with the fantastic idea of chivalry to women and blind eye to time, place and person, the Hindus of that period never tried to chastise the Muslim women-folk for their wrongs to Hindu women, even when the former were many a times completely at their mercy.

The hatred in Savarkar is so powerful that while castigating Muslim women as a class at least at one place he puts a question mark between the expression *'fair (?) sex'*. Savarkar's perception of the problematic is thus clear. Muslims, both men and women, were defiling the chastity of Hindu women by design and the perversely virtuous Hindus have not paid them back in the same coin. Again, this problematic is not confined to the past alone. We have already referred to his hagiographer citing Savarkar's rebuke of Shivaji in the context of the Indo-Pak war of 1965.

To choose Shivaji for the rebuke for misplaced chivalry and a perverse/notion of virtue is extremely significant. Apart from being a popular hero, Shivaji is the central figure in the Hindu communalist reconstruction of medieval Indian history. He is almost a cult figure and is held in high esteem for his qualities of character and leadership. His treatment of the daughter-in-law of the Muslim governor of Kalyan is naturally reversed in chronicles as well as in popular memory and literature as a model of conduct befitting a noble king and a chivalrous hero. Savarkar rebukes him precisely for this conduct thus challenging the notion of sanity and moral value implicit in such reverence. Here, let us have Savarkar himself on Shivaji and his interpretation of the import of this chivalrous act:

Even now we proudly refer to the noble acts of Chhatrapati Shivaji and Chinaji Appa, when they honourably sent back the daughter-in-law of the Muslim governor of Kalyan and the wife of the Portuguese governor of Bassein respectively. But is it not strange that when they did so, neither Shivaji nor Chinaji Appa should ever remember the atrocities and the rapes and the molestation perpetrated by Mahmud of Ghazni, Muhammad Ghori, Alla-udin Khilji and others on thousands of Hindu ladies and girls like the princess of Dahir, Kamaladevi, the wife of Karnaraj of Karnawati and her extremely beautiful daughter, Devaladevi. Did not the plaintive screams and pitiful lamentations of the millions of molested Hindu women, which reverberated throughout the length and breadth of the country, reach the ears of Shivaji Maharaj and Chinaji Appa ?

The souls of those millions of aggrieved women might have perhaps said 'Do not forget, O Your Majesty Chhatrapati Shivaji Maharaj and O! Your Excellency Chinaji Appa, the unutterable atrocities and oppression and outrage committed on us by the sultans and Muslim noblemen and thousands of others, big and small. Let these sultans and their peers take a pledge that in the event of a Hindu victory our molestation and detestable lot shall be avenged on the Muslim women. Once they are haunted with this dreadful apprehension that the Muslim women too, stand in the same predicament in case the Hindus win, the future Muslim conquerers will never dare to think of such molestation of Hindu women.

But because of the then prevalent perverted religious ideas about chivalry to women, which ultimately proved highly detrimental to the Hindu Community, neither Shivaji Maharaj nor Chinaji Appa could do such wrongs to the Muslim women.

It was the suicidal Hindu idea of chivalry to women

which saved the Muslim women (simply because they were women) from the heavy punishment of committing indescribable serious crimes against the Hindu women.

Their womanhood became their shield, quite sufficient to protect them.[38]

We have referred to how such historical perspectives come close to the narratives preserved and transmitted through oral traditions, family recollections and other informal and not-so-formal channels. What one must recognise is the agonising conflict between the tempting 'lessons' of such narratives on the one hand and the values of decency and civilisation on the other. This conflict is very real for anyone who consciously or subconsciously bases his perception of the self and the other on such narratives. One is exhorted to take revenge, to pay back in the same coin, to prove his potency by raping a woman of the 'Other'. But for many people, their sense of values becomes a barrier between the temptation such exhortations provide and any actual action they may lead to. Even in the minds of the most degenerate of people, normally there is a contrasting notion of moral virtue, which works as a controlling device in a complex way and separates the private confession or bragging (about having done it) and the public posture of innocence (or having acted under the force of circumstances). No matter how frequently it is done, there is still a kind of resistance to upholding rape as a 'moral act'.

Savarkar breaks down this resistance with one decisive stroke by removing the conflict between virtue and perversion. He does it boldly and unhesitatingly by systematically turning virtue itself into perversion, and that too, as the natural moral of a grand story — by lambasting none other than Shivaji himself. The perspective is structured as a tale of heroic deeds and horrible defeats. So, even the conduct of a hero like Shivaji is to be condemned if it upholds a moral barrier for the construction of baser instincts as the valid political mode. The sexuality of women is nothing but an arena, a medium, a symbol; just as you die for holding the honour of your national flag and consider it your national duty to save the flag from the enemy, so also your attitude towards women should be the same, that is, uphold the dignity of yours and violently defile the others as retribution or pre-emption.

*The Six Glorious Epochs* is really not a work of history in an academic sense of the term. Rather it is a work of moral philosophy, which replaces God by nation and brings the latter forth as an equally transcendental and mystified category, as the primary referent of moral discourse. This moral philosophy deliberately aims not only at lowering but totally eliminating the barrier between the perpetrator and abettor at one level and temptation and hesitation on the other. When a Rithambhara or an Uma Bharati calls those Hindus who believe in non-violence, secularism and decent moral values, *'hijras'* she is quite in tune with Savarkar who castigates Hindu society in exactly the same vein. It is in his discourse that, both explicitly and decisively, foul becomes fair and fair becomes foul.

It is indeed an irony that in the end of *The Six Glorious Epochs*, Savarkar describes his own work *Indian War of Independence 1857*, written in 1909 as 'written from the standpoint of the Hindu nation'.[39] In fact the so-called 'standpoint of the Hindu nation' in that book was very different, actually diametrically opposed to the 'standpoint of the Hindu nation' as evolved in the post *Hindu pad-padshahi* phase of Savarkar's work. In that book Savarkar could write of Maulvi Ahmed Shah,

> The life of this brave Mohammadan shows that a rational faith in the doctrines of Islam is in no way inconsistent with or antagonistic to a deep and all powerful love of the Indian soil and that the true believer in Islam will feel a pride to belong to and a privilege to die for his mother country.[40]

Savarkar concludes his saga of 1857 by quoting from a *ghazal* composed by Bahadur Shah Jafar. *The Six Glorious Epochs* is actually a culmination of a process which begins precisely with *Hindutva* where the Hindutva world-view is articulated in an abstract way and reaches its high water-mark in the narrative enunciation of *The Six Glorious Epochs*.

Savarkar had long ago done in the discourse of values what was done in Surat in the realm of behaviour. He turned the Muslim into an outcast outside the pale of society, almost a sub-human species not to be given the benefits of human values and virtues. In this process, history is only deployed to prove and communicate an essentially moral point, which is extremely simple : Rape per se is not a crime. In fact, it is a valid weapon in the warfare with Muslims. To consider it morally abhorrent in all circumstances irrespective of any consideration given to time, place, persons and context, is, according to this point of view, a perversion of virtues, and it is this that is historically responsible for the defeats and humiliation of the Hindu nation.

The heroes in Surat were thus trying to do away with this perversion, which is responsible for their humiliation, as they had been enjoined to do. They were not raping innocent female individuals but were punishing the active abettors of crimes against the Hindu nation, particularly against Hindu women. They were not rioting, but they were fighting a battle in a millennium-old war. Their acts had less to do with religious ritualism and more with a ferociously authoritarian nationalism. Those leading intellectuals who talked loud and long about Taslima Nasreen, maintained a studied silence on Surat, but by their rationalisation of the program as a 'just punishment' are also only contributing their part to the philosophical task of making foul fair and fair foul quite in tandem with Savarkar and his ilk.

Secular discourse has thus stagnated and to refer to the degeneration of the communal discourse as if there ever was a decent and cultured one and to contrast Savarkar with Vinay Katyars and Rithambharas is in itself an ironical sign of the stagnation and inadequacy of the secular discourse.

## VII

In the course of our argument, we have referred to the *Mahabharata* story of Draupadi. The religiously revered text of the *Mahabharata* has faithfully preserved Draupadi's cry of anguish and her intrepid questioning of the patriarchal constructs of womanhood and morality while faced with the traumatic ordeal of being disrobed in the Royal Court; she questions such an assembly where there are only those who do not speak out the essence of religion: that religion, which is not based on truth and finally that truth itself, which is pierced through by deceit and deception. It is also culturally very significant that Draupadi is eventually saved in her humiliating distress, not by her righteous, noble and manly husbands, but by the so-called effeminate god Krishna.

Draupadi is the mythological archetype of the sexually awakened woman, who affirms herself and is recognised as such. It is such sexually awakened women that the patriarchal cultural discourse is mortally afraid of. It is probably a coincidence but an extremely loaded one that in this land of Sitas, Savitris and Padminis, one rarely finds a woman with the name Draupadi.

It is indeed a great threat to the communal and fascist world-view to have sexually awakened women because such women, by their sheer numerical strength, reduce the space of authoritarian semiotics exactly by half. Such women defy the entire construct of history, culture and moral values. They refuse to identify themselves only as symbols of honour and as means of procreation. To foreclose such an awful possibility, it is incumbent upon the communal-fascist discourse to reiterate woman's status as a symbol of honour and as a means of retribution. The seemingly contradictory connotations of the status are actually two sides of the same coin, just as the sophisticated ideology of rape as a political weapon and the actual participants in the spectacle of politically connotative rape are two shades in the same spectrum. Surat epitomises one and Savarkar the other. And both are mortally afraid of Draupadi— the sexually awakened woman affirming herself and being recognised as such.

## Notes on legends

1 Draupadi, according to the *Mahabharata*, one of the most revered and feared texts of the Hindus, was the shared wife of five Pandava brothers (so called after their father Pandu). The eldest of the Pandavas, Yudhisthir, was called Dharmaraj (morality personified) and was very fond of the game of dice. It was while playing dice with his villanous cousin, Duryodhana, that he gambled away not only his kingdom, but also Draupadi. She was saved from the ordeal of being publicly disrobed by Lord Krishna.

   Draupadi represents the courage to question blind orthodoxy and the claims of moral superiority made by the elders and divines. Many times in the story she is rebuked for this. Her friendship with Krishna is fairly unconventional in terms of the kinds of relationships that were 'sanctioned'.

2. Padmini, according to Rajput bardic legend, was the most beautiful and noble of women, queen consort of the king of Chittor. Allaudin Khilji (1296-1316 AD) of the Delhi sultanate invaded Chittor in order to take Padmini by force or deceit. Padmini committed sati in order to guard her honour and died on the pyre of her husband. This legendary account is not confirmed by chronicles or other historical evidence.

3. The mythical figures of Sita and Savitri are generally supposed to symbolise the virtues of an ideal woman, most important of which is total identification with the explicit and implicit wishes of the husband.

## Notes

1  *The Mass Psychology of Fascism*, London, Pelican Books, 1975, p. 138.
2  Begum Anis Kidwai, *Azadi ki Chaon Mein* (Hindi), Delhi, National Book Trust, 1990. pp. 156-7 and p.338.
3  The construction of woman as a symbol of national honour and sovereignity of the state becomes very clear in the Indian state's response to the problems of women abducted during the partition riots of 1947. The government's policies were formulated with a view to retrieving the 'national honour' and not with the perspective of woman as an individual who could have a say in her own destiny. For a detailed and well researched treatment of this see: Ritu Menon and Kamla Bhasin 'Recovery, Rupture, Resistance: Abduction of Women during Patrition,' *Review of Women Studies, Economic and Political Weekly*, April 24, 1993.
4  Asghar Ali Engineer, 'Bastion of Communal Amity Crumbles,' *Economic and Political Weekly*, February 1993, p. 263.
5  Jan Bremen, 'Anti-Muslim Pogrom in Surat,' *Economic and Political Weekly*, April 17, 1993, p. 741.
6  Sudhir Chandra, 'Of Communal Consciousness and Communal Violence: Impressions from Post-Riot Surat' *Economic and Political Weekly*, September 11, 1993, p. 1883.
7  Ibid, p. 1883.
8  G P Deshpande, 'Polity and Culture in the Wake of Ayodhya', *Economic and Political Weekly*, February 6, 1993, p. 219.
9  Ibid.
10 According to Dayananda Saraswati, such books are akin to 'food contaminated with poison' and ought to be discarded. See his *Satyartha Prakasha* (Hindi), Delhi, Dayanand Sansthan, 1974, p. 52.
11 Kenneth W. Jones, *Arya-Dharma: Hindu Consciousness in 19th Century Punjab*, Delhi, Manohar Publishers, 1976, p. 125.
12 Sudhir Kakar, *Intimate Relations: Exploring Indian Sexuality*, Penguin, New Delhi, 1990, p.1.
13 Sudhir Kakar, *Shamans, Mystics and Doctors*, Delhi, Oxford University Press, 1982, p. 87.
14 Bhagwan Josh, 'Women and Sexuality in the Discourse of Communalism and Communal Violence,' paper presented at a seminar on 'The Problem of Violence' at the Indian Institute of Advanced Studies, Shimla, September 9-13, 1991. Mimeograph, p. 6.
15 Kenneth W Jones, *The New Cambridge History of India: Socio-Religious Reform Movements in British India*, Delhi, Orient Longman, 1989, pp. 44-45.
16 Urvashi Butalia, 'Community, State and Gender: On Women's Agency during Partition' *Review of Women Studies, Economic and Political Weekly*, April 24, 1993.
17 Vinayak Damodar Savarkar, *Hindutva: Who is a Hindu* ? (sixth edition), Delhi, Bharti Sahitya Sadan, 1989, p. 4.
18 Vinayak Damodar Savarkar, *The Six Glorious Epochs of Indian History*, p. 124, Delhi, Rajdhani Granthagar, 1971, 'A word in confidence' (translator's note).
19 Ibid, p. 124.

[20] Dhamanjay Keer, *Veer Savarkar*, Bombay, Popular Prakashan, 1966, p. 539.
[21] Bhagwan Josh, op.cit. p. 7.
[22] *The Six Glorious Epochs of Indian History*, p. 71.
[23] Ibid, p. 104.
[24] Ibid, p. 85.
[25] Ibid, p. 131.
[26] Ibid, p. 141.
[27] Ibid, pp. 129-30.
[28] Ibid, p. 146.
[29] Ibid, p. 167.
[30] Ibid, p. 169.
[31] Ibid, p. 181.
[32] Ibid, pp. 174-75.
[33] Ibid, p. 176.
[34] Ibid, p. 177.
[35] Ibid, p. 178.
[36] Ibid, p. 180.
[37] Ibid, p. 181.
[38] Ibid, p. 461.
[39] *The Indian War of Independence 1857*, Delhi, Rajdhani Granthagar, 1986, p. 456.

# Muslims and Hindus
# Men and Women

## *Communal Stereotypes and the Partition of India**

### URVASHI BUTALIA

This paper grows out of a study I have been engaged in for some
years now. Begun as an oral history of partition, the study has
grown in many different directions. One of these is the question
of the experiences of women and an exploration of the many
inter-layered meanings and nuances of what one might call the
gender question at the time of partition. Until recently, little
attention has been paid to this question: rather, it has been
assumed that partition was in many ways, a gender neutral
process.[1] Recent work by historians and others has proved this
wrong and increasingly, gender is beginning to form one of the
starting points of enquiry into this major historical event which
continues to dominate the lives of many north Indians today.[2]

As I have begun to go more deeply into a study of partition, I
have come increasingly to the conclusion that it is not enough
just to visibilise women—who may have been hitherto invisible—in the history of partition, although that is without doubt
an important part of the enterprise; rather I feel gender has to
form an essential category in any understanding of partition. It
provides, in many ways, and to certain aspects, not just *an*
*i*mportant key but *the* important key, without which our understanding of partition is incomplete.

* I am grateful to Uma Chakravarti and Tanika Sarkar for their helpful comments
on this essay. Much of the work here would not have been possible without the
generous research assistance of Subhadra Sanyal.

There are many points from which one can approach a gendered history of partition. The violence that accompanied partition marked women and women's bodies in particular ways: we know of the rape and abduction that happened on a mass scale, of the cutting off of women's breasts, the tattooing of their bodies. We know too that in many places women were killed by their families, in others they took their own lives, and in some they also participated in the violence. (I have spoken of these in my paper referred to earlier) The dramatic changes wrought by partition in what was hitherto seen as the 'normal' life of families, communities—caused by the dislocation, the mass deaths, the forced migration—all of these led to another little discussed aspect, widowhood, destitution and loneliness for women (in the parlance of the Indian state women left without male protectors after partition were termed 'unattached'). Many women were unexpectedly rendered single as would-be partners died, or disappeared, and the 'marriageable', age passed. Paradoxically, for others, particularly those of the middle classes, mass scale refugeeism following on partition enabled their entry into different professions, among the most 'suitable' of which was social work. A gendered history of partition would thus explore how women were centrally implicated in the realignment of family and community identities, in the making of a national identity, in the communalism that so deeply marked this particular historical process. I am not attempting such a history here. In this paper I wish to build on my earlier work and take forward some of the arguments that were embryonic at the time in order to examine and unravel only one aspect of this complex question: that of the constitution of the identity of the 'Hindu' woman. I look at this through the prism of the concern reflected by the state and others about the raped and abducted woman and at how the harsh reality of what happened to women's bodies was deployed—and continues to be so—for purposes of nation making on the one hand, and retribution and revenge on the other. My main concern in this particular essay is to examine, how two different discourses, one, an overtly communal one, that of the Rashtriya Swayam Sevak Sangh (RSS) as seen through its mouthpiece, the *Organiser*, and the other, a statedly secular one, that of the Indian Legislative Assembly, constructed this identity, and the common and different concerns they reflected. In both of these, arguments and discussions about the Muslim state (i.e. Pakistan) and its subjects (i.e. Muslim men), the Indian state (defined as secular but often understood to mean Hindu) and its subjects (Hindu and Sikh men) were conducted with a sub-text, the body of the Hindu woman. Why did it become so important to define and fix such an identity? And why did the question of the Hindu woman's body, her sexuality become so important for two such different entities as the state and the RSS?

1947 was a complex moment in Indian history: a time of euphoria and achievement, a time at which Indians could congratulate themselves at having gained indpendence, but also a time of violence, loss, mass deaths, uprooting and communalism. In an insightful article on the reconstitution of Urdu writing and publishing after partition Aijaz Ahmed reminds us that 1947 was a moment of triumph not only for anti-colonial nationalism but also for communalism. In its consequences therefore, he says, it became the source of further communalisation of the politics that emerged on both sides.[3]

Ahmed adds that the reconstruction of partition history has tended to pose nationalism and communalism as entirely distinct, the former being associated purely with the creation of Pakistan, 'as if Indian nationalism itself was some pristine thing unsullied by the many compromises and adjustments it had made, at different junctures, with both the Hindu and Muslim communalists'.[4] What actually happened, he points out, was that with the principal strains of Muslim communalism being contained so to speak, in the shape of a state outside India, and 'on the strength of the monumental bitterness unleashed by the Partition, Hindu communalism could itself gain unprecedented respectability. Thus it was that many of its precepts became part of the general common sense and some of its positions were gradually adopted, in whatever mystified forms, even by sections of the liberal, secular, intelligentsia.'[5]

What were the consequences of this increased communalisation for women and how were they implicated in it? How did the ideas put forward by Hindu communalists gain acceptance vis a vis women? On the Indian side, when many communal stereotypes passed into public memory, and communalism itself gained unprecedented respectability, what sort of stereotypes became the staple of public memory? This question becomes particularly important not only because women could not have remained immune from the communal nature of partition but also because, with the increased visibility of women in communal parties today, and the sustained attempts being made by the Hindu right to address and mobilise the vast mass of women into communal campaigns, the resources and repertoire that are being deployed and drawn upon are often those that (while they may have existed earlier, and many did) were rendered respectable and acceptable at a time extremely charged in communal terms. The passage of time, and the difficulty both in personal narratives, and in written history, of facing up to the kinds of experiences that women went through, have also helped to render such stereotypes more 'acceptable'. When skilfully deployed, several of these find resonances and echoes, often in the most liberal of minds. This makes it increasingly difficult to speak of the 'Hindu right' as something that is located 'out there', at some point distant and distinct from the 'secularists' or the 'liberal intelligentsia'. Rather, what the last few years have brought before us most forcefully is the need to explore the many layers of sedimented ideologies which lie within us, and to begin dismantling these in order to approach long term action.

## II

The story of partition, the uprooting and dislocation of people, was accompanied by the story of the rape, abduction and widowhood of thousands of women on both sides of the newly-formed borders. The mass movement of people on foot, by bus, train, cart, left women, children, the aged and infirm, the disabled, particularly vulnerable. Little is known of the histories of these people and how they dealt with the trauma, pain and dislocation of enforced migration.[6] Because the state played a major role in the rehabilitation of widowed and destituted women, a rich literature exists on this. In the Legislative Assembly debates, newspaper records, police records and others we find, too, a considerable amount of discussion on raped and abducted women. Paradoxically, however, it is in oral narratives that there is, by and large, a silence on the abducted woman.

At least two women, to my knowledge, have written extensively about women (these are Kamlaben Patel and Anis

Kidwai),[7] and one (Damyanti Sahgal) I have interviewed at length. In my encounters with their work and their selves, I was initially struck by how difficult they had found it to write about their experiences and their work. Kamlaben, who worked with Mridula Sarabhai in rescuing abducted women, took some 20 years to write of her experiences because she found them too painful and disillusioning. Anis Kidwai, who worked in the Muslim refugee camps in Delhi, was advised by her brother not to publish her work and it is only in the last decade that it has become available. In my interviews with her, Damyanti Sahgal, who worked as Premvati Thapar's deputy in the recovery programme of the central government of India, insisted that there was little point in my interviewing her, because she had nothing to say or tell.

Why had these women chosen to remain silent? And indeed why had their families 'aided' in the imposition of such silences? What was it about the experiences of women that collective memory seemed to want to block out? Further questions came up: why, I asked myself, had families, men, women I had spoken to made no mention at all of the question of abducted women? Chivalrous women, for example those who had committed mass suicide in order to save themselves from being converted to the 'other' religion, were the subject of much discussion. In remembrance services in gurudwaras they were honoured and their *shahidi* (martyrdom) valorised. Widowed women seemed to have been accorded a dignity and social status which was quite unusual for a society that has traditionally derided widowhood as being the woman's fault. Indeed widowed women became a symbol of the state's benevolence and assumption of the role of parent. But with abducted women, the story was quite different. In families, while people were open in recounting many aspects of the tales of trauma, loss and dislocation, they never mentioned abductions. Those who did speak, or rather hint at, them, mentioned them always in the context of other families ('did they tell you it happened in their family?') not of their own. Thus the silence of history was compounded by a familial silence where, while some stories of partition were kept alive in collective memory, others had been obliterated. It was as if, by being abducted (as if they had somehow done this to themselves) the women themselves were to blame.

This silence is all the more surprising when one sees the

dimensions of the problem. Literally thousands of women were abducted in what became two free countries. Abduction is a catchall description that has come to be used for all women (and some men) who disappeared during the confusion of partition. While it is true that many were abducted, it is equally possible that many may have gone of their own accord. Nonetheless, for their purposes, the two states treated all women missing, or living with men of the other religion after a particular time, as abducted women.[8]

On the basis of complaints received from relatives the two countries compiled lists of missing women. While there is no way of ensuring that the figures were reliable (for instance a complaint about a particular woman could often be filed separately by three relatives, and this would then appear in a list three times at different places), some figures did find their way into public record. From these it seemed as if the number of Hindu and Sikh women abducted in Pakistan was roughly 33,000 (this did not include women from Kashmir and it was felt that if these were added the figure could well have reached 50,000). Lists received from Pakistan showed the figure of Muslim women abducted in India to be around 21,000. Whether or not these lists were accurate, they did serve to point to the size of the problem. It was because of this that the Indian state decided to mount what came to be known as the Central Recovery Operation, to locate, recover and, if necessary, 'rehabilitate' abducted women. Shortly after partition the Indian state also launched what was to become another of its major operations, that of rehabilitating widowed women, providing them with homes and jobs, as well as with psychological and moral support. In my larger work I have made a brief comparison of these two parallel but very different operations; here, however, I will not go into the question of widowhood.

As early as September 1947 the Prime Ministers of India and Pakistan met at Lahore and took a decision on the question of the recovery of abducted women. In a joint declaration they voiced what they felt was the main responsibility of the state:

> Both the Central Governments and the Governments of West and East Punjab wish to make it clear that forced conversions and marriages will not be recognised. Fur-

ther, women and girls who have been abducted must be
restored to their families, and every effort must be made
by the Governments and their officers concerned to trace
and recover such women and girls.[9]

Later, in December of the same year, this joint appeal was
given executive strength through an Inter Dominion Treaty in
which both countries resolved that all women abducted or forcibly married after March 1, 1947 should be restored to their
familes and that a joint organisation of both dominions would be
set up to carry out the necessary rescue work. A sub-committee
was set up which was to submit a report in three days on what
steps needed to be taken. Between them, the governments also
decided to collect particulars of abducted women, to broadcast
joint appeals for recovery, to organise transit camps in every
district for housing abducted women while they awaited their
transfer to a central camp to be set up in each dominion, exchanging weekly statements regarding the number of abducted
women, etc. A book published in 1952 by the Central Recovery
Organisation in India gives a district by district list of Hindu and
Sikh women who went missing or were presumed abducted in
Pakistan.[10] The Pakistan newspaper *Dawn* (founded by Jinnah)
published regular appeals for information about abducted
women, asking people to supply full details of where the woman
was last seen, and so on.

Almost from the beginning the recovery operation was fraught
with difficulty and tension. In the early stages Pakistan protested
against the involvement of the Military Evacuation Organisation
and suggested that its duties should be confined only to guard-
ing of transit camps. The actual work of rescue, they suggested,
should be given to the police. The Indian government was reluctant to do this because they claimed that in many instances the
police themselves were the abductors of women. Abduction by
people in positions of authority happened on both sides. Kirpal
Singh cites several cases. In one, two assistant sub-inspectors
of police went to recover an abducted woman and themselves
raped her.[11] In Montgomery, a tahsildar of Dipalpur, while
participating enthusiastically in broadcasting/publicising appeals for information about abducted women, is said to have
kept an abducted woman with him for some eight months.[12]

The question of abductions by police officers was taken up at the Inter Dominion Conference in December 1947 and later in January of the next year. India blamed Pakistan because they said that it had suddenly closed five districts of West Punjab to Indian social workers and police, claiming that they were close to the theatre of operations in Kashmir.

While the 3 September agreement quite clearly specified that abducted persons (The Act defined an abducted person as 'a male child under the age of sixteen years or a female of whatever age who is, or immediately before the 1st day of March 1947, was a Muslim. . .')[13] had no real choice in the question of their recovery, and this was reiterated in the Inter Dominion Treaty, it appears from government records that this was a question of some debate between Pakistan and India. Pakistan is said to have argued that some women were happy in their new surroundings and had offered resistance to being restored. The Deputy High Commissioner of Pakistan is said to have written to the Chief Secretary, East Punjab, thus: 'One . . . has written to say that his daughter. . . . aged 13 years, has been kept by one. . . son of. . . Jat of village Bhoma District Amritsar. In reply to his request for the recovery of the girl he was informed by the Indian Military authorities that his daughter did not wish to leave her husband.' One abducted woman is reported to have said to the District Liaison Officer, Gujranwala: 'How can I believe that your military strength of two sepoys could safely take me across to India when a hundred sepoys had failed to protect us and our people who were massacred ?' Another such statement was: 'I have lost my husband and have now gone in for another. You want me to go to India where I have got nobody and, of course, you do not expect me to change husbands each day.' A fourth said, 'But why are you particular to take me to India ? What is left in me now of religion or chastity ?'[14] Whether or not we should take these statements at face value, is a question that is beyond the scope of this paper. Nonetheless, these statements do testify to a certain reluctance on the part of some women to be 'recovered' and it is also clear from Indian records that many women did refuse to come back. The recovery operation lasted several years and during this time, women had perhaps 'settled' into families, some had 'accepted' their fate, some had had children and therefore many did not want to face a second dislocation. Social workers such as Kamlaben, Anis Kidwai and Damyanti Sahgal who worked in the Central Recovery Programme spoke eloquently of the women who did not want to return, of those who were torn about what to do with their children. Born of Muslim fathers, for Hindu families these children would be living symbols of the pollution of the race and therefore could not be integrated into Hindu society. The fear was not unfounded: when women did return, often families would not accept them back. Those who had children were even more difficult to accept and many were forced to choose between their children and their 'families'.

According to Rao, in support of its arguments Pakistan had produced declarations to this effect which were attested by magistrates. The Indian side viewed this with some scepticism, but eventually a compromise was worked out according to which 'women who ostensibly professed reluctance to be sent back to their original fold were to be segregated in special camps and there exposed to a process of resolute persuasion.'[15]

The agreement later became an ordinance (promulgated on January 31, 1949). Shortly afterwards, in the same year, the Abducted Persons Recovery and Restoration Ordinance became an Act. Interestingly, there was no parallel legislation on the Pakistan side although there was an Ordinance under which the Pakistan state operated. The Act provided for the setting up of a joint tribunal to deal with disputed cases. It is interesting to ask why the Indian government felt compelled to go in for such legislation at all, as by the time it was enacted, the bulk of the recoveries had already taken place (the figure dropped steadily after that) and according to Kirpal Singh, the majority of women recovered were not those who had been reported lost. The Act remained in force till 1957 when it was withdrawn because of considerable opposition. It was also because of this opposition that at the Indo Pak conference held in May 1954 it was discussed that some way should be found to ensure that abducted persons were not forced to go to the other country against their will. Special homes were then set up where unwilling persons could be housed and given time to make up their minds without 'fear or pressure'. How much of a choice this actually gave women is another question.

### III

On 29 December 1949 the front page of the *Organiser* carried a story entitled: 'Pakistan the Sinner: 25,000 Abducted, Thousands sold'. The story ran as follows: 'For the honour of Sita, Sri Rama warred against and destroyed Ravana, when filthy Khilji beseiged Chitoor its thousands of women headed by Rani Padmini all clad in gerua [saffron] saris, mounted the funeral pyre smiling, ere the mleccha [impure] could pollute a drop of the noble Hindu blood. Today, when tens of hundreds of Hindu women are spending sorrowful days and unthinkable nights in Pakistan, the first free government of the Union of Indian Sovereign Democratic Republic has nothing but a whimper for them.'

This article, and its subsequent accusation that Pakistan actually deserved the epithet 'Napakistan' (impure) was typical of the kind of rhetoric the *Organiser* voiced regularly in the years following immediately on partition. The rape and abduction of Hindu and Sikh women by Muslim men formed the backdrop against which accusations were levelled at Pakistan for being barbaric, uncivilised, lustful. The very formation of the nation of Pakistan out of the territory of Bharat (or, as we shall see later, the body of Bharatmata) became a metaphor for the violation of the body of the pure Hindu woman. The Indian state was regularly assailed for its failure to protect its women and to respond to Pakistan, the aggressor state, in the language that it deserved. More than ever, the need of the hour for Hindus was to build up 'a strong and virile state backed by a powerful army',[16] because, as one Chaman Lal, author of *Hindu America* put it, 'we have become such extreme pacifists that despite receiving kicks. . .we continue to appeal to the invaders in the name of truth and justice.'[7] If the invader was to be responded to in kind, what was required for the removal of this grave 'national' weakness was the 'Kshatriyaisation' of the Hindu race.[18]

For many writers in the *Organiser* the rape and abduction of women was a shameful, but predictable, event for what else could be expected of Pakistan, a nation 'built on the predatory desire for Hindu property and Hindu women [which] took practically no steps to checkmate the lust and avarice of its champions.'[19] There was, however, another reality. Muslim women had also been abducted by Hindu and Sikh men. How could this be explained? In the debates in parliament this was seen as an 'aberration', these men had clearly fallen victim to 'evil passions'. For the *Organiser*, the answer was rather similar. In an article entitled 'During the War of 1947' the writer claimed:

> During the Hindu Moslem War in the Punjab in the summer of 1947 passions ran high. Lakhs of people were slaughtered on both sides. But the war—the worse than war, abduction—on women, *a notorious and age-old practice of Muslims* (my italics) made the Nation writhe in pain and anguish. Thousands of Muslim women, widowed and abandoned, were left in Hindu majority areas also. But as soon as recovery work started, most of them, till then sheltered by the Hindus, were handed over to the authorities. Hardly any Muslim women remain in Bharat against their wishes. *It is significant to note that some of them were abducted by Muslims themselves.* (my italics)[20]

Hindu men thus, while occasionally falling victim to evil passions, are by and large harmless, even weak, and certainly not lustful. 'The Hindu mind,' we are told, 'is broad enough to do justice to others but not bold enough to demand justice.'[21] This is because India has a great tradition, a magnanimous culture that has ensured that:

> throughout the ages and even at the pinnacle of her armed might, when she could easily have swept the continent she never assumed the tyrant's role. While other people take pride in savage campaigns launched by their ancestors for enslavement, exploitation and forcible proselytization of their brother human beings, India, pregnant with the wisdom of her illustrious seers and true to her hoary culture, remembers only the key days of her glory when the impact of her glorious civilization was felt far and wide.'[22]

This ancient tradition is what makes the Hindu male tolerant and civilised, such that, even having abducted Muslim women, he is willing and ready to hand them over to the state or the authorities, the moment the call is given. It is also this tolerance—hitherto important—which has, in the moment of crisis, rendered the Hindu male incapable of protecting his women. This is why then, the call to arms, to fight and retaliate in the language of the Muslim state.

In a similar vein we are told by one writer that:

> Tens of thousands of our pious mothers and sisters who would faint at the sight of blood, were kidnapped and sold for so many rupees, annas, pies. I have seen some of them recovered from that holy land. Their foreheads bore tattoo-marks declaring them 'Mohammad ki joru', 'Mian Ahmed ki joru', 'Haji Hussain ki joru', etc., etc . . .
>
> Their [that of refugees in general] early and effective absorption in the economy and society of the regions of their adoption is the primary duty of every national of Hindustan. The task is not easy. It bristles with difficulties. That is obvious. But no less obvious is the fact that the problem is *a challenge to our manhood, no less than to our nationalism*. (my italics)[23]

For many writers of the *Organiser* during this period it becomes important to establish the purity of Mother India, the motherland which gave birth to the Hindu race and which is today home to the Hindu religion. The country, whether referred to as Bharat, or Hindustan, is imaged in feminine terms, and the partition, as a violation of its body. One issue of the *Organiser* (August 14, 1947) has a front page illustration of Mother India, the map of the country, with a woman lying on it, one limb cut off and severed, with Nehru holding the bloody knife responsible for doing the severing. Of Bharat Mata we are told that 'it is this steadfast faith in her religion that has saved Hindustan from extinction through countless centuries. . . she has run the gauntlet of conquest and bondage, she has been wrought upon by fear, persuasion and temptation to fling away her old faith and choose another but she refused to part with her religion which is her soul.'[24]

In this homily there is a lesson too for those abducted women who have so readily fallen prey, or chosen to accept the religion of the 'other'. If Hindu women are thus 'good' mothers, the very real fact of their cohabitation—enforced, perhaps even voluntary— with Muslim men represents a real threat to this ideal and therefore has to be dealt with. It is their husbands and brothers who have to fight for them, to go to war, even 'to burn themselves to ashes' if need be, and to bring them back into the fold despite their 'pollution'. As 'Kamal' (a pseudonym for a regular writer) puts it, 'Not only was Bharatvarsh our mother and we its children, she was the Deity and we her devotees. She was sacred. To go out was to go to foreign, impure, barbaric lands and so a purification on return was necessary.'[25] Another article quotes Ram as saying to his brother: 'O Lakshman, this golden Lanka doth not please my heart. The Mother, the country of our birth, is sweeter than the joys of heaven itself.'[26]

In sharp contrast to the image of the Hindu mother is that of the Muslim woman who appears only infrequently in these pages. In an article entitled 'Life in Sind', Hoondraj Kriplani bewails the   fact that Hindus are being abused and insulted at every step: 'Even in your own house you are not safe. Muslim women would enter your house on the pretext of enquiring whether you have anything to sell. And after a few minutes they will tell you that they have come to stay. You cannot drive them out, for you dare neither touch them nor get them removed by anyone else. . . .' He goes on to add an ingenious warning to his Hindu brothers: 'You may persist for two or three days in living with them, but then, of course, there is the real danger of these Muslim women crying aloud at night. And then where do you stand?'[27] At another point, in a regular column entitled 'Indraprastha Calling' we are told, in a question and answer exchange (albeit in a tongue-in-cheek fashion) that a Muslim woman was known to have given birth to cartridges![28]

The pages of the *Organiser* are rich in this kind of rhetoric and concern and are no more than what one would expect from an overtly communal journal of this kind. This brief sketch will, I hope, suffice to point to some of the major strands of thinking on the question of women. I want now to turn to some of the debates that took place in parliament on the issue of the recovery of abducted women and to see what kinds of echoes we find here for the thoughts and ideas we have met in the *Organiser*.

## IV

The legislation being debated in 1949 in the Indian legislative assembly was the Abducted Persons Recovery and Restoration Act, an extension of the ordinance on the subject that the state had issued. The Act had to do with the recovery of Muslim women who had been abducted by Hindu and Sikh men. The Assembly had an extended debate on the Act, to which more than 70 amendments were moved, representatives of the government were called to question on various points, but in the end, it was passed virtually unchanged. For our purposes, it is interesting to see how the passage of this Act, and the accompanying debate, provided an opportunity for Indian members of parliament to pronounce their views on Pakistan, a country they saw only in rather stark terms. The debate also allowed the newly formed nation to define itself vis a vis its 'Other', and to present itself as caring, secular, tolerant, rational, modern—in other words, everything the other was not.

Members of the Assembly who spoke in the debates were of all hues. It is striking, however, to note how closely what they said mirrored a great deal of what we have met with in the *Organiser*. Perhaps this ought not to seem surprising: yet this was the very Parliament wherein the identity of the nation was now being forged on what it defined as 'secular' and 'modern' lines. The first concern was that Pakistan had not returned women in sufficient numbers, more especially not in the same kinds of numbers the Indian side had returned Muslim women. Several members expressed shock at this, and at the fact that Pakistan had shown itself less than willing to keep to the terms of the agreement. This, to them, was a reflection of two things: the typical, uncivilised character of Pakistan (made up, as it was, of Muslim men who had fought for a communal state and who were therefore communal by nature) and the much more humane approach of the Indian state. At the same time the Indian state's 'inaction' in this matter was also seen as a lack, a sign of weakness on its part and its inability to draw the other country in line. Professor Shibban Lal Saxena (UP General) said he was deeply dissatisfied at 'the failure of our government to be able to infuse a proper spirit in the other Dominion to restore our sisters to us.'[29] He suggested India retaliate and do something commensurate with the gravity of the situation, not only because that was the right thing to do 'by our sisters' but also because India had (in the manner of the *Organiser*) a 'tradition'. 'Even now,' he said, 'the Ramayana and Mahabharata are revered. For the sake of one woman who was taken away by Ravana the whole nation took up arms and went to war. And here there are thousands and the way in which they have been treated . . . . Our sisters from Kashmir were actually sold in the bazars and whatnot was done to them.' [30] He went on to add that when there was a dispute with South Africa the Indian government had reacted by merely imposing sanctions, a clear sign of its weakness, when much stronger action was called for. There were other criticisms and a suggestion that restoration of Hindu and Sikh women abducted in Pakistan should have formed part of the Ceasefire Agreement.[31]

As with the *Organiser*, the *Ramayana* and *Mahabharata* provided important reference points here too, as did the call to 'open war if need be'[32] to get back Hindu women. Another MP asserted:

> If there is any sore point or distressful fact to which we cannot be reconciled under any circumstances, it is the question of the abduction and non-restoration of Hindu women. We all know our history of what happened in the time of Shri Rama when Sita was abducted. Here, when thousands of girls are concerned, we cannot forget this. We can forget all the properties, we can forget every other thing, but this cannot be forgotten . . . . As descendants of Ram we have to bring back every Sita that is alive.[33]

The feeling that Pakistan needed to be brought in line was echoed by others who felt, to use the words of Pandit Hriday Nath Kunzru, that the restoration of Muslim women to 'their rightful home' (i.e. Pakistan) was a 'great moral duty'. 'We cannot refuse to fulfil our obligations because others decline to fulfil theirs.' He was of the view that Pakistan should be made to feel that it was not an act of merit but of degradation to keep unwilling persons within its own territory and to 'compel them to give up their own religion and to embrace Islam.'[34]

Suggestions for retaliatory action were, however, turned down by the government's representative. In response to Pandit Thakur Das Bhargava's statement that he saw no reason why 'a country is not justified in keeping these [Muslim] girls as hostages for some time. . . as a matter of policy it should have been done,'[35] Gopalswamy Ayyangar, speaking for the Indian government, held that such behaviour did not behove a 'civilised' government. Rather, it was India's responsibility, given its modern, secular, rational, outlook, to persuade the other country to behave in a manner that would be 'consistent with its claim to be a civilised government.'[36]

Like its men, the Muslims who had abducted Hindu and Sikh women, Pakistan too became tarred with the same brush. It was not civilised, it had not displayed moral standards. Renuka Ray from West Bengal asserted that 'India is not going to succumb to the ideas of Pakistan. India has her own objectives and standards and whether Pakistan comes up to them or not, it does not mean that India is to go down to the level and the lack of moral standards displayed by Pakistan.'[37]

By showing concern for Muslim women abducted, forcibly converted and sometimes forcibly married within its territories, the Indian state was showing itself to be civilised, modern and secular. The modernism was, however, tempered by the ancient tradition of the *Ramayana* and the *Mahabharata* which enjoined protection of womenfolk, as well as chivalrous and honourable behaviour. Pakistan, by contrast, in the eyes of Indian parliamentarians, had no such commitment to secularism, nor any such ancient tradition to draw on, for this was a Hindu tradition and Pakistan was a Muslim state. Despite the excessive concern for the rights of 'our sisters' (i.e. abducted Muslim women) to live a life of their own, and the constant reiteration of their innocence, members of parliament were also keen to establish that abductions had not taken place in their states, that there the social order was intact. When one member asked a hypothetical question, using UP as an example, about abductions in that state, a member from UP came back and asked why he had spoken of UP and why not of Bihar. It was clear that while concern was being voiced for the fate of 'our women' held in the other dominion, and they were 'pure' at least in intent if not in body, it was somehow not desirable that abductions should have taken place on the soil of this or that state. Not because abduction in itself was reprehensible, but because the presence of abducted women somehow affected the character of the state.

## V

A piece of its territory had been lost, and lost to a 'barbaric' religion, to 'communal' people. Mother India, the nation, imaged throughout the nationalist movement in feminine terms, had been violated, her body truncated, never to be recovered. The *Organiser*'s front page picture of the map of India tracing the outlines of the female body, arm outstretched into what formed Pakistan, with Nehru holding a knife that had severed the arm from the body, is a graphic and powerful reminder of this. The violation and rape of the body of the nation was mirrored in the violation and rape of the bodies of its women. And while the loss of the nation's body was irrecoverable, the bodies of women could be recovered, had to be recovered.

I do not wish to suggest that both discourses we have looked at are identical. There are differences which I will examine shortly. Despite these, however, the overall picture has a disturbing similarity. Pakistan, the state, emerges as barbaric, lacking in civilisation, reason, as well as morals. If Pakistan is barbaric, its men are violent, aggressive, fanatical, uncivilised, virile, sexually active and lustful. Its women are not to be trusted for they can draw unsuspecting Hindu men into their net. India, the Hindu nation, by contrast, is seen as secular, tolerant, rational, civilised, modernising, yet rooted firmly in tradition. The hidden or absent referrent, whose 'absent presence' (if one may use such an expression) informs and underlies much of the discussion, is the abducted Indian (read Hindu) woman. She is the one whose loss, through abduction, causes concern. It is this and her violation, through rape, that reflects on the weakness and emasculation of Indian men, and, in the eyes of some, the Indian state. And it is the suggestion that she may actually wish to stay with her abductor/rapist or that she may not wish to return to her family/husband, that she may actually exercise agency on her own behalf, that becomes unacceptable. The sexual chaos that this very real possibility represents, the 'unleashing' of women's sexuality that it can suggest, is something unsanctionable, both for Indian men, and for the Indian state. The Central Recovery

Operation was thus, at one level, an attempt to reintegrate and relocate abducted women into the restructured family, community and nation.

Defining the identity of the Hindu woman also becomes important because each Hindu woman is mother India in her individual capacity, and their collective energy, the basis for the real mother India. These identities are constructed at different, overlapping, levels. In the *Organiser,* all abducted women are innocent victims, the resisting woman does not exist. This representation is important as it enables an instrumentality of revenge and retribution in what comes increasingly to be referred as a long-term war (see, in this connection, Purshottam Agarwal's essay in this volume). Overlying the innocent victim, and completely obliterating the resisting, therefore sexual, woman, is the image of the mother, caring, nurturing, compassionate, desexualised, of whose pure womb sons are born to further the cause of the Hindu *rashtra.* As Sumati Ramaswamy points out: '. . . the representation of the nation or the community as a self-less and compassionate Mother allowed it to be abstraced from the public sphere of politics and self-interest and put on a pedestal as an iconic subject of affection and devotion.'[38] This process simultaneously 'fixes' the identity not only of the Hindu woman, but also the Hindu man, the Muslim man and the Muslim woman. Kumkum Roy, writing in this volume, explains why such an exercise becomes important where Hindu women are concerned:

> Focusing on this form of womanhood rests implicitly (and occasionally explicitly) on a number of assumptions — that Hindu women are different from non—Hindu women, that they are different from Hindu men and that they are a homogenous category. In other words, possible differences along caste/class/regional lines are glossed over, a specific gendered understanding is centralised, and a communal identity is sharpened — if not created. There is thus a tendency to universalise and generalise on the one hand, and to differentiate on the other, to sustain an impression of sameness and uniqueness at two mutually reinforcing levels.[39]

A similar instrumentality does not inform the discourse of the state which is more nuanced, complex and differentiated. In acting to recover abducted women the state is, at one level, responding to the very legitimate claims of the community (both men and women for complaints were filed by both) on it. In doing so, it violates the rights of some of its citisens—those who did not wish to return. While this is the material reality, at the symbolic level, for the post-partition fragile, and deeply contested state, the process of recovering its women becomes one of restoring its legitimacy and the nation's honour. It is also, for a state that sees itself as civilised, the civilised thing to do. The imaging of the nation as simultaneously mother, home and family, provides a powerful underpinning for the state to see itself as caring parent, concerned for the fate, and future, of its citizens. It is this concern that makes it necessary to recover the mothers of its future citizens.

The *Organiser*—and I am not suggesting that all writers in this magazine have an identical underlying concern—has, on the whole, a different agenda. If for the state it is important that women be brought back into the fold, for the *Organiser* the opposite is true. Abducted and raped women must stay where they are, in a state, if you like, of *permanent* rape because it is this that will enable Hindu men to avenge themselves on those responsible for this condition of their 'sisters', every Sita and Draupadi.

This is not a specious claim. That this concern provided a strong motivation for action is evident in many different ways. In 1990, while working on a report on communal violence in the Nizamuddin basti in Delhi, a group of historians interviewed BL Sharma, a senior member of the Vishwa Hindu Parishad in Delhi. Sharma told them that his turning to militant Hinduism had directly occasioned by the tales of the rape, violation and abduction of Hindu women by Muslim men during partition. It was this that had led to his becoming a member of the RSS. [40] Not surprisingly, it did not seem to count that Hindu men too had played no mean role in the rape and abduction of Muslim women, or indeed of Hindu women. What had overwhelming importance was the rape, by the 'Other', particularly as this proved yet again that Pakistan was a nation built on the 'predatory desire for Hindu property and Hindu women.'

In the India of the nineties, the images of raped and abducted women, the metaphor of the violated body of the nation, continue to be repeatedly used to generate what one might call a new political economy of violence. Such violence, directed against the minority community, is directed also against women of the minority community in particular ways: rape, leading to impregnation with the seed of the 'superior' or 'pure' race. As other writers in this volume have pointed out, the mass rape of Muslim women in Surat in the aftermath of the destruction of the Babri masjid was articulated, by the Hindu right, as revenge and retribution for the rape of Hindu women during partition. In an interview with a group of college students Krishna Sharma of the VHP said: 'Hindus must make sure that they are feared by others. We have to prove our mettle. If they rape 10-15 of our women we must also rape a few to show them that we are no less.' (See *Interviews* in this volume). While one form of such revenge is rape, a second is to target younger, presumably fertile women (and men) and to kill them—the women often by stabbing in the womb—so that they will not reproduce.

Women and property are inextricably linked in much of the discourse we have seen. This is a motif that recurs in almost all communal rhetoric today: if the 'predators' (men) have designs on and the desire for women as property, the 'victims' equally see the violation of those women as a violation of their property. In much sectarian violence in India today the 'losses' of partition, in terms of women and property, provide powerful referrents. There is also a material reality to the loss of property: in Bhagalpur, Surat, Bombay the attacks on Muslims had to do not only with their 'Otherness' in terms of religion, but with more material things. In Bhagalpur the riots took place at a time when the crop was ready to be harvested. Mass desertion by Muslims meant this was now 'ripe' to be stolen by others; a community that was particularly targeted was the weavers of Bhagalpur, famed for their silk. Not only were they killed, but their looms were viciously destroyed, leaving them with no possibility of economic recovery. In Bombay, it is now well known that apart from the 'communal' motivation behind the killing of Muslims, there was too the very real reality of the value of the real estate they were sitting on.

Unlike at the time of partition, this property is now 'internal'—it cannot be broken away, but it can be taken away from its owners by other means. And these go hand-in-hand with the violation of the women of the victim community. In Bhagalpur, younger women were especially targeted for killing in order to 'stop them breeding like pigs', while in Surat the story of the rape of women needs no elaboration.

Nonetheless, while the *Organiser's* rhetoric may have been aggressive and full of falsehoods, and the state's more differentiated, the latter still legitimised various forms of communal stereotypes. Indeed, the highly charged communal climate in which the debates were conducted, did impinge on the Legislative Assembly and its 'acceptance' or 'endorsement' of anything that can even mildly be seen as communal. This is a matter of concern for a state whose very identity was, and continues to be presented as a secular one.

Today, we can see a much clearer recharging of these myths, a circumstance which is increasingly visible from 1984 on. Women are being especially targeted, pulled out as primary victims, and this goes hand-in-hand with their rise as significant actors in communalism. The ground that the state and the *Organiser* occupied in part at the time, has almost totally been given over to the latter, and to related organisations of the Hindu right. In a sense, while the state did share some of the assumptions of the *Organiser*, it could still act as a moderating influence, a tempering force. Today there is no such space for the state to assume this role because there are too many other preoccupations, and in 'real' terms the issue does not exist. There are no abducted women to recover. Their abduction at partition has entered the realm of 'myth' in a way that they can be pulled out and deployed with ease. How can the state then deal with myth, with belief, with intangibles ? And if the state cannot, what can small groups do ? It is the work of such groups that can and does provide the beginnings of answers to this question.

## VI

What purpose is served, one may well ask, by the above examination ? Is the exercise merely an academic one, or does it have any meaning beyond the needs of historical research ? I have tried to show here how in communal violence in contemporary India, stories of the rape and abduction of Hindu and Sikh women have formed the subtext and also the overt motivation for the violence that is visited upon minority communities, and in specific ways, on minority women. A matter of concern is the very real circumstance that in every such instance of violence, whether it is Bhagalpur, or Khurja, or Surat or Bombay, there is very little outrage or outcry from people we might loosely define as 'liberal' or even broadly 'secular'. Indeed, the only people who seem to act, respond, take up issues, are civil liberties, anti-communal and women's groups. The 'inability' to respond to the agenda being set by the Hindu right on the part of secular and liberal people has been critiqued as the failure of secularism in India. This critique has also been very eloquently and effectively countered, so I shall not go into it here.

Instead, I would like to suggest that not enough attention has been paid to the highly selective and manipulative process by which myths and stereotypes about the marauding and libidinous Muslim, the innocent and motherlike Hindu woman, the tolerant Hindu man, have entered and entrenched themselves in public memory and consciousness. The construction of this picture leaves out many things, not least of which is the fact that rape and abduction took place on both sides, as did violations of women's rights. Hindu, Muslim and Sikh men were equally guilty. I think we need also to remind ourselves of where such manipulation wishes to place and fix women, and how important it is to counter such manipulation if we are to preserve any of the precious few gains the women's movement has made in the last few decades. In other words, the meaning, for someone like me, of such an excercise, does not lie only in a search for patterns and motivations, but in providing an understanding from which informed action can take place within the women's movement.

## Notes

[1] Although earlier histories and documentation of partition, such as Kirpal Singh's *Partition of the Punjab* and Satya Rai's *The Partition of India*, make mention of the experiences of women and children, they do not focus on these in any special way. More recently, my own larger work 'Community, State and Women's Agency: Women's Experiences during Partition' in *Economic and Political Weekly*, Review of Women Studies, April 1993, and a somewhat extended version of this article in Oxford Literary Review, January 1995, has examined this question. It has also been looked at by Ritu

Menon and Kamla Bhasin in their 'Recovery, Rupture, Resistance: The State and Women during Partition' also in the same issue of *Economic and Political Weekly*, and, most recently, Veena Das has also looked at women, drawing largely on the research done by Ritu Menon and Kamla Bhasin.

Just as the story of women's experiences during partition has not received much attention from historians, so also, the history of partition has, by and large, been mainly a constitutional history, or what one might call 'history from above'. It is only now that it is becoming clear that one needs to re-examine partition not only for gender but for other experiences. My own larger work looks at untouchables, children, and others on the fringes of society.

2   See articles cited above.

3   Aijaz Ahmed, 'Some Reflections on Urdu', *Seminar* 359, July 1989, 25.

4   ibid.

5   Ibid.

6   See my essay 'Listening, for a Change: Oral narratives of Partition,' paper presented at a seminar on Northern India and Independence, Nehru Memorial Museum and Library, December 1993, and also Urvashi Butalia, ed., 'Memories of Partition', *Seminar* 420, August 1994.

7   Kamlaben Patel, *Mool se Ukdhe Hue* (Hindi), Bombay 1990. Anis Kidwai, *Azadi ki Chaon Mein* (Hindi) Delhi, 1989.

8   The first disturbances took place in Punjab in March 1947 when a number of Sikh majority villages in Rawalpindi district came under attack. Thus it was assumed that the beginning of March could therefore be taken as a sort of cut off date: all Hindu and Sikh women found to be living with Muslim men after that date could be assumed to have been abducted.

9   U Bhaskar.Rao, *The Story of Rehabilitation*, Delhi, Publications Division, 1967, p. 30.

10  Central Recovery Organisation, *Non Muslim Abducted Women and Children in Pakistan and Pakistan Side of the Cease Fire Line of Jammu and Kashmir State*, Government of India, Ministry of External Affairs, 1952. Till this time, the names of abducted people had not been made public out of consideration for the families. This was the first time that such a list was actually being released.

11  Kirpal Singh, *The Partition of the Punjab*, Publications Bureau, Punjab University, Patiala, 1972, p. 171.

12  Ibid.

13  Abducted Persons Recovery and Restoration Act, 1949.

14  All the above examples are from Kirpal Singh, op. cit. pp. 170-71.

15  Rao, op. cit. p. 35.

16  *Organiser*, 10 July 1947. A great deal of detailed work on the RSS and the Organiser has been done by Paola Bacchetta. See, particularly her 'Communal Property/Sexual Property: On Representation of Muslim Women in a Hindu Nationalist Discourse,' in Zoya Hasan, ed., *Forging Identities: Gender, Communities and the State*, Delhi, Kali for Women, 1994.

17  *Organiser*, 10 July, 1947.

18  *Organiser*, 10 July, 1947.

19  *Organiser*, December 14, 1949.

20 *Organiser*, December 14, 1949.

21 *Organiser*, November 30, 1949.

22 *Organiser*, 10 July 1947.

23 *Organiser*, 13 November, 1948.

24 *Organiser*, 25 Setpember, 1947.

25 *Organiser*, 19 August 1948.

26 *Organiser*, 5 August 1948.

27 *Organiser*, 18 December, 1947.

28 *Organiser*, 23 October 1947.

29 India: Legislative Assembly Debates 1949, p. 709. All subsequent references to the Legislative Assembly Debates are from the same year.

30 Ibid.

31 Ibid.

32 Ibid, p. 718.

33 Ibid, p. 752.

34 Ibid.

35 Ibid, p. 764.

36 Ibid.

37 Ibid, p. 716.

38 Sumati Ramaswamy, 'En/gendering Language: The Poetics of Tamil Identity,] in *Comparative Studies in Society and History*, 1993, vol 35 (4) 713.

39 Kumkum Roy, 'Where Women are Goddesses, the Gods Rejoice' in this volume.

40 P K Dutta et al, 'Understanding Communal Violence: Nizamuddin Riots,' *Economic and Political Weekly*, November 10, 1990.

# Communalising Gender
# Engendering Community
## Women, Legal Discourse and the Saffron Agenda

RATNA KAPUR and BRENDA COSSMAN

## Introduction

The discourse of democracy and fundamental rights have become powerful weapons in the hand of the Hindu right to
further their Hindutva campaign. Secularism, in their hands, has
become a way of challenging the identity of minority communities. Equality has become an implement for reinforcing dominant Hindu norms, and attacking the 'Other' for violating these
norms. In this paper, we explore the way in which these concepts
of secularism and equality have become the site of a contest for
meaning, as the Hindu right seeks to redefine these concepts in
accordance with Hindutva's vision of the relationship between
religion and politics and of the role of women in Indian society.

This redefinition is part of a much broader campaign. The
Hindu right is engaged in a discursive struggle, that is, in a
contest over the way in which individuals understand the world
around them. Hindutva represents a particular set of beliefs and
categories; it is a way of giving meaning to the world and of
organising social institutions. The Hindutva campaign is also
ideological, that is, it is related to the social, economic, and
political conditions of contemporary India, and to the legitima-
tion of social and political power. It is part of a contest over the
dominant or hegemonic way of understanding the world, and of
establishing an understanding that contributes to the legitima-
tion of social power and inequality.

Hindutva is not, at least not yet, an ideologically dominant discourse, but rather, is involved in a discursive struggle for ideological dominance. These discursive struggles are ongoing at many levels—historical, political, cultural and economic. Our focus is on the struggle for meaning and dominance within the field of law—particularly, on the struggle to redefine the concepts of secularism and equality. As we will attempt to illustrate, these concepts have become the site of a contest for meaning over the role of religion in Indian politics, and over the role and identity of women in Indian society.

This legal discourse plays an important role in the re-articulation of community and gender identity — mutually constituting identities that are central to the Hindutva campaign. Community and gender, or more specifically, religion and equality are often seen as conflicting, and oppositional. Indeed, the conflict between the right to freedom of religion and women's right to equality has proved explosive, often resulting in communal disturbances, as witnessed in the cases of Roop Kanwar and Shah Bano. The conflict is understood as one of balancing essentially oppositional rights. This understanding, however, has failed to appreciate how this conflict between religion and equality represents a broader discursive struggle over both community and gender identity by the forces of Hindutva. It is only through the deconstruction of oppositions—between religion and equality, between community and gender—that we can begin to understand the impact of these discursive struggles on women. We will attempt to illustrate the ways in which the discourses of religion and equality, and of community and gender are mutually constituting in the Hindutva discursive strategy, i.e., women are constituted in and through communal identity, and conversely, community is constituted in and through women's gender identity.

In the first section of the paper, we briefly consider the discourse of Hindutva, and the way in which Hindu communalists are attempting to forge an ideologically dominant discourse through a broad range of discursive fields, including law. In the second section, we examine the discursive struggles that are taking place over the meaning of secularism and freedom of religion for ideological hegemony. We review competing understandings of secularism, and attempt to illustrate the way in which the Hindu right is appropriating a particular understand-

ing of secularism to advance its Hindutva agenda of establishing
a Hindu *rashtra*.

We then turn to examine the discursive struggles that are
taking place over the meaning of equality, particularly sexual
equality. In this section, we review the competing understandings of equality, and of gender difference and how they become
the site of the broader discursive struggle of the Hindu right for
ideological hegemony. We examine the paradoxical ways in
which the Hindu right has seized hold of the competing understandings of equality and gender difference, in order to reassert
the traditional role of Hindu women in the family and in society.
At the same time, we examine how the discourse of equality and
gender difference is deployed to attack the Muslim community
and the discriminatory treatment of Muslim women. The final
section examines how women are mutually constituted through
the discourses of gender and community. At the same time, we
expose the internally inconsistent statements on Hindu women
within the Hindu right.

## Communalism and the Hindu right

Communalism has been defined as a discourse based on the
'belief that because a group of people follow a particular religion, they have as a result, common social, political and economic interests'.[1] It is a discourse that attempts to constitute
subjects in and through community attachment, particularly
through religious community.[2] It constitutes the way in which
these subjects see and give meaning to the world around them.
Through communal discourses, subjects come to understand the
world around them as one based on the conflict between religious groups; Indian society is understood as fractured by the
conflict between these groups. This community identity becomes
the basis for social, economic and political demands,[3] and for
political mobilisation around these demands. Through the discourse of Hindutva, Hindu subjects are constituted to understand this fractured society in a particular way.

At the heart of Hindutva lies the myth of a continuous thousand year old struggle of Hindus against Muslims as the structuring principle of Indian history. Both communities are assumed
to have been homogenous blocks—of Hindu patriots, heroically
resisting invariably tyrannical, 'foreign' Muslim rulers.[4]

More recently, it is said, the policy of appeasing minorities—i.e., of special treatment for Muslims and other religious minorities — has perpetuated the oppression of Hindus. The contemporary social, economic and political malaise that is gripping Hindu society is seen as the result of this policy of appeasement. The answer to this crisis, according to the Hindu right is a Hindu *rashtra*—India must be a Hindu state. Only then can Hindu culture and pride be restored. The subjects of Hindu communalist discourse are being constituted in the world around them through this lens.[5]

The discourse of communalism is, at the same time, ideological. In speaking of communalism as ideological, we are highlighting the connection between ideas and material structures; and the way in which these ideas are used to legitimise relations of domination. Both of these themes are emphasised in much of the contemporary literature on Hindu communalism. The recent surge in the Hindu right is seen to be in part a response to the economic, political and ideological crises of cotemporary India — to the failure of modernisation, to the crisis of governability, and to the demise of nationalist, democratic ideologies in post-colonial India. These discourses are seen to be related to the material conditions—the current political and economic reality.[6] This surge in Hindu communalism is also related to the role of the discourse of Hindutva in legitimating and supporting the political agenda of an aspiring political elite. Hindu communalists are seeking to forge an ideologically dominant discourse, through the organisation of consent and the production of common sense, which will, in turn, increase the support for the BJP and the Sangh *parivar* more generally. The increasing support for the Sangh *parivar* has demonstrated that a large group of Hindus are beginning to accept the Hindu communalist version of history and politics as universal and natural. The discourse of 'Muslim domination', 'appeasement of minorities' and 'Hindu pride' has become commonplace. And as this discourse becomes more commonplace, so the support for the BJP continues to grow.

The Hindu communalist discursive struggle for ideological hegemony stretches across a broad range of discursive fields—history, politics, economics. Our focus is on the struggle for meaning within the field of law, as legal discourse becomes yet another contested site. Law has long played a contradictory role in mediating social conflict. As an official, through relatively autonomous discourse of the state, law plays a role in legitimating unequal power relations, as well as in challenging them.[7] While it is a hegemonic discourse, its relative autonomy from other branches of the state creates the possibility of it operating as a counter-hegemonic discourse. The legitimacy of law resides in its purported objectivity and universality, and to sustain this legitimacy, the rule of law must appear to be equally applicable to all of its subjects. These values of legal liberalism create law's counter-hegemonic potential.[8]

In the sections that follow, we will explore the counter-hegemonic legal strategies of the Hindu right. The focus will not be on legal cases or legislation, but rather, on legal discourse. We will examine the way in which the Hindu right is challenging the dominant meanings of legal discourse, and seeking to redefine these concepts for its own purposes, i.e. in accordance with its vision of Hindutva.

### Discursive struggles: contested discourses of secularism and freedom of religion

The legal and political concepts of secularism and freedom of religion are currently the site of discursive struggles for ideological hegemony. The Hindu right is seeking to displace the dominant meanings of the legal concepts, and to redefine these concepts in accordance with their vision of the appropriate relationship between religion and politics—a vision which at its most extreme threatens to undermine the very spirit of secularism. In this section, we explore the contested discourses of secularism and freedom of religion, and the ways in which the communalist version is being deployed in their campaign towards Hindutva.

Secularism is widely accepted as a cornerstone of Indian democracy.[9] There is, however, no similar consensus on the meaning of this concept. Indeed, secularism has come to mean many things to many people. At least two different conceptualisations of secularism can be identified in Indian legal and political discourse. In the first approach, secularism is understood as the separation of religion and politics. Within this formal approach to secularism, there can be no state involvement in religion and no law based on religion. The state must maintain a position of strict neutrality and impartiality towards religion. Freedom of religion is based on a liberal understanding that asserts each individual is free to follow the religion of her choice without state interference. The formal approach has, by and large, been rejected as Western, anti-religious and inappropriate in the Indian context.[10]

In the second approach, secularism is based in the Gandhian notion of *sarva dharma sambhava*—the equal respect of all religions. This approach is not based on the separation of religion and politics, but rather, on the equality of all religions within political as well as private life. This version of secularism:

> ... implies not the distancing of religion from the state
> but a continuum of all religions with the politics of the
> state. In this secular vision is also emphasised the equal-
> ity of all religions, and impartiality of the state. The
> impartiality of state vis-a-vis all religions is stressed, as
> the state itself is supposed to be the representative body
> of all religious communities.[11]

*Sarva dharma sambhava* has been widely accepted as the meaning of secularism in India, and it is this approach that has dominated legal and political thought since Independence.[12] It has similarly been widely accepted that the concept of freedom of religion in Indian constitutional law is one that has allowed state intervention in religion.[13]

There remain, however, diverse opinions on the precise meaning of this concept; particularly, on the meaning of the equal respect for all religions. The meaning of secularism is dependent on the meaning to be given to the concept of equality. Equal respect for all religions could mean that all religions must be treated equally, i.e., treated the same in law. Alternatively, it could mean that religions should be equal in result, i.e., the law may have to treat them differently to ensure that they are treated equally.[14]

Both of these approaches to secularism have been subject to criticism. The first approach to secularism—the wall of separation between religion and politics—has been rejected in India as Western, hostile to religion and thus inappropriate in the Indian context. While there are certainly some important limitations to this approach to secularism, particularly in the context of India, the characterisation of this approach as hostile to religion is somewhat misdirected. This criticism is based on the history of secularism in the West, and particularly on the First Amendment to the United States Constitution which provides that the state shall make no law in relation to religion. This anti-establishment clause, as interpreted by the United States Supreme Court, has proven to be extremely problematic. The problem, however, is not one of being hostile to religion. Many have argued that the strict state non-intervention and neutrality required by the anti-establishment clause only serves to reinforce the power relationships of the status quo, 'Neutral means might not produce neutral results, given historic practices and social arrangements that have not been neutral.'[15] Indeed, surface neutrality of these policies ignores, and risks reinforcing their non-neutral impact. Practices that may appear to be neutral as between different religions may in fact be premised on the norms and practices of the majority. State neutrality, in the face of divergent practices between majority and minority groups, often serves to reinforce the majority practices, and the power of the majority to define the norm. The majority's practices become the unquestioned norm, against which any difference is measured, and in turn, denied. In the context of the United States, this has often meant reinforcing the dominant protestant norm of the majority, and failing to accommodate the norms and practices of religious minorities.

The second approach to secularism—*sarva dharma sambhava* — has also been the subject of considerable criticism as the dominant model in India. Insofar as this approach is based on the equal respect of all religions, and thus, on the recognition of different religious communities, it can be seen to reinforce and reinscribe these differences. *Sarva dharma sambhava* does not transcend the categories of communalism, but rather, is based on and operates to reinforce these communalist categories. Many writers have observed that Indian secularism is not the antithesis of communalism, but rather, a product of many communalisms.[16] Upadhyaya, for example, has argued that the *sarva dharma sambhava* approach to secularism has been an underlying cause of the communalisation of Indian politics.[17] He argues that this vision of secularism, in which the state is envisioned as 'the representative body of all religious communities' becomes a majoritarian secularism, in which 'the religion of the majority ultimately exercises the decisive influence in the state structure.'[18] In this view, *saarva dharma sambhava* as an approach to secularism operates to reinforce the very categories of community, and in turn the forces of communalism that ultimately threaten to undermine secularism.[19] As the next section will explore, these limitations with the *sarva dharma sambhava* approach are vividly illustrated by the way in which this approach to secularism has been deployed by Hindu communalists.

## Secularism and the Hindu right

It is within the context of these competing discourses that the concept of secularism has become a site of a broader discursive struggle for ideological hegemony by Hindu communalists who have cast their position as a secular one.[20] Some have argued that the claim to secularism by the Hindu right is nothing more than a sham. While there is no question that the effect of the communalist discursive strategy is to undermine the very spirit of secularism, the strategy cannot be so easily dismissed. Rather, a more detailed examination of this discursive strategy reveals how skilfully the Hindu right has deployed the discourse of secularism. Through the adoption and manipulation of a particular understanding of secularism, the Hindu right is seeking to redefine the role of religion in Indan politics, and in so doing is redefining the concept of secularism beyond recognition.

Hindu communalists explicitly argue in favour of *sarva dharma sambhava*, and positive secularism.[21] This discourse of the BJP and the RSS is based on a particular vision of equal respect for all religions, i.e., formally equal treatment. Within this view, the equality of all religions requires that all religious communities be treated the same in law. Any special or different treatment, on the basis of religion, is seen to violate secularism:

> The idea of a theocratic State is an anathema to the Indian mind. The BJP believes that the State in India has always been a civil institution which respects all religions equally and makes no discrimination between one citizen and the other on the grounds of language, caste or religion.

It is the duty of the State to guarantee justice and security to all minorities — linguistic, religious or ethnic. The
BJP considers that it is also imperative for national inte-
gration that minorities do not develop a minority complex.[22]

The same emphasis on formally equal treatment can be seen
in RSS political rhetoric. In a typical statement, an RSS publication states: 'The RSS . . . never demands any special rights to the
Hindus. At the same time, it is against giving any concession to
other religious minority groups and it opposes religious discrimination.'[23]

The particular meaning that the Hindu right gives to *sarva
dharma sambhava* is one based on formally equal treatment. Accordingly, any laws or policies that provide special treatment
for minorities are opposed as pseudo-secularism, and appeasement of minorities.[24] Article 30 of the Constitution, which allows
minorities to run their own educational institutions, and Article
370 which provides special status for Jammu and Kashmir, are
thus opposed on these grounds. It is similarly this emphasis on
secularism as equal treatment that informs their support for a
Uniform Civil Code, that is, all religious communities must be
treated exactly the same. In contrast, the prevailing notion of
secularism in Indian constitutional law and politics, which has
allowed for the special treatment of minorities is cast as 'pseudo-
secularism'.[25]

Beneath this discourse of secularism and equality, however,
the emphasis on equal treatment is but a thinly veiled attack on
the legitimacy of minority rights. Not only is any special protection for the rights of religious and ethnic minorities explicitly
rejected, but through this approach communalists are attempting to establish majority norms as the ostensibly neutral norms
against which all others are judged. Their norm is a Hindu
norm. In their vision, the role of the state in religion is not one of
neutrality at all, but of fostering the Hindu nation. In this approach, the discourse of secularism operates to reinforce the
norms of the dominant Hindu community. We can see the paradox of this vision of secularism carried to its contradictory
extreme. The practices of the Hindu majority come to be viewed
as neutral, and the state in turn is seen to be acting neutrally

when it reinforces these practices. Thus, Hindus do not need 'special rights' because of the extent to which all legal rights come to be based on Hindu cultural norms and practices.

In some of the more extreme statements of the RSS, the true spirit of this version of secularism is evident. Deoras, for example, in defending the secularism of the RSS and of Hindu *rashtra*, has argued that only Hindus are capable of real secularism.

> If secularism means treating all religions on an equal footing, proselytisation and secularism cannot go together. Those who believe in conversion do so because they feel that their religion is superior to all others. Their organisations therefore can not claim to be secular. Hinduism, on the other hand, does not believe in conversions and Hindus have never been proselytisers. As such, organisations of Hindus alone can truly be secular.[26]

There is a perverse logic to this RSS argument, based on their ability to define the terms of debate. Secularism is defined as the toleration of all religions; Hinduism is defined as the only religion with a true tolerance for all other religions; thus, according to these terms, only a country based on Hinduism can be truly secular. Within this vision, secularism becomes a state based on a single religion. There are yet more extreme voices within the Hindu right, whose vision of the relationship between religion and politics is one of convergence. Some sants and sadhus unabashedly advocate a religious state, arguing for example for a return to the laws of Manu. Within this vision, secularism collapses into its antithesis—a theocratic state.

While the Sangh *parivar* does not always speak with a single voice on the question of secularism, the communalist discourse appeals to an understanding of secularism that radically departs from accepted definitions. Within this more extreme vision there is of course no separation of religion and politics. But even as measured against the standards of *sarva dharma sambhava*, the Hindu communalist vision undermines the spirit of secularism. There is no real respect or accommodation for any other religion. The state becomes a Hindu *rashtra*, and politics thereby become Hindu. Moreover, there is no real respect for other religions, in so far as these religions are not seen to be as tolerant as Hinduism, and therefore, not as worthy of respect. Rather, within this version, the objective becomes the assimilation of minorities, into the broader and ostensibly more tolerant fabric of Hinduism. This discourse of secularism thus represents no more than the politics of Hinduism, and freedom of religion represents the assimilation of religious minorities.

The ability of the Hindu right to deploy this discourse of secularism brings into focus many of the criticisms that have been made of this approach. The failure to separate religion from politics enables the supporters of Hindu *rashtra* to cast their arguments in the discourse of secularism.[27] Further, as invoked by the BJP and the RSS, the discourse of secularism, with its emphasis on equal treatment, reinforces the categories of communalism, and the power of the dominant religious community to establish the norm, against which all others are judged.[28]

## Discursive struggles: contested discourses of equality and gender

The legal and political concept of equality and particularly of sexual equality, is also the site of discursive struggles. The Hindu right is seeking to redefine these concepts in accordance with their visions of the role of women in Indian society. This is a contest over the constitution of gender identities, i.e., over the power to define who and what Indian women should be. In many respects, this discursive struggle parallels the contest over secularism and freedom of religion. Indeed, as we will argue, these struggles are overlapping and mutually constituting.

### Equality and gender difference

Equality has eluded any simple or uniform definition. There have been a number of competing visions of equality—competing visions which parallel the debates around secularism. At least two approaches to equality are clearly identifiable in political and legal discourse: a formal and a substantive approach.[29]

In the formal approach, equality is seen to require equal treatment, i.e., all those who are the same must be treated the same. It is based on treating likes alike. Accordingly, equality is equated with sameness. Only individuals who are the same are entitled to be treated equally. This initial definitional step can effectively preclude any further equality analysis. If the individuals or groups in question are seen as different, then no further analysis is required; difference justifies the differential treatment. Accordingly, when groups are not similarly situated, then they do not qualify for equality, even if the differences among them are the product of historic or systemic discrimination.

In contrast, the substantive approach to equality is seen as sometimes requiring different treatment, i.e., those who are different may have to be treated differently in order to be treated equally. It is based on the recognition that equality sometimes requires that individuals be treated differently. This approach is extremely critical of the formal model of equality, and its emphasis on sameness. The focus of a substantive equality approach is not simply with the equal treatment of the law, but rather with the actual impact of the law. The explicit objective of a model of substantive equality is the elimination of the substantive inequality of disadvantaged groups in society. The focus of the analysis is not on sameness or difference, but rather on disadvantage. Substantive equality is directed at eliminating individual, institutional and systemic discrimination against disadvantaged groups which effectively undermines their full and equal social, economic, political and cultural participation in society. The central inquiry of this approach is whether the rule or practice in question contributes to the subordination of the disadvantaged group.

In constitutional and political discourse, no one vision of equality is unequivocally dominant. Although the formal model of equality has been predominant in constitutional case law, some incursions have been made toward substantive equality.[30] Even within this prevailing context of formal equality, preferential treatment and 'compensatory discrimination' to improve the position of disadvantaged groups has been an accepted part of the discourse of equality.[31] Further, this formal vision of equality has not always dominated social and political discursive fields.[32]

The debate over the meaning of equality is further complicated in the context of women, and gender equality. The question of the relevance of gender difference becomes the site of further contests. Three approaches to the question of gender difference can be identified. In the first, women are understood as different from men—more specifically, as weaker, subordinate and in need of protection. In this approach, any legislation or practice that treats women differently from men is justified on the basis that women and men are different, and that women need to be protected. This approach tends to essentialise difference, i.e., to take the existence of gender difference as natural and inevitable. There is no interrogation of the basis of the difference, nor consideration of the impact of the differential treatment on women. In the name of protecting women, this approach often serves to reinforce their subordinate status.

In the second approach, women are understood to be the same as men, i.e., for the purposes of law, they are the same, and must be treated the same. In this approach, any legislation or practice that treats women differently from men is seen to violate the equality guarantees. This sameness approach has been used to strike down provisions that treat women and men differently. It has, however, also been used to preclude any analysis of the potentially disparate impact of gender neutral legislation. According to the sameness approach, it is sufficient that women and men be treated formally equally. Any recognition of gender difference in the past has been perceived as a tool for justifying discrimination against women.

In the third approach, women are understood as an historically disadvantaged group, and as such, in need of compensatory or corrective treatment. Within this approach, gender difference is often seen as relevant, and as requiring recognition in law. It is argued that a failure to take difference into account will only serve to reinforce and perpetuate the difference and the underlying inequalities. In this approach, rules or practices that treat women differently from men can be upheld, if such rules or practices are designed to improve the position of women. If, however, the legislation or practice is based on a stereotype or assumption that women are different, weaker or in need or protection, it would not be upheld. This approach argues that gender differences must be taken into account in order to produce substantive equality for women.

In the context of gender equality, the protectionist approach has been and continues to be dominant, although the sameness approach is increasingly evident.[33] These approaches to equality reflect the prevailing and competing discourses on women more generally. The protectionist approach reflects patriarchial and familial discourses, in which women have traditionally been constituted as different and weak, as wives and mothers, as inferior and subordinate. The sameness approach reflects a liberal discourse which constitutes women as equal to men. While this liberal discourse has made some inroads, the patriarchal discourse remains powerful, and continues to inform the political and legal claims that women make to equality.

The particular meaning of political claims for equality, and in particular, for women's equality is thus far from self evident. Equality, and women's equality, like secularism, means many things to many people. It is within the context of these competing discourses that the concept of equality has also become a site of a broader discursive struggle for ideological hegemony being waged by Hindu communalists. It is part of a contest over the meaning of equality, and the role and identity of women in Indian society. Communalists have seized hold of these competing visions of equality and gender differences, in their attempt to rearticulate a traditional role for women in society. Through a manipulation of particular understandings of equality and gender difference, they are seeking to undermine the very spirit of the concepts of equality, particularly, of gender equality in much the same way that they are undermining secularism.

The BJP approach to equality seems unequivocally formal, i.e., individuals who are the same should be treated the same. References can be found throughout BJP literature and speeches to the importance of non-discrimination, and to the equal treatment of all citizens. Indeed, it is this formal understanding of equality that informs their position on secularism, i.e, the equal respect of all religions, in their view, involves treating all religious communities the same.[34] Additionally, it is this formal approach to equality that underlies the BJP's opposition to Article 30 and Article 370 of the Constitution, as well as their support of a Uniform Civil Code, and to the replacement of the Minorities Commission with a Human Rights Commission.

The RSS approach to equality is less clear. On the one hand, their rhetoric often echoes the equal treatment approach of the BJP, particularly in relation to religious minorities. 'Equal treatment', and 'equality before the law' are invoked to attack any special treatment of minorities.[35] However, these same RSS ideologues have displayed a rather different approach to equality.

Golwalkar explicitly rejected the 'Western' concept of equality.[36] In contrast to this understanding which, in his view, emphasizes 'equality of men'. . .on the material plane because all men were equally in need of all . . . basic material needs',[37] Golwalkar argues that it is only on the spiritual plane that it can be said that all men are equal. 'It is in this sense, the same spirit being immanent in all, that men are equal. Equality is applicable only on the plane of the Supreme Spirit. But on the physical plane the same spirit manifest itself in a wondrous variety of diversities and disparities.'[38]

Golwalkar argues that 'disparity is an indivisible part of nature and we have to live with it', and concludes that harmony, not equality, should be the organising principle.[38]

A similar emphasis on harmony is echoed by contemporary RSS leaders. HV Seshadri writes:

> The principle of equality propounded by Hinduism envisages an all round harmonious synthesis. . . . All members of a family mete out equal treatment to each other and they also perform different rules. It is possible because they love each other and they live in harmony. The body of man itself has different organs which perform diverse functions but a harmonious order prevails among them. Hence the Hindutva and RSS primarily lay an emphasis on harmonious order.[40]

Based on this vision, Sheshadri concludes: 'We cannot contemplate a society, a life or a world without the elements of diversification. When we visualise the unity in diversity, we would be able to bring equality and harmony.'[41]

Equality, in the RSS view, does not mean that all persons must be treated the same. Rather, equality means harmony within difference. This view seems to contemplate equality as harmony within explicitly unequal material conditions. The RSS redefinition of equality thereby undermines the very spirit of both formal and substantive equality.

The Hindu right's approach to women and women's equality is found somewhat more sporadically in BJP and RSS literature and statements.[42] The discourse on women is often characterised by its strikingly religious overtones defining women in the images of Hindu goddesses and consorts—as mothers and wives, dutiful and sacrificing. For example, in a recent statement of its commitments, the discussion of women begins with the statement that 'BJP looks upon womankind as *Matri Shakti*'.[43] This image of the Hindu woman as *matri-shakti* has been evident in a number of controversies in which the BJP has been involved. In the controversy around Uma Bharati, who was alleged to have had a romantic involvement with another BJP member, the focus was on Uma Bharati to prove and publicly proclaim her chastity—not on the man with whom she was alleged to have had the affair. It is women, not men, who must be chaste and pure, and who must, like Sita, go to great lengths to prove their purity.[44]

The attitudes of the BJP leadership in the context of the Ram Janmabhoomi movement have also exemplified the way in which women are seen primarily as mother figures. Vijayaraje Scindia stated at the *kar seva* held in 1991 that mothers and wives of *kar sevaks* who sacrificed their lives for the temple construction were worth worshipping.[45] Women are intended to inspire and strengthen not so much through example, but through sacrifice and tears.

However, the BJP does not always deploy this religious and obscurantist rhetoric in their representation of women. The party's policies on women are often cast in the discourse of equality. 'The BJP pledges itself to restore to women the position of equality with men that the Indian tradition proposed and accepted.' [46]

The discourse of equality is fused with the more fundamentalist discourse that seeks to reclaim a glorious and ancient past. The objective of equality thereby becomes the restoration of women to the position that they once enjoyed in this 'Golden Age'. It is in this emphasis on returning to the past that the BJP distinguishes its position from the women's movement, particularly in the West. The Mahila Morcha writes, for example:

> We conceptually differ from what is termed as the women's liberation movement in the West. We require a sort of readjustment in the social and economic set up. No fundamental change in values is desirable. Women in India ever [sic] had a pride of place within the household, and the society. That has only to be re-established and re-affirmed.[47]

The BJP's understanding of the 'equality' to which women are to be restored further emerges in their statements and policies on women. While the BJP has generally adopted a formal approach to equality, the equal treatment of women and men is not what they seem to have in mind. In a telling statement, the BJP asserts: 'Men and women are equal but they are not the same'.[48] With a single stroke, the BJP both invokes the discourse of women's equality, and at the same time undermines any real entitlement to it by stating that women are different. Their formal approach to equality is coupled with a protectionist approach to gender difference. Since sameness is the prerequisite for equality, women, who are different, do not have to be treated the same.

The way in which women are to be treated, and the position of 'equality' to which they are to be restored becomes increasingly evident in the BJP policies on women. This policy focuses on women's traditional roles in the family. For example, health care, particularly maternal and natal care, are taken up, as are smoke-less chulhas and sanitation facilities for poor rural and slum women. Policies that reinforce women's role in the family as mothers and wives are supported as part of women's equality rights. In so doing, the Hindu right reinforces the assumption of natural and essential differences between women and men. Women are mothers and wives—they are *matri shakti*—they are different, and these differences must be honoured and protected.[49]

Mridula Sinha, president of the Mahila Morcha, has expressly stated that women's role in the family is primary in their programmes and activities for women: 'We maintain that the family and its unity must be maintained. Too much of freedom to women would break the nuclear family and we resist this.'[50]

The extent to which BJP policy supports women in their traditional family roles is further highlighted by the political issues that are expressly excluded from their agenda. For example, writing in regard to the UN conference on Women in Nariobi:

> The BJP women's wing expressed its profound appreciation of the conference. However, it also expressed its sharp disagreement with certain subjects that were discussed at the conference, subjects that are antithetical to Indian social order and our cultural moorings. Evalua-

tion of women's domestic work in terms of money is an insult to Indian motherhood . . . Likewise the demand for legal sanction of lesbianism is too vulgar and irrelevant in the Indian context.[51]

Wages for housework and lesbianism are both considered to be antithetical to Indian womanhood—defined in and through women's natural roles as mothers and wives. Wages for housework and lesbianism undermine these roles; thus, they cannot be supported.

Political claims that, in their view, go too far beyond these traditional roles are dismissed. Atal Bihari Vajpayee's statement is particularly revealing. 'Women who want to become men and want to make other women (like) men are worthy of ridicule.'[52] Implicit in this statement is the assumption of natural differences between women and men. These differences can be strategically deployed to justify any differential, protective and discriminatory treatment. To argue counter to their policies—to argue that any particular legislation discriminates against women—is met with the refrain that women are trying to become men. Political claims that go too far beyond the traditional roles of women in the family are rejected as attempts to make women into men, and thus ridiculous.

It is important to recognise that the BJP policy on women also includes issues of women's education and employment—issues which seem to bring women out from within the narrow confines of the family. The BJP has identified women's socio-economic dependence as a main cause of women's oppression, and accordingly, the party supports programmes designed to improve their socio-economic status, including increased employment opportunities, particularly in areas that 'suit women most'.[53] Women's illiteracy is also seen to contribute to this poor status, and must therefore be eliminated through improved access to education.

However, even the support given to improving such educational and employment opportunities for women is justified in the name of the family: 'An Indian woman will command the affection of the father, the love of the husband, and the respect of her son only when she has been provided with equal rights and opportunities.'[54]

Women's role in the family as mothers and wives remains the cornerstone of the BJP approach to restoring women to the position of equality reserved for them in Indian tradition. We can begin to see the extent to which the traditional discourse of women as *matri shakti* infuses the BJP policies. Indeed, it is this image of *matri shakti* that can be seen to underlie the very understanding of women's equality. 'Man and woman will remain the two wheels of the chariot of the family, and the nation. There can be no better concept of unity and equality of man and woman than the concept of "Ardhanarishwar".'

We can also begin to see here echoes of the RSS vision of equality, that is, of equality as harmony in diversity. Equality does not mean treating women the same as men. Nor does it mean compensating women for the ways in which they have traditionally been disadvantaged. Rather, it means an affirmation of the difference between women and men. These different roles of women and men, in the family and in society, are affirmed and celebrated as a harmonious synthesis.

The BJP approach to equality within the context of women thus remains somewhat elusive. They seem to appeal, on one level, to a formal approach to equality, coupled with a protectionist approach to difference, infused with religious and patriarchal discourses that ensure that women do not have to be treated the same as men. Yet, at a deeper level, it is apparent that the very meaning of the concept of equality begins to shift away from sameness and equal treatment towards difference and different treatment. In both approaches, however, we can begin to see one of the many paradoxes in the discourse of equality as deployed by the Hindu right, i.e, of legitimating their arguments with the liberal legal discourse of equality while at the same time, using this discourse to reinforce traditional images of women, and undermine any substantive claim to gender equality.

Moreover, in both approaches, the power to define gender difference is crucial. This definitional power, while relying on a multiplicity of non-legal discourses, also resides in law, that is, law has the power to decide which gender differences are relevant in which context. Legal discourse both reflects and reconstitutes particular understandings of gender difference. Within the framework of Hindu communalist discourse, the aim is to deploy this definitional power to reconstitute a traditional and patriarchal understanding of gender difference, and of identity for women. Legal discourse or more specifically, legal discourses of equality becomes an important dimension of the strategy of reconstituting gender identity.

The BJP's formal approach to equality is, at the same time, being used to claim the sameness of all women, and that all women must be equal. This claim is but a thinly veiled (and often not veiled at all) attack on the Muslim community and the discriminatory treatment of Muslim women, When the BJP argues that all women must be treated equally, they mean that Muslim women should be treated the same as Hindu women. In this respect, their approach to equality corresponds to their approach to secularism, where any recognition of difference is seen to constitute a violation of secularism. Thus, any recognition of difference as between the women in different religious communities is seen to violate the constitutional guarantees of equality, which in their view, require the formally equal treatment of all those who are the same. Muslim women, as women, should be the same as Hindu women—and thus they should be treated the same in law.[56] We can thus begin to see a second paradox in the way in which the concept of equality is used in Hindu communalist discourse. The formal discourse of equality in the context of women is thereby deployed to undermine the equality of minority religious communities. Treating the Muslim community equally means treating them like the Hindu community, which means in effect, subordinating Muslims to Hindu norms and practices.

The paradoxical ways in which the discourse of equality is invoked by the BJP is vividly illustrated in their response to the Shah Bano case, and particularly to the enactment of the Muslim Women's Protection Act. The BJP opposed the Act, on the ground that it violated the rights of Muslim women.[57] The Muslim community, supporting this Act, was thereby constituted in terms of its opposition to women's equality. Yet, both the Act, and its alternative—Section 125 of the Criminal Procedure Code—are based on treating women differently from men. Women are different from men and need to be protected from men. The discourse of equality is at one and same time being used to reinforce the idea that all women are or should be the same, but women are not and should not be the same as men. It is being used to undermine the recognition of differences as between different religious communities, while affirming the recognition of differences as between women and men.

This response to the Shah Bano controversy begins to reveal the extent to which the discourses of secularism and equality are mutually constituting. In the BJP's view, the Act violates both secularism and equality. It violates secularism because the Muslim community is treated differently. It violates equality because Muslim women are treated differently from Hindu women. Both discourses are used to reinforce the image of the Muslim community as 'Other'. And in so doing, the discourse of equality is, in effect, being used to undermine substantive equality, that is, real equality between women and men, and substantive secularism, as also equal respect and accommodation for minority communities.

Equality, in the hands of the Hindu right, remains an elusive, but enormously useful concept. It is, on the one hand, consistently deployed as equal treatment to attack the rights of religious minorities. Yet, within the context of gender, such consistency evaporates. Equality is sometimes deployed as equal treatment, but coupled with a protectionist approach to gender, infused with religious and patriarchal discourses that ensure that women do not have to be treated the same as men. It is also deployed as harmony in diversity. The approach is fundamentally contradictory. In the context of religious minorities, there is no talk of harmony in diversity; only of a quest for assimilation and sameness. But in the context of women, i.e., of Hindu women, there is a celebration of difference, and a quest for harmony. Beneath the surface, the discourse of equality in Hindutva becomes a tool for dismantling the rights of religious minorities, and masquerading the continued inequalities of gender and community.

## Redefining women: the mutually constituting discourses of gender and community

These discursive strategies over the meaning of equality are part of broader discursive struggles to rearticulate the meaning and identity of Indian women, and the meaning and identity of the Indian community. The importance of reconstituting gender identity for the Hindu right is intricately connected to the project of reconstituting communal identity. Recent work on nationalism has begun to explore the ways in which sexualities and gender identities, particularly women's sexualities are constituted in and through discourses of nationalism; and conversely, the ways in which nationalisms are at the same time constituted in and through the discourses of sexualities.[58] A similar analysis can be made in relation to communalism, that is, that the discourses of sexuality and communalism are mutually constituting. Images of women, of motherhood, of family have been central in the symbolic constitution of communities; and of communal identity. As Amrita Chhachhi writes 'women become the symbols and repositories of communal/group/national identity', and fundamentalism 'constructs notions of femininity and masculinity as symbolic of the community'.[59] Women's identity becomes partially constitutive of the identity of the community, and as such, community cannot be separated from women's identity. Any attempt to change women's role or position within the family/community/nation is thereby perceived as an assault on the community—on the very identity of the community. It becomes a symbolic attack on the communal identity.

The constitution of women's identity in and through the discourse of nationalism and communalism is not, however, monolithic. Rather, women's identity is constituted through multiple discourses of nationalism and gender, sexuality and community. Even within the Sangh *parivar*, the discourses constituting the Hindu woman are multiple, and at times, seemingly contradictory. Both BJP and RSS discourses on women are characterised by internally inconsistent statements. For example, most moderate voices within the Rashtrasevika Samiti and the BJP Mahila Morcha oppose sati, whereas some of the more extreme voices have supported a woman's right to choose to commit sati. Similarly, moderate voices support the legislative changes that have been made to Hindu personal law, and argue for a similar reform of Muslim law through a Uniform Civil Code. BJP policy even speaks of ensuring women's equal access to their husbands' property. Yet, many RSS ideologues, sants and sadhus express their opposition to the reform of Hindu personal law, and argue for the restoration of the laws of Manu.[60] A revised social science textbook for high schools, issued by the BJP government in Uttar Pradesh, states that the reforms in Hindu personal law, in the Hindu Widow Remarriage Act, the Hindu Women's Property Rights Act, 1937, the Special Marriage Act, 1954, and the Hindu Marriage and Divorce Act, 1955 have lead to 'disorganisation within the family. The total result of these progressive legislative measures. . . in favour of women is tension and strife in the family.'[61] Recently, some sants and sadhus have even argued in favour of the restoration of Hindu polygamy.[62]

Within the Sangh *parivar*, we thus can see at least two distinct positions constituting the Hindu woman—a moderate/conservative position and a fundamentalist position. Underlying these different positions is a common thread—of women as *matri shakti*, as wives and mothers, as strong Hindu women. At a deeper level, however, we can see at least two different discourses constituting the Hindu woman: a 'traditional' discourse in which she is celebrated as *matri shakti*; and a 'modern' discourse in which she is the bearer of rights.[63]

Both the moderate and fundamentalist positions contain elements of these discourses of modernity and tradition. For example, the moderate voice of the BJP Mahila Morcha contains very strong traditional overtones in their emphasis on women's role in the family as wives and mothers. The Rashtrasevika Samiti which brings women out of their homes and their traditional roles is careful to defer to the priority of the family. The sevikas work with and through the family of its members, and are careful not to challenge the family's ultimate authority over its members, particularly its female members.[64]

Similarly, even the more fundamentalist discourse contains elements of modernity. For example, in the debate around Roop Kanwar's sati, some of the more fundamentalist voices within the BJP—the same voices that had openly deplored the enslavement of Muslim women in the Muslim Women's Act—publicly defended Roop Kanwar's sati. Vijayraje Scindia defended the tradition of sati as a part of 'our' cultural heritage and argued that it was the fundamental right of all Hindu women to commit sati should they choose to do so.[65] The statement amounts to a careful intermingling of two discourses: tradition and a modernist appeal to liberal rights discourse. Women are constituted through the religious discourse in which the good wife performs the ultimate act of self sacrifice. This image is reinforced with the modern discourse of women choosing to exercise their rights. Both the discourses of tradition and modernity are used to legitimise the act of sati, and the loopholes in the anti-sati legislation—an act that any approach concerned with the substantive equality of women would condemn as being at least as 'retrograde' and 'anti-woman' as the passing of the Muslim Women's Bill. Yet, the discourses of tradition and modernity, religion and liberalism, are carefully and insidiously manipulated to justify - even celebrate—the oppression of women in Hindu communities.

There is another level at which these discourses of tradition and modernity appear contradictory. The BJP, particularly the Mahila Morcha, support policies that would improve the socio-economic position of women, and thereby increase women's opportunities for economic independence. Similarly, RSS women are empowered through physical and intellectual training, and many are encouraged to work outside of the home.[66] The modernising influence in the constitution of the Hindu woman thus sits in awkward juxtaposition to the more traditional discourses. Women's increased independence, particularly, their socio-economic independence, creates the material conditions for women to exist outside of the family. The modernising discourses thus create the very possibility for a break from the traditional roles ascribed to women within the fundamentalist position.

Yet, these discourses may not be as contradictory as they initially appear. First, it is important to recongnise that the discourses of tradition are thoroughly modern discourses.[67] In the context of the Hindu right, the discourse of tradition is part and parcel of the reconstruction and political deployment of history from a communal perspective.[68] Further, as Chhachhi has observed, the development of state-sponsored religious fundamentalism goes alongside the increased demand for women's labour market participation. She argues that in this respect, religious fundamentalism may be providing an important new legitimating ideology, to keep women under patriarchal control, at the same time as they are moving beyond the narrow confines of the private sphere. We can see this discursive strategy in the context of the new Hindu woman of Hindutva. The constitution of the new Hindu woman—a woman who may be educated, and who may work outside of the home, a woman who is strong and powerful, inside her family, and her community—is still a woman constituted through traditional discourses of *matri shakti*, as mother and wife; and of Sita, as chaste, pure and loyal. The new Hindu woman is strong , but she is strong in restoring the glories of an ancient past, a past which, as reconstructed through communal discourses, accords a particular role for women in the family, and in society: dutiful wives, and self-sacrificing mothers. Any additional roles that women may perform are ancillary to these. Indeed, women's work and education are seen as a means of strengthening their roles in the family.

In this communalist discourse, although women are seen as different from men there is a strong emphasis that they should not be weak. Rather, the Hindu right seeks to reconstitute women as strong. The RSS policy takes a strong stand against violence against women, including organising women to defend themselves. A strong Hindu woman is seen as essential for the constitution of a strong Hindu society, since women are responsible for raising the new generation, with appropriate values and discipline. Strong Hindu women are to be important conduits of a strong Hindu culture. This constitution of the identity of the Hindu woman is an essential part of the process of constituting a new definition of nation and Hindu identity—a nation and identity that is both 'traditional' and modern.

The construction of Muslim women's identity is similarly constituted through multiple discourses within the Hindu right. However, as we have begun to see, within Hindutva, the Muslim woman is constituted in very different terms. The construction of the Muslim woman sits in sharp contrast to the Hindu woman—she is the oppressed and subservient 'Other'.[69] This Muslim woman is also the product of a paradoxical mix of traditional and modern discourses. But, unlike the Hindu woman, she is neither respected as mother, nor is she the subject of rights. Saving Muslim women from their oppression becomes the justification for not respecting the practices and beliefs of the Muslim community, and indeed, the basis for subordinating this community to Hindu rule. Muslim women and in turn the Muslim community are constituted as the antithesis, as the binary opposition of Hindu women, and the Hindu community. Muslim women are what Hindu women are not. Moreover, this opposition is a hierarchical one—Hindu is dominant and superior, Muslim is subordinate and inferior. Through this construction of the Muslim woman as 'Other', the Muslim community as a whole is judged and subordinated.

The strategy is strikingly similar to the discursive strategies of British colonialism, justifying its rule through the subordinated position of Indian women.[70] Muslim women in Hindu communalist discourse, like Indian women in British colonial discourse, are defined in opposition and subordination to women in the dominant group. The product of this Hindu fundamentalist discourse of equality and secularism is a somewhat contradictory image—Muslim women are different, but they should be the same. The unstated norm or reference point against which these women are measured is the Hindu woman, the unstated norm against which the Muslim community is measured, the Hindu community. By making Muslim women the same, they would in effect be 'de-Muslimised', i.e., they would no longer be constituted through the discourses of their community. And in turn, their community could no longer be constituted through the discourses of gender. This discursive strategy of the Hindu right is skilfully constructed to strike at the heart of identity — the intersection of community and gender. Further, as in colonialism, this strategy operates to deflect attention from the subordinated condition of women within the dominant community. In the context of Hindu fundamentalism, attention is turned away from the subordination of women within Hindu culture. Rather than considering the oppression of women within their own community, this fundamentalist discourse attempts to refocus attention on the harm done to women within the Muslim custom of *iddat* and *mehr*.

## Conclusion

In this article, we have attempted to illustrate the extent to which legal discourse, specifically, the concepts of secularism and equality have become the sites of contested meanings, as the Hindu right seeks to redefine these concepts in accordance with its vision of Hindutva. These efforts at redefinition are part of a broader discursive struggle for ideological hegemony being waged by the forces of Hindutva. Legal discourse has become one among many fields that the Hindu right has sought to occupy, in rearticulating the meaning of community and gender, the role of religion in society, and the identity of women. Further, we have attempted to illustrate the extent to which the legal discourses of secularism and equality, and of community and gender, are not oppositional, but rather, mutually constituting. The Hindu right is seeking to reconstitute women in and through the image of the Hindu nation, and of reconstituting the nation in and through the image of Hindu women.

The question that we must at least begin to address is how we might counter these discursive strategies of the Hindu right. More specifically, we must consider how to reappropriate the discourses of secularism and equality from the communalists. In the comments that follow, we do not purport to answer these questions in any definitive manner, but rather, only to offer some preliminary and tentative suggestions for beginning this essential and urgent task.

As a first step, it is important that those who are opposed to the surge of the Hindu right and their communalist agenda enter the fray of this discursive struggle with a clear vision of secularism and equality. Our understanding of secularism and equality must be clearly and concisely articulated as an alternative to the meanings deployed by the Hindu right.

One option is simply to defend the dominant meanings of secularism and equality from the assault by the forces of Hindutva. However, our discussion has suggested that neither the formal approach to secularism nor the formal approach to equality, is adequate. These formal approaches and their emphasis on strict neutrality, reinforce the dominant norms of the status quo: dominant religious norms in the context of secularism, and dominant gender norms in the context of equality. Indeed, as we have suggested, the success of the Hindu right lies in the very limitations of the traditional understandings of secularism and equality, and the ability of the communalists to manipulate these meanings to their own ends. Countering the Hindu right need not simply entail a reassertion of the dominant discourse. Rather, the need to resist the Hindutva agenda provides an important opportunity to re-evaluate this discourse, and redefine these concepts.

There are several options for defining secularism. One is to reclaim *sarva dharma sambhava* from the Hindu right, but to contexualise the equal respect of all religions within a substantive approach to equality. Equal respect for all religions would not mean equal treatment, but rather, equality in result. Substantive equality for religious minorities may require differential treatment, i e., in order to compensate for past and continuing disadvantage, and to protect cultural and religious differences, minorities may require special treatment. Accordingly, laws that treat minorities differently, such as Article 30 and Article 370 of the Constitution would not be seen to violate the principles of secularism and equality, but rather, as essential to the realisation of substantive secularism and substantive equality.

This approach has certain advantages: it uses the specifically Indian version of secularism, and allows for the protection and support of minority rights. The problem however, is that religion and politics are not separated. To the extent that we accept that the communalisation of politics has resulted from the failure to clearly demarcate the spheres of religion and politics, then this reformulation of the *saarva dharma sambhava* will not resolve the underlying problem of communalism.

A second option is to adopt and synthesise the best features of the prevailing approaches to secularism, while moving beyond the limitations of each. Secularism could be based on both the separation of religion and politics, and the equal respect of all religions. In contrast to *sarva dharma sambhava*, this approach would begin with the argument that religion and politics must be separated; that is, it is only through this separation that the communalisation of politics can be reversed. The approach should not be seen as anti-religion. It is simply based on the belief that politics and religion should be separate spheres. Within this approach, religion is recognised as an essential part of individual and group identity. But, it is kept apart from politics.

This approach to secularism recognises that the equal respect of all religions, particularly, of religious minorities, may require state intervention. Freedom of religion must guarantee that individuals and groups are free to practice their religion in spheres outside of the state. However, since state neutrality can reinforce the norms and customs of the dominant religious community, the protection of freedom of religion for religious minorities may require state intervention. It is an approach based on a substantive model of equality, which recognises that affirmative state action may be required to correct historic and systemic disadvantage. Thus, laws that treat minorities differently, such as Article 30 of the Constitution, or the Minorities Commission, within this approach, could also be seen to be an important part of the realisation of substantive secularism and substantive equality. This is not to suggest that differential treatment is *always* required. Rather, this approach would direct attention to whether state intervention and differential treatment is required to protect freedom of religion for the minority in question, and would allow such treatment if it is so required.

Similarly, in the context of equality, we would advocate a substantive approach which would direct attention to whether particular laws or practices contribute to the subordination of disadvantaged groups, or to overcoming that subordination. Such a substantive approach to equality could in turn lead to more appropriate understanding of gender and of the relevance of gender difference. The substantive approach would consider whether particular rules, norms or practices reinforce the subordination of women, or contribute to overcoming that subordination. The relevance of gender difference would not be a question of always treating women the same, or always treating women differently. Rather, the substantive approach allows for a more contextually specific analysis of the objectives and effects of particular laws or practices on particular women.

Such a substantive approach to both secularism and equality would be an important advance over existing understandings of these concepts. These substantive approaches would better capture the spirit of the Constitution, and the kind of protection it contemplates for historically and socially disadvantaged groups. Further, these approaches could go some considerable distance in revealing and correcting the distortions of the Hindu right's approach to these concepts.

Models of secularism and equality alone cannot displace the growing influence of the discourse of Hindu communalists. We must then struggle to displace Hindutva, and to establish alternative visions of secularism and equality as dominant in legal discourse. In this endeavour, we must recognise that legal discourse is not simply the preserve of lawyers, judges and academics. The success of the Hindu right has lain in its ability to popularise its versions of secularism and equality. Its vision of secularism as the formally equal treatment of all religions, with no special treatment for any group, is becoming part of the common sense of increasing numbers within the Hindu community. References to 'pseudo-secularism', 'appeasement of minorities', and 'no special rights' abound, even amongst those not convinced of or converted to Hindutva. Debates over the real meaning of secularism continue to rage not simply in intellectual circles, but in the popular media. The legal discourse of secularism and equality have become part of the popular consciousness. Although the Hindu right has not yet been successful in displacing dominant meanings and establishing a new discursive hegemony, its victory to date lies in having popularised these debates, and its versions of these concepts.

To counter the forces of Hindutva, our visions of secularism and equality must displace the versions of the Hindu right in the popular consciousness. The currency of the debates regarding secularism provides a window of opportunity to do so. However, it is important that we do not simply adopt the popularising strategy of the Hindu right. Our versions of secularism and equality must not simply be popularised, they must be democratised. The populist and essentially majoritarian approach of the Hindu right must be transformed into an authentically democratic approach. Majoritarianism must give way to a respect for minority rights, the very cornerstone of democracy. Within such a democratic framework, we can then use the currency of the debates to articulate and debate our versions of secularism and equality.

We must at the same time recognise that the struggle against Hindutva will not always be a direct one of engaging with and challenging their distorted versions of secularism and equality. The struggle must also take many indirect forms. We must be careful that our other political strategies do not inadvertently play into the communal hand. As feminists, for example, we need to adopt more complicated understandings of gender identity in our own strategies, and recognise the extent to which gender and community are mutually constituting. We cannot, for example, afford to emphasise gender based discrimination in situations which may only serve to reinforce communal identities. Discrimination against Muslim women is only the most obvious example of how feminist issues can and have been appropriated by the Hindu right.

We must be able to negotiate our way through the complex web of interlocking discourses of gender, community and religion, through which women are constituted. Women's identity is never based on gender alone. Our strategies for addressing women's oppression must thus develop more complicated understandings of identity, which embrace these mutually constituting discourses.

Finally, in attempting to draw attention to the role of legal discourse, we are not suggesting that law has a leading or even a central role in the discursive struggles of the Hindu right. Our objective has simply been to highlight the extent to which legal discourse is one of the many discursive fields that the Hindu right has sought to occupy. And although solutions to social and political problems rarely lie in law alone, as long as the Hindu right continues to try to advance its agenda through the redefinition of such basic legal concepts as secularism and equality, it will be essential that those of us opposing Hindutva continue to struggle to occupy this field.

## Notes

[1]   Bipin Chandra, *Communalism in Modern India* , Delhi, Vani Educational Books, Vikas Publishing House, 1984, p.1.

[2]   Ibid.

[3]   See Asghar Ali Engineer, 'Hindu-Muslim Relations in Contemporary India - An Analytical Approach' in *Beyond Darkness - Some Reflections on Communalism* , Bangalore, CIEDS Collective and EKTA, 1990) discussion on p.64.

[4]   Tapan Basu, Pradip Datta, Sumit Sarkar, Tanika Sarkar, and Sambudha Sen, *Khaki Shorts Saffron Flags: A Critique of the Hindu Right* , Delhi, Orient Longman, 1993, p.2.

[5]   There is considerable debate about whether the current phase of Hindu communalism can be accurately characterised as 'fundamentalism'. More specifically, there are questions about the relationship between revivalism and fundamentalism, and whether fundamentalism is applicable to Hinduism. See James Warner Bjorkman, ed., *Fundamentalism, Revivalists and Violence in South Asia*, Delhi, Manohar, 1988. As recent literature has begun to explore, fundamentalism has become a phenomenon that eludes any simple or self- evident definition, and important work has begun to be done on identifying and examining the features of fundamentalism in historically and materially specific contexts. See generally, Linoel Kaplan, ed., *Studies in Religious Fundamentalism*, London, MacMillan Press, 1987; also Bronislaw Misztal and Anson Shupe, eds., *Religion and Politics in Comparative Perspective:*

*Revival of Religious Fundamentalism East and West,* Praeger, Westport, 1992; Martin Marty and Appleby *The Fundamentalist Projects* , 1993, vols.1 - 3.

Our preliminary observations suggest that the current phase of Hindu communalism has become fundamentalist since the rise and increased participation of the Vishwa Hindu Parishad in the activities, indeed the very identity of the Sangh *parivar*. Some of the features of fundamentalism that we have identified which characterise Hindutva ideology include the use and abuse of religion for political support through religious zealotry; the glorification of the past and appeal to a former golden age; and the construction of an enemy or 'Other'. However, more historically and materially specific work needs to be done on identifying the nature and characteristics of fundamentalism in the Indian context.

6   For example, Amrita Chhachhi has argued that the legitimacy of the post-colonial state is in crisis, partly because it has been unable to tackle the proliferation of movements for regional autonomy, competition for economic resources and decentralisation of power, resulting from uneven regional development. It is no longer able to derive legitimacy from the anti-colonialist nationalism of the post-independence period. 'The centralising tendency of the state requires some ideology of unity. It is here that Hindu fundamentalism could provide the new hegemonising ideology of nationalism.' Amrita Chhachhi, 'The State, Religious Fundamentalism and Women: Trends in South Asia', Working paper, Sub-series on *Women, History and Development: Trends in South Asia* (The Hague: Institute of Social Studies, 1988) p.11.

Both the centralising tendency and the crisis of legitimacy have been accentuated by the current economic restructuring — the new economic policies being implemented by the current government in accordance with the structural adjustment requirements of the IMF. These structural adjustment policies, although involving privatisation and deregulation of industry, require a strong state to be successfully implemented. Moreover, currency devaluation and high inflation is resulting in a deterioration in standards of living, which in turn only further contributes to the legitimacy crisis of the state and to its need for a new legitimating and hegemonising ideology. At least in the short term, these new economic policies may only result in an intensification of the material conditions that have contributed to the growth of Hindu fundamentalism.

7   For a discussion of the contradictory role of law in women's struggles for social change in India, see Brenda Cossman and Ratna Kapur, 'Women and Poverty in India: Law and Social Change' *Canadian Journal of Women and the Law* .

8   See Laclau and Mouffe, *Hegemony and Strategy: Towards a Radical Democratic Politics*, London, Verso, 1985, on the democratic potential for new social movements created by the principles of equality and liberty. See Alan Hunt 'Rights and Social Movements' 17 *Journal of Law and Society 309* ,1991,; Amy Bartholomew and Alan Hunt 'What's Wrong with Rights?' 9 *Law and Inequality* 1, 1990, arguing on the counter-hegemonic potential of rights discourse. For a different view, warning that both progressive and reactionary social movements can be mobilised through rights discourse, see Judy Fudge,

'What Do We Mean by Law and Social Transformation?' 5 *Canadian Journal of Law and Society* 48, 1990; and Judy Fudge, 'The Public/Private Distinction: The Possibilities of and Limits to the Use of Charter Litigation to Further Feminist Struggles' 25 *Osgoode Hall Law Journal 485*, 1987; also Carol Smart, *Feminism and the Power of Law*, London: Routledge, 1989.

9  The term 'secular' was not inserted in the Constitution by the Constituent Assembly, although there had been considerable discussion and agreement regarding the secular nature of the Indian state. 'Secular' was inserted into the Indian Constitution by the 42nd amendment passed in 1976.

10  It has been argued that Nehru favoured this approach to secularism. See Pradeep Kumar 'Nehru, Congress, and Secularism' 27:39 *Mainstream* June 24, 1989, 25-26, 35.

11  Prakash Chandra Upadhyaya, *The Politics of Indian Secularism: Its Practitioners, Defenders and Critics*, Occasional Papers on Perspectives in Indian Developement, Nehru Memorial Museum and Library, Number XI, January 1990, p.85.

12  See Anil Nauriya in 'Relationship between State and Religion: Antinomies of Passive Secularism' in *Beyond Darkness*, op.cit. Most authors agree that the Indian state has not adopted a wall of separation between religion and the state as exists in the American Constitution, and thus not adopted a formal approach to religion and secularism: see 'Secularism: Constitutional Provision and Judicial Review' in G S Sharma, ed., *Secularism: Its Implications for Law and Life in India*, 1966; V P Luthra, *Concept of Secular State and India* Bombay, Oxford University Press, first edition, 1964, pp.44-47; A R Saiyed 'Secularism in Retreat: The Communal Secular Paradox in India' in B Chakrabarty, ed., *Secularism and Indian Polity*, Delhi: Segment Book Distributors 1990, p. 147. See also A R Desai 'Congress (I) Communist parties and Communalism' 19:30, *Economic and Political Weekly* 1196 (July 28, 1984).

The bills introduced in Parliament in the monsoon session of 1993 on religion were intended to adopt the *sarva dharma sambhava* approach to secularism. The Constitution (80th Amendment) Bill 1993 provided that the state should have equal respect for all religions. However, while the Bill was in committee a provision was added to it providing that the state shall not profess, practise or propogate any religion. The addition went beyond the *sarva dharma sambhava* approach insofar as it attempted to separate religion from politics. The second bill, the Representation of the People (Amendment) Bill 1993, sought to prohibit any political party from using a religious name and deregister any party that sought to promote religious disharmony and enmity and thereby also represented an effort to delink religion from politics.

13  The Constitution itself and many other legislations allow the state to interfere in religious matters. The right to freedom of religion is laid down in Articles d25 and 26. Article 25 entitles all persons to freely practise their religion subject to public order, health and morality. Furthermore, the state is entitled under article 25 (2) (b) to make laws for social welfare and introduce social reforms. Under this sub-clause, it can eradicate social practices which stand in the way of the country's progress: see State of Bombay, A 1962 SC 853; Taheer Mifuddin v. Tyebhai Moosaji A 1953 Bom 183. The

state is further permitted to intervene to regulate the secular activities of religious Endowments, Madras V Lakshmindra Swamiar A 1954 SC 282; Shri Govindlalji v. State of Rajasthan A 1963 SC 1638. However, decisions have tended to treat Article 26 as independent from Article 25, thus increasing the scope of religion and the activities that are considered integral to a religion, and reducing the scope of the state's authority to intervene.

14  See discussion below in notes 29 to 33 on the formal and substantive models of equality.

15  Martha Minow, 'The Supreme Court: 1986 Term—Foreword: Justice Engendered' 101 *Harvard Law Review* 10 (1987).

16  For a similar discussion on the ways in which nationalism has been misunderstood as the antithesis of communalism, and the ways in which nationalism has drawn on communalist notions and symbols, see Gyanendra Pandey, *The Construction of Communalism in Colonial Northern India* , Delhi, Oxford University Press, 199). See also Romila Thapar 'Imagined Religious Communities? Ancient History and the Modern Search for a Hindu Identity' 23:2 *Modern Asian Studies* 209, 1989; and Chandra op.cit., on the ways in which the history of communalism has similarly been imagined and constructed.

17  Upadhyay argues, 'By declaring that religion was at the heart of politics (Gandhi) fully legitimised political use of religious belief systems. Ever since Gandhi's ascendancy in the Indian National Movement, therefore, the separation of religion from politics has been impossible for the dominant political forces of the country. From this point onwards, commitment to secularism ceased to imply an opposition to the religious-political model of propaganda and mobilisation.' Upadhyaya op.cit., p.90.

18  Ibid., p.85. Upadhyaya further develops this argument of the majoritarian nature of Indian secularism in 'The Politics of Indian Secularism' 26:4 *Modern Asian Studies* 815, 1992.

19  Anil Nauriya, argues that the concepts of secularism are inadequate in their passivity. He argues that one can neither be neutral toward nor have equal respect for the impact of religious practices on social life. Nauriya, op.cit. pp. 56-57.

20  Upadhyaya, argues that the consensus on the value of secularism, and conversely, the evils of communalism have become so prevalent that virtually all parties, including the most communal, reject the label of 'communal' and present themselves as secular. Upadhyaya, op.cit., pp 3-4.

21  The BJP Manifesto states: "The BJP believes in positive secularism which, according to our constitution-makers, meant Sarva-Dharma-Samabhava and which does not connote an irreligious state", as quoted by L K Advani in his speech to Parliament, November 11, 1990. Similar statements are seen in RSS literature, from Golwalkar to the contemporary ideologues such as Deoras and Malkani.

22  Ibid.

23  K Jayaprasad, *RSS and Hindu Nationalism*, Delhi, Deep and Deep, 1991, p. 93; Nana Deshmukh, *RSS: Victim of Slander*, Delhi, Vision Books, 1979.

24  'Towards Ram Rajya, Mid Term Poll to Lok Sabha, May 1991—Our Commitments,' Delhi, Bharatiya Janata Party, 1991 states on p-4: 'Article 30 permits minorities to run their own schools. It will be rationalised and suitably

amended to ensure justice and equality to all irrespective of religions'. The document similarly recommends that the Minorities Commission 'which entertains complaints of discrimination only from minority sections' should be replaced by a Human Rights Commission 'to look into complaints of injustice against any section of society'. Similar references to pseudo-secularism and appeasement of minorities are repeated in BJP speeches. Advani repeatedly attacks pseudo-secularism and appeasement of minorities in his speeches. A typical example: '...secularism has come to mean a premium on belonging to a minority' in 'Secularism, A Premium on Belonging to a Minority' interview with Advani in *Blitz* Magazine, reproduced in *Nation's Hope* 1991, pp. 24,25.

25  This understanding of secularism has come to have many academic proponents as well. See for example, N.S. Ghelot, ed., *Politics of Communalism and Secularism: Keeping Indians Divided*, Delhi, Deep and Deep Publications,1993, which includes several articles arguing against special protections for minorities and pseudo-secularism.

26  *Balasheb Deoras Answers Questions*, Banglore:,Sahitya Sindhu, 1984, p. 53. See also K Suryanarayana Rao, *Hindu Rashtra: Not Merely a Slogan But The Vibrant Reality* , Madras, Vigil, 1990) arguing that 'only a state with such universal Hindu ideas can uphold all the modern secular and democratic values.' (no page numbers)

27  Upadhyaya argues that the problem lies in the failure to define secularism as the separation of religion and politics. 'This has created a situation in which even openly communal individuals and groupings have hijacked the appellation of secularism to justify their own positions, and in this sense, lead to the absence of any real secular advance'. Upadhyaya op.cit., p.4.

28  For a more detailed discussion of the competing approaches to secularism, and the way in which Hindu communalists have sought to deploy the discourse of secularism to advance their Hindutva agenda, see R Kapur and B Cossman 'More Than a Matter of Words: Secularism (s) and the Challenge of Hindutva' *The Thatched Patio*, vol.6, No.1, January/February 1993.

29  For a detailed discussion of these competing models of equality, and the ways in which these approaches have informed Indian Constitutional law, see Ratna Kapur and Brenda Cossman 'On Women, Equality and the Constitution: Through the Looking Glass of Feminism' 1, 1993, 1 *NLSJ*.

30  See Abdul Aziz v. Bombay, A 1954 SC 321; Kerala v N M Thomas, (1976) SCR 906; Shamsher Singh v. State, A 1970 P.&H. 372.

31  These special measures are sometimes understood as part of equality, and other times, cast as necessary exceptions to equality. See Kapur and Cossman, 'Women Equality and the Constitution,' op.cit.

32  This debate over competing visions of equality was recently the subject of political controversy with the Mandal Commission, and reservations for scheduled and backward castes. Debates over the meaning of equality raged in the media. On one side, it was argued that reservations violated equality - that equality required that everyone be treated equally. On the other side, it was argued that reservations were fundamental to equality—that equality required   disadvantaged groups to be treated differently. These debates highlighted the contested meanings of equality as a political and legal concept

in Indian society. Indeed, the political paralysis brought about by the Mandal Commission illustrates how deeply divisive and controversial the competing concepts of equality remain in contemporary political and social life.

[33] For the protectionist approach, see Raghuban Saudagar Singh v. State of Punjab, A 1972 P.&H. 117; Shahdad v. Mobd Abdullah, A 1967 J&K 120; Soumithri Vishnu v. Union of India, A 1985 SC 1618; Thamsi Goundan v. Kanni Ammal A 1952 Mad. 529; Mt. Choki v. State of Rajasthan, A 1972 Raj 10. For the sameness approach see C B Muthamma v. Union of India and others, A 1979 SC 1868. The corrective approach has had only a marginal influence: Partap Singh v. Union of India A 1985 SC 1695. See generally Kapur and Cossman, and especially 'Women, Equality and the Constitution', op.cit.

[34] A policy statement from the BJP National Executive Meeting, January 1986, Chandigarh, states 'The Bhartiya Janata Party urges the. . . Government to so conduct itself that no citizen gets any feeling that he is discriminated against, or unfavourably treated.'

[35] See for example, H V *Seshadri, The Way*, Delhi, Suruchi Prakashan, 1991, speaking (on p-5) of the majority Hindu community, who states, 'Give us also the rights which are now enjoyed by others. Apply the principle of equality before the law to all. Stop discrimination against us.' See also Seshadri 'Strange Political Diction', *Organiser*, February 4, 1990; Balasaheb Deoras frequently invokes the same rhetoric of equal treatment and equality before the law. For a typical example, see ' Bharat Bhoomi is Hindu Bhoomi'. Address of RSS chief Shri Balasaheb Deoras, *Organiser*, October 14, 1990.

[36] M S Golwalkar, *Bunch of Thoughts*, Banglore, Vikrama Prakashan, 1966, p.16.

[37] Ibid., p.18.

[38] Ibid.

[39] Ibid .p.p. 19-20.

[40] Seshadri further develops this analogy of family: 'The young child in the family holds the parents and his elders in high regard, but the elders do not treat the child as low. Similarly, there can be inequality on the basis of intelligence and wisdom. But the Hindu view point does not allow to treat them as higher or lower classes'. Sheshadri, op.cit. p.113.

[41] Ibid. p.115.

[42] It is important to recognise that there is no clearly uniform position within Hindutva discourse, but rather an array of positions ranging from the more progressive to the more fundamentalist. For example while some of the more authoritarian statements from RSS ideologues such as Hedgewar and Sarvarkar appeal to the laws of Manu, just as contemporary sants and sadhus within the BJP agitate for a return to Manu, moderates within the BJP, as well as the women's wing of the BJP and the RSS deny any support for such a reinstatement. See for example Vajpayee's interview in *Sunday Magazine* February, 1993, and Tanika Sarkar's work on women in the RSS, 'The Woman as Communal Subject: Rashtrasevika Samiti and Ram Janmabhoomi Movement', 26:35 *Economic and Political Weekly*, August 31, 1991, 2057-62. In our discussion, we draw from a broad range of at times contradictory statements, in an attempt to discover the common threads that run through these divergent positions.

43    'Our Commitments' op.cit., p-25. For a discussion of this *matri shakti* identity
      for women in RSS ideology, see Ish Mishra 'The Women's Question' in
      *Communal Ideologies: A Study in the Ideologies of Rashtriya Swayam Sevak Sangh
      and Jamaat-E- Islami*', Delhi, Centre for Women's Development Studies, n.d.

44    To a somewhat lesser extent, Hindu fundamentalists also offer women a
      renunciatory mode of existence, which allows women to escape from the
      domesticity that has been available to them. It is this renunciatory mode that
      has created the possibility for women such as Uma Bharati and Sadhvi
      Rithambhara to occupy such a high profile position within the Hindu right.
      At a more community based level, the Rashtrasevika Samiti—the
      women's wing of the RSS—provides intellectual and spiritual training for
      women, thus both affirming their religiosity, and providing them access to a
      world of knowledge and spirituality from which they have been excluded. It
      is, however, important to recognise that the Samiti is careful to ensure that
      the power of the family to make decisions regarding its members, particu-
      larly regarding its female members, remains unthreatened, and the decision
      for a woman to marry trumps her own decision to participate in the Samiti.
      Thus the renunciatory mode does not completely escape the role of women
      as *matri shakti*. For an excellent discussion of women in the Rashtrasevika
      Samiti, see Tanika Sarkar, See also Basu et al, op.cit., pp. 41-44, 78-87.

45    'Women Ram Bhakts Make History', *Dashak ke Jharokhe Main*, Delhi, Mahila
      Morcha, BJP, 1991, p.112. See also the following statement by P K Roy,
      'Operation Ayodhya' in *Nation's Hope* '. . . It look them ( *kar sevaks*) six days to
      reach the periphery of Ayodhya, accepting the hospitality of the villages on
      the way. Many elderly women blessed them before bidding them farewell. "I
      could not control my tears at such send off by villagers for whom we were
      strangers. Despite their poverty, they looked after our every comfort, pool-
      ing their resources. Women collectively prepared food. And they forced
      food packets on us for the way," said one *kar sevak*!! Roy, op.cit., p.16.

46    Bharatiya Janata Party, *Our Five Commitments*, 1984 ; See also Mridula Sinha
      'Women's Equality—Miles to March' *Organiser*, September 1, 1985, p.7 re-
      garding the position of the BJP Mahila Morcha on equality.

47    'Women's Decade: Mahila Morcha Response' in *Dashak ke Jharokhe Mein*,
      p.120 Mridula Sinha, in 'Women's Equality - Miles to March' writes: 'In spite
      of all this glorious background the Indian woman today has to fight a
      sustained and long-drawn battle to achieve the goal of complete equality.
      This can be fulfilled not by blind imitations of the modes and techniques of
      struggles adopted by the so-called liberated women of the west.' Ibid. A
      similar, though more extreme position is found in the writings of RSS ideo-
      logues. K R Malkani, in *The RSS Story*, Delhi, Impex India, 1980, argues that
      'the position of women is better in India than anywhere else in the world'.
      On p.175 he writes that the RSS . . .' would consider women's libber's as the
      worst enemies of woman kind'.

48    *Our Five Commitments*, op.cit., p.18.

49    In this respect, the BJP can be seen to be appealing to and reinforcing the
      dominant familial ideology, which has traditionally constituted women as
      wives and mothers, in and through the family. For a discussion of familial
      ideology, see Michelle Barrett *Women's Oppression Today*, London and New

York, Verso, 1988, and Michelle Barrett and Mary MacIntosh *The Anti Social Family*, London and New York, 1991.

50 'Wooing the Half that Matters' *The Sunday Times of India*, January 21, 1991, 14-15, p.15

51 *Dashak Ke Jharoke Main* op.cit., p.3.

52 Ibid., p-4.

53 *Our Five Commitments*, op.cit., states 'Another sure way of producing security for women is to enlarge the employment in areas and sectors that suit them most.' Policy statements include a concern with women's employment. While there is little elaboration as to what these areas might be, another document provides that women should be primary school teachers: 'Our Commitments' op.cit., p.25. The Mahila Morcha, on the other hand, has stated that training for women should not be confined to such traditional areas as sewing and toy-making, but rather should 'be expanded to cover areas like light engineering': *Dashak ke Jharokhe Main*, op.cit., p.121. See also 'BJP Mahila Morcha Decries Rising Crime Against Women' *Organiser*, September 15, 1985, p.14.

54 Sinha, op.cit, p.5.

55 Ibid.

56 Sinha writes 'It is a tragedy that in the eyes of the law, the concept of Indian womanhood is non-existent. They are Hindu women, Muslim women, and Christian women . . . The emancipation of the Indian women will remain a far off cry as long as a Uniform Civil Code is not passed.' Ibid. The BJP Mahila Morcha has repeatedly campaigned in favour of a UCC 'so as to equally cover all Indian women', 'BJP Mahila Morcha Decreis Crimes Against Women', op.cit., p.14.

57 "The National Executive [of the BJP] regards this move to amend section 125 CrPC as retrograde, anti-women and a surrender to obscurantism and bigotry". BJP National Executive Meeting, Chandigarh, 1986, op.cit.

58 See in particular A Parker, M Russo, D Sommer and P Yaeger, eds., *Nationalisms and Sexualities* 1992, New York, Routledge

60 See Manini Chatterjee, 'Strident Sadhus: Contours of a Hindu Rashtra', *Frontline*, January 16-29, p.4. See also an interview in *Frontline*, July 30, 1993,p. 28, in which Swami Nischalanando identified 'the Hindu Code, family planning, the Sati Act' as three areas in which the government has unduly interfered in religious matters since Independence, and which must be undone.

61 As quoted by Sherna Gandhi; 'Status of Women: The Other Casualty', *Sunday Observer*, February, 21-27, 1993.

62 Chatterjee, 'Strident Sadhus' op.cit., p.5. Swami Muktanand Saraswati for example was quoted as stating: 'There should be no laws regarding marriage. Today, a Hindu can marry only one woman while a man can have five wives. Why should a law be there? If a man wants to have 25 wives, let him'.

63 Many 'traditional' discourses are as much a product of colonialism as are the 'modern' discourses of liberalism. For example, notwithstanding the British colonialist policy of non-intervention in the personal affairs of the various communities, the extent to which personal laws were the product of a complex history of intervention, codification and reform of customs and

practices is well documented: see Archana Parashar *Women and Family law Reform In India, Uniform Civil Code and Gender Equality*, Delhi, Sage Publications, 1992.

[64] See Tanika Sarkar, op.cit., 2062.

[65] See *Patrika*, October 12, 1987, New Delhi. See also Indu Prakash Singh and Renuka, 'Sati: The patri-politics', paper presented at The Status of Widows, Abandoned and Destitute Women in India' Workshop, April 22-24, 1988 pp. 2-3, criticising the notion that sati is a voluntary act.

[66] Tanika Sarkar, op.cit., 2062; see also Basu et al, op.cit., pp 84-87.

[67] See Caplan op.cit., on the extent to which, as he states on p.5 'fundamentalism must be seen as quintessentially modern in the sense that it constitutes a response to events and conditions in the present.' See also Misztal and Shupe, op.cit.

[68] See for example Romila Thapar 'Imagined Communities' *Modern Asian Studies* 23:2 (1989), 209-31.

[69] Himani Banerji observes that the images of Muslim women in Hindutva demonstrate the ultimate version of contempt for women. Muslim women are portrayed as 'ignorant and superstitious slaves of Muslim men', who 'breed like rabbits, and are incapable of knowledge or spirituality'. See 'Women Against Communalism', *Sanchetana*, February 1991, (Calcutta) 2-3.

[70] Laura Nader, 'Orientalism, Occidentalism and the Control of Women', *Cultural Dynamics* 3, 1989; Lata Mani 'Contentious Traditions: The Debate on Sati in Colonial India' in Kumkum Sangari and Sudesh Vaid *eds.,Recasting Women: Essays in Colonial History* , Delhi, Kali for Women, 1989, pp. 88-127.

# The Frying Pan or the Fire?*

*Endangered Identities, Gendered Institutions and Women's Survival*

## VASANTH KANNABIRAN and KALPANA KANNABIRAN

After November 1984 and the massacre that followed Indira Gandhi's assasination it was clear to all of us that to survive and remain politically relevant we had to start addressing the issue of communalism and its impact on women. Hyderabad itself has had a tortured history of communal tension and violence right from the forties and memories of the Razakars and police action weave in and out of each outbreak of violence. But it was 1984 and the glaring evidence of the state's complicity in communal violence that finally destroyed any shred of faith that had remained regarding the myth that the state is secular. Many cherished assumptions collapsed and we had to start afresh. We realised that we could no more treat issues of dowry or rape unproblematically; that to ignore communal or caste politics would only mean to be either swept aside or co-opted by it. From the position of seeing women as sufferers and victims of caste/community violence we began to see that this violence structured the definition not only of women but of community, caste and nation.

In this article we try to search through some of these assumptions and look at their connections. The most critical issue from the point of view of human rights is the violent

* We are indebted to Nilanjana Chatterjee, Rhoda Reddock and Jasodhara Bagchi for critical comments on earlier drafts of this article.

polarisation of difference and attempts to hegemonise on the basis of this difference, along various axes of power and privilege. As feminists we share concerns that question every such attempt to hegemonise on the basis of difference. Every one of these attempts is targeted against a group that is perceived as opposing dominant interests and is premised on the control over women. Further, these attempts use a rhetoric that violently expropriates women's personhood and rights. In the course of this article we also hope to problematise violence and secularism, removing them from the realm of binary opposition, rhetoric and abstraction to the concrete ways in which they get played out.

A look at violence against women in a communal situation informs us of the very specific implications that violence in identity politics has for women. Anticipating our argument we can perhaps say that the identity of a community is constructed on the bodies of women. This identity formation works in two ways — both of which are violent and are defined by and through the aggression on women of particular communities. First through the rape of women of minority or subordinated groups — religious as well as caste groups — which is also the rape of the community to which the woman belongs. The justification for this act of violence is provided by demonstrating the 'inherent immorality' of the community and its individual members. This is also an assertion of difference and separateness and a reinforcement of the aggressor's position in the right. The second way in which identity is constructed is through the allegation by the dominant group of the rape of and aggression on their women by men of minority communities, an allegation which serves to justify dominant caste/community hegemony, by demonstrating the 'lack of character' of minority men who show scant respect for women. This affects the perception of minority women as women who by virtue of belonging to 'characterless' men, become women without character. This then creates a condition for the total refusal of safeguards—constitutional or otherwise—for women of these minority groups. Public/political discourse on women is aimed at first classifying them by caste and community, creating levels so that different classifications can co-exist and separating the 'normal' from the 'abnormal' within each level and between levels. Those who are perceived as being outside the 'normal' cannot assert a legitimate claim to protection from the state: not just the women, but the communities they belong to.

To elaborate this point a little, while the predicament of minority women and dalit women is much the same, they are situated at different levels. Women of minority communities are located outside the Indian state, as it were. Constructing their 'otherness' then is the beginning and the end of constructing the 'otherness' of their community vis-a-vis the 'Indian community'. Dalit women, on the other hand, exist within the Hinduised Indian state and their 'otherness' is constructed in a manner that reinforces the upper caste Hindu norm — one that is essentially an undesirable 'aberration' within Hindu society and one that destroys the 'Hindu fabric' from within. The upper caste Hindu therefore sees himself as being threatened and under attack from two sides: from the outside, by immoral (in the wider sense of the term) minorities and from inside by 'unclean castes'. And women form the core target in both the perception of this threat as well as the use of violence to suppress it.

Old wives' tales told in shocked tones in the family amply illustrate this. One was that Hindu women had to start wearing blouses as otherwise the Muslims would grab their breasts and pull them away. The other was the real story of a young brahmin widow who had gone through her husband's funeral ceremonies which included her tonsure and the stripping of her ornaments, then eloped with a Muslim. Within weeks she was sighted with her hair grown and her earlobes pierced Muslim-style — wearing several earrings. Given the crucial symbolic significance of the purity and chastity of the shaven widow for orthodox traditional Hinduism these stories illustrate for us how deep-rooted the anxieties and fears concerning Muslims can be. What would happen if large numbers of shaven widows began to prefer multiple earrings and a full life to the shadowy existence they were condemned to? 'Desecration', a story by Ruth Prawer Jhabvala, makes an interesting connection for us in this context:

> The fact that she was a Muslim had a strange fascination for him. Here too he differed from the Raja Saheb: as an educated nobleman, he had transcended barriers of caste and community. But for Bakhtawar Singh these were still strong. All sorts of dark superstitions remained

embedded in his mind. He questioned her about things he had heard whispered in the narrow Hindu alleys he came from—the rites of circumcision, the eating of un-clean flesh, what Muslims did with virgin girls. She laughed, never having heard of such things. But when she assured him that they could not be true, he nodded as if he knew better. He pointed to one of his scars, sustained during a Hindu-Muslim riot that he had sup-pressed. He had witnessed several such riots and knew the sort of atrocities committed in them. He told her what he had seen Muslim men do to Hindu women. Again she would not believe him. But she begged him not to go on; she put her hands over her ears, pleading with him. But he forced her hands down and went on telling her, and laughed at her reaction. 'That's what they did', he assured her. *'Your* brothers. It's all true.' And then he struck her, playfully but quite hard with the flat of his hand.[1]

A little later, he forces her to kneel and say her prayers and derives great pleasure in sexually assaulting her while she re-cites the prayer.

The threat to the community is defined as the threat to the chastity of women of the community/caste and the threat is challenged through the violent expropriation of the chastity of the target group which is synonymous with the aggression on women of these groups. Further, since the struggle for hege-mony/power is carried out on women's bodies, establishing control over women by rape or demonstrating a violation of one's women by rape then becomes a legitimate means of carry-ing out this struggle.[2]

Women are implicated in inter-caste and communal violence in ways that underscore the fact that while for men the demand for human and democratic rights does not necessarily entail a loss of community, for women, on the other hand, an assertion of democratic rights by definition denies them a space in the com-munity. Religious fundamentalism, communalism and caste chau-vinism assert a control and hegemony that is antagonistic to women's interest in democracy or claims to human dignity.

We see that in the old traditional community both men and

women had clearly defined roles and responsibilities. With the growth of capitalism and the emergence of the nation state however, the old communities shrink into the private sphere with a fringe of religious and cultural practice that is not quite private and still not the large public sphere. Men become citizens and claim democratic rights in these new spaces which are essentially alienating. However, they still look back and actively depend for their sense of identity and rootedness on the old community which has now shrunk to family and a religio-cultural fringe. Women then take on the added responsibility of absorbing and nurturing this need for stability on the part of men. Their own community however shrinks to the family and religious community/caste. To bring the rhetoric of rights then into this shrunken and fragile space is as one judge observed, to 'let a bull into a China shop'. The price women pay for their own identity in the community and the protection it guarantees is the sacrifice of their democratic rights.

It would be useful, perhaps, at this point to look briefly at the many-layered context in which identity is constituted. First, there is the existence of different religions, for instance, Buddhism, Christianity, Hinduism, Islam, Jainism, Sikhism and Zoroastrianism. Each of these religions has different sects, with widely divergent religious practices often with conflicting interests; within each sect again there are sharp hierarchies based on class and in Hindu and Christian sects on caste as well. Added to this, are the twenty odd official language groups, with each state speaking a different language with a different script. A cultural hegemony is also constituted along the lines of language, with the most visible opposition being between the Hindi speaking states of central and north India and the non-Hindi speaking states of the west, east and south. Within each language group again consider the countless dialects which constantly resist cultural and political domination by the official dialect. Finally, take the sharp polarisation of interests between the tribal population, which is large and extremely oppressed, and the non-tribal population, which actively promotes the alienation of the tribals from their land, forests and customary rights. The Indian state, as we shall see, participates actively in the creation of polarised interest groups on every one of these fronts, and is complicit in the violence that often erupts in the confrontations (both actual and potential) that weave into and through each other to constitute the complex phenomenon that we call identity politics.

Secularism in India has been officially defined as a positive respect for all religions, which would mean a non-interference in religious (and social) practice. While it is necessary to separate religion from the state and democratic processes through the institutionalisation of secularism, the history of 'secular politics' in India has consistently foregrounded the absorption of majoritarian consciousness in state processes — whether it has to do with rhetoric, public ceremonies, the official sponsorship of religious heads (Hindu, upper caste, male), the donning of religious garb and symbols (the sudden public appearance of Indira Gandhi's *rudraksha* beads or NTR's saffron robes for instance). This means in practice that it is possible to divorce the rhetoric and definition of secularism from its practice by the state and its representatives. It is also possible then to use the current definition of secularism to justify the continuation of oppressive social institutions and justify the public practice of religion by representatives of the secular state. What are socio-religious practices? The veil is social practice; discriminatory inheritance laws are enshrined in religion; the restitution of conjugal rights as a male prerogative is social practice; caste based oppression is codified in Hindu religion; female infanticide and female foeticide are social practices; strict codes of dress and mobility for women are social practices; marital violence is social practice; rape is social practice; one could go on endlessly. . .and every one of these social practices is welded to the question of identity and gender. The redefinition of secularism therefore is an explicitly feminist concern.

The question that begs an answer then is, what are the implications that secularism thus defined bears for women? As A R Desai points out:

> The state and the ruling class have never clearly defined the basis of morality which should permeate the cultural climate of the country. It has nowhere been formulated how the state wedded to a respect for all religions should act if different religions and sects within religions prescribe diverse, contradictory, discriminatory and unequal and opposite prescriptions of beliefs and practices,

and generate conflicting institutional forms and social rituals, founded in injustice and discrimination against other groups and citizens. Should the state, in the name of respect for all religions, both in public and private, permit these contradictory, iniquitous, discriminatory and hostility generating values and practices among citizens? ... It has also never been clearly stated whether the value systems and practices which are adhered to by atheists, materialists, agnostics or rationalists should be equally respected. If so, should the religious and moral practices and rituals which offend them be permitted to be publicly performed in the name of respect for all religions?[3]

This last concern is real because here Desai is not speaking of a small group of urban educated intellectuals. India has had a very strong and visible communist presence for at least six decades now, not to mention the Socialist Party and a section of rationalists.

In a very important sense therefore, it is precisely the rhetoric of secularism that has laid the basis for the politics of identity that is being played out in India today. The current debate on the failure/success of secularism has been generated by the upsurge in violence between the Hindus and the Muslims, and the rapid spread of Hindu nationalism in the country.

In order to understand the various dimensions of this polarisation we need to return to the context in which it occurs and is sustained. The post colonial state, at the time of its conception, was to be an instrument of social transformation, as well as one that would execute ameliorative strategies vis-a-vis disadvantaged/underprivileged groups in society. In realising its purpose, the state was to be relatively autonomous of dominant/vested interests. Although, as Kothari argues, this conception of the state was by no means radical, the very fact of its relative autonomy could allow the space for the politicised oppressed to foreground socially purposive ends in the agenda.[4] There are various dimensions to this question of autonomy, especially in the Indian context. Most importantly, there was the problem of translating political independence into economic self-reliance. The national goals of undertaking social transformation at home while pursuing economic self-reliance vis-a-vis global capitalist centres could only be realised by a highly centralised state.

It is important at this point, for us to consider how far this was possible given the actual nature of the post colonial Indian state. It was a state that had assumed political power with the least disturbance to existing power and class relations in society. State power was 'transferred' and 'appropriated' rather than 'conquered', 'destroyed' and 'transformed'. So, while the realisation of 'national goals' was predicated on the vision of an activist state that was also highly centralised, in reality, there was a general consensus among the privileged few that the state would not interfere with the concentration of wealth and power within society.[5]

This consensus was one that involved a collaboration between the state, Indian big business, foreign capital and eventually also the rural elite. This consensus was not without its share of internal contradictions and tensions. Some of the most obvious areas of tension were the definition of the limits of state power and central power, of the private domain of custom, usage and religion, the tension between the public and private industrial sectors, and the tension in the protection of the privileges of the farm lobby.

Further, certain prerequisites for equal citizenship, like the right to work, the right to shelter, the right to education etc., were not explicitly stated as fundamental rights in the Indian Constitution. In an already sharply hierarchised society, this resulted in a further deprivation and exploitation of large sections of the population. What happened as a result was the increasing alienation of the Indian state from the people, both at the central and regional levels, making repression the only way for the state to retain effective control over the people and contain the growing discontent and disenchantment among the youth and masses of the oppressed who began to search for solutions in radical left politics.

At yet another level, during the process of modernisation, the state had begun to address the problem of 'integrating' women into development and into production. With the penetration of capital, women have been drawn into a monetised system which, while retaining its feudal exacting character, has deprived them of the traditional supports and rights that eased their burden slightly. Development thus further marginalised women by addressing only their practical needs and confined them to their reproductive roles by refusing to tackle the gender division of labour. Besides, the whole process of development has systematically depoliticised and invisibilised women's subordination through its policy of addressing women's practical needs and of confirming women's place firmly within the home and family.

How does this tie up with the escalation of violence against women on the one hand and, on the other, the agendas of the increasingly powerful fundamentalist organisations, particularly the Hindu nationalists, who are looking for ways in which to expand their ranks? This rapid modernisation has a critical impact on the condition of women. On the one hand, we see an apparent erosion of certain traditional patriarchal boundaries while at the same time there is a shriller and more strident reassertion of gendered identity and redefinitions of masculinity and femininity.

With modernisation and consequent urbanisation, increasing numbers of people of both communities—impoverished by the desertification of the countryside and failure of crops — migrate to urban areas in search of employment and survival. However, they find themselves uprooted and increasingly alienated from a socio-cultural context. At this point the pressure is on women to provide rootedness and a sense of community and continuity. The growing helplessness that men experience in a hostile environment is sought to be compensated by a reassertion of power and control over women within the family. Further, to use Kothari's argument, the agenda of transnational capital decrees a global homogenous culture which accompanies the generalisation of a utopian model of economic development.[6]

The main vehicles for this global homogenous culture are the middle classes who now become the primary targets that set the tone of 'social goals'. These social goals are defined in terms of caste and class, in a manner that is opposed to affirmative action for disadvantaged castes on the one hand and asserts the need for a Hindu nationalism on the other. This complete absorption in a consumerist lifestyle by the middle classes which is tied to an increasing polarisation of class, caste and community interests has very specific implications for women. One witnesses an increase in family violence resulting in what has come to be vulgarly known as 'dowry deaths' among the middle classes. One also witnesses the transformation of the middle classes into effective vehicles of communal and caste propaganda.

Television, which significantly, is state owned in India, is an important instrument of this transformation. Look at the propagation of the legend of Rama for instance. The process of modernisation generates a need among Hindu fundamentalists to redefine Hinduism as an ideology compatible with modernisation.[7]

Modernisation is integrally linked to the growth of capitalism. In terms of its religious associations, capitalism is often believed to thrive among Semitic religions such as Christianity and Islam. The argument would then run, according to Romila Thapar, that if capitalism is to succeed in India, then Hinduism would also have to be moulded to a Semitic form, although this desired change is often disguised in the theory that what is actually happening in the resurgence of Hinduism is a turn to Hindu traditions. The political exploitation of the worship of Rama, for instance, has not only been visible but has been forced to the forefront in recent months, culminating in the fall of a government. This has added yet another dimension to the ways in which the Rama *katha* has been used. The worship of an incarnation was now being used to build up a political base among the populace. The first step in doing this however, was to annul different versions of the story and to project a single one as the authentic one. This is done through the medium of television which is rapidly replacing even entrenched oral traditions. The version selected for projection is a Hindu Vaisnava text familiar to people of the Indian Hindi belt and a literate few elsewhere. It bears serious implications for our understanding of the ways in which women are re-located within this context and how notions of femininity and masculinity get reconstituted.

On the one hand there is an extreme polarisation and hierarchisation of male-female differences and, on the other, there is an emphasis on caste purity which gains a new authenticity and currency. So while the worship of Rama sets itself up against Islam, it also sets up a very definite hierarchy within. Further, it polarises regional differences and sets up a hegemony of the Hindi speaking north against the south. This has very serious consequences for the large numbers of south

Indian working class migrants in the north. Witness the large scale dispossession and evacuation of south Indians in the recent riots in Bombay, which started out as a Hindu-Muslim confrontation, but soon spread to include not just religious minorities, but immigrants as well—most of whom belonged to the working classes.

At the same time, in the working classes, women are drawn out of their traditional spaces and provide cheap labour, competing in a sense with men in the labour market. They are therefore constantly apologetic about appropriating the breadwinning role of men. The men's need for power and the women's need to compensate for their appropriation of male space leads to an escalation of family violence. There is also a growing need for cultural specificity, and the assertion of a cultural identity. In this assertion, women are required to wear the markers, and are expected to assume the role of the bearers of tradition. Exploiting this need for a cultural context, communal forces recruit men from these classes into their ranks to provide a broadened mass base and street power. The emotions that are evoked are those of machismo — emotions that impact directly and violently on women within the home and without. The need for this assertion is itself poignant, springing from the insecurity and anxiety of a community that is uprooted and dispossessed, where men depend on women's wages (as distinct from their labour within and without the home). For the sense of impotence that the man as breadwinner experiences, their women compensate with their dignity and their very lives. Outside the home, the assertion of a cultural/communal identity takes an extremely violent form with women being the primary targets. This is despite the fact that communal rhetoric focuses on 'protecting women'. This, we argue, is only logical because the notion of 'protection' is predicated on the sense of property. And property needs to be guarded against assault and appropriation from outside and subject to strict, if necessary violently enforced, control with the group.[8]

The state itself is a repressive apparatus that depends on the politics of masculinity to sustain its control. Power is strategic for the state and it exercises and retains power by actively institutionalising a hegemonic masculinity. And it is this masculinity which is the underbelly of street power and a lumpen

culture that legitimises and provides popular support for the
state with all its contradictions arising from its communal, caste
and class interests. The patriarchal state can be seen, then, not as
the manifestation of a patriarchal essence, but as the centre of a
reverberating set of power relations and political processes in
which patriarchy then connects the state, family violence, religious fundamentalism, and caste chauvinism.

The spaces in religion and ritual that were traditionally
women's spaces have now been appropriated by communal
mass organisations. Festivals which upto this point were celebrated within the local community and the extended family,
and were primarily the responsibility of women, and provided
avenues for their cultural expression, have now been taken over
by communal forces and celebrated with the aggressive use of
technology and mass mobilisation. The celebration itself ceases
to be one of a particular deity or occasion. It is a celebration of
the community's capacity to aggress. This inevitably fuels a riot.
As increasing numbers of men get recruited into these
organisations, they are killed, hurt, or arrested and the responsibility for ensuring the survival of the family falls even more on
women.

While women are the most vulnerable in a riot situation, we
also see that women often share the communalised consciousness that targets them. We come across women hiding bodies of
riot victims, sheltering rioters and participating actively in communal propaganda. Our experience in the women's movement
has shown that women have very definite interests in caste and
community. They experience the negation and insecurities that
communities and caste groups feel, and derive power and strength
from belonging to these groups. The new communal phase, as
Tanika Sarkar argues, 'enables the woman's self constitutions as
active political subject in dangerously unprecedented ways'.[10]
For women who feel the need for religious involvement, and
especially those whose men are involved in these organisations,
this provides an opportunity to draw themselves out of a restric-
tive domestic space into a vast and virile environment. During
communal riots in Ahmedabad and Hyderabad for instance, and
in caste riots, women have played an active part marching and
shielding rioters from the police. This seems to typify a general
trend among the upper caste Hindus.[11] The underside of their

participation in communal organisations is the militant assertion by women of their caste identity. In the recent massacre of dalits by upper caste Reddi landlords in Tsundur in Andhra Pradesh, Reddi women, for the first time, played an active, public role in defending their men. Their defense, interestingly, was a collective public declaration that they (and there were three hundred of them) had been raped by the dalits in that village.[12]

It would not be true to say that women are drawn into these organisations by their men. Women have never been mere victims or passive recipients. They see themselves as crusaders for a cause — protecting what they see as the identity and integrity of the nation; the cause of Hindutva. Women then are caught in a bind: between their democratic rights and gender justice on the one hand and the fact that their gender idenity is tied to their community/caste identity on the other. There is a sense in which they are trapped without a community. At another level the assertion of community identity traps women. That is, we see that women's access to the 'larger causes' of nation or freedom is mediated by men, family and community. They are without nation. And one senses this tension in Mahatma Gandhi who made the struggle for freedom a sacred duty, raising it above family and community and thereby releasing women to enter the struggle. Yet, in countless individual cases he advised women to wait and obey parents or husbands who were unwilling to let them go. In times of upheaval women find legitimate space which disappears in conditions of normalcy leaving them once again within/without community. We cannot afford today to underestimate, even less ignore, the impact and strength of the resurgence of communal and caste violence.

As the articulation of women's issues grows sharper, it has led inevitably to a greater political understanding of the specific ways in which most issues that concern a third world country (whether it is international funding, privatisation, militarisation or environmental degradation) impact on women.

The complexity of the issues that concern us has several layers. On the one hand we need to be sensitive to the specifities of concrete realities and avoid the tendency to generalise or draw broad conclusions that would blur critical differences in experience. At the same time we are confronted with the fact that every incident in one part of the region sets off a succession of reactions and responses in the other countries. Rising fundamentalism in one country is immediately sought to be matched by its neighbours or used (BJP support for Taslima Nasreen of Bangladesh, for instance). We see that the rise in communalism/ fundamentalism is also closely linked to structural adjustment policies in the region. How then do we forge links across national, religious and linguistic boundaries in a common cause while keeping constantly before us the diverse and explosive nature of the problems we confront? How do we struggle against the tremendous erosion of democratic spaces and human rights that women face today and still retain a measure of the self consciousness and humility we need to ensure that we do not eliminate difference?

*Note*: A part of this essay was presented by Kalpana at the South Asian Feminist Workshop, Colombo, March 1992, in a paper entitled "Rape and the Construction of Communal Identity". This essay was discussed and presented by us at a joint seminar at Hunter College, The City University of New York under the title "Problems of Survival: Women and Communal Violence in India' in March 1993. Some of these ideas were developed in the Rockefeller Residency Program in the Humanities, Spring 1993 Public Lecture delivered on 6 May 1993 at Hunter College, CUNY by Kalpana. The lecture was entitled 'The Women's Movement and the Politics of Identity in Contemporary India'.

## Notes

[1]  Ruth Prawer Jhabvala, 'Desecration', in *Out of India: Selected Short Stories*, John Murray, 1986, p.279.

[2]  The category of rape includes every act of sexual aggression on women.

[3]  A R Desai, 'Caste Violence in post Partition Indian Union', in A R Desai (ed), *Repression and Resistance in India*, Bombay, Popular Prakashan, 1990.

[4]  Rajni Kothari 'State and Statelessness in Our Time', *Economic and Political Weekly*, vol.XXVI, nos. 11 & 12, Annual number 1991 pp.553-58.

[5]  Amiya Kumar Bagchi, 'From Fractured Compromise to Democratic Consensus: Planning and Political Economy in Post Colonial India', *Economic and Political Weekly*, vol.XXVI, nos. 11 & 12 , Annual Number, 1991.

[6]  See note 4 above.

[7]  Romila Thapar, 'A Historical Perspective on the Story of Rama', in Sarvepalli Gopal (ed), *Anatomy of a Confrontation: the Babri Masjid-Ramjanmabhumi Issue*,

New Delhi, Penguin, 1991, pp. 141-61. The discussion at this point draws heavily from this article.

8   See Ritu Menon and Kamla Bhasin, 'Recovery, Rupture, Resistance: Indian State and Abduction of Women During Partition', *Economic and Political Weekly*, XXVIII 17, April 24, 1993, pp. WS2-WS11.

9   R W Connell, *Gender and Power; Society, The Person and Sexual Politics*, Polity Press, Cambridge, 1987, p.130.

10  Tanika Sarkar, 'The Women as Communal Subject: Rashtrasevika Samiti and Ram Janmabhoomi Movement', *Economic and Political Weekly*, XXVI, 35, August 31, 1991.

11  Urvashi Butalia, 'Community, State and Gender: On Women's Agency During Partition', *Economic and Political Weekly*, XXVIII: 17, April 24, 1993, pp. WS12-WS-24.

12  Vasanth Kannabiran and Kalpana Kannabiran, 'Caste and Gender: Understanding the Dynamic of Power and Violence', *Economic and Political Weekly*, September 14, 1991.

# Redefining the Agenda of the Women's Movement within a Secular Framework

## FLAVIA AGNES

### A new challenge to existing social movements

Bombay has the reputation of having been the home of many progressive social movements during both the pre- and post-independence periods. Although the first communal riots recorded in the history of Bombay took place as early as 1893,[1] during the period when the city grew into an industrial capital it became increasingly cosmopolitan, with the migrants providing the necessary dynamism for the growth and expansion of the city. It was also its openness to migrants that made Bombay so attractive to the many refugees who took shelter here after partition. Although post-partition Bombay has seen a number of riots, these have not ruptured the fabric of social life in any significant way.

This is what made the scale and intensity of the riots which followed the demolition of the Babri Masjid at Ayodhya so surprising for the people of Bombay. They dealt a serious blow to the cosmopolitan and progressive image of the city. The city which had welcomed refugees of all natural and and man-made calamities and had provided them with the basic minimum means of sustenance, witnessed a large-scale exodus. Many of its age-old trades as well as its valued traditions went up in flames with the tacit approval of thousands of spectators.[2]

The riots posed a new challenge to the social movements in the city. Every stone, every pebble thrown by the frenzied mob became the touchstone upon which their work had to be tested. And sadly, faced with this new challenge, they failed miserably. It was evident that building a secular force had not been on their agenda and hence they could not counter the rising wave of communal passions. The feeble voice raised by a few groups was drowned in the sea of venom and hatred into which the city had plunged. Even worse, some trade unions and community organisations became the fertile collective ground on which this venom was nurtured and nourished.

As the city 'went back to normal' and the organisations tried to pick up the threads of their work, they sensed a sharp cleavage. The beneficiaries of a programme or the members of a union had been divided into two sectors — the majority and the minority. The question foremost in the minds of secular-minded persons was an obvious one. Why had this happened? And when? Where did they go wrong? Did the venom of communalism spread overnight? If not, was there any way in which they, as secular-minded people or groups, had consciously or unconsciously participated in this process? The riots affected different social movements in different ways. Since my work has primarily been within the women's movement, I will pose the questions within its confines.

## The women's movement in India

Around the late seventies and early eighties the autonomous women's movement began to take shape mainly around the issues of rape and bride burning. The groups which mushroomed in various cities consisted of women from left and liberal backgrounds, many of whom were professionals from the middle and upper strata of society.[3] To focus attention on the issues, women walked the streets in protest marches and shouted slogans.

The initial spontaneous protest marches led to more sustained activities such as counselling and support services.[4] Women from both lower and middle strata approached such centres for help in crisis situations. These centres subscribed to a pro-women ideology which can be termed broadly feminist, although some groups refrained from using this term. They challenged the traditional and conservative role of women as subordinate partners within domestic and social relationships.

Although the groups remained small in number, the movement was highly visible as it received wide media publicity. This acted as a pressure tactic and the state was forced to respond. Women's issues were placed on the agenda of state-sponsored development schemes, social work programmes and sociological research. The government set up anti-dowry police cells to help victims of domestic violence. There were also several cosmetic efforts at legislative reform although the inadequately formulated laws did not have the desired effect.[5]

While the counselling centres remained at the crisis intervention level, several community groups and non-government organisations (NGOs) formulated programmes to address economic issues of concern to women, particularly in the unorganised sector. Some of these NGOs were headed by women who subscribed to this new ideology and hence were able to transgress the narrow boundaries of 'women's welfare' and incorporate the new concept of 'women's empowerment'. Although they did not directly challenge the subordinate role of women within marriage, or address 'personal' issues such as domestic violence, they indirectly helped in the empowerment of women through development work.[6]

The autonomous women's movement focussed on issues which challenged patriarchal power structures within a broad liberal framework. There were several instances where the movement addressed issues concerning dalits, tribals and landless labourers.[7] Activists involved in the movement also provided relief during communal riots and worked in broad secular fora.[8] During community conflicts and their resultant police excesses or during human tragedies, women's groups were able to place gender concerns on the agenda of human rights and civil liberties groups.[9] But overall, the movement worked on the assumption that gender lines can be drawn up clearly and sharply in a patriarchal society and within these parameters sexual assault and domestic violence affect women equally across class, culture and religious barriers.

## Secular culture as an agenda

The leaders of this autonomous movement remained predominantly urban and upper class Hindu. Their work centred mainly in areas away from and outside their own immediate neighbourhood and community context. In order to reach out to women from a different class, caste and culture and to propagate the new ideology of the strong and assertive woman, the movement adopted a populist approach and relied upon mythical symbols of Shakti and Kali to convey the newly constructed feminist ideology. The movement relied more upon myths and fictions rather than on the history of a pluralistic society that encompassed within its framework the cultural idioms of minority communities.

The intention of using the symbols from the dominant religious culture was not to propagate Hindu ideology. But since the movement did not have 'secularism' as one of its prime objectives, no conscious efforts were made to evolve alternate symbols. Hence the cultural expressions with which women who were in the forefront were familiar had surreptitiously crept into the women's movement.

The feminist movement also had to constantly counter the allegation that it was 'Western'. So in order to establish its 'Indianness' it relied on Hindu iconography and Sanskrit idioms denoting woman power, thus inadvertently strengthening the communal ideology that Indian, Hindu and Sanskrit are synonymous.

Within this social milieu of a high caste Hindu culture, the handful of minority women who were vocal and articulate had also internalised the dominant culture and hence did not protest against this trend. On the contrary, in order to prove their secular credentials they willingly divorced themselves from their own traditions and cultural symbols of women's strength and power and accepted not just these symbols but also the food habits and dress codes of the dominant section.

## Women and communal forces

With women's concerns gaining prominence in both governmental and non-governmental organisations during the eighties, women's issues became an important agenda for all political parties. Initially, political parties refrained from raising issues of domestic strife and male dominance within party organisations. The women who needed support against violent husbands or male colleagues had to approach a women's organisation to deal with this issue. This conservative approach was maintained not for traditional and reactionary reasons of preserving the family but more in order to preserve the existing status quo among party cadres. But, over the years some party-affiliated women's organisations started addressing issues of women's oppression within the family through counselling centres.[10]

In Bombay during the mid-eighties, the Shiv Sena (a communal party), which was gaining popularity within the lower middle class, was able to mobilise a large number of women around support activities such as income generation, creches, and mid-day meals for children, civic amenities, ambulance services etc. The movement also appropriated cultural fora of public celebrations of Hindu festivals like Ganesh Utsav and Satya Narayan Pooja which had been popularised by Tilak during the nationalist struggle in pre-independence India. In addition, the sons of the soil theory propagated by the Shiv Sena had also managed to carve out a special niche for women. As mothers of these sons of the soil the women were given a special role and responsibility: they had to defend their sons when the latter were arrested, and bring them up to be brave and loyal to the soil.

Through a systematic hate campaign the Shiv Sena was able to whip up communal tensions among their women cadres. The image of the modern Hindu woman which was constructed while advocating the communal Hindu ideology was not that of a traditional subservient and docile domestic being but a new modern Durga, the destroyer of evil, an angry and rebellious woman. This construction of the modern Hindu woman closely resembled the Indian construction of the new 'feminist' woman.

This new woman could come out on the streets with as much ease as the men from the community to avenge their wrongs. And in this action she had the blessings of the party and community leaders. Hence women found this role not only exciting but also more comfortable than one which involved protesting against a violent husband or a rapist from within the community. In this latter role, they would not have the protective mantle of the party nor the blessings of community elders.

Through a process of selection, Hindu communal forces usurped the external usages popularised by the feminist movement such as protest marches and road blocks (which are contrary to the conservative domestic role of the traditional Hindu woman) while at the same time rejecting the movement's ideological stance. The irony lay in the fact that the communal parties were able to mobilise women far more easily using the image of the modern Durga than the movement which had popularised these forms in the first place.

To its dismay the women's movement found that the new-found strength, the shakti of the modern Durga was not directed against violence within the home and community but was directed externally towards the Muslims — both men and women. In this process the myth that all women are equal and could be mobilised around a common issue on a common platform lay shattered.  The validity of slogans such as 'Sisterhood is Power-ful' or *'Hum Sub Ek Hain'* (We  Are One)  was threatened. But what was even more distressing was that women from communal organisations mouthed slogans coined by the women's movement *'Hum Bharat Ki Nari Hain; Phool Nahin Chingari Hain* (We are the women of India, not delicate flowers but smouldering embers) while leading demonstrations during the riots or while the Babri Masjid was being torn down.

## Merging demands: obscenity and the Uniform Civil Code

The merging of lines between communal forces and women's organisations did not stop at the level of symbols and slogans but also found an expression through some of the more concrete demands raised by the movement.

Obscenity was one such issue. Women's groups had taken up a campaign against obscenity in the media. The aim was to protest against using women's bodies as sex objects or portraying women in derogatory and subservient roles. The campaign received the support of all sorts of people—from Victorian moralists to Hindu revivalists. The issue also became very popular with communal parties. In Bombay the women's wings of the Shiv Sena and BJP organised demonstrations and stormed the Doordarshan studio to protest against the late-night screening of classic films on television including those which portrayed women in assertive roles.[12]

In the hands of communal forces the issue took a dangerous turn and somehow got pulled into another communal campaign aimed at curtailing the freedom of speech and expression on secular issues. Shiv Sena activists forced the Film Makers Combine (FMC) to sign an undertaking that they would not portray the demolition of the Babri Masjid, or show *maha aratis* (which had led to communal frenzy in Bombay in the month of January) or any other issue that might 'hurt' Hindu sentiments in films. Included in this agreement was a clause that women would not be portrayed in derogatory roles.[13]

The second issue was the demand for a Uniform Civil Code. The women's movement had led a sustained campaign for reforms within the segregated and religion-based marriage laws and had pressurised the state to evolve a non-sexist secular code. This demand found an echo in a similar demand by communal forces.

Family laws in India are termed 'personal laws' and are divided along religious affiliations rather than territorial jurisdiction. Even after independence no effort was made to evolve a Uniform Civil Code despite the constitutional mandate that stressed the necessity for such a code.[14] The ruling party, in order to lure the minority vote, continued to sacrifice the rights of minority women. Examples of this can be found in laws governing Christian and Muslim minorities. The only exception is the recent reform in laws governing Parsis.[15]

The archaic and anti-women Indian Divorce Act was enacted by the British in 1869 (it was meant for foreigners and native Christians) to facilitate the smooth functioning of the colonial regime. But today it is applicable to Indian Christians (who are referred to as 'native Christians' in the Act).[16] Under Section 10 of the Act, while a man can get a divorce on the grounds of adultery the woman has to prove an additional ground such as cruelty or desertion.[17] Repeated pleas to change this oppressive provision by Christian women's organisations[18] as well as recommendations by the Law Commission, have fallen on deaf ears.[19]

In a similar vein, the Dissolution of Muslim Marriages Act of 1939 governing the divorce of Muslim women, which has no provision for custody of children or for maintenance, has remained unchanged. Further, the customary privilege of the Muslim male to a unilateral *talaq* (divorce) is held valid in spite of protests from Muslim organisations.[20]

But the most stark example of this tendency was the passing of the Muslim Women's (Protection of Right to Divorce) Act 1986. A judgment in 1985 (popularly known as the Shah Bano judgment)[21] which reaffirmed the divorced Muslim woman's right to maintenance, aroused the wrath of some leaders of the Muslim community because of certain adverse comments made by the judiciary against Islam. Widespread protest by Muslims in different parts of India led to passing of laws which deprived divorced Muslim women of their hard-won right to maintenance under a secular code.[22]

It was not surprising that the demand for a Uniform Civil Code raised by the women's movement aroused contradictory responses from fundamentalists belonging to both the majority and minority communities. It was opposed strongly by Muslim and Christian religious leaders who projected it as a threat to their cultural identity and a violation of the fundamental rights guaranteed by the Constitution.[23] But it became an important plank upon which a hate campaign against Muslims could be built. Through it, Hindu communal organisations were not only able to gain popularity among Hindu males who envied their Muslim counterparts their 'freedom' to practice polygamy,[24] but could also pose as the champions of the women's cause.

### The myth of a progressive Hindu Code

There was a very clear difference between the demand made by the women's movement which was based on a pro-woman, secular and non-sexist ideology and the anti-Muslim demand of the communal forces. But this did not clearly manifest itself through well publicised campaigns. Although most of the initiators of the women's movement were culturally Hindu they perceived themselves as secular people. Hence they did not focus sharply and minutely on the existing Hindu code and did not attempt to challenge the sexist bias within it.[25] At another level, however, the movement was able to rally around important cases initiated by a few minority women challenging the sexist biases within their personal laws.[26] This resulted in the women's movement focussing primarily on lacunae within laws governing minority communities, and not really examining Hindu laws which were also in need of reform.

Perhaps a few examples of the extent of sexist biases within laws governing Hindus are necessary to clarify the issue. The first and concrete example is the Hinduisation of the Special Marriage Act. While the Muslim Women's Bill, which deprived

Muslim women of their right to maintenance under a secular code was strongly criticised, the amendment of 1976 to the Special Marriage Act of 1954 went unnoticed. This was the forerunner to the Muslim Women's Act and the first instance, after independence, when the trend towards a uniform secular code had been reversed. A religious group was taken out of the purview of the secular code and placed within the purview of a code based on religion. By this amendment if two Hindus married under the Special Marriage Act then the secular code which granted equal rights to men and women — the Indian Succession Act of 1925 — would not apply to them and parties would continue to be governed by the Hindu Succession Act which ensured male coparcernary rights.[27]

The amendment was both anti-women and anti-minority, it sought to protect the property interests of a Hindu man who married any woman within the broad Hindu fold, by not depriving him of his coparcenary rights. Since the concept of coparcenary (through which a male at birth becomes a partner in the ancestral property; a woman can never be a coparcener) per se is anti-women this amendment was *de facto* against women's rights. At another level, it served as a deterrent to a Hindu male wishing to marry a woman from the minority religious communities because then he could be penalised and made to forfeit his rights to ancestral property.

This amendment aroused no public furore from progressive organisations. Perhaps it is apt to point out that this amendment was passed at a point in history when the legislature enacted major changes in laws governing women's rights, as a response to the Status of Women Committee Report of 1974—*Towards Equality* and to the International Women's Year, 1975.

Several other lacunae within the Hindu Code also went unnoticed. For instance, the procedure of solemnising the Hindu marriage at one level remained Brahmanical but at the another level the code validated customary rituals and ceremonies. To this confusion Hindi films have contributed their bit by creating a fiction that exchanging garlands or applying *sindoor* (vermilion) to the forehead of the woman constitutes a valid marriage. This confusion, coupled with non-registration of marriages, has enabled the Hindu male to contract second marriages with impunity.

In divorce proceedings a Hindu man can, at his whim and fancy, admit either his first or his second sexual relationship as a valid marriage. This places the woman in a polygamous relationship which is extremely vulnerable, while it permits the man to enjoy the fruits of the relationship without any financial responsibility. When the man refuses to validate the marriage, the woman loses not only her right to maintenance but has to face humiliation and social stigma as a 'mistress'. So much is at stake for the woman that it is not an uncommon sight at the family court in Bombay for two women, who are vying with each other for the status of wife, to come to blows. Only the Hindu Marriage Act permits such scope for ambiguity regarding the solemnisation of marriage. Under other laws the officiating priest has to provide the necessary document by way of a *nikah nama* or he is required to register the marriage with the Registrar of Births, Deaths and Marriages.

In criminal prosecutions for bigamy under Section 494 of the Indian Penal Code, years of litigation fail to end in a conviction for the errant man because courts have adopted a rigid view that only *saptapadi* and *vivahahoma* are valid marriage ceremonies.[28] If, in the case of a second marriage it cannot be proved that these ceremonies have taken place, the courts will hold the second marriage to be invalid even though the couple have been living as husband and wife and the community has accepted them.[29] Hence the progressive sounding provision of monogamy has not only turned out to be a mockery but has in fact proved to be more detrimental to women than the uncodified Hindu law which recongnised the rights of wives in polygamous marraiages.[30]

The constitution of coparcenary concepts within the Hindu Succession Act denied equal property rights and the right to the ancestral home and property to women.[31] Daughters had equal rights only in the self-earned property of their fathers. This provision made it easy for men to turn their self-earned property into a joint property and deny women equal property rights. While introducing the provision of property rights to women in Parliament, this lacuna was pointed out to appease the Hindu revivalists who had vehemently opposed the provison granting property rights to women.[32] Some southern states like Tamil Nadu, Andhra Pradesh and Karnataka have tried to rectify such discrimination to women through state amendments.[33]

Under the Hindu Adoption and Maintenance Act, a Hindu wife can neither adopt nor give her child in adoption.[34] The father remains the natural guardian of the child (under the Hindu Guardianship and Adoption Act). But based on the deep-rooted desire to control women's sexuality, the law continued its distinction between legitimate and illegitimate children and made mothers the natural guardians of their illegitimate children, absolving the fathers of any moral responsibility towards the child.[35] A similar anomaly is that while, at one level, equal property rights were denied to the Hindu woman both in her ancestral as well as marital homes, under some strange and perverse notion of equality she was called upon to pay maintenance to her husband, a provision which does not exist in other personal laws.[36]

But, unfortunately, none of these anomalies and anti-women biases within the Hindu code received wide media publicity. They remained hidden in statute books and legal manuals. The women's movement did not rally around litigations challenging these anti-women biases in its campaign for a uniform secular code. Hence the demand by the women's movement could not clearly position itself away from the sexist Hindu code. Almost by default, the movement contributed to the fiction popularised by the Hindu fundamentalists that the Hindu code is the perfect family code which ought to be extended to other religious denominations in order to 'liberate' women.

The women's movement could not thus allay the fears of minority women that the Hindu code would not be thrust upon them under the guise of 'uniformity' in order to crush their cultural identity. Already burdened under sexist and archaic laws, women of minority communities would now have to bear the brunt of this 'default' as well. In addition, the severe opposition from fundamentalists of both Christian and Muslim communities to the Uniform Civil Code and assertion of their cultural identity means obstacles to the rights of minority women.

## Women's rights within communal organisations

Till recently the women leaders of communal organisations had advocated a conservative role for women. The public statements of Rajmata Vijayaraje Scindia and Mridula Sinha (of the BJP Mahila Morcha), supporting the practices of sati and dowry are well known. Although out of the 200,000 *kar sevaks* who went to Ayodhya for the destruction of the Babri Masjid 55,000 were women, their role was mainly behind the curtain, cooking and feeding their male counterparts.[37]

However, as large numbers of women enter the public arena under the banner of communal forces, the older and conservative notions about women's role and status in society will give way to a struggle for equality within the organisational structure. This can be seen from the recent rebellion among a group of BJP women MPs on behalf of Uma Bharati who had had sexist insult and abuse heaped on her by a party member. Newspapers have reported rumblings of discontent in the Mahila Morcha of the BJP which is demanding a broader representation within the organisation. Even the most conservative Hindu organisation, the Rashtriya Swayamsevak Sangh (RSS) imparts physical training with a special accent on the martial arts to its women members, the Rashtra Sevikas.

Indicating this shift in the party's attitude to the women's question, Mridula Sinha stated in an interview that women leaders are working on a perspective paper on 'BJP and Women'. She added that it is important that women know their rights and only education and independence will enable women to have access to these rights.[38] Further, she condemned the Muslim Women's Act as a backward step. According to her, the BJP has never discouraged women from standing for elections. During the 1989 elections the BJP fielded the highest number of women that is, 5.5. per cent as compared to the 4.5 per cent by the Congress and 3.3 per cent by the Janata Dal.[39]

Even the Shiv Sena has been taking a more active interest in women's issues in recent times. In a case where a minor domestic worker was repeatedly raped by her employer (which resulted in pregnancy), the issue came into public attention when a Shiv Sena MLA raised it in the state legislature. The Shiv Sena has also been reporting rape cases, at times even more promptly than some newspapers. For instance, a case of gang rape of a teenager which occurred on 17 November was reported in *Samna,*the mouthpiece of Shiv Sena, on 18 November and the same news item appeared in the *Times of India* five days later on 23 November, 1993. The Hindi version of the same paper *Dopahar ki Samna* also carried a sensitive and informative report denouncing police inaction and corruption while investigating rape cases. The writer provided accurate statistical information and lamented the delays and humiliation caused to women in courtrooms. Interestingly, two other articles on the same page were: an editorial on the Kashmir issue which blamed Pakistan and stated that it was time to disrobe Benazir (The exact words used are—*Benazir ka lehanga utarne ka yeh sahi vakht hai* and *Clinton ko batana zaroori hai ki Benazir ki choli ke peeche kya hai*. This is the correct time to desrobe Benazir and Clinton should be told exactly what lies behind her blouse), while a third article on the demolition of the Babri Masjid stated that the destruction of the Masjid was essential not just to assert Hindu identity but to preserve democracy and human values in society.[40]

## New challenges during the post-riot phase

With women's concerns gaining prominence everywhere, women's organisations will be forced to choose their political allies within the existing political set up. For instance the recently constituted women's commissions both at central and state levels will be broad forums which include representations from women's organisations along with other political parties. While this will provide the opportunity to influence policy decisions, the representatives will have an option either to be co-opted by the ruling party or form broad alliances with the opposition, including communal organisations. The question which needs to be addressed is whether women's interests will be strengthened by joining hands with communal forces in broader fora, as this could amount to a tacit endorsement of their propaganda. Or should commitment to secularism and minority rights be a pre-condition to forming coalitions for women's rights?

While these issues have not been adequately addressed, the complexities of the post-riot situation have brought minority concerns centre stage. Some groups feel that women's issues can no longer be addressed merely within a patriarchal framework along gender lines but have to be re-examined within the newer challenges to democracy, secularism and minority rights. The questioning does not limit itself to controversial issues like personal laws but extends even to seemingly non-controversial issues like domestic violence.

Here is one example of the choices which were thrust upon women's groups in the context of the riots. Around October, 1992, the Joint Commissioner of Police (Bombay) Mr R D Tyagi, issued directions to the subordinate police stations that cases of domestic violence should not be registered against women who do not bear visible marks of physical injury on their person. This direction was a setback. It is through a sustained campaign that a special provision was incorporated within the Indian Penal Code—section 498 (A)—which recognised both physical and mental violence against women within the matrimonial home.[41] Although the officer later retracted his statement, to counter the allegation that women misuse this provision, a seminar was planned with police and legal authorities and was scheduled for January, 1993.

But the riots of December 1992, drastically changed the original context of the seminar. In the wake of the large-scale police brutality where groups of young boys of the minority community picketing on the roads to protest the destruction of the Babri Masjid were shot down by the police, the faith of the minority community in the law enforcing machinery had totally broken down. Large numbers of Muslim youth with bullet injuries were forced to hide in their homes for fear of being locked up if they came into the vicinity of police stations.[42]

In such a situation where a whole community was being targeted thus, the issue of domestic violence had lost its earlier context. By organising a seminar on domestic violence women's organisations would be helping the police to defuse the more pressing issue of police excesses during the riots. Interaction with the law enforcing machinery in a forum on women's issues would amount to condoning their brutality towards Muslims.

The police, too, were eager to arrest Muslim men under any pretext. They would have entertained a Muslim woman's complaint on violence with undue eagerness and responded to it promptly. Viewed within the context of the women's movement, this could have been an ideal situation, but the response would, in fact, be anti-Muslim rather than pro-women. By applauding this move on the part of the police, women within the movement would be segregating the issues affecting Muslim women into isolated compartments of gender and religious identities.

During these months of political instability the number of women approaching agencies for help had decreased. The number of Muslim women following up their court cases had gone down even more drastically. Law and order had broken down and violence and instability had corroded the social fabric, an essential pre-condition for raising the question of domestic conflict. Interestingly, faced with violence and hostility at a broader social level, women seemed to have lost the limited space to challenge male violence in the domestic sphere. In the face of such adversity, they lost faith in courts, and police. This is not, however, to say that they were not mindful of the violence and male authority within their homes. It was simply that they felt they had no forum left to address it.

### Extended social space for women during conflict

Ironically, the social space which is denied to women in peace time was now being offered to them on a platter in the face of grave adversity. Women from both communities were being used or became willing martyrs in aid of the community, defying traditional norms and roles. In predominantly Muslim localities women became the buffer between the police and the community youth, and suffered many casualties.

The elderly neighbours of 50 year old Neelam Bano who was shot dead on 8 December, 1992 in a slum in Bandra East say, 'As the police opened fire, a group of us elderly women came out. We did not let the boys come out as the police might fire at them. We did not think that the police would fire at a group of elderly women.'[43] In many *bastis* (shanties), while men went into hiding, the women braved bullets to protect the children with a great sense of pride and honour. It is the women who stood in long queues to claim relief at the collector's office or went to police stations to lodge complaints.

On the other side, the Shiv Sena was able to mobilise a large section of women (even at midnight) to hold up traffic and to demonstrate outside police stations to protest against the detention of Hindu youth. Women slept on the roads to prevent army trucks from entering the area to rescue Muslim hostages or put out fires.[44] The slogans which its left groups had used to strengthen collective action were now used to whip up communal frenzy among violent mobs. For instance the slogan—'*Hum se jo takarayega, mitti me woh mil jayega*' (Those who confront us will be destroyed ) rent the air.

All of this did not mean any improvement for women within the home: those who threw stones at the Muslim men and helped in the violence and looting, would nonetheless have to approach women's organsations for help in problems of domestic violence etc., in peacetime.

With the Muslim community the equation was in reverse. Community leaders who were fighting for legitimacy and a right to a dignified existence in a riot-torn situation, became allies of women activists in anti-communal fora. But at that moment women did not dare to question them on their views on the Shah Bano judgment or the triple *talaq* ( divorce). And even as activists were being welcomed with open arms during peace rallies they were apprehensive that riot time allies might become peace time adversaries. The same men may deny activists access to the women of their community once 'normalcy' returned, for after all, then their (the activists') work would be 'threatening'.

## A moment for reflection

Women leaders of left political parties such as Ahilya Rangnekar CPI (M), while confronting the fact that women had played a significant role in the riots, admitted that the left parties and women's organisations had failed to counter communalism.[45] It was evident that gender unity could not withstand communal hostility.[46] The section of women who are traditionally the most difficult to mobilise, housewives, had responded to the call of Hindutva and marched under the banner of the Shiv Sena and the Durga Vahini, the women's wing of the VHP. Sadhvi Rithambara and Uma Bharati addressed mammoth public meetings of devout followers and became the living incarnations of shakti.[47]

The riots dealt a severe blow to the premise that the women have a separate existence away from their communal identity where they can discuss problems of rape, divorce and maintenance on a common platform. The same issues affect different women in different ways at different times. Activists also realised that their allies and adversaries would change depending upon external realities. If social action means reacting to external social reality, then as the external reality changes, the internal positions will have to be redefined or else the movement itself will become redundant in the wake of the newer challenges.

In conclusion, it is necessary to emphasise that this critique of the movement is made from within, and by someone who has participated in all the different stages of the development of the movement. The contradictions and confusions are as much a part of the movement as its gains and are signs of a movement which is alive and growing, which is reformulating its positions in response to external shifts in the configurations of power.

The women's movement does not stand in isolation and is an integral part of other social movements. Hence the contradictions and ideological shifts expressed here within the context of the women's movement hold true for other social movements as well. During the last decade the trade union movement in Bombay has become communalised with the Shiv Sena dominating many important trade unions in the city. The Sena-dominated unions in Larsen & Tubro, Oberoi Towers, Bombay Dyeing and other private companies not only led riots but also demanded that Muslims be removed from the workforce.

The hostility towards Muslims was not limited to Sena-dominated unions but was also widespread among left party affiliated unions. In the course of my discussions with trade unions of the left it became clear that even these unions were not entirely exempt from being communalised, and this resulted in several instances of violence and arson in factory premises. This led to large scale absenteeism of Muslim workers. Less than 30 per cent of the Muslim labour force in the organised sector returned to work even after a month of the riots. In an effort to restore normalcy, establishments like the Tatas issued a public statement inviting the Muslim workers back to work and promising them adequate protection. But some others sent their Muslim workers on leave on the grounds that they could not guarantee their safety.[48] The severe blow to the commercial activities of the trade centre led industrialists like JRD Tata and Nani Palkhivala to demand a partial emergency or to declare the city as Union Territory in order to bring the riots under control.[49] This is an indication of the extent to which the trade union movement was divided.

Analysing these developments, one trade union member explained that the Shiv Sena had been able to provide the space to the workers for cultural assertion, however narrow and exclusionary in nature it might be. On the other hand, the left organisations had rallied mainly around economic and political issues which had resulted in limiting their scope.[50]

Dalit and other caste-based movements also had to confront similar issues. The Hindu community, which had been divided along caste lines on the Mandal issue, now stood united against Muslims. Progressive organisations which had supported the Mandal campaign found that this alliance could not withstand the stress of communal pulls. Within the government bureaucracy those who held 'reserved' posts expressed deep-rooted communal biases even while implementing relief programmes declared by the government. In Dharavi and other bastis the corporators belonging to the Republican Party, a political forum of the Dalits, led the riots against the Muslims. Shanta Dharia, a Republican Party woman corporator, was shot down by the police while she was leading a rioting mob.[51]

The experience of the Bombay riots posed a new challenge to progressive movements in the city. In the process groups were forced to question the premise that progressive movements are per se secular. It is evident that deep-seated communal biases can be overcome only when secularism becomes an important agenda and a conscious political choice for any progressive movement.

For the women's movement, the challenge has become even more complex, particularly in the context of minority rights versus women's rights in the current political controversy over the Uniform Civil Code. The support by communal organisations to this issue has placed the women's movement in an awkward position. It is true that the hardships and suffering experienced by women of all communities — minority as well as majority — cannot be swept under the carpet or glossed over with the rhetoric of freedom of religion. Nevertheless, the women's movement cannot isolate itself from the political realilty confronting the country.

Laws have to be enacted in Parliament and debated by the elected representatives of the people. It is within this segment that the women's movement will have to find its allies. Since political parties can no longer be rated simplistically as being pro or anti women, alliances will have to be formed keeping in mind other parameters — secularism versus communalism, imposition of majority will upon the minority and commitment to the basic structure of the Constitution as laid down by the Supreme Court.

With women's rights being pitted against minority rights, the demand for the former can no longer be limited to simply working towards a code that ensures uniform rights to women of all communities. The strategy will have to be more complex to encompass the diversity of women's lives if it is to break the current political stalemate and bring concrete relief to women who are trapped under the present socio-economic and political system.

## Notes

1   Jim Masselos, 'The City as Represented in Crowd Action', *Economic and Political Weekly* January 1993, Vol 38, no 5, p.182 .

2   For a detailed account of the Bombay riots see two articles titled 'The Winter of Discontent' (pp.12-42) and 'A City at War With Its self' (p.43-108) by Clarence Fernandez & Naresh Fernandes in Dilip Padgaonkar, ed., *When Bombay Burned* Delhi, Times of India publications, 1993.

3   Forum Against Oppression of Women, Bombay; Stree Sangharsh, Delhi; Stree Shakti Sanghatana, Hyderabad; Sachetana, Calcutta.

4   Saheli, Delhi; Vimochana, Banglore; Women's Centre, Bombay; Ahmedabad Women's Action Forum (AWAG), Ahmedabad.

5   Flavia Agnes , 'Protecting Women Against Violence?' *Economic and Political Weekly* , April 1992, p. WS-19

6   Annapurna, Bombay; Self Employed Women's Association (SEWA), Ahmedabad; Working Women's Forum, Madras; Women's Voice, Bangalore.

7   Sunderlal Bahuguna, 'Herstory - Women's Nonviolent Power in the Chipko Movement, *Manushi*, No.6, 1980, 34; Fatima Burnard, 'Despite Heavy Odds - Organising Harijan Women in Tamil Nadu Villages', *Manushi* No.19, 1983, 33; Alaka & Chetna, 'When Women Get Land - a Report from Bodhgaya', *Manushi* No. 40, 1987, 25; Peter Custers, 'Women's Role in Tebhaga Movement - An Interview with Bimla Maji', *Manushi* no 32, No2, 1986, 28.

8   Madhu, Kishwar, 'Gangster Rule - The Massacre of the Sikhs, *Manushi* No.27, 1984, 34; SEWA Report on Communal Violence, 'Why This Slow Murder', *Manushi* No. 33, 1986, .5; Sonal Mehta, 'We Know the Weapons Will Finally Turn on Us. Recurrent Anti Muslim Riots in Ahmedabad', *Manushi* No.36, 1986, 7; Lalita Ramdas & Jaya Srivastava, 'From Day To Day - Envisioning Tomorrow—Working with Victims of Anti Sikh Riots at Tilak Vihar' *Manushi* No.36, 1986, 35;

9   'Civil Rule Threatened in North East', *The Lawyers* Vol.4 No.2, February, 1989. 24; Shashi Sinha, 'Bhopal - How Women Suffered', *Manushi* No. 29, 1985, 36;

10  Bharatiya Mahila Federation of CPI; Janwadi Mahila Samiti of CPI (M); Mahila Dakshata Samiti of Janata Dal and Stree Mukti Sanghatana of Lal

Nishan Party.

11 During its early days (in the late seventies) the Shiv Sena popularised the slogan 'Amchi Mumbai, Marathi Mumbai' (Our Bombay, Marathi Bombay). This slogan apparently expressed the growing dissatisfaction of the Marathi middle class youth against 'outsiders' — mainly south Indians and Muslims who were alleged to have been responsible for the growing unemployment of 'Maharashtrian' youth. The Sena urged these 'sons of the soil' to take up arms against the outsiders. It is this population of disgruntled Maharashtrian youth that forms the backbone of the Sena in Bombay today.

12 When Doordarshan started a programme of late-night screenings of English classics, the women's wing of the BJP and Shiv Sena stormed the Doordarshan premises demanding a ban on these films on the grounds that they corrupt the minds of young children. The portrayal of women's desire was termed as obscene by these women. Interestingly though, there was no protest from them against films such as *Pati Parmeshwar*, *Suhagan* and others which show women in subordinate roles. Soon after the riots the same women's groups led a demonstration against a film sponsored by the National Film Development Corporation (NFDC), *Dharavi*, in which Shabana Azmi was in the lead. They succeeded in stopping its screening. This time the reasoning was that Shabana Azmi was 'anti-national'.

13 See Seema Sinha, 'SS-BJP "Emergency" on Bollywood Resented', *Indian Express*, 12 May 1993. Some of the conditions accepted by the Film Makers Combine are:

1. Any member of the film industry who is not a member of the political party should not criticise or condemn Hindus involved in the Ayodhya movement or *maha aratis*.
2. In case such persons do want to criticise then they should officialy join a political party of their choice and then exercise their right to criticise the Hindu movement.
3. No new films should be launched with artistes whose nationalist credentials are under suspicion.
4. Artistes shown in nude pictures, magazines and the like will be banned from starring in films by the FMC.

14 Article 44 of the Constitution states. 'The State shall endeavour to secure for its citizens a Uniform Civil Code throughout the territory of India. Although this is not a fundamental right which can be enforced in a court of law, it is a directive principle for the governance of state policies and hence becomes a Constitutional mandate for the State.

15 Amendments to the Parsi Marriage & Divorce Act, 1936 by Act 5 of 1988 (with effect from 15th April, 1988).

16 The Indian Divorce Act was to be a residual act meant mainly for European Christians, as the 'natives' were governed by their own customary laws in matters of marriage and divorce. The various British Charters in the initial phase of Company rule retained the power to adjudicate in different civil matters—matrimonial, succession, inheritance, etc., with customary tribunals. Hence people who were not governed by any customary or caste-based laws, for example the European Christians, did not have a forum to adjudicate in matrimonial matters.

Later, through a Letters Patent issued under the Royal Seal in 1861, the High Courts in the Presidency towns of Bombay, Calcutta and Madras were conferred the jurisdiction over matrimonial matters. It was under this power that the Indian Divorce Act was passed in 1869.

17 Heera Nawaz, 'Section 10 of the Indian Divorce Act —Need for Amendment', *The Lawyers* Vol.3, 1988, No.10 ,14.

18 Joint Women's Programme, 'Christian Women Demand Reform', *Manushi*, No. 33, 1986, 34

19 Law Commission of India. 90th Report on The Grounds of Divorce Among Christians in India, S.10 Indian Divorce Act, 1989, 1983.

20 Shikhare , 'Talaq Mukti Morcha in Maharashtra', *Manushi* No.32, 1986, 23

21 Mohd. Ahmd Khan V Shah Bano Begum AIR 1985 SC 945;

22 The Muslim Women's Act excluded a divorced Muslim woman from the purview of the beneficial social legislation under Section 125 of the Criminal Procedure Code of 1973 which provides for maintenance of wives, children and parents.

23 Articles 25-28 of the Constitution guaranteeing freedom of religion.

24 To give an example in State of Bombay vs. Narasu Appa Mali *AIR* 1952 Bom.84 it was contended that banning polygamy among Hindus violated the provision of equality under article 15 (1) of the Constitution.

25 'Law: Is a Father Natural Guardian—Hindu Guardianship Act Challenged', *Manushi* No.35, 1986, 33; Smt. Madhu Bala vs. Arun Khanna—*AIR* 1987 Delhi 81 reported in 'Natural Mother as the Custodian of Her Child', *The Lawyers* Vol. 4, No.10, 1989, 17; Shamona Khanna , 'Challenging the Unequal Position', *The Lawyers* Vol.7 No.4, 1992, 28.

26 Challenge to the Inheritance Laws of Syrian Christians by Mary Roy [Mary Roy vs. State of Kerala AIR 1986 SC 1011] and Challenge to s.10 of the Indian Divorce Act by Mary Sonia Zacharia [Mary Sonia Zachariah v. Union of India (1990) [Kerala Law Times (KLT) 131] These litigations were supported by Christian Women's organisations i.e. Young Women's Christian Association (YWCA) and All India Council of Christian Women (AICCW) and the Joint Women's Programme (JWP). Similarly, the issue of triple talaq was raised by the Talaq Peedit Mahila Morcha, Pune. Shahnaz Sheikh filed a case in the Supreme Court challenging various discriminatory provisions under the Muslim Personal Law in 1984 (see 'Abusing Religion to Oppress Women', *Manushi* No.22, 1984, 9; ' Challenge to the Muslim Women's Act', by P.K.Saru reported in *'Hazir Hai'*, *The Laywers*, Vol.2, No.11, 1987, 23. The cases are pending in the Supreme Court.

27 Section 21 (A) of Special Marriage Act, 1954, Instituted by the Marriage Laws (Amendment) Act 1976 (68 of 1976) Section 22 (with effect from 27 May, 1976)

28 Section 7 (1) & (2) of Hindu Marriage Act, 1955. The *saptapadi* marriage is performed by the bride and bridegroom taking seven steps round the nuptial fire. A Hindu marriage is deemed to be solemnised on completion of the seventh step, as per case law on this issue. A *vivahoma* is the chanting of specific hymns, at the nuptial fire, by the officiating priest.

29 Bhau Rao v. State of Maharashtra AIR 1965 SC 1964; S. Varadarajan v. State of Madras AIR 1965 SC 1564; Priyalatha vs. Suresh AIR 1971 SC 1153.

[30] Anupama Pradhan v. Sultan Pradhan 1991 Cri. L.J.3216

[31] Section 6 of the Hindu Succession Act, 1956; See P M Bhakshi, 'Partition Rights of Female Hiers' *The Lawyers* Vol.3 No.43, 1988, 14.

[32] Archana Parashar, *Women and Family Law Reform in India,* Delhi, Sage Publications, 1992, p. 128.

[33] Heera Nawaz, 'Equal Property Rights to Women in Karnataka,' vol.3 No 6, 1988, 16.

[34] Section 8 (c) of the Hindu Adoption and Maintenance Act 1956.

[35] Section 6 (a) & (b) of Hindu Minority and Guardianship Act, 1956.

[36] Section 24 & 25 of the Hindu Marriage Act, 1955. See also Shamona Khanna, 'Padmasini's Quest for Justice' *The Lawyers,* February 1992 ,25. Also note that the 1988 amendment to the Parsi Marriage & Divorce Act, 1936 has granted Parsi men the right of maintenance under Sections 39 and 40 of the Act.

[37] Diva Arora ,*The Telegraph,* 27 December, 1992.

[38] Tanika Sarkar ,'The Crucible that Moulds,' *Pioneer,* 23 December 1992.

[39] Manira Alva, 'Women's Issues: The Primary Party positions', May, 1993.

[40] The Hindi Tabloid *Dopahar ka Samana* dated 18 November, 1993 pp.1 and 4

[41] Meena Menon 'Tyagi Slams Door on Battered Women' in *Times of India,* 28 October, 1992 and 'Pact on Definition Arrived - Mental Torture of Women' *Times of India,* 6 November, 1992.

[42] Madhu Kishwar, 'Safety is Indivisible - The Warning from Bombay Riots', *Manushi* No.74-75 P.2.

[43] Interviews Muslim women in a documentary by Madhsree Dutta titled 'I Live in Behrampada' (1993).

[44] Flavia Agnes 'Behrampada - A Besieged Basti', *Manushi* No. 74-75, 8.

[45] Sharmila Joshi, 'Women as Messengers of Peace', *Independent* 10 March, 1993.

[46] Kalpana Sharma 'Can Gender Unity Override Communal Hostility?' *The Hindu,* 7 March, 1993.

[47] *Sunday Observer,* 31 January, 1993.

[48] 'The Bombay Riots—the Myths and Realities—A Report', by Lokshahi Hak Sanghatana and Committee for the Protection of Democratic Rights, Bombay, March 1993 p.87.

[49] Ibid.p 10.

[50] This was discussed by Dr Vivek Monteiro of the Centre for Indian Trade Unions (CITU, affiliated to the Communist Party of India, Marxist) and Meena Menon of the Indian Federation of Trade Unions (IFT, affiliated to the Communist Party of India, Marxist Lenninist) at a seminar in Bombay (February 1993) in a panel discussion entitled 'The Nation, State and Indian Identity.' It was substantiated by veteran trade unionist Bagaram Tulpule who chaired this session.

[51] 'The Bombay Riots — the Myths and Realities— A Report,' p. 6

# Feminism Inverted
## *The Gendered Imagery and Real Women of Hindu Nationalism**

AMRITA BASU

'If Shahabuddin has drunk his mother's milk,
I have also drunk my mother's milk.'

*Sadhvi Rithambara*

'My mother was a very strong woman. She had to struggle to
support her children and maintain her land. I have tried to
follow her example.'

*Uma Bharati*

'My mother died when I was a baby;
I was nurtured by my motherland.'

*Vijayraje Scindia*

If one was to imagine the gendered imagery and female leadership associated with Hindu 'communalism', the images that
come to mind are of women as self-sacrificing, long-suffering,
non-violent victims.[1] Such images find fullest expression in
Gandhian nationalism. But associations of women with pacifism
even figure in many agrarian social movements of which the

*Paola Bachetta, Mary Katzenstein, and Mark Kesselman provided insightful
comments on an earlier draft of this paper. I am also grateful for research and
writing support from the Amherst College Research Award and the John D. and
Catherine T. MacArthur Foundation.

Chipko movement is a prime example.[2] These images derive their force partly from their singularity: to represent the diversity of women's life experiences might undermine their iconic roles.

Like the independence movement and subsequent social movements, Hindu nationalism has sought legitimacy in notions of selflessness, sacrifice and martyrdom. Along with anti-colonial nationalism, it has liberally employed gendered images and appeals. However Hindu nationalism represents a departure from earlier forms of mobilisation with respect to its uses of gendered images and the place of real women in two respects. First, a number of women enjoy greater prominence in Hindu nationalism than have women in the nationalist movement. Second, the female leadership of the Hindutva movement does not advocate pacifism. While their directives are most specifically targeted at Hindu men, this female leadership implicitly sanctions and indeed encourages women's exercise of violence.

Vijayraje Scindia, Uma Bharati and Sadhvi Rithambara, the three women who have emerged as the most powerful orators of Hindu nationalism, defy the gendered images of earlier movements in a number of ways. None of them is particularly nurturing; one among them is a mother and her estrangement from her son is widely known. Regardless of the personal hardships they may have experienced, they depict themselves as powerful agents rather than passive victims. Most strikingly, all three women openly espouse violence against Muslims.

Moreover these women's backgrounds and life histories do not conform to a singular model of Indian womanhood. While Vijayraje Scindia is a member of an affluent, upper caste princely family, Uma Bharati and Sadhvi Rithamabara are from relatively poor, lower caste, rural backgrounds. Vijayraje Scindia, who has long been active in party politics, joined the Jan Sangh because of her disillusionment with the Congress party. By contrast, Uma Bharati and Sadhvi Rithambara were afforded their first opportunities for political activism through the Ram Janmabhoomi campaign.

Even the personal appearance and demeanour of these women are strikingly different. Vijayraje Scindia is an elderly matron who dresses in white, as is customary for widows, and radiates an aura of piety and sobriety. By contrast, Sadhvi Rithambara exudes a passionate rage that is said to have instigated riots in many places where she has delivered public speeches; Uma Bharati is a spirited, extroverted woman, who seems to revel in the role the press accords her of the 'sexy *sanyasin*', (a person who has taken religious vows including vows of celibacy). As I left her apartment after an interview, Bharati was striking the poses of a film star for a photographer who was doing a feature story about her for a glossy Hindi magazine.[3]

I decided to focus on Rithambara and Bharati because as single, militant, young women of modest backgrounds, they mark a striking departure from women both in positions of leadership and in fundamentalist movements in South Asia. I included Vijayraje Scindia in my analysis because of her prominence in the Vishva Hindu Parishad (VHP) and Bharatiya Janata Party (BJP), as its former vice president. The difference in her background, compared to that of the two other women, fruitfully suggested the diversity of female images and roles in the Hindutva movement.

My comparison of these three women leaders of the Hindutva movement prompted me to raise a number of questions. As noted earlier, in contrast to most other movements in which women have figured only as symbols, images and abstractions, the Hindutva movement seemed to be challenging the most important iconic representation of women, namely their association with non-violence. How did women's espousal of violence further the cause of Hindu nationalism? Conversely, were women's interests served by a movement that espoused violence against a relatively powerless minority community? Or did Rithambara, Bharati and Scindia, as `real' as they appeared to be, serve as icons within the Hindutva movement?

I unravel the puzzle concerning the prominence of these three women by exploring the peculiarities of communalism in India. As I will suggest, in contrast to fundamentalist parties and movements that are preoccupied with restoring women to their traditional roles, the BJP 'combine', which is governed by expediency, presents itself as a champion of women's rights.[4] However from a feminist vantage point, women only figure as a means of furthering an electorally driven communal strategy.

My interest in Rithambara, Bharati and Scindia precludes confining attention to any single organisation, for these three women have been active in the Rashtra Sevika Samiti (the women's organisation affiliated with the RSS), the Durga Vahini (the VHP affiliated women's organisation) and the BJP Mahila Morcha (women's organisation). However since I am primarily interested in the explicitly political dimensions of women's activism, I devote greater attention to the BJP than to its affiliated organisations.

## The powers of renunciation

There is, amidst their many differences, one striking similarity between Scindia, Bharati and Rithambara, that is critical to the project of Hindu nationalism. All three women are celibate: Vijayraje Scindia is a widow and Uma Bharati and Sadhvi Rithambara are *sanyasins* (*Sadhvi* means celibate).

Their chastity heightens their iconic status for it is deeply associated in Hinduism with notions of spirituality, purity and otherworldliness; these qualities also make these women reliable spokespersons for the future Hindu *rashtra*.

Renunciation—both sexual and material—exercises enormous moral force in India. Its most important exponent historically, Mahatma Gandhi, could unify diverse regional, caste, religious and class groups because he seemed to transcend their particularistic loyalties. RSS *pracharaks'* (preachers) claims to be nationalist similarly rest partly on their ascetic life style, which in turn connotes sacrifice, martyrdom and selflessness. Simply put, it is difficult to imagine that people who eat, dress, and live simply could be corrupt, ambitious and cruel.

Further elaborating the implications of renunciation, the BJP distinguishes itself from other political parties by its supposed indifference to power. Thus it can accuse the Congress party, without a trace of irony, of engaging in 'vote bank politics' —of appealing to particular caste, ethnic and religious communities out of electoral expediency.

That the BJP, as a parliamentary party, should be so openly and closely associated with the VHP, a religious organisation, and the RSS, a para-military organisation, constitutes an anomaly within the Indian political context. One might speculate that women's mediating or liminal roles help to strengthen ties between these organisations. The very contrasts between these three women are critical to the BJP combine's attempt to reconcile diverse organisations and constituencies. While Vijayraje Scindia presents herself as a seasoned politician with a historical memory of what Congress once promised and has failed to deliver, Bharati and Rithambara reflect the impatience of youth. Whereas Vijayraje Scindia appeals to the declining feudal classes, Bharati and Rithambara appeal to the upwardly mobile lower middle classes. 'The BJP is a natural choice for people like us who do not have name or fame but are drawn to the party by our commitment to the cause', Bharati observed in an interview.

Flouting the Constitution's secular injunction to keep religious organisations out of electoral politics, Uma Bharati and Vijayraje Scindia assert that their political activism grows out of their commitment to their religious and cultural heritage. Similarly, their militance is a constant reminder that the BJP is not only a parliamentary party but also a potentially subversive mass movement.

If male *pracharaks* are highly respected, the status of female *sanyasins* is even more elevated. Hinduism considers women's sexuality both powerful and dangerous.[5] Conversely, a celibate woman may be freed from numerous social conventions and restraints to denounce the political class. Rithambara has called Mulayam Singh Yadav, the former chief minister of Uttar Pradesh, *ullu ka patha* (a curse which translates as son of an owl), former prime minister V P Singh a hypocrite, and the Imam of Jama Masjid a buffalo; she often uses the term *napunsak* (eunuch) for politicians. In one cassette, she reviles Mulayam Singh Yadav for calling members of the VHP and Bajrang Dal (its youth organisation) drunkards when he is intoxicated by his love of power.

The popularity of Rithambara's cassettes seems to reflect a widespread hatred of politicians which is rooted in turn in Hindu conceptions of the inferiority of the worldly domain of political life compared to the other-worldly domain of religion. Women are well suited to make this critique of the political world from the distance afforded them by the protective inner sanctum of the home. But Muslims, with the support of some Hindu traitors, now threaten to shatter that private domain by violating both Hindus' sacred places and their women. This betrayal justifies Rithambara's rage and enables her to flaunt the seemingly powerful, no doubt inspiring confidence in those who are angry but disempowered.

The power of Rithambara's appeals also lies in her ability to combine allusions to classical myths, legends and poetry with the symbols of everyday life. I attended a VHP rally outside New Delhi where Rithambara spoke in melodic couplets. She said:

> ... Muslims, like a pinch of sugar, should sweeten a glass of milk; instead, like lemon, they sour it. What they do not realise is that a squeezed lemon is thrown away while the milk that has been curdled solidifies into *paneer* (cheese). So Muslims have two choices: either to live like sugar or like wrung lemons.

These melodic couplets paraphrase the writings of the famous poet Tulsidas in which lemons figure as symbols of selfishness. By contrast, milk is associated with the cow and the mother, both of which are revered in the Hindu tradition, and connote self-lessness. The image of lemon curdling pure milk might even be interpreted as a sexual metaphor in that it alludes to the defiling of the feminine purity associated with cows and milk. The verses imply that even a minority can bring ruin to the society. Thus Muslims must choose between assimilation and death.

Far from repudiating the cassettes of Uma Bharati and Sadhvi Rithambara, the BJP accorded these women greater prominence as they became more militant and vociferous, by nominating them to run in the parliamentary elections. Rithambara and Bharati are vital to the BJP's attempt to eschew its elitist charac-ter. Both women seemingly embody a subaltern perspective: they are low caste, relatively poor, and female. They thereby serve to bolster the BJP's fallacious contention that the Ram Janmabhoomi campaign originates at the grassroots level. Fur-thermore, their dismissal of reason in favour of raw emotion provides a powerful affirmation of the BJP's attack on what it considers the Congress party's pseudo-secularism, rationalism and westernisation.

The BJP is faced with a serious contradiction between its need to foster Hindu-Muslim violence in order to gain Hindu votes and its desire to depict Hindus as victims whose violence is defensive and reactive. Given the realities of economic and political life, the BJP cannot plausibly allege that Muslims dominate Hindus today. But it can justify Hindu violence by pointing to the sexually predatory Muslim male and the vulnerable Hindu woman.

However, the more difficult question remains why Uma Bharati and Sadhvi Rithambara, who have themselves suffered as a result of their class and gender, should advocate genocidal violence against a relatively powerless minority community. Although Vijayraje Scindia's participation in the Jan Sangh might be attributed to her landowning, princely background why has she become a leading exponent of militant Hindu nationalism? Furthermore to what extent do Rithamabara, Bharati and Scindia appeal to 'ordinary' Hindu women?

## The gender logic of women's violence

If feminism entails some recognition of gender inequality and expression of solidarity with other women, it is difficult to accommodate Scindia, Bharati and Rithambara in even the most expansive definition of feminism. At their most benign they render Muslim women invisible; more often they seek to annihilate Muslim women. Yet all three women have found within Hindu nationalism a vehicle for redressing their experiences of gender inequality and for transgressing sex-typed roles.

Let us begin by analysing the attributes of Rithambara and Bharati that have brought them into the public eye, namely, their speech. (Although Scindia is not highly visible as a public orator, she spoke in an extremely militant fashion when interviewed.) It may be liberating for women, who are continually enjoined to be decorous, to be praised for their good citizenship when they deliver loud, angry, coarse public speeches. As women they may have particular license to speak from emotion rather than reason. For example, when Uma Bharati tells Hindu men to act like lions rather than frogs, she assumes the tones of a wife chiding her negligent husband. In public speeches, their use of vulgar expressions and their ability to address men with familiarity and condescension transgresses traditional gender roles and expresses both their anger and agency. Jolting her audience to rid themselves of inhibitions as she expresses herself with humour and wrath Sadhvi Rithambara delivered a speech in Khurja on December 5, 1991 which I attended. She cried out: 'Whatever we do, Muslims do the opposite. We Hindus write from right to left, they do the opposite, we worship cows, they kill cows, we eat with our mouths; tell them to do the opposite . . . .'

The concept of displacement may help explain Hindu nationalists' aggression towards Muslims. Pursuing the Lacanian view that enjoyment is ultimately enjoyment of the Other, Slavoj Zizek argues that conversely, hatred of the Other is a hatred of our own excess of enjoyment. He suggests:

> We always impute to the "other" an excessive enjoyment; s/he wants to steal our enjoyment (by ruining our way of life) and/or has access to some secret, perverse enjoyment. In short, what really bothers us about the "other" is the peculiar way it organizes its enjoyment: precisely the surplus, the "excess" that pertains to it— the smell of their food, their "noisy" songs and dances, their strange manners, their attitude to work . . ."[6]

What makes this argument so germane is the preoccupation of Hindu nationalists with the supposed strength, virility and aggression of Muslim men. Hindu communalists speak incessantly of how much meat Muslims consume, the numbers of children they bear, and their physical stamina. These images must be set against the colonialist images of effeminate, weak Hindu men that Mahatma Gandhi so ingeniously inverted. They particularly connote envy when expressed by *pracharaks* who have renounced meat, sexuality, marriage and family.

The BJP has made the raped Hindu woman symbolic of the victimisation of the entire Hindu community. What makes this symbol so effective is that it recalls the violence that women routinely suffer. Paradoxically, by according recognition to violence against women, the BJP pays a back-handed tribute to the Indian women's movement. Recall that the catalyst to the emergence of a nationwide feminist movement was the rape of a tribal girl in 1979. By castigating violence against women, the BJP also co-opts one of the major grievances of the women's movement, which it deeply resents for supposedly contributing to the disintegration of the Hindu family.

In the case of Hindu women militants like Bharati and Rithambara, it would appear to be anger against Hindu men in their own community that is displaced onto Muslim men. Recall their fury at the rape of Hindu women—which is actually far more often committed by Hindu than by Muslim men. Note their mockery of Hindu men, and their assertion of their own strength as women. When Rithambara repeatedly states that

Hindus have been exploited because of their selflessness, passivity and generosity, she is restating a widely held grievance by women about their relationship with men.

There were few issues that Uma Bharati said enraged her more than sexual exploitation. She spoke vehemently against the exploitation of women's bodies in advertising and the media and favoured strict censorship laws to control pornography. Above all, she expressed outrage about rape.

> In my constituency, a twenty-five year old boy raped and killed a six year old girl and threw her body in the well. The police are looking for him. I have announced that if I find him, I will kill him myself with my bare hands, and I mean it, I would. I think that rape has declined in my constituency because people know how it enrages me.

Displacement may also assume another form for Bharati and Rithambara: their own assumption of the activist roles they advocate for Hindu men. Most writers on the subject assume that nationalist appeals to defend the motherland are directed at dutiful sons. However, this supposition neglects the strength of the mother-daughter bond in favour of the much vaunted mother-son relationship. When asked what had politicised her, Rithambara responded: 'If Shahabuddin has drunk his mother's milk, I have also drunk my mother's milk.'[7] Thus while the overt pretext for her speeches may be to goad men into activism, she is suggesting that devotion to the motherland is as much an inspiration to dutiful daughters as to filial sons.

When I asked Uma Bharati what had politicised her, she spoke at length about the powerful influence of her mother. Uma's father had died when she was eleven years old, leaving her mother to support her and five older siblings. Difficult as this would be under any conditions, matters became much worse when some relatives attempted to take over the family land. Her mother was determined to retain the land. One day she set out on foot to appeal to the chief minister for help. It took her a month to reach Bhopal, some 300 kilometres from their village. Uma Bharati recalled,

> When she reached the CM's [chief minister's] bungalow, she kept requesting appointments to meet with him but

he would not give her the time. For weeks she sat by the gate and watched his car come and go; he would not even look in her direction. Finally she lay down on the road in front of the gate and said that she would rather be killed by his car than sit there unnoticed. In the end the CM saw her and helped her.

In this account, the land figures not as an abstraction but as the source of the family's material sustenance; similarly, the link between the mother and the land is not figurative but real. For Uma's mother to fulfil her maternal responsibilities, she had to depart from conventional female roles to fight for her rights. The story reveals why Uma came to believe that access to power was critical to attaining independence as a woman.

Vijayraje Scindia said that her mother died when she was a baby; Hindu *rashtra* had taken the place of the mother she longed for. She admitted to having shown favouritism towards her son when he was young. But once her children grew up, her relationship with her son had become embittered. By contrast, her daughter, Vasundhara Raje, divorced her husband and lived with her mother and child in the family compound. Most importantly, she followed her mother's lead in politics. Vasundhara Raje was elected to parliament on a BJP ticket.

Vijayraje Scindia, Sadhvi Rithambara and Uma Bharati have all transgressed gender roles in both private and public domains. Unlike the vast majority of Indian women, none of these three women is economically dependent on fathers, husbands or sons; none of their identities is defined by their roles as wives and mothers. All three women have realised considerable political ambition and yet masked it with the aura of religious and nationalist commitment.

Religious devotion has always provided Hindu women the opportunity for some degree of collective identification and freedom from domestic drudgery. While Hindu nationalism may heighten these possibilities, it does not necessarily entail a deepened understanding of gender asymmetry. The differences here between Uma Bharati and Vijayraje Scindia are informative.

Reiterating a position that she had made publicly, Vijayraje Scindia defended sati in an interview with me. Referring to religious scriptures, she drew a highly questionable distinction between voluntary sati, to which she attributed a glorious tradition, and the coerced sati of recent times, which she considered immoral. She was evasive when asked how she would describe Roop Kanwar's sati, saying that it must have been wrong if in fact it had been coerced but she could not be sure. In other respects she remained committed to asymmetrical gender roles. She argued that Indian religion and culture supported the notion that women's primary duties were as wives and mothers.

By contrast, Uma Bharati vehemently opposed sati in any form and denied that it was sanctioned by Hinduism. She recalled that many esteemed widows in the epics, including Ram's mother Kaushalya, in the *Ramayana*, had not become satis. 'When women commit sati', she commented bitterly, 'it has more to do with property than religion', alluding to in-laws' attempts to prevent their widowed daughters-in-law from gaining control over the dowry they brought with them at marriage.

Uma Bharati explained that her religious training, which began when she was only six years old, had provided her the opportunity for a formal education, extensive travel within India and Europe, and an escape from both arranged marriage and manual labour on the family land. 'Religion earned me my freedom', she commented wryly:

> It doesn't always work that way; my mother did not want me to become a *sanyasin* so I only began wearing saffron after she died in 1982. She wanted me to remain an independent woman and to fight for my rights. She used to tell me that marriage is not everything; sex is not a sin. Maybe she was a Christian in a former life . . . .

Bharati denied that Hinduism was responsible for the oppression of women:

> In India, women are oppressed because people are uneducated and deceived into believing that religion dictates women's inferiority. I am very religious and I don't believe that is what Hinduism says. After all, look at Sita. She did not always obey. Sita went her own way and committed suicide in the end rather than following her husband's orders. So why should women demean themselves?

The aura of religious devotion even enabled Bharati to carve out a distinctive personality and appearance. Her saffron robes always looked brighter than most and she sported a jaunty short haircut which she claimed was necessitated by her religious devotion. She claimed that the only way she could enter the disputed structure in Ayodhya on October 30, 1990, when it had been cordoned off to the public, was by shaving her head and dressing like a young boy. In her speech at the Jaipur plenary of the BJP which I attended in the winter of 1990, she described the circumstances as follows:

> I was feeling guilty about not having reached Ayodhya on October 30th and I had to repent. I loved my hair. But I went into a temple and called a barber. He did not understand that I wanted him to shave my head; he thought I wanted a bobcut. Once my head was shaved, even though the security at Ayodhya was very tight, I sneaked through.

Hindu nationalism provided both Bharati and Scindia the opportunity to pursue their ambitions and develop their capabilities as women. However in keeping with the differences in their age, class and caste backgrounds, these women held strikingly different positions on women's issues. Whereas Scindia spoke the language of religious conservatism, Bharati spoke the language of women's rights. Note that even Bharati's seemingly liberated views only pertained to *Hindu* women. It is difficult to reconcile her bigotry towards Muslims with feminism or any other form of humanist thinking.

Two questions remain to be explored: to what extent do Rithambara, Bharati and Scindia speak to women activists within the Hindutva movement? Which aspects of the BJP combine's ideology and platform have encouraged their militance? Conversely, does their expression of their own subjectivities conflict with the logic of Hindu nationalism?

Interviews with BJP women's organisation and Durga Vahini members in numerous cities in north India revealed that they held Bharati, Scindia and Rithambara in great esteem and rarely found their positions extreme. Many women praised their strength, courage, and oratory powers and claimed to have been inspired by their leadership. Indeed, the president of the local women's organisation in the town of Kotah said that their Durga Vahini had responded to Rithambara's calls by training its members to use guns, in preparation for the final battle in Ayodhya.[8] In the riots that spread across north India following the destruction of the mosque in Ayodhya on December 6, 1992, Hindu women often goaded crowds to attack Muslim families and properties.[9]

One of the most important ways in which Bharati and Rithambara have reached women is by politicising the domain of personal life. Their attention to questions of public and private morality appears to hold great appeal for women. Furthermore, their cassettes have enabled house-bound women to become intimately familiar with their views. The closest historical parallel is MK Gandhi's ingenious involvement of women in spinning, *swadeshi*, and other anti-colonial activities that could be performed within the home.

The government's half-hearted attempt to ban the controversial tapes only increased their desirability. I accompanied a group of BJP party workers during a house-to-house electoral campaign in the Chandni Chowk constituency of Delhi in preparation for the 1991 parliamentary elections. On the streets, party workers shouted the standard electoral slogans. But when they entered the courtyards of people's homes, shouts of 'Jai Shri Ram' and *mandir vahin baneyenge* (we will build a temple at that spot!) filled the air. Cassettes blasted the speeches of Rithambara and Bharati. Significantly, men predominated on the streets, women in the inner courtyards of the houses.

### The political logic of Hindu nationalism

In different ways, Bharati, Rithambara and Scindia have all used the opportunities offered by the Ram Janmabhoomi agitation to advance their personal and political agendas. However, their emergence within the particular context of Hindu nationalist mobilisation is not merely fortuitous. While the BJP is in important respects deeply patriarchal, it has sometimes advanced women's rights in order to fulfil its more critical objective of isolating and vilifying the Muslim community.

Since the BJP is often mistaken for a fundamentalist party, it may be useful to elaborate the distinctions between fundamentalism and communalism.[10] Fundamentalist parties' attempts to reorder society are guided by an orthodox, or what they would consider an authentic interpretation of religious scriptures. One important aspect of this attempted return to tradition concerns the resurrection of older forms of family organisation and women's roles within them. Notions of community honour thus become contingent upon safeguarding women's sexual purity and domestic roles.

By contrast, the use of religious appeals, the role of the high priests of Hinduism and references to the authority of religious texts is at best ornamental to the BJP's designs. Even its conception of a Hindu *rashtra* is ill-defined and idiosyncratic. Familial imagery plays an important part in the BJP's nationalist ideology but strengthening the family and women's domestic roles is not an intrinsic part of Hindu communalism. As a result, both the gendered imagery and the actual roles of women in Hindu nationalism are far more diverse than in fundamentalist depictions. While the RSS may idealise women from the epic literature who embody notions of suffering and self-sacrifice, they also celebrate brave and powerful women who use violence if necessary to protect their communities. Nor has the BJP opposed women's legal and political rights that would accord them greater equality with men.

As a result, at several gatherings of women that the BJP convened, its leaders challenged women's subordination. For example at the BJP plenary in Jaipur in 1991, some of its top ranking leaders, including MM Joshi, AB Vajpayee, Vijayraje Scindia, and Uma Bharati, acknowledged women's suffering and extolled their strength. Atal Behari Vajpayee wryly commented: 'We have created only two roles for women: as either *devis* or *dasis* (goddesses or slaves) to the exclusion of other roles. But women are above all human beings who deserve respect and justice'. He spoke of the hardships that working-class women endured because laws requiring employers to provide creches at worksites and equal wages had not been implemented.

Tara Bhandari, a prominent Mahila Morcha member, spoke about the problems of child marriage, dowry deaths, and sexual harassment, and said that only if women organised collectively to assert their interests would the government be responsive to their problems. MM Joshi, who had just become president of the

BJP, stated:

> You greeted me with the slogan 'Dr Joshi, we are with you.'
> But I would change the slogan to say: '*Mahila shakti*,
> (woman power) we are with you in struggle!' for the
> struggle should begin with you. In India, as in other parts
> of the world, women face discrimination . . . I have been
> inspired by my mother who struggled a lot with her in-
> laws . . . Mother struggled for 84 years to put an end to out-
> dated traditions in her in-laws' home . . . That's why I am
> telling you to struggle too . . . Please forgive me for saying
> that you have to change yourselves, for women forget their
> own sufferings when they become mothers-in-law. Many
> homes celebrate when a boy is born and grieve when a girl
> is born . . . you have to change all of this . . .

These statements by no means demonstrate the BJP's commitment to women's liberation, among other reasons because these
views were not typical of the BJP leadership as a whole. However, they demonstrate the BJP's recognition that its popularity
among women rests at least partially upon its appeals to their
interests as women.

The most important BJP stance concerning women is its support for a Uniform Civil Code on matters governing the family,
which is presently governed by religious law. The BJP's support
for the Uniform Civil Code is designed not only to gain women's
support but also to highlight the repressive aspects of Muslim
law. 'I feel for my Muslim sisters', Uma Bharati commented, 'but
they do not seem to feel for themselves. How can they agree to
wear the *burqa*? How can they abide by Muslim law?'

The BJP decries the 'pseudo-secularism' of the Congress
because it shied away from passing a common civil code. Furthermore, personal law, Uma Bharati argues, defies the spirit of
the Constitution. Unlike Congress, we say 'one people, one nation, one law', boasted Mridula Sinha, the national president of
the BJP women's organisation.[11]

The acid test of the BJP's intentions judged by feminist standards, however, is whether women stand to gain from the stances
it has taken. The Uniform Civil Code that the BJP envisages
seems to be modelled after Hindu law; in its present form it
would be unlikely to significantly benefit Hindu women. While

Bharati spoke privately against women's oppression and Tara Bhandari and others paid lip service to it in public speeches, the BJP women's organisation has not organised around issues like rape, female foeticide and dowry deaths, the real violence that women confront in their everyday lives.

The very metaphor of the nation as family mystifies hierarchies of power in both contexts. Just as a nation must be ruled by powerful, centralised, authoritarian leadership, so too might one assume the necessity for patriarchal domination of the family. Furthermore, the idea that the nation, like the family, is an organic construct suggests that women's roles within the family are biologically determined. Mridula Sinha stated emphatically, 'For Indian women, liberation means liberation from atrocities. It doesn't mean that women should be relieved of their duties as wives and mothers.' Mohini Garg, the all India secretary of the BJP women's organisation echoed her thoughts: 'We want to encourage our members not to think in terms of individual rights but in terms of responsibility to the nation.'[12] Set against the statements of Atal Behari Vajpayee are those of KR Malkani, another top-ranking BJP national leader, who extols the elevated position of women in Indian society and concludes that women's primary responsibilities are to their families.[13]

If in some respects the BJP seeks to strengthen the family, it also seeks to redistribute patriarchal authority among Hindu men. Acharya Giri Raj Kishore, the joint general secretary of the VHP, recalled that as the *kar sevaks* returned from Ayodhya, they stopped at homes along the way where women would wash their feet.[14] Normally, he continued, women would only wash their husbands' feet but the *kar sevaks* were god's disciples. Thus all Hindu men became deified as if they were husbands while conversely all women become subordinated in the same manner as Hindu wives.

If the BJP combine has fostered activist roles for women around the Ram Janambhoomi issue, it has also undermined the long term prospects for women's activism. While the speeches of Bharati and Rithambara may have great popular appeal, at a deeper level, they doubtless intensify fears of women's irrationality in the public domain.

Furthermore, while Rithambara, Bharati and Scindia often subvert their iconic status by expressing their personal ambi-

tions and fears, the BJP also upholds unsullied images of femininity. For example, the Sita who featured in the famous television series, the *Ramayana*, was silent, decorous, glamorous and
subservient. The BJP actually nominated Deepika Chikalia, the
actress who played the role of Sita, to run on a BJP ticket in the
1991 parliamentary elections. Throughout the campaign, her
demeanour remained exactly the same as in the television series:
unable to represent herself, she had to be represented.

As a result of its deep-rooted mysoginism, women who join
the BJP often find their political ambitions frustrated. Uma Bharati
became embroiled in a conflict with Sunderlal Patwa, the former
Chief Minister of Madhya Pradesh, which made her the object of
a rumour campaign. Her opponents claimed that Bharati was
having an affair with Govindacharya, the former BJP general
secretary. Bharati further sensationalised the drama by informing the press that she had taken an overdose of sleeping pills; her
secretary had saved her just in time. 'People are very narrow
minded and old fashioned, especially when it comes to women',
she told a reporter from the *Indian Express*.[15] The vendetta against
Bharati may have reflected resentments on the part of the entrenched upper caste male leadership of the party at the meteoric
rise of a lower caste woman.

## Conclusion

Are there Uma Bharatis, Sadhvi Rithambaras and Vijayraje
Scindias in other religious nationalist movements or do they
emerge from the unique circumstances of Hindu nationalism?
What significance do these models of female leadership have for
'ordinary' Hindu women?

It is difficult to hazard any generalisations about the extent to
which the 'Sadhvi phenomenon' exists elsewhere without undertaking comparative analysis. Women's identification with
moral and religious concerns finds some parallels in reform
movements dating back to the nineteenth century in diverse
national locations. The forms of women's activism I have described also resemble right-wing racist movements in Germany,
France and the United States. However, at least in the contemporary context, there are few accounts of comparable forms of
women's leadership in religious fundamentalism and right-wing
racist movements.

At the broadest level of generalisation, the decline of the paternalistic state in the advent of economic liberalisation, and the moral decay of Indian political life, creates the space for the growth of xenophobic militance. Politicians and political parties no longer seem accountable to their constituencies. They also seem to find it less necessary to conceal their crass greed for power.

This context has seemingly contradictory implications for the emergence of militant female leadership. On the one hand the overall decay of the political system has made their cruel injunctions to violence much less shocking today than they would have been even a decade earlier. One might even speculate that Indira Gandhi inspired figures like Rithambara through her appeals to a Hindu constituency, strong-arm tactics, and subtle attempts to depict herself as Mother India.

On the other hand, these women's popularity appears to be linked to their vehement hatred for the state. Indeed their antipathy for the state and for Muslims is often difficult to disentangle. The very concept of appeasement, for example, blames the state and Muslims for their opportunism and conversely implies that Hindus are victims of both forces.

Other political groups, particularly on the far left, have provided equally forceful critiques of the state. The unique contribution of Hindu nationalists, however, is to couple their trenchant critique of the existing state with implicit support for a stronger and more paternalistic state. Female ascetics can claim to recognise greed and corruption from their position of selflessness, suffering and martyrdom. But given their vulnerability to sexual exploitation, they also recognise the need for law, order and morality to reinvigorate political life.

One of the central themes that runs through Rithambara's cassettes is the notion that India has lost its moral bearings. As to when and why this crisis began, she provides no analysis; she is equally critical of MK Gandhi and of VP Singh. Rather, she implies that the political arena is synonymous with selfishness, the religious arena with selflessness. Ostensibly—and ostentatiously—locating herself outside the domain of political power, she is well situated to make her critique. Her speeches also imply that the present crisis is the product of modernity. Things have deteriorated to the point that everything is now bought and sold, she asserts: minds, bodies, religion, and even the honour of our elders, sisters, mothers, and sons. 'We cannot auction our nation's honour in the market of party politics', she cries out in a cassette recording. In a sweeping gesture she links commercialisation, the commodification of labour, and sexual exploitation. The antidote to this evil is intense political engagement combined with asceticism, which renounces material possessions, sexuality and physical labour.

In her exhortations against corruption, immorality, materialism and modernity, Rithambara speaks the language of religious fundamentalism. However, the movement that has supported her rise—and that she has helped generate—is not fundamentalist. Rather its political expediency has enabled Hindu nationalism to decry the degraded position of Muslim women in order to demonstrate its own superiority in a manner that is reminiscent of colonialist depictions of degraded Indian womanhood.[16] At the same time, Hindu communalism has allowed its women activists to express their own subjectivities. The BJP's stance on female seclusion illuminates these themes.

The BJP decries the system of female seclusion as a product of Muslim rule in two ways: ignoring social structural bases of seclusion among Hindus, it argues that Muslims brought *purdah* (literally curtain; seclusion) to India and Hindu men also secluded women to protect them from Muslim male aggression. The prominence it accords to Rithamabara, Bharati and Scindia seems designed in part to signal the greater liberation of Hindu than of Muslim women (which is ironic because Scindia practised public seclusion until she was widowed in 1957). Similarly, its support for a Uniform Civil Code seems designed to depict the Muslim community as retrograde.

Thirdly, and most specific to Hindu nationalism, the 'Sadhvi phenomenon' finds inspiration in certain aspects of Hinduism. While Hinduism cannot be made responsible for the rise of these militant women, it would be myopic to claim that there is nothing Hindu about Hindu nationalism. Although its growth is primarily a political phenomenon, it has skilfully appropriated certain aspects of Hinduism in ways that have some important implications for women.

Hinduism provides a rich terrain for gendered nationalist imagery for it closely associates the land with female properties. Furthermore, unlike many religions, Hinduism rejects the notion that women are inherently weak and passive; they are often dangerous because they are powerful and vindictive. The varied personalities of female deities in Hinduism may inspire a range of female persona in political life. While men dominate organised religious worship, women orchestrate religious observance within the home. Indeed, religious observance has always allowed women considerable opportunity to express their subjectivities as women. Hinduism also enables renunciation, which may be especially liberating for women since it allows a rare opportunity for escaping domination by parents, husbands, and in-laws.

The acceptance by Hindu men of women's political activism may be related to their belief that we are experiencing a period of chaos that has both religious and political underpinnings. The political uncertainty associated with the breakdown of the Congress party provides evidence that we have entered the chaotic age of *kaliyuga* in which normative restraints on social conventions can be relaxed. Paradoxically, Hindu nationalists have helped bring about the chaos of which they speak.

Women may be especially well situated to restoring harmony because of their liminality. In patriarchal, patrilineal societies like India, women are considered outsiders to the nuclear family; similarly their class status is indeterminate until they marry, at which point it is determined by their husbands. As liminal beings, women are ideally suited to the nationalist project of reconciling the interests of diverse classes, castes and organisations.

Women may also have license to challenge the unethical nature of political life because of the widely held belief that women possess a higher morality than men. Bharati, Scindia and Rithambara may particularly inspire confidence for they appear to have been forced into political activism by their religious devotion; appearing—often deceptively—to have no axe to grind or personal ambitions, they can act as the moral guardians of (Hindu) society.

The account I have provided makes it difficult to sustain the notion that women are less violent than men. To assume as some scholarship on both women and nationalism does, an organic connection between women, morality, and pacifism reflects a deep-rooted essentialism. But as unethical as they may be, all three women are deeply concerned with moral questions and deeply troubled by the erosion of moral values from the political sphere.

More broadly, Hindu nationalism shares with pacifist movements a preoccupation with questions of private and public morality. They both also uphold organic conceptions of citizenship which, in turn, often associate femininity with nature. Indeed the moralistic character of Hindu nationalism, particularly its sexual puritanism, encourages women's espousal of violence to rectify the unethical nature of the social order.

The gains that these women have achieved through their engagement with Hindu nationalism would be less likely by virtue of their sex were it not for this political engagement. Unlike most South Asian women who achieve political prominence because of their relationships with influential men, these three women are relatively independent of men in both their personal and political lives. The ironies of their realising their subjectivities as women through Hindu nationalism might be attributed in part to the very nature of patriarchal domination which denies women both a self and a cohesive, proud collective identity. Conversely, the realisation of women's personal subjectivities and political ambitions may well be premised upon their denial of collective identification with other women.

If a gender logic underlies women's militant leadership, what is its relationship to the broader logic of Hindu nationalism? The position that these women occupy seems to partially serve both their own purposes as well as those of the BJP. From the BJP's perspective, their iconic status is useful in mobilising dutiful sons into politics while keeping women out of 'real' power. Although at times they pose an embarrassment or inconvenience because they are too loud or too ambitious, these women have never openly challenged the men who run the BJP.

Viewed from the perspective of these women, we find within their gendered appeals the resonance of their real life experiences as mothers and daughters, victims and agents. In some respects their religious aura protects them from the slander that women often face when they enter political life. It also enables them to mask their personal ambitions and thereby partially conform to conventional gender roles. However, their iconic status also confers upon them the illusion of power.

If part of my project is to explain the emergence of militant female leadership, another is to explore the differences in the ways in which their messages are received among the varied social groups that constitute the BJP combine. The public speeches of Bharati, Scindia and Rithambara seem to chide and challenge men while comforting and inspiring women. The message they convey is that women can assume activist roles without violating the norms of Hindu womanhood or ceasing to be dutiful wives and mothers. The support of prominent men in religious and political life not only legitimates their roles but also bridges the chasm between good citizens and devoted wives and mothers.

In visiting riot-devastated communities in which Muslim women were raped and their children butchered, I often wondered why most Hindu women who were present neither expressed compassion nor remorse. As the voices of Rithambara and Bharati echo through my mind, the answer becomes clearer: Hindus are victims, they tell us; by virtue of being Hindu, they can neither be communal nor aggressive. According to this perverse and tragic logic, the rape of Muslim women is not 'real' violence for Muslims can never be victims. The disembodied words of Rithambara are filtered through a cassette recording:

> ... Hindus, who can never be communal, are today being branded communal. They [Muslims] murder with impunity And people are silent. But we are defamed when we cry out in pain!

Uma Bharati adds: [17]

> ... The Koran exhorts them to lie in wait for idol worshippers, to skin them alive, to stuff them in animal skins and torture them until they ask for forgiveness. Our heritage enjoins repentance even if an ant is killed underfoot.

What makes the logic of the Hindu women who have framed this appeal so chilling is that it is wholly self-serving: not only does it respond to their deep sense of injury but it also provides the pretext for their activism. The constitution of the identities of Rithambara, Scindia, Bharati and their countless Hindu sisters is enabled, in other words, by the thrill of wringing imaginary lemons to destroy real human life.

## Notes

1. The term communalism refers to partisanship or chauvinism deriving from religious identity; communal conflict occurs between members of different religious communities, most often Hindus and Muslims. The term is misleading because of its assumption that such prejudice and conflict is religious in nature. However, I use the term in part to differentiate Hindu nationalism or communalism from relgious fundamentalism with which it is often confused.

2. See Amrita Chhachhi, 'Forced Identities: The State, Communalism, Fundamentalism and Women in India,' in Deniz Kandiyoti, ed., *Women, Islam and the State*, Philadelphia, Temple University Press, 1990; Madhu Kishwar,'Nature of Women's Mobilization in Rural India: An Exploratory Essay,' *Economic and Political Weekly*, December 24-31, 1988, 2745-63; for a somewhat different analysis, Gail Omvedt, *Reinventing Revolution: New Social Movements and the Socialist Tradition in India*, New York, ME Sharpe, 1993; and Vandana Shiva, *Staying Alive: Women, Ecology and Development*, Delhi, Kali for Women, 1989.

3. Personal interview, Uma Bharati, December 1991. All subsequent quotes (not attributed to her cassettes) are from here.

4. The term 'BJP combine' refers to the BJP and its affiliates, the RSS and the VHP, and their affiliates.

5. Susan Wadley, 'Woman and the Hindu Tradition,' *Signs*, Vol 3,1, 1977, 113-25.

6. Slavoj Zizek, 'Eastern Europe's Republics of Gilead,' *New Left Review*, No 183, 1990, 54.

7. Interview, P Nagarjuna, *Sunday Chronicle*, May 5, 1991.

8. Personal interview, Prema Rao (pseudonym), Kotah, Rajasthan, 1991.

9. I visited a locality in the BHEL industrial township of Bhopal in January 1993 where the residents described a woman who was a municipal councillor and a BJP member. A few weeks earlier she had rushed to the scene of a riot and goaded Hindu male youth into further violence against Muslims. See also, Madhu Kishwar, 'Safety is Indivisible: The Warning from Bombay Riots,' Kalpana Shah, Smita Shah and Neha Shah, 'The Nightmare of Surat,' *Manushi*, 74-75, 1993.

10. See Dipankar Guha, 'Communalism and Fundamentalism: Some Thoughts on the Nature of Ethnic Politics in India,' *Economic and Political Weekly*, Vol XXVI, Nos 11-12, March 1991, 573-82.

11. Personal interview, Mridula Sinha, 1991, New Delhi. All other statements are based on this interview.

12. Personal interview, Mohini Garg, 1991.

13. Malkani made this statement to a group of women journalists and activists in New Delhi. It was reported in *The Times of India*, February 15, 1992.

14. Personal interview, Acharya Giri Raj Kishore, 1992.

15. *Indian Express*, Feburary 19, 1992.

16. See Lata Mani, 'Contentious Traditions: The Debate on Sati in Colonial India,' in Kumkum Sangari and Sudesh Vaid, eds., *Recasting Women: Essays in Colonial History*, New Delhi, Kali for Women, 1989.

17. This translation of a cassette by Uma Bharati appears in Madhu Kishwar, 'In Defence of Our Dharma,' *Manushi*, No 60, 1990, 4.

# Heroic Women, Mother Goddesses
## Family and Organisation in Hindutva Politics

TANIKA SARKAR

## I

The emergence of a women's movement within the Hindu right may lead us to reassess certain assumptions about women's relationship with violence, religion, politics and the contemporary urban middle class culture. In moments of mass violence the only women who have engaged our attention so far have been the victims from the vulnerable community who need to pick up the pieces of a shattered community life and laboriously, painfully, begin a healing process. Within religion, women are usually regarded as quietist devotees who use its mythical and ritual resources to create an autonomous cultural space that wrests from patriarchy some relief and even power. They are vested with a more intimate and deeper relationship with and a custodianship of authentic religious traditions of the community. As far as politics goes, the thrust of research has been towards debating their location within mass nationalism, with only occasional glances at women of the left. The cultural aspects of upper-caste urban middle class life, especially the tenor of change from the eighties have not yet drawn much systematic attention and we operate with nebulous impressions of a new kind of market formation that is dominated increasingly by commodities and images flooding in from the West.

The study of the women of the Hindutva brigade is not to invalidate these assumptions but to add to them very different experiences of contemporary Indian life that may open up other trajectories. I wanted to place the women of the right at the intersection of all these processes — politics, violence, the new middle class and religion. At the same time, while it is important to see the formation as overdetermined by these multiple experiences, in the ultimate analysis I recognise the fundamentally political nature of the agenda, however much it may project itself as religious or cultural. In fact, the women's movement of the right reveals the political possibilities and resources of the new culture and religion of the middle class.

The need to precisely assess the gender politics of the right is linked up with a larger compulsion to understand the specificities of rightwing politics in India. Despite the continued existence of a 70 year-old, self-multiplying, innovative and uniquely experimental semi-fascistic formation in our country, we tend to veer away from any focussed encounter with it. The right is constantly dissolved into either an economic conjuncture that may or may not be conducive to fascism[1] or it is written about as a hard form of nationalism, born out of a westernist modernity. The accent then inevitably shifts to the history of mainstream nationalism which totally ignores the specific mediations of the Sangh family[2] or mentions the Sangh as a communal discursive pattern whose ideology is not seen to be anchored in socio-economic conjunctures and political contingencies.

After the Ramjanmabhoomi movement reached a climax around 1990, Sangh politics at last became a matter of overwhelming concern. The focus, however, was on one member of the family — the BJP — and its machinations for the takeover of state power.[3] This, to my mind, is a fragmentary and seriously incomplete and limited way of looking at the right. The right aims at nothing short of transforming the upper-caste/middle-caste leaders of Hindu society individually and collectively. It is this larger and ultimately far more crucial ambition which opens up a space for the political importance of the women of the Sangh family.

## II

The Rashtriya Swayamsevak Sangh, the most effective organiser and bearer of the politics of the Hindu right, and the founder and teacher of a whole range of mass and electoral wings tied to its training programme and general guidance, was founded in 1925, at a time when Indian nationalists had already been able to organise one of the largest mass movements in history. It was set up as an alternative to the politics of mass anti-colonial struggles since it neither joined nor initiated any anti-British movement upto Independence and its only activism was expressed in anti-Muslim violence. Its ideological guru, Savarkar, had turned away from participation in the politics of revolutionary terror-ism before he evolved an agenda for the Hindu right. The Rashtrasevika Samiti, its women's wing, was set up in 1936.[4]

The Gandhian struggle had, from the early twenties, gradu-ally involved women from urban middle class, as well as from peasant and tribal backgrounds in open, mass movements. From the late twenties a vibrant left wing tradition of working class politics also emerged, pitted against the colonial state and its allies—a predominantly European class of industrial capitalists. Women were prominent occasionally as union organisers and as working class militants.[5] In the early thirties the revolutionary terrorists of Bengal began to invite women cadres into their ranks as full-scale comrades in arms, rather than as mere providers of logistic support. The women of the Hindu right, therefore, had a wide array of political alternatives, of models of activism to choose from. The decision to stick to the politics of the right was, there-fore, not exercised in a vacuum but it was an informed choice. It is important to recuperate this counterpoint, since any choice made by women is often assumed to be made out of helplessness and an absence of alternatives towards empowerment.

Lakshmibai Kelkar, the mother of a Maharashtrian RSS vet-eran, persuaded the RSS *Sarsanghchalak* Hegdewar in 1936 to help her set up a separate women's wing. Upto this time, the RSS had been confined to an uncompromisingly upper caste highly educated middle class base, largely from the deeply privileged Maharashtrian brahmin group. The women came from identical backgrounds, from nearly identical families. This was the first front that the RSS founded, after a gap of eleven years of its own foundation. It was also after a fairly long period of persuasion from Kelkar, who had initially wanted the all-male Sangh to open itself up to women members, and eventually got Hegdewar's help in setting up a women's wing as a compromise gesture. The foundation of the Samiti was, then, a departure and a new turn in RSS strategy. What lay behind this decision?

The thirties were a time of rapid left advance in Indian politics, of consolidation of peasant and trade union fronts, of unity among socialistic elements both inside and outside the Congress. The United Front tactic of the Communist International, which advised communist parties of colonised countries to join mass anti-colonial movements even under a nationalist bourgeois leadership, had helped Indian communists significantly to establish themselves as a national presence and to enlarge the political possibilities of their working class and peasant fronts.[6] A more telling challenge came from the rapid organisational initiative of low-caste politics that threatened not only to challenge upper-caste authority, but to break away from the Hindu political constituency altogether. The crisis coincided with an enlargement of the scope of electoral politics. Under the circumstances, the decision of untouchables to form a separate political constituency would permanently affect the definition of the Hindu community and would fatally circumscribe the scope of established upper-caste authority.

There was, then, a crisis in the politics of social base and of mobilisation. The RSS tackled it in its own way. It did not develop other thrust areas immediately, socially or even geographically. It only accepted the demand of the women of its own families for a public political space and for a non-domestic existence and organisation. The Samiti could form daily centres for physical, martial and ideological training. But no other forms of politics were made available to it. The women stayed out of anti-colonial mass struggles as well as out of women's organisations that had been debating and agitating over issues of gender justice and rights in autonomous, middle class organisations. Ideological instruction consisted of a violent creed of patriotism where the Motherland and the community were seen to be threatened not by the British but by the Muslim.

Yet the departure did not lead to a significant broadening of the RSS gender ideology as a whole. We must note that while the name Rashtriya Swayamsevak Sangh means 'Nationalist Volunteers', the term Rashtrasevika denotes women who serve the nation. The difference in the names is significant in several ways. It not only relegates women's work within the Samiti organisation to a domestic role, but also consigns their domestic labour firmly to the sphere of humble service. The sense of autonomy and self-choice that are associated with the word 'volunteer' are notably missing. In the formative period of the Samiti, neither Hegdewar nor his successor, M S Golwalkar, the super ideologue of the RSS, attached much importance to women's formal organisational work, and the Samiti led a low-priority, non-innovative, routine-bound existence. In Golwalkar's corpus of writings, women are predominantly mothers who could help the Sangh cause most by rearing their children within the RSS framework of *samskaras* — a combination of family ritual and unquestioning deference toward family elders and RSS leaders.[7] The crisis, therefore, led to an intensive self mobilisation on a broader basis that encompassed its own women. This response is fairly typical of RSS strategy. After the Emergency had been imposed, for instance, it went in for large-scale primary school formation, to train the children of the urban upper caste trader-service sectors, its standard class base. This mode of progress does not expose the women of the Hindutva brigade to polluting lower-class/caste milieus or take them away from familial environs. It does not confront them with the larger problems of their socially exploited sister, so that the Hindutva women are never forced to choose between gender and their own class/caste privileges. It keeps them tied to family interests and ideology while spicing their lives with the excitement of a limited but important public identity. The Samiti seeks to deepen the conformist character of its constituency by diverting their attention away from concern about victims of social oppression and their own class/caste complicity with existing orders of power relations to an alleged non-concretised notion of Muslim oppression of Hindu women through the ages. From Savarkar's formative writings on Muslim rule in India, the stereotype of an eternally lustful Muslim male with evil designs on Hindu women has been reiterated and made a part of a historical common sense.[8] The stereotype helps to restrict the concern of women within the desired framework. From certain affirmative actions undertaken during the V P Singh government, the women of the RSS combine (the RSS, BJP, VHP and affiliated groups) have reason to fear an imminent breach of their upper caste movements. Their caste and class position therefore ensures that they lend their commitment exclusively to a highly militant yet socially conservative movement.

It is interesting that on their daily training grounds an identical schedule has always been followed by both the RSS and the Samiti. There are regular physical training programmes for women, with a special focus on the martial arts, including practice in shooting. RSS-run schools, similarly, teach exactly the same course to their boys and girls. When the Samiti was first established, it was certainly most unusual, if not a transgression, for respectable women to go through such exercises. The only parallel in those times would have been with the terrorist women of Bengal. Those women, however, were prepared to leave home while the Samiti originally had no plan of direct political action.

Lakshmibai Kelkar, the founder of the Samiti, was keen that her girls must have strong, trained bodies. The aspiration seems curious, given the fact that it was put to no active or public use for a long time to come. We shall see later that the cult of the strong physique came to include an extra meaning for women, over and above that inscribed within the organisation by the founders. At the same time, body-centred practices for women have old and varied meanings and values within different currents of Hindu patriarchy. A variety of physical rites and rituals meant to preserve her virtue and family welfare are taken to constitute nearly the entirety of prescribed religious activity for the pious Hindu woman. Late nineteenth century Hindu revivalist-nationalists, from whom the RSS drew much inspiration, added another meaning to such practices. The Hindu woman's body, hemmed in with scriptural ritual, was imagined as a pure space that escaped the transformative effects of colonisation, whereas the Hindu man, seduced by the operations of western power and knowledge, had surrendered himself and had lost his autonomy. The woman's body, having passed through the grid of Hindu ritual exercises, therefore alone remained, for these Hindus, the site of an existent freedom as well as the future nation.[9]

The Samiti has preserved the accumulated meanings but transformed the essential rituals. The symbolic function of ritual has been interpreted literally with the mystical notion of female virtue and power materialistically translated as sheer physical strength. Possibly the influence of contemporary eugenics was at work; a healthy feminine body would bear strong children. From the turn of the century, many high-born militant Hindus have been anxiously preoccupied with the supposedly higher fertility rate of Muslims and low-caste Hindus that seemed to doom the leadership of upper-caste Hindus in Indian society.[10] The incarcerated and leisure-softened bodies of upper-caste women would also be regarded as inadequate vessels to bear the soldiers of the imagined Hindu nation. Since all fascist movements cast their men as able soldiers and killers, their women are invariably asked to ensure exceptionally healthy bodies that would guarantee the production of the most efficient combatants.[11]

## III

The RSS response to the political crisis of the thirties might seem inappropriate, given the limited base that they could command. Surely, women of their milieu, of their families, did not require immediate attention and organisational investment formally, since their consent to RSS politics was more secure than that of any other category? The investment would seem blatantly uneconomic unless we have a precise and careful understanding of its broader strategy and political vision.

It is an inch by inch, person by person mode of advance which brings to mind the Gramscian model of molecular hegemony. It places more importance on a totalitarian conquest of the existing base than on a thinly spread out numerical expansion. An active mobilisation of women was also a priority, since even among socially privileged castes and classes women have a relatively insecure and tenuous location.

Even after the Samiti had been founded, M S Golwalkar, second *Sarsanghchalak* and supreme ideologue of the RSS, restricted his observations on Hindu women to a 'Call to Motherhood'. The women of upper-caste and middle class families had to manage the home front and to keep it free of individualistic aspirations, of libertarian tendencies, of democratic relationships within the family. 'Let our mothers make the children wake up early in the morning, make them salute their elders, and offer worship to the family deity.' They should teach girls to avoid European dress and not to 'expose their bodies more and more' and their children to resist 'a blind aping of the West'. They should keep alive the observance of sacred occasions and ceremonies and take children on regular visits to temples. They must also teach them literacy, but the teaching of 'noble *samskaras*' or a pious disposition was far more useful than formal learning. *Samskaras* would include deference to family elders, Hindu historical heroes and deities and to RSS great men. They would thus at once encompass the family, the Sangh and the nation into one single whole which the mother's mediation renders an intimate reality.[12]

In Golwalkar's authoritative pronouncements on the woman's role, there is a strong accent on learning the value of deference within the family. The mother mediates the process of the complete submersion of the child within such a family. The child learns obedience to the Sangh which appears to him as an extension of the familial space, demanding, initially, the same ideological teaching and personal bearing. On all important Samiti occasions, mothers bring their children over, as do non-Samiti wives of RSS members. The Samiti, I was told, was second home to the small children. At a Delhi Samiti, office bearers told me that even though the Samiti encourages girls to go in for higher education and professions, they also insist that they teach them unquestioning obedience to family decisions even when families decide against education and career. Their success was ensured by their supplementary role in maintaining and deepening family discipline.[13]

In the Samiti literature, motherhood is remarkably emptied of its customary emotional and affective load and is vested with a notion of heroic political instrumentality. The Hindu heroes, we are told, reared their children to teach them to die for the Motherland. In recent times, the VHP woman ascetic leader Sadhvi Rithambara reiterated the same message in her audio cassette which was the most potent VHP instrument for whipping up anti-Muslim violence. The nationalist martyr Bhagat Singh's mother, she narrates in her apocryphal story, wept after the son's execution, not because her son was dead, but because she had no other son who could die a similar death. The accent was on her lack of motherly grief, her eagerness to re-experience the loss. A transgressive departure from the model of natural or ideal motherhood, but stripped of all libertarian or larger human possibilities. The point is that the Samiti makes departures in norms and conventions, it expands the horizons of domesticity and adds serious, politicised dimensions to femininity. At the same time, the thrust of the transformation is to obliterate the notion of selfhood, to erase concern with social and gender justice and to situate the public, political, extra-domestic identity on authoritarian community commands and a totalitarian model of individual existence, every particle of which is derived from an all-male organisation which not only teaches her about politics but also about religion, human relationships and child rearing.

The mother is pivotal to the RSS scheme of mobilising its own family. Golwalkar also advised her to make 'useful contacts among the women folk within the neighbourhood and carry out programmes which would inculcate our cherished ideas among them and their children.'[14] Mothers, then, are political creatures and agents and we will not grasp the deeply political import of this agenda unless we are clear about the directly political and not merely ideological significance of everyday relations, personal disposition and habits, of domestic ritual and practice within the RSS scheme for hegemony, and the full significance of the much used and key term *'samskaras'* in the Sangh vocabulary. The mother is to instil habits of deference, of obedience, of respect for the RSS version of patriotism. She should scramble the child's earliest notions of history, mythology and patriotism through moral lessons about 'faith in Dharma and pride in our history', and instructions about *'tirthas* and temples'. The importance of learning them in earliest infancy when critical faculties are not aroused, of learning them through stories whose format demands a suspension of questioning and passive listening is enormous. As to how important the lessons in Dharma and history, pilgrimages and temples lumped together are, should be evident in the success of the Ramjanmabhoomi campaign which pitted a Muslim king against the sacred figure of Ram, and insisted that the destruction of the Babri Mosque was not only a religious but also a patriotic duty. One cannot learn these lessons too young.

## IV

In a bitterly ironic inversion of women's former invisibility in the domain of public violence, large numbers of women have been extremely active and visible, not only in the rallies and campaigns but even in the actual episodes of violent attacks against

Muslims. The complicity has also involved an informed assent to such brutalities against Muslim women as gang rapes and the tearing open of pregnant wombs in Bhopal and Surat in December 1992 and January 1993 — informed, because these episodes had been widely reported and publicised and there was no way that these women could have escaped knowledge of them. We will explore the factors in their social experiences that have enabled their politicisation on precisely these issues and agendas, and reflect on the large meanings and implication of women establishing themselves as political subjects through an agenda of hatred and brutality against a besieged minority.

I shall argue that the new communal phase enables the women's self-constitution as active political subject in dangerously unprecedented ways.

*Kar sevikas* have been mobilised from what are traditionally some of the most conservative backgrounds — upper, middle ranking service sector and trading families. The very limits of the movement may then be taken as signs of strength within a different kind of reading. Nor can we draw false comfort from any illusion that these women are not speaking their own minds, their own words. Pradip Kumar Datta who visited Ayodhya in January 1991, speaking to a bunch of male satyagrahis was, for some time, faced with an array of archaeological-cum-historical arguments as well as the standard Rashtriya Swayamasevak Sangh (RSS) definition of Bharat as *pitribhumi, matribhumi*, and *karmabhumi*. Then Chandravati, a woman from Aligarh, excitedly broke into the conversation and introduced a very different note: *Yahan aye hain khoon barsane ke liye ... mandir ka arth hai mulla ko phansi lag jai ... Mulayam aur VP ko phansi lag jai* ...(We have come here to shed blood . . . the meaning of temple building is that mullahs should be hanged, Mulayam and VP should be hanged.) The whole discussion subsequently shifted to a markedly more violent plane.

Each of the *kar sevikas* interviewed — those affiliated with VHP as well as those not so affiliated — played a distinctive individual variation on the themes of Ramjanmabhoomi and Hindutva. For Vijay Dube, a would-be *sanyasin* from Ghaziabad, Hindutva implied a sweeping, millenarian vision of collectivity ('*sumiti*') '*Yeh [Hindustan] samudra jaisa gambhir hai, akash jaisa vyapak hai . . . Hindu hi adi ant hai* (This country is as deep as the ocean, as endless as the sky . . . the Hindu is the beginning and the end.) Unlike other religions, Hinduism is not time-bound but eternal. It is not an individual but a collective experience. It finds its centre of gravity in Ramjanmabhoomi which then becomes: *'Hamara servaswa dharam ki bat nahin hai, sarvasaarvaswa hai'* (It is everything to us, it is not just a matter of religion: it is all, it is our everything.) With the liberation of Ayodhya, *'poora vishwa badal jayega ek nayee shrishti ka nirman hoga.'* (The whole world will change, a new creation will come into being.)

For Mithilesh Vashisht, a VHP worker from Modinagar, on the other hand, the value of the Ramjanmabhoomi movement lay in the assertion of strength and self-respect against oppression: *'Atyachar, anyachar, anyaya nahin sahenge, har cheez ki seema hoti hai'* (We will not tolerate oppression and injustice, everything has limits.) Another (unidentified) woman intervened with a more poetic-mythical version of the necessity: *'Yeh hamara ang hai, hamara abhushan hai . . . Krishna bhagawan ka chakra hai'* (This is a limb [of our body], our ornament . . . it is the 'chakra' of Lord Krishna) All *kar sevikas* were bursting with speech — with arguments and descriptions—each had an accent very distinctively her own. Within a hitherto limited social and geographical scope then, the Ramjanmabhoomi movement seems to have enabled major breakthroughs in women's political self-activisation, unwitnessed in earlier communal upsurges.[15]

In a curious way the present movement inverts the usual pattern of symbolisation within national and earlier communal movements. So far, in both, the fetishised sacred or love object to be recuperated had been a feminine figure — the cow, the abducted Hindu woman, the motherland. When we interviewed B L Sharma secretary of the VHP Indraprastha unit in April 1990, he had woven an entire anti-Muslim tirade around the figure of the repeatedly raped or threatened Hindu woman. The Sanatan Dharmi and Arya Samajist office-bearers extended the image into that of a perpetually exposed and endangered motherland.[16] Here, however, the occupied 'janmabhoomi' belongs specially to a male deity, and women are being pressed into action to liberate and restore it to him, to bring back honour to Ram. Ram's army of monkeys and squirrels has now acquired a new combatant and Sita's sex is coming to the rescue of Ram—an inversion of the epic narrative pattern where Ram and his army had to rescue Sita. The reversal of roles equips the communal woman with a new and empowering self-image. The woman has stepped out of a purely iconic status to take up an active position as a militant.

In this context, the very careful and significant handling of the Ram *lalla* (infant Ram) image acquires a new meaning. Stalls in Ayodhya sell a large number of stickers and posters depicting a chubby infant baring his pink gums in a toothless smile. Local legend has it that in 1949, just before the deity miraculously reinstalled itself within the mosque, a police constable had found a dark and lovely child playing by himself in that corner: the homeless baby had come back home to claim his patrimony. The VHP video-cassette produced by Dr J K Jain, *Bhaye Prakat Kripala*, reproduces the event over a long time, with the child within the mosque displaying himself in a variety of 'cute' poses and eventually stringing a bow. We must remember that the *Ramayana* and the *Ramkathas* resonate with the many losses of Ram: he loses his kingdom, his father, he is a figure bathed in tears, a reason, perhaps, why the common man and woman can identify more with him than with other mythical heroes. The entire series of deprivations has now been collapsed into the shape of that irresistible human idol — the deprived male infant. On top of that, within the mosque and next to the main deity, is an icon of the crawling Ram *lalla* — a posture traditionally associated with the baby Krishna — and linked in a long chain of associations with emotional and aesthetic structures. While the appeal of the homeless baby would be a general one, it would be especially poignant for women. Readings of recent events that insist on a monolithic militarisation of Hinduism by present iconic trends, therefore, miss out on the versatility which is perhaps their most remarkable feature. While the Ram *lalla* appeals to the mother in a woman, the warrior Ram probably simultaneously arouses a response to an aggressive male sexuality.

All this, as I have said earlier, is a relatively new development. Up to the middle of 1990, well after the *shilanyas* (ceremonial laying of the foundation stone) ceremonies with their attendant riots, there was practically no literature by women that VHP or RSS offices sold regularly. VHP news sheets that covered *shilapujan* (ceremonial worship and consecration of bricks) and *shilanyas* ceremonies gave no space to women's writings. Even Rithambhara's cassette addresses exclusively men in its invocations to rise and fight: *'Vir bhaiyon, jago'* (Brave brothers, awake.) Her speech obviously targets women listeners as well. There are intimate references to domestic politics among mothers, sisters and daughters-in-law, to women's work within the home. Yet each time the call for action is issued, it is addressed to brothers: 'You have to make yourselves into a clenched fist, my brothers.' 'You have to make yourselves into motherhood: remember how Bhagat Singh's mother was found crying after his death, not because she had lost her son, but because she had no other son to be martyred.' Even the Rani Jhansi is invoked as the mother of a brave patriot.

It is true that the *Bhaye Prakat Kripala* casette inserts the warrior figure of a queen as an adversary of Babar, and, within the current movement, Sadhvi Rithambhara, Uma Bharati and Vijaya Raje Scindia are endowed with an exalted position. They remain exceptional, rare figures, however. Upto this point, then, women are still the productive womb, mothers of heroes. Their presence was minimal on the crucial days of 30 October and 2 November, 1990.

## VI

The Rashtrasevika Samiti has kept a remarkably low public profile through the six decades of its existence. Even though it is one of the oldest women's organisations in the country, its total membership is about a lakh now and is largely restricted to traditional RSS and BJP bases — Maharashtra, Karnataka, and Andhra Pradesh. The Delhi wing was formed in 1960 and now includes about 2,000 members. *Shakhas* (a local branch in the RSS, where members and recruits meet for education and training) are located almost entirely in middle class areas: Karolbagh, Patel Nagar, Janakpuri, Naraina Vihar, R K Puram, Lajpat Nagar, and Kamla Nagar. Volunteers come from enterprising trading families or from middle-ranking government service backgrounds. The VHP Mahila Mandal, which started operating in Delhi from the 1980s, has about 500 members. The two mass fronts of the VHP — the Bajrang Dal and the Durga Vahini — are strictly segregated.[17]

The growth in spatial, numerical and social terms has been quite low compared to the Delhi-based radical women's organisations which have come up much later, or mass women's organisations under left political parties. The All India Democratic Women's Association, linked to the Communist Party of India (Marxist), CPI(M), was founded in 1981 and now has a membership of about 29 lakhs (29,00,000), overwhelmingly rural in composition. The Janawadi Mahila Samiti, its Delhi branch, has about 15,000 members, with large bases in labouring areas. The comparison is relevant since the VHP Mahila Mandal and the Rashtrasevikas also work (unlike other voluntary women's organisations) in close collaboration with an electoral party and a number of affiliated mass organisations.[18]

What does the apparent contrast between the austere reserve of these organisations and the recent flamboyant wave of a militant reclaiming of the public spaces by Hindu women denote? Is it a break, a radical departure, or the culmination of a long drawn-out strategy? Or is it a consciously planned extension in activity and concerns that stretches out old boundaries?

## VII

It seems that we can usefully approach this problem through an extended reference to the very well-known cassette of Sadhvi Rithambhara. One remembers that voice only too well: high-pitched, shrill, breathless, delivering a non-stop harangue with no modulation. The voice seems always almost about to crack under the sheer weight of passion. The overwhelming and constant impression is one of immediacy, urgency, passion, spontaneity. For over sixty minutes, extreme stress is continuously conveyed and the speech seems to be improvised as if on a battlefield — an inspired voice speaking recklessly from the gut. The later ban heightened the earlier impression of impending martydom, while legends about the 'martyrs' of 30 October and 2 Novembe subsequently fed back into the effects of the cassette. The cassette, then, is not a finished product but one that grows with events.

New technology opens up unprecedented audio-visual possibilities for political messages and stretches boundaries of orality. The startling impact of the original *maidan* speech becomes simultaneously preserved and fixed and can duplicate its own efforts endlessly, to ever-growing audiences, in changed political conditions. By preserving and replaying the human voice and the spoken word, a different kind of impact is attained from the one that results from re-reading a written text. The latter also grows and acquires new meanings over time but it remains an individual exercise that involves the text and the reader in a private relationship. The speech on the other hand, is based on a public relationship of a speaker addressing an entire congregation and proceeds through a continual interchange of passion between the speaker and the listeners. New technology is able to recapture that exchange *ad infinitum* for freshly or differently constituted congregations, and, at the same time, allows the first message to fatten on new meanings and associations gathered from the movement unleashed by itself, growing from its own self-fulfilling prophecies. Rithambara's words on martyrdom would have much enlarged and transformed meanings for people listening to them after 30 October, 1990.[19]

Technology naturalises the intended effect to such an extent, and covers its own traces so completely, that we forget that what we are listening to is recorded speech, and not a live recording of an actual speech either. That sustained high pitch and that non-stop delivery would be impossible to improvise without breaks or modulation. It is a studio composition, an artefact which, with meticulous deliberation and co-ordination, pieces together, over long stretches, a carefully rehearsed address. The greatest success of technology lies neither in preservation nor in duplication but in its naturalising abilities, in its self-effacement.

Such an understanding of this speech may illuminate the complex organisational structure within which the Samiti is located. Without drawing an exact and mechanical parallel, and without reducing the Hindutva movement to a mere contrived effect, we can still relate the impression of spontaneous militancy to an elaborate and finely-tuned institutional structure and a shared ideological stockpile that tie together a wide range of party organs, mass fronts and movementalist bodies to the apex body — the RSS. Each individual organisation—the BJP, the VHP and their various fronts— has developed its own distinctive thrust area and all have internally circulating members. A senior VHP Mahila Mandal leader, in 1991, went over to help out with

BJP Mahila Mandal work. Rashtrasevikas claim to have trained the Durga Vahini for the *kar seva*, even though the Durga Vahini is affiliated to the VHP.[20] Almost all BJP women MPs are members of the Rashtrasevika Samiti. Co-ordination, in fact, stretches beyond the core institutional cluster. Rashtrasevikas are offered hospitality for their training camps by Sanatan Dharma mandirs and Arya Samajist Dayanand Anglo Vedic (DAV) Schools. The Samiti is closely associated with a chain of nursery schools run by the Saraswati Shishu Mandir, which is an RSS outfit. The VHP headquarters at Ramakrishna Puram in Delhi houses one of those schools. The school at Naraina Vihar (Delhi) has a very distinctive visual plan and layout. Instead of the usual pictures of flora and fauna or of nursery tales that decorate conventional nursery schools, walls on one side display frescoes of historical Hindu heroes locked in battle against Muslims. On the other side are portraits of 'Hindu' freedom fighters protesting against the British with appropriate messages inscribed below. The central building has the map of *Akhand* Bharat (undivided India) draped around the figure of Bharatmata with the entire *Bande Mataram* hymn inscribed below it. The DAV school on Aurobindo Marg follows an almost identical visual display.

An intricate and delicately-balanced system of interlocking personnel functions and interests is ultimately monitored by the apex parent organisation, the RSS. The Sangh calls itself a family, not a political organisation. As proof of this it claims that all its members are equal and uniform in dress, disposition and functions. This stems from a peculiar notion of what a family is, since there cannot be a family without women in it and there cannot be a family that is ever undifferentiated in functions and habits. Only by developing a women's wing, then, does the family metaphor partly realise itself. The Rashtrasevika Samiti was, after all, the first affiliate that the RSS helped to foster, although a good eleven years after its own foundation. The family model is, in some ways, more than just a metaphor. All the Samiti members that I talked to had male relatives in the RSS. In fact the striking ease and self-confidence that animate the very vocal participation of even junior office-bearers in a discussion with their elders may partly be explained by the status of their male relatives within the Sangh. This might carry greater importance than the order of ranking within the Samiti itself.

The organisational principles of the Sangh provide the pattern for the Samiti. The Samiti does not have internal elections and the *pramukh sanchalika* (chief organiser) nominates her successor. Office-bearers are selected by senior members. The Samiti *pracharikas* (propangandists) are unmarried women, advocating celibacy that characterises RSS *Sarsanghchalaks* (chief leaders), all of whom so far have been bachelors. Much of the RSS ritual is also replicated within the Samiti. The strict and detailed code of regulations for setting up and disbanding the daily *shakha*, a physical and martial arts training (the Samiti provides for lessons in yoga, sword and lathi play, judo and stengun fighting), regular *boudhik* or ideological discussion and the discipline and protocol within *shakha* programmes are common to both. Whereas the RSS observes six annual festivals—five of which are connected with traditional religious events and the sixth, the Shivaji Utsav, is a Hindu nationalist celebration—the Samiti observes five and omits the non-traditional festival. The major hymns are also more or less the same and are recited individually as well as collectively in exactly the same order. At the same time, a fine tension exists between vociferous claims to complete autonomy and pride in sharing the RSS heritage. Vidushi, a young office-bearer, told me rather defiantly that the two bodies are totally distinct as two railway lines are, which run parallel, and yet are always separated. The analogy, however, comes straight from M S Golwalkar.[21] In a different sense, too, as we shall see later, the Samiti supplements certain kinds of Sangh work, thereby reiterating, in a way the conventional place of the Hindu *dharma patni* (wife by sacred ritual) within the household—a related yet subordinate sphere.

In the *boudhik* sessions within the Samiti, I came across the same finished structures of thought, the same basic themes on which variations are played by Rashtrasevikas, the BJP, the VHP, individual *kar sevaks* and *sevikas* and loose fragments of which have come to constitute parts of popular common sense among non-affiliated informal support groups for Hindu *rashtra* (Hindu nation). The RSS occasionally plugs into a whole range of otherwise radical issues—ecology, world peace, interrelated critiques of western materialistic and rationalistic and monolithic notions of truth that lead to imperialist suppression of non-western identities.

I shall summarise here a single theme which I heard being expounded at a Samiti training camp and which I read up in Samiti and RSS literature. This was the symbolism of the *bhagwatdhwaj*, or the saffron flag which, is ritually worshipped at the beginning and end of each *shakha*. The discourse starts with the unique philosophical concept of tolerance within Hinduism—*Sarva dharma samabhava* — which celebrates pluralism and the many equally valid ways of reaching god. This very pluralism and tolerance, however, is taken to characterise a single national ethos which is essentially Hindu, and to which all immigrant religions into India have adapted themselves. The notion of an essentially Hindu national ethos came under attack when 'fanatic' Muslim rulers ruled the land and tried to destroy it with 'brute strength'. The British, however, 'planned to subvert the Hindu mind itself'. This was achieved through a seemingly superior and successful mode of Western knowledge which induced self-forgetting and which substituted alien categories of thought for self-knowledge. The perception of a single national ethos was broken up and Indian history was restructured to prove that the nation means simply a geographical space inhabited by different but equal communities, each with its separate ethos. This false and alien notion of secularism destroyed the single shared culture and fractured the sense of wholeness, led to communalism and violence, and eventually culminated in the partition of the country. The Sangh aspires to recuperate that essential wholeness through its struggle for a Hindu *rashtra*. An RSS pamphlet, *Vishal Hindu Bharatiya Samaj Bhavi Swayam Sevak*, puts it: '*Sangh samaj me sanghathan nahin, samaj ka sangathan hai*" (The Sangh is not an organisation within society, it is organisation of society.)

Our true history today (so the discourse ran) is folded back into certain symbols that have resisted western distortion. The saffron flag, used in the past by Maharana Pratap and Shivaji, is one of them. At the National Flag Committee deliberations even Maulana Abul Kalam Azad had apparently accepted it as our national flag, but Jawaharlal Nehru, the alienated, '{wrong-headed' secularist that he was, refused to do so. Yet another symbol is the hymn *Bande Mataram* which captures the essential entirety of Bharatmata and for that reason must be recited in its entirety—*akhand* recitation being the equivalent of *akhand* Bharat.

This was apparently substituted by *Jana gana mana* as our national anthem which Rabindranath Tagore had actually composed to welcome George V. The story is of course a complete fabrication, but was reiterated by a whole range of Samiti members with complete assurance.[22]

## VIII

Somewhat like the Sangh, but much more emphatically so, the Samiti leaves alone charity or social welfare work and has no interest in union activities. Numerical expansion or extensive mobilisation has not, then, so far been the primary concern which explains their low growth rate. It is an intensive physical and ideological training-centre out of which a small group of hand-picked cadres is regularly selected and sent out to circulate among the affiliated organisations and movements.

This kind of intensive mobilisation works best during its initial, formative phase within a 'same class' situation where recruits and teachers do not constantly need to break down boundaries within their own disposition and habits to communicate and interact with one another. Mobilisation is then horizontal unlike the vertical spread of radical women's organisations which reach out to less privileged sisters as soon as they form themselves. The breadth of the latter's concerns and connection is undoubtedly their greatest initial ease in interaction among all its members. A VHP worker described the Sangh-Samiti combine as engaged in class work rather than in mass work. Class here refers to a classroom situation where all participants usually share the same social milieu. The description is quite precise since the training is pedagogical in a very total sense. Not just the arguments but an entire mode of arguing, a particular disposition is slowly nurtured with the person, leaving a distinct mark on the more engaged activists — a calm, quiet confidence, an unhurried, patient and seemingly reasonable exposition which proceeds by agreeing with the other person as much as possible and then gently suggesting and building up its own basic themes.

For the Samiti, the daily *shakha* is not the sole or even the most major form of activity. The family concept is extended to cover the members' families in a number of ways. The Samiti's guardianship role in the case of unmarried girls is carefully meshed in with an acknowledgement of the primary rights of the family. If the family obstructs a girl's desire for further studies, a particular profession, or a late marriage, the Samiti at first tries persuasion. If this fails completely, the family's decision stands. The same policy is followed over problems of the girl's boyfriend or self-choice in marriage. Rekha Raje, a *pracharika*, hastened to assure me that the Samiti tries to fill up their time with 'health' pursuits and such 'problems', therefore, rarely arise. If they do, the Samiti first inspects the boyfriend. If he is found to be suitable, it then tries to persuade the family. Again it is the family which must ultimately decide and on no account should the girl be encouraged to disobey.

Prospects of persuasion are enhanced and problems of divided loyalties averted by regular visits to the girl's home and the systematic cultivation of warm personal connections. A young Samiti member told me that they make a point of visiting each other's homes and dropping in for tea whenever they happen to pass that way, so that the entire family is included within the circle of the Samiti solidarity. *Adhyapikas* (women teachers) from the *shakha* go over regularly to discuss a member's behaviour and prospects with her relatives. The Samiti is then carried right into the heart of the domestic space and ceases to be an institution within the public sphere. Even if the girl's own connections with her *shakha* snap for some reason, durable contacts have been made with the parental family and the zone of influence permanently expanded. For small towns, where individual Samiti workers find it difficult to keep a *shakha* going, the Samiti sends instructions every three months, keeping the member posted on Samiti developments, rituals to be observed within this period and on how to attain a base among women of her acquaintance on a non-formal basis.[23] At Khurja in western UP, Prabha Aggarwal, coming from a staunch RSS family, managed to set up a *shakha* which acquired 50 members.[24] A scandal involving a local BJP *pracharak*, however, made parents withdraw their daughters from the *shakha*. Prabha now follows the 'correspondence course' of posted instructions, and spreads Samiti festivals and rituals on a home-based format. The local Saraswati Shishu Mandirs do the rest of the propaganda work, on school premises.

Solidarity and warm supportiveness are more actively expressed when Samiti members take turns with cooking and nursing whenever there are major illnesses in a member's house. The *shakhas* have a strictly local character and these gestures enable them to strike deep roots in the entire neighbourhood. When a girl marries into a non-RSS family and her new domestic situation prevents active *shakha* work, senior *shakha* members regularly visit her in-laws and strike up a close relationship with them. The married girl then acts as a pivot within a new domestic set up, a new neighbourhood. The Samiti, in fact, encourages her to drop *shakha* work for the first few years after marriage, until her status in her new home is firmly established and her Samiti friends are accepted by the entire family. If, however, the in-laws still discourage a connection with the old *shakha*, she is again not advised to assert her choice. Her old Samiti members, of the local branch, keep in close touch with her and her family. She is given a few easy exercises that may be done even within a fairly crowded home and she is told to teach them to women relatives in the new family. She is also advised to establish herself as an ideal counsellor and arbiter to enable her to informally discuss the ideas she received during her *shakha* days or which her Samiti members have kept her attuned to. One can see how useful such a loose and informal network would be in inculcating notions of 'Hindutva' and Hindu *rashtra* over a long period of time, and then, swiftly linking them up with a particular agitation which would find a ready support base without any direct and immediately organisational investment.

Gradually, the woman's reputation as a dependable adviser and friend in need will spread to the women in the neighbourhood and enlarge and stabilise a circle of dependents and listeners. For the women within the kinship network and the immediate neighbourhood, the presence of such a woman ensures an informal forum for the discussion of general topics. In this way she fills up a crucial gap and appeases a very real hunger for serious intellectual discussion among women, a need which traditionally only religious topics used to meet. Women's religiosity is usually explained in terms of certain emotional, cultural or social needs. One vital function of religion is rarely taken into account, that it alone gives her access to a world of meanings enclosed in epics, allegories or other forms of religious texts that she can interpret and dwell on, and thereby transcend her own immediate and closed world of limited experience. The Samiti partly continues these themes and partly weaves them into a different and larger political fabric. A Haryana housewife-turned-activist told me that for her the highest value of the Samiti lay in exposing her to the world of thinking beyond household, or personal matters. Golwalkar had seen a lot of possibilities in such household-cum-neighbourhood circles for women working for the Sangh and these possibilities have been much extended since his time.

Informal training for unaffiliated wives of RSS activists is yet another important field for Samiti work. At a Samiti training camp, a whole session was reserved for them, followed by a joint lunch and a group discussion on their problems and possible activities. I found that the wives were as familiar with Samiti activists and activities as any formal member. I met a schoolteacher, wife of an RSS activist, who has been married for five years, before which she had had no contact with that organisation. Although not a member of the Samiti herself, she managed single-handedly to persuade her entire body of colleagues to join a day-long protest fast at Ajmal Khan Park, Delhi, after the 30th October deaths. Her accounts of the Samiti and the Sangh were as detailed and as confident as those of any activist's. Her work, she told me, was manifold. She has to coach her two tiny children thoroughly in the daily Sangh mantra recitations and cultivate proper *samskaras* (traditions) in them. Along with other wives of RSS activists, she makes it a point to take her children to Samiti ceremonies from an early age so that it becomes a second home to them. Another function was to help out with needy RSS families in her locality. Her husband, for instance, would tell her if one of them was getting a daughter married. In that case all the wives of RSS activists would divide up parts of the dowry to be collected among themselves. They would also get together to help out if an ailing RSS member or someone in his family suddenly needed blood. RSS members are required to donate blood and keep their certificates precisely for this purpose — to have access to the blood bank in emergencies. Apart from being a far-sighted and practical form of support, this probably fosters the notion of a blood brotherhood. In her place of work the wife is expected to gather influence and respect for her ideas and attitudes. Much of the Samiti's activity is then informal, but no less effective for that reason.[25]

Is the Samiti then merely filling up a space marked out for it by the Sangh for its own purpose? And, if so, does not this conclusion contradict a statement that I had made earlier — that the strength of the movement lies in the exhilarating possibilities it creates for certain sections of deeply conservative women, in its being an expression partly of their own creativity?

I think that the original parameters worked out by *Sarsanghchalaks* have proved to be flexible and accommodating. The major body of Golwalkar's instructions had carved out a sort of '*Lakshmangandi*' of faithful motherhood, within which the properly instructed mother carefully guards her children from corrupting western influences and instils in them the right *samskaras* — filial piety, knowledge of patriotic heroes and of religious texts. Rashtrasevikas have travelled a long way since then without overtly resisting the original instructions. The gap between the original impulse and the new self-definition may or may not open up fissures within the movement, depending upon the versatility and suppleness of the Sangh ideology.[26]

Somewhat different forces seem to be working within the Samiti itself, although it would be false and crude to posit a clear dichotomy between the two: to see one as potentially feminist and the other as overly fundamentalist. At the Delhi office of the Samiti in 1991, I was told quite frankly that the decision to train *kar sevikas* was the result of an internal debate that was eventually won by younger Samiti members. The charges against Uma Bharati, by sections of the party leadership, inspired a group of BJP women MPs to come out in criticism of the leaders. It was a remarkable instance of an inner party dispute on a gender issue.[27]

The differences of emphasis between men's and women's accounts of the Samiti's history are interesting. In the first place, there are somewhat different origin-myths of the organisation. Neither the authorised history of the Samiti, nor the account of a senior *pracharika* had mentioned that Hegdewar was approached to admit women to the Sangh. They are equally silent about the fact that he had refused and had asked Lakshmibai Kelkar to set up a parallel organisation. An RSS publication, however, wrote about it and claimed that he had convinced Kelkar about the problems of a common organisation. Samiti narratives, then, seem to push the fact of the refusal out of sight. Official Samiti history has a somewhat different explanation for the event that had led to its establishment. It says: *Hindutva jagaran ka pramukh dheyya lekar is swatantra sangathan ka shubharambha hua* (This independent organisation made its auspicious beginning with the primary aim of awakening Hindus). On the other hand, Rekha Raje, a *pracharika*, recounted how, on a train journey, Kelkar had witnessed the rape of young girl by goondas. She clarified 'in response to my question' that the rapists were not Muslims. The girl's husband had been present there, but he proved helpless. Kelkar realised that since Hindu husbands could not help their wives, women had to protect themselves. Whereas the edge in this story is turned against Hindu failures (the Hindu male's lust and the Hindu male's cowardice), the official text overlays that version by the more amorphous aim of '*Hindutva jagaran*'.

The self-definitions of the Samiti place primary emphasis on physical courage, on a trained, hardened female body. The Sangh agrees with its supreme importance and then goes on to list 'intellectual grasp of the values of Hindu culture and devotional attachment to the ideals of Hindu woman-hood.' A Samiti publication puts it even more strongly: *Swasangrakshanksham nari ki samaj me adhik pratishtha hoti hai* ( A woman who is able to defend herself gets a higher status in society.) The specific deity that embodies their aspirations is the eight-armed Durga, a militant icon who subsumes Saraswati, Lakshmi and Kali. Sevikas see themselves as full-fledged soldiers in an impending apocalyptic war. Their pre-prandial mantra translates as follows: 'Our limbs have been nourished by our Motherland and we must give them back to her in her service.' Asha Sharma, in charge of the Delhi organisation, explained that the mantra tied the theme of patriotic sacrifice with that of active combat. She agreed that when war is mentioned, they see a civil war as a possibility. The patriotic war in whose aid the female body is being trained, then seems to be a war against the Muslims. The large place that the myth of 'Muslim lust' occupies within the general mythology of Hindu communalism would also explain the need for self-strengthening.[28]

Yet we must remember the oral version of the origin-myth — Hindu goondas raping a girl in the presence of her Hindu husband — and also the reference to the larger status of the

'*Swasangrakshanksham nari*' within her own social milieu. Defence against attackers, and respect within her own environment, is then the implicit sub-text which might, in everyday calculations, become a more powerful motive force and a more real compulsion than the ultimate political intention of '*Hindutva jagaran.*'

The force of the compulsion becomes clearer when we consider the milieu from which the Samiti mobilises its cadres. As we have seen earlier, sevikas come from upwardly-mobile, trading or middle ranking service sectors, which are fertile breeding grounds for dowry murders. Women's organisations deal with huge numbers of divorce or maintenance suits at this social level. They are familiar with the violence and oppression that flourish against women here. In the large northern cities, if not in the small towns so far, education and professional opportunities for women have come late but they have come in big way. Nor are families opposed to women's employment, since they are a valuable source of extra income. Thrust into public and mixed spaces for the first time, women encounter all the time, new forms of overt or covert sexual discrimination and violence. Small wonder, then, that the physical-training programmes of *shakhas* have proved to be extremely attractive, with their promise of a powerful body and the self-confidence that it generates. The empowered body would be a shield against gender oppression within domestic as well as within public spaces.

We may, then, assume that despite the overarching aim of Hindu power, the woman needs to utilise Samiti facilities against her own hostile environment as well. The problems of the newly-mobile professional woman are often discussed in the Samiti journal, *Jagriti*. An article narrated how the author withstood the offensive behaviour of a police officer to whom she had gone to report a street accident. Several others take up similar problems. With suggestions and examples, they try to project the image of a responsible and confident woman-citizen who would know how to exercise her civic rights even in this chauvinistic world.

Authoritative statements on the women's location in Hindu society tend to make entirely positive assessments. The *pramukh sanchalika's* speech at the 1990 annual Samiti conference proclaimed, rather grandly, that 'the women of India have always been free.' A lead article in *Jagriti* ('*Rashtra ka Adhar Nari*') elabo-

rated the assertion, tracing a history of her power with highly
selective examples from Manu to the present Ram movement. At
the same time, other assessments also jostle for space. '*Nari
Jagaran*', an article in *Jagriti* postulates that oppression of women
is a deep-rooted social condition, and that only an organised
women's movement can resist and change it. It does not equate
the women's movement in India with the Hindu movement.
Whereas the earlier article I have referred to, was highly critical
of the international women's movement as allegedly being shaped
by a corrupt, westernised modernity, the latter legitimises them.
Yet another article, '*Parivartit Parivesh Me Bharatiya Nari*', is
extremely critical of Indian men for obstructing the entry of
women into politics. Entering politics is described as a condition
of protecting women's rights. A basic conflict of gender interests
is seen to underlie social divisions of other kinds, and communal
identities are not believed to interfere at this point.

It is interesting to find that whereas writing by leaders —
Golwalkar, official RSS statements, Samiti leaders' pronouncements — applauds the new Hindu woman for apparently resisting the trap of westernised modernity, women's own articles in
Samiti publications, when dealing with everyday problems, are
scarcely concerned with the so-called danger of surrendering
traditional virtues to modernity. In fact, the new Hindu woman
is often cast in a mould that comes close to the pattern of
bourgeois feminism. As an article in *Jagriti* put it:

> In order to attain the comprehensive development of
> women, it is extremely important for them to be eco-
> nomically independent. Therefore, in order to ensure
> economic independence, they need reservation in em-
> ployment, and they need women judges to conduct all
> cases related to such issues.

The Hindu woman, is, therefore, to be a person with professional and economic opportunities, secure property-ownership,
legal rights to enforce them, and some degree of political power
to ensure her rights.

How would the new Hindu woman relate to Hindu tradition?
I feel that tradition exists as a cherished but remote icon, requiring ritual worship but seldom brought out for daily use or
inspection. Very often the question of religious faith is displaced

on to the realm of patriotic faith. The greatest triumph of the present communal movement has been to blend two potent sources of emotional involvement—*desh bhakti* and Ram *bhakti* — (devotion to the country and devotion to Ram) into a homogeneous whole. Adherents now use them interchangeably. When Pradip Kumar Datta asked *kar sevika* Vijay Dube how Ram came to mean so much to her, she immediately traced back its source to her childhood experience of the China war and the passions it had aroused in her. Patriotic faith, in her case, was the original impulse that had fuelled religious passion, and she herself was not aware of any distinction between the two.

Verdicts on specific gender questions within present Hindu society seemed, on the whole, modernistic. A young activist protested that there could be no such thing as voluntary sati. 'It isn't possible. Why should a woman wish to burn?' She conceded that it could be done out of 'depression and frustration' — that is, as a mark of weakness and not as a mark of moral strength. Neighbours and relatives, however, must shore up her will to live. The Samiti, theoretically, does not ban inter-caste or even inter-communal marriage provided, of course, the family agrees. The cover page of *Jagriti* depicts two women crouching in a helpless posture against a dark background. A young, rather grim looking woman, steps out of that frame on to the radiant half of the page with an uplifted head. There are no Hindu marks on her body — no veil, no *sindur*, no *bindi*. She wears sandals, her sari is draped tightly around, her whole stance is free, even aggressive. Of course, she does wear the Samiti uniform — a purple-bordered white sari. The magazine is almost uncompromisingly non-'feminine' in nature, making no concessions to conventional women's topics. There are no hints on beauty aids, no cookery or embroidery section, no advice on child rearing. Stories are scrupulously bare of the individual romantic element. They deal, instead, with the romance of Hindu civilisation or that of modern patriotism.[29]

Women's power is a theme that is celebrated, occasionally, in grotesque circumstances. At the Ayodhya *kar seva*, at a peak point in a violently communal agitation, women were chanting the beautiful feminist slogan: '*Hum Bharat ki nari hain, phul nahi chingari hain*' (We are the women of India. We are sparks, we are not flowers.) When Pradip Kumar Datta asked some of them why Sita was absent in their invocations to Ram, the men fell silent, but women had their answers ready. One said that this was Ram's birthplace and not Sita's and this accounts for her absence. But Vijay Dubey had a more effective answer: Shri actually means Sita; hence in the chant Shri Ram, Sita is placed before Ram. Datta asked: 'You mean that Sita is contained in Ram?' 'No' said Dubey, 'Sita comes before Ram.' In a VHP children's publication, *Hanuman ki Kabaddi,* Hanuman says he is neither Ram's *bhakt* (devotee) nor Sita's, but he is the *bhakt* of Sitaram.[30]

I do not want to convey the impression that a sort of women's liberation is going on happily within a somewhat unfortunate Hindutva framework. The limited public identity that has become available to these women is made conditional on their submission to a new form of patriarchy. When I asked Asha Sharma where the Samiti differs from other women's organisations, she replied: 'We do not believe that in marital disputes the husband is necessarily to blame. When we arbitrate, we do not take the woman's side, we are neutral. We will tell the woman that she must do everything to preserve her home life. We are not wreckers of homes.' They do not offer legal counselling to women, nor is divorce at all encouraged. Dowry is called an evil, but its practice is obviously not banned among Sangh or Samiti members. Samiti members, in fact, collect dowry for poorer sisters. When *kar sevikas* at Ayodhya were asked if their status would improve in Hindu *rashtra,* one of them said yes, because Muslims would not be allowed to have four wives. That alone would ensure greater respect for women. She could not, on the spur of the moment, conceive of any other possibility for herself.

The same silence surrounds the question of caste. It is formally denounced and there is community dining to ensure the absence of distinctions. Yet the caste system is never made a theme for discussions or criticism in their study-sessions. Class-struggles are yet another field of resounding silence and non-involvement.

## Conclusion

One important way of looking at women's relationship to the right — and it is a way that the RSS itself prefers to project — has been to obliterate the political movement from the frame of references and to fill up the space exclusively with religious compulsion. The political movement, since it is in Ram's name, presumably then ceases to be political, and only then becomes a movement women can identify themselves with. The visibility of women coincides, we must remember, with the simultaneous visibility of ascetics in the movement. Both are there to make the same point. It would seem that people who have been traditionally aloof from the realm of power politics are now 'spontaneously' coming forward to assert the Hindu faith, and that professional politicians of the BJP are humbly and faithfully following the commands of the whole people.

There are three sets of underlying assumptions behind this opinion. First of all, women are depicted as a homogenous mass and are identified with the common folk or the whole people. Women's presence in the movement is then used as a sign of the movement's ubiquity, its universality. The social base of the women of the Hindu right, however, is easily identified as overwhelmingly upper-caste, middle class, and urban. A Delhi office holder has, for example, frankly admitted the middle class character of the movement.

The second and third unstated assumptions are interrelated. There is a notion that faith is timeless and above historical change and political manipulation. It further assumes that any demand made in the name of a religious issue always harks back to this timeless faith and not to any modern variant that can be open to political appropriation. There is also a conviction that women are custodians of this eternal faith, and that they can respond to a call that comes from the heart of age-old Hindu beliefs.

Here we need to remind ourselves that prior to the Ram Janmabhoomi movement, no traditional text, ritual, or myth ever made a statement that Ram's birthplace had been made into a mosque, or that it was a matter of religious duty to build a temple on the site of the Babri Mosque. The most sacred vernacular version of the *Ramayana* that is in use in northern India and is revered by the VHP was written after the presumed destruction of the alleged temple, and yet there is no mention of that event in the text, nor any injunction laid on Hindus to build the temple. Women are, therefore, not responding to a call of eternal Hindu feelings, but to certain contemporary transformations that are grafted onto a crucial cluster of Hindu institutions — temples, big religious foundations, and monastic establishments that are now acting as auxiliaries of political parties and organisations. They are not acting according to time-honoured ritual or texts or devotional traditions; instead they are accepting versions of faith that have been created by high-tech modern media — video films, audio cassettes, the televised version of the epic. Recognition of this puts a very different complexion on both the presumed immutability of faith and tradition and women's relationship to them.

Finally, there remains the vexing question of whether this movement, despite women's growing commitment to it, authentically expresses the empowerment of women or reflects a manipulated, constructed 'false' consent and intentionality. Two separate questions and problems are tied to this — the question of 'real' interests, and the question of power. No feminist can possibly argue that the movement can contribute anything to the broad rights of women. We have explored its uncompromising orthodox compulsions as well as the positively fundamentalist tendencies. Yet among women of a specific conservative milieu it certainly has bestowed a degree of empowerment and a sense of confidence and larger solidarities. It has brought them into activist, public roles, and has thereby probably increased their bargaining power within their homes, as political activism invariably does to some extent. It has allowed them to go beyond a purely domestic or feminine identity. At the same time, this limited yet real empowerment leads them to a complicity with fascist intolerance and violence, toward the creation of an authoritarian, anti-democratic social and political order. Eventually, it is going to lead these women, in the name of the feigned authenticity of indigenism, to resisting notions of justice, even for their own sex. In Iran, masses of women have supported compulsory incarceration of women, and in Nazi Germany women agreed to give up their right to vote.

This brings us to the question of manipulation. Gender, like class, does not have an emancipatory potential that is 'natural' or innate. Gender power grows from a sense of solidarity to being a force for itself only through intervention, contestation, and an exercise of and struggle over choices. Certainly, a feminist consciousness does not nestle within a woman, ready to attain progressive self-realisation within a congenial environment, but is acquired through bitter conflicts and problems of choices — within herself, most of all. The point about the women of the Hindutva brigade is not that they are simply being conned into belief, for the same applies to men. Our interviews with women demonstrators at Ayodhya convinced us that their affirmation of the Ramjanmabhoomi issue was no mindless gesture but a highly informed conviction. The point is to assess the nature of the issues they assent to.

Self-assertion through violent communalism is probably accompanied by a certain growth in self-confidence that the Samiti has generated over several generations. We cannot write off the gender ideology of the Hindu right as unproblematically fundamentalist despite its overarching conservative patriarchalism which we have noted. For a certain section of affluent, middle class women of north Indian cities and towns, where women's education and professional opportunities have come rather late, the Samitis do offer a limited but real empowerment. These upwardly mobile trading or service sector families are breeding grounds for dowry violence and murder. Women are also being thrust into mixed public spaces and jobs for the first time and face new forms of sexual discrimination and violence. Physical training programmes, with their assurance of tough, hardened bodies and the attendant self-confidence, help them to negotiate the newly founded extra-domestic identities.

The limits of equality should be noted. The RSS continues to plan and lead every step of the movement and the RSS remains an all-male body. This means that women are necessarily excluded from the highest decision-making bodies. In a sense, the dazzling presence of the spectacular triad— Sadhvi Rithambhara, Uma Bharati, Vijayaraje Scindia—is meant to blind us to the crucial absence of women at the heart of effective action.

Equality in the political role and violence develops within an overall context where the women of the Hindutva brigade stay out of contemporary women's agitations for enlargement of gender rights and justice which have been one of the most potent forms of radical politics in the country today. In recent months there has been an open turn towards unabashed fundamentalism. The VHP leader Bamdev has asked for a restoration of male polygamy and the abolition of divorce among Hindus and BJP women leaders like Vijayaraje Scindia and Mridula Sinha have defended widow immolation. The VHP woman leader Krishna Sharma has demanded that women should return to their homes unless they are impelled by dire economic necessity. She has also defended dowry and polygamy as traditional resources and signs of cultural automomy that alienated pseudo-secularists have made into a bogey.[31] The earlier pride in a reformed Hindu family law, which the BJP had used as the sign of Hindu superiority over the backward conservative Muslims, seems to have become a somewhat outmoded rhetoric.[32] It seems that Hindu patriarchy, uncontaminated by western influence, has once again emerged as the embodiment of preferred values. And once again, women must forget about gender rights to ensure community supremacy.

Perhaps, a subsidiary reason would be that the Hindu right always tends first to stereotype the Muslim and then proceeds to appropriate the features of that stereotype for itself, out of a profound yet unstated conviction in the superior political strength of the Muslim community. The Muslims are fanatical about Islam — and Hindus are asked to put the community and religion above every other consideration. The Muslim breaks temples — and so the Hindu must wreck a mosque. Muslim polygamy has always been seen as a ploy for overpopulating the country with Muslims and a sign of irrepressible virility. It is also a right, a privilege that the Muslim male has in excess over that of the Hindu male.

The main reason, however, would relate directly to the contradictory pulls within the movement which makes it imperative to foreground women and, simultaneously, to limit and contain the consequences of their prominence, and the enlarged bargaining power that their politicisation could fetch within the family. The recent growth of urban consumerism, so much of which targets the woman, expands their claim to a larger share of the family budget. It is also the site of an individualism, not based on a notion of rights but on consumerist preoccupations and demands, on a new self-image, fashioned by the ad culture. This puts new strains on relating to women as older forms of control begin to slip. While professional women have access to unprecedented self-reliance, even housewives, faced with the ad culture and the shopping arcades, seek out things that are specially meant for themselves. Older ways of feminine domesticity and patriarchal control face new strains — the more so, since the new consumerism is largely the basis of the new middle class prosperity and self-advancement. And the Sangh *parivar* is, above all, based on this middle class.

At this moment it becomes imperative to recover and articulate explicitly the submerged patriarchal norms. The televised version of the *Ramayana* epic which was made to coincide with the building up of the Ramjanmabhoomi movement, restated the older codes of patriarchal command through the irresistible, erotic appeal of the self-abnegating figure of Sita. Also, now that the movement has transcended the boundaries of carefully trained Samitis and RSS families, and encompasses much of the urban middle class which, despite its support, is insufficiently indoctrinated in the broader RSS *samskaras*, controls need to be spelt out precisely. More of its women are joining white-collar jobs and that has the threat that they may succumb to the more militant varieties of trade union politics. A broader normative disciplining is a safeguard against that.

The language in which the Hindu right restates its patriarchal purposes points to a larger imperative. The assertion of the greater dignity, even sacrality of the chaste and good Hindu woman covertly substitutes for, and ultimately displaces, a demand for equal rights. The Hindu right depends on a seemingly radical contestation of 'modern secularism', a critique of modernity that opposes the liberal theories of rights that it considers an alien and alienating colonising influence. In their place it tries to claim the existence of 'traditional' notions of community obligations and mutuality. The claim can establish itself through a suppression of the historical realities of caste and gender asymmetries. The non-historicised claim of a sustaining, nurturant Hindu community and tradition is then used to undercut radical attacks on Hindu gender and social hierarchies, of demands for equal rights and affirmative action. However, it does not frontally oppose these demands since that will demystify the notion of a nurturant Hindu community. It will also reduce eventually the potential mass base of the right which cannot hope to ride a 'Ram wave' for ever. It therefore concentrates attack on the notion of equal rights on different grounds. It denounces its

pseudo-secular nature since it suffers from contaminated historical origins, having reached this country through the colonial
connection and western education. An indigenist reasoning is
used to oppose the notion of civil liberties, democratic rights,
social equality and gender justice. At the same time, it manages
to conceal its socially inegalitarian face and wear a spuriously
radical demeanour since it is apparently contesting colonial resi-
dues.

## Notes

1. Left political observers seem to be reluctant to focus on aspects which do not relate to the material and class base of political formation. It is a curious reluctance, since Marx, in his historical writings, analysed the practice and character of decisive political actors with great care and insight.
2. A telling example will be Gyan Pandey. His focus on a rather undifferentiated and monolithic colonial discourse and its nationalist derivatives completely ignores the Indian right as a participant in the making of communalism.
3. From the early nineties Indian journalism produced an impressive corpus on the BJP.
4. Tapan Basu et al, *Khaki Shorts and Saffron Flags: A Critique of the Hindu Right*, Delhi, Disha Books, 1993.
5. See Radha Kumar, *The History of Doing, An Illustrated Account of the Women's Movement and Feminism in India*, Delhi, Kali for Women, 1993.
6. Sumit Sarkar, *Modern India: 1885-1947*, Delhi, Macmillan, 1983.
7. M.S. Golwalkar, *Bunch of Thoughts*, Bangalore, Vikrama Prakashan, 1980.
8. See Purushottam Aggarwal's article in this volume.
9. Tanika Sarkar, 'Rhetoric against the Age of Consent: Resisting Colonial Reason and the Death of a Child Wife,' in *Economic and Political Weekly*, 4 September, 1993.
10. P K Datta, 'Dying Hindus: Production of Hindu Communal Commonsense in Early 20th Century Bengal' in *Economic and Political Weekly*, 19 June 1993.
11. See Claudia Koonz, 'Mothers in Fatherland: Women in Nazi Germany,' in Beidenthal and Koonz, eds., *Becoming Visible: Women in European History*.
12. Golwalkar, op. cit.
13. For my interviews with office-bearers, see 'The Woman as Communal Subject: Rashtra Sevika Samiti and Ramjanmabhoomi Movement' in *Economic and Political Weekly*, 31 August 1991.
14. Golwalkar, op cit.
15. I am indebted to P K. Datta for the taped interviews.
16. P K Datta et al, 'Understanding Communal Violence: Nizamuddin Riots,' in *Economic and Political Weekly*, 10 November, 1990.
17. Interview with office-bearers of Rashtra Sevika Samiti in December 1991 and January 1992.
18. Interviews with office bearers of Janwadi Mahila Samiti in December 1990.

20 Interviews with Samiti and VHP Mahila Mandal office bearers in January 1991.
21 *The Women as Communal Subject*, op. cit.
22 Ibid.
23 Ibid.
24 Interview with her family members at Khurja, March 1991.
25 'The Woman as Communal Subject', op. cit.
26 Ibid.
27 Ibid.
28 Ibid.
29 Ibid.
30 P.K. Datta's interview with *kar sevikas* at Ayodhya, op cit.
31 Anita et al, see article in this volume.
32 I am indebted to Dr Zoya Hasan for this observation.

# Hindu Nationalism and
# the Construction of Woman

## The Shiv Sena Organises Women in Bombay[1]

### SIKATA BANERJEE

### The feminisation of violence in Bombay

The politics of Hindutva[2] pursued by the Bharatiya Janata Party[3] (BJP) and regional parties such as the Shiv Sena in Maharashtra forms the context for frequent incidents of communal violence in India. However, even a populace hardened by the reports of constant communal conflict was shocked as arson and murder raged through the city of Bombay during the months of December 1992 and January 1993. The Shiv Sena, a Maharashtra political party, which jumped on the Hindutva bandwagon, openly declared its involvement in various attacks on Muslim life and property in Bombay.[4]

The violence in Bombay included not only men but also a surprisingly large number of women. The Shiv Sena mobilised women to block the arrest of several of its leaders, to prevent fire engines from going to Muslim areas engulfed by fire and even to loot stores and attack Muslim women. Many disparate voices bear witness to the feminisation of violence in Bombay. A male Shiv Sena leader makes the following comment:

> At Radhabhai chawl[5] they (i.e. Muslims) bolted the door from the outside and set it on fire. And all our (i.e. Hindu)[6] children, families, they were roasted, . . . when this hit the headlines the next day, even my wife told me 'I should offer you bangles now'[7]. What are we? In our own country Hindus are being burnt' and everybody got

down into the street and the situation went out of control. Thousands of women also came down. They were so hostile. So hostile.[8]

A feminist activist supports the Shiv Sena leader's observation:

A very, very, disturbing aspect of these killings was that women were some of the most aggressive participants in the riots . . . There were cases of women assaulting other women.[9]

This paper focuses on the feminisation of violence in Bombay and its implications for female activism. Violent feminine action, although not unheard of, is not very common in India. Indeed, in the past, reports of female involvement in violent situations in India have tended to emphasise women's peacemaking role:

The fact that other community women being present did not deter the women from coming for the meeting, shows how overwhelmingly these women wanted peace and normalcy in the area. Women having links with various parties were also present. They painted a banner saying 'Women Want Freedom From Communalism'. They drew their own symbols of peace: homes, trees, children. They also resolved to work for communal harmony.[10]

Nonetheless, in the recent Bombay riots women actively took part in looting, assaults, and violent demonstrations. This rather unconventional role of women in the Bombay violence is a result of the Shiv Sena's efficient mobilisation of Hindu women, coupled with its impressive clout within the Bombay political community, which it chooses to wield aggressively.[11] Indeed the Shiv Sena's celebration of Shivaji's destruction of Mughal (read Muslim) power and its emphasis on the militant, masculine, Marathi persona almost conflates violence and action in its political vocabulary. Consequently, the Shiv Sena women have incorporated this vocabulary.

The active participation of women in the public arena of violent politics under the aegis of a Hindu fundamentalist organisation is an unusual social phenomenon as the Hindu right has never officially critiqued the patriarchal norms that delegate women to the private sphere where their primary roles

are as wife and mother. This phenomenon signals that the politics of Hindutva is creating a social niche for women that challenges the notion of female emancipation Indian feminists have
been trying to disseminate in India. They view the Shiv Sena's
successful mobilisation of women as a direct threat to their
efforts as it only offers a limited sense of emancipation and
ignores the larger issue of patriarchal oppression.[12] I realise the
term 'feminism' includes a vast array of theoretical perspectives
that range from Marxist feminism to Postmodern feminism.[13]
However, all would agree that the role of women in the family[14]
underlies the complex structure of patriarchy. Women must
transcend their roles in the private realm as wives and mothers
to achieve any sort of liberation. In contrast, the Shiv Sena has
introduced a notion of female power that glorifies women's roles
as wives and mothers.

This paper will not judge whether the Shiv Sena's view of
emancipation is 'false' or whether the feminist perspective yields
'true' liberation. The Shiv Sena's success in mobilising women is
of concern because in the name of Hindutva women have committed violent acts that implicate them in the death of over a
thousand people in Bombay. If feminists (or others) wish to
challenge the Sena's successful mobilisation of women, a close
analysis of its political practices and the context within which
they play out is in order.

## Theoretical framework

Many political scientists have pondered the answer to the question Ted Gurr posed so succinctly: Why (do) Men Rebel? or in
this case: Why (do) Women Rebel or Organise?[15]

In comparative politics, the literature on revolution and/or
agrarian radicalism grapples with the issue of popular mobilisation
and action.[16] The answers to the question posed above have
usually been framed within a materialist or structural framework.
People rebel when, as James Scott has pointed out, anger born of
exploitation is not enough to facilitate collective action.[17] So how
does anger flowing from economic deprivation or any other
perceived exploitation such as cultural dominance become
translated into violent political action? Theoretical accounts point
to such intervening structural factors as leadership, state action,
patterns of land ownership and party politics. However, there is

one intervening factor that such accounts either ignore or allude to perfunctorily: identity. Identity is either viewed as immutable or seen as the superstructure that hides the hard political or economic base. But the manner in which people define themselves and their membership in a community is important as it forms the normative basis of political action. Identity draws on the grammar of everyday life. In other words, daily communication takes place because ordinary people have a shared intersubjective cultural context which forms the basis for why they feel an affinity for a certain identity and for other members who share this identity. This solidarity based upon a common identity ignites the social dynamite created by a conjunction of certain structural factors. This identity is not primordial nor is it immutable. Symbols and rituals which define the boundaries of community are constantly changing and have multiple interpretations.

Identities are fluid and multiple. They are fluid in that over time new interpretations of an identity may emerge. For· example, the nature of a Hindu identity was redefined as the nineteenth century Hindu reform movement constructed a response to colonial charges of primitivism and barbarism against this 'native' religion.[18] Identities are multiple in that during one particular period there may be various interpretations of one identity contesting for dominance. For example, in contemporary India, 'Indian' may mean a secular citizen (this is the official view) or it may signify a member of the Hindu religion (this is the view advanced by the forces of Hindutva). Similarly, many conceptualise Hinduism to be centred on a monolithic brahminical tradition (a view held by certain fundamentalist religious leaders in the Hindu nationalist fold) while others challenge the brahminical view by claiming that the crux of Hinduism lies in India's pluralist folk culture. Similarly, 'woman' as a category may be open to multiple interpretations.

Feminist analyses acknowledge that identity is a slippery notion and do not claim that the 'woman' is easy to locate. A debate still rages in feminist theory about the exact definition of 'woman'. Who is the 'woman' that forms the basis of feminist action? Robin Morgan in *Sisterhood is Powerful*[19] chooses to construct 'woman' by drawing upon what she perceives as shared universal experiences of male domination. Her definition is attacked by Third World and minority feminists who accuse her of erasing diversity amongst women. They state that there is no single 'woman' but a variety of women shaped by differences in class, race, culture and sexual orientation. The woman that Morgan creates is not universal 'woman' but a white, middle class, woman privileged over all others. More recently, feminist theory has become fragmented as voices of many women struggle to be heard and 'woman' is constructed in a myriad ways. Some welcome this fragmentation and flux[20] while others[21] deplore the recognition of excessive diversity as being paralysing.

The feminist framework's notion that 'woman' is an identity that is fluid and constructed rather than immutably determined provides a framework through which to analyse the Shiv Sena's skilful creation of a female identity through a network of symbols and rituals. Yet, the construction of 'woman' is only one part of the relationship forged between the Sena and Hindu women. This party's efficient mobilisation at the grassroots level, its provision of tangible benefits and its focus on a homogeneous, mass base provided the *structural* context for its success in organising women. A consideration of structural factors is important in that a constructed identity has no practical meaning unless it is woven into the material reality of life. Further, people think and communicate about the material basis of life through ideas that shape their identity as *Hindu* or *Indian* or *woman* or *Hindu woman*. The following section briefly sketches the political and economic reality underlying the Shiv Sena's call for action.

## The material context of the riots

Two factors—a crisis of governability and the deindustrialisation of Bombay—create a background of economic and political frustration which was translated into successful political action by the Shiv Sena.

*The crisis of governability*: In *Democracy and Discontent*,[22] Atul Kohli focuses on India's growing crisis of governability. He points to the following causes of the state's declining capability to govern in India: the changing role of the elite and the decline of the Congress Party's dominance in Indian politics, weak and ineffective political organisations and the mobilisation of new groups for electoral participation. These factors are also found in the state of Maharashtra as the Congress party which has domi-

nated in politics is weakened by internal factionalism and unable
to accommodate demands made by groups mobilised by competing political parties such as the Shiv Sena. The effectiveness of this
government was exemplified by the government of Naik which
was in power during the riots. This government's vacillating
stance towards growing violence and its absolute inability to
maintain order provided the ultimate proof that the state did not
have the political will or power to govern. Simultaneously, citizens freely speculated about Sharad Pawar's (Naik's party rival,
ex-Minister of Defence and, at the time of writing Chief Minister
of the state of Maharashtra) involvement in the riots.[23] When the
populace of a state freely admit that their representatives actually
instigate political violence it becomes clear that any popular faith
in the government as a symbol of law and order has been eroded.

*The industrialisation of Bombay:* Fifty per cent[24] of Bombay's population lives in horrific urban slums. Indeed Bombay has the
dubious honour of being home to Asia's largest slum: Dharavi.
The population of these slums keeps growing as migration from
surrounding rural areas continues unabated. This economic crisis has been further exacerbated by a phenomenon referred to as
the 'deindustrialisation' of Bombay. The number of jobs in the
manufacturing sector is decreasing while the only new jobs
being created are in the service sector which require sophisticated training and skills not available to the urban poor:

> The situation is even worse today because of the over-
> all decline in employment in the commercial capital.
> Between the sixties and eighties, nearly nine lakh manu-
> facturing jobs were lost. Textiles, in fact, have made
> way for chemicals as the city's major employer. In the
> eighties the total employment in the organised sector
> declined from 12.6 lakhs to 11.7 lakhs.[25] The flip side is
> the sharp rise in the number registered at employment
> exchanges. With the structural changes in the Indian
> economy, Bombay is likely to witness a further shift
> from manufacturing to the service sector where occu-
> pations like data processing call for education and
> skills.[26]

The failure of the 1982-83 labour strike,[27] which was a last
ditch effort by the textile workers who formed a majority of the

employed in the organised sector to save their jobs, created a feeling of anger and disillusionment. This anger provided an explosive background against which the Sena's political practices unfolded. As the organised sector shrunk, the unorganised sector (daily wage labour, street vending, domestic employment) expanded. But these occupations do not pay well and offer no job security. Rather than dissipating the feeling of economic deprivation, these jobs actually increased frustration, as many skilled factory workers who turned to these occupations out of desperation resented their fall in status. This is the context in which the Sena's political message created an identity that empowered women (who frequently were the wives, sisters and daughters of the male labourers) trapped within a net of economic and social frustration.

### The Shiv Sena and the construction of woman

The Sena has created a clever balance between tradition and change. On the one hand, women are taught to stay within the bounds of Hindu womanhood as the Sena organises traditional female ritual which emphasises women's primary role as wives and mothers. On the other, women committed violence because they were organised, encouraged to transcend their domestic role and made a part of political spaces. Many Indian feminists see this strategy as dangerous, because they believe it creates an illusion of emancipatory change while keeping patriarchal institutions in place.[28] Tanika Sarkar argues in this vein when she records a similar process of female 'liberation' initiated by the RSS[29] among middle class women:

> Where would feminists stand in relation to this manifestation of women's power? For there is no denying that the organisation does enable a specific and socially crucial group of middle class women in moving out of their homebound existence, to reclaim public spaces and even to acquire a political identity, and give them access to serious intellectual cogitation.[30]

But, she also notes:

> We know the costs only too well . . . . Political involvement has reached its culmination in an authoritarian

Hindu right that promises no liberation . . . accepts final commands from an all-male leadership that refuses any debate on Hindu patriarchy.[31]

She articulates the dominant fear amongst feminists in India as well as Bombay. The Shiv Sena organises women by arranging:

> concrete area-wise programmes for women in every one of their *shakhas*[32] like the creches[33], like the income generating programme (e.g. rolling papads). And having all these cultural festivals like *haldi-kumkum*. Very slowly it is being developed I think for the last five years or so. Particularly lower middle class women (are) being consolidated. That's why they can come out.[34]

One would assume that the creches and income generating programmes encourage women to be economically self-reliant or at least to contribute to the family income while the public celebration of rituals and a system of political iconography strengthen their roles as wives. The images embedded in the Sena's political message are open to a wide range of interpretations of female power. On one hand, income generation projects imply a view of women as workers. Economic means may provide some autonomy. On the other hand, the celebration of rituals like *haldi-kumkum* or *Shiva-ratri* emphasise the role of women as wives. Haldi or turmeric is ritualistically applied to a young bride and kumkum is the ritual mark of married women. *Shiva-ratri*, or the night of Shiva, refers to a rite wherein single women pray for a husband like the Lord Shiva. This two-pronged strategy can be interpreted three ways. One, the Sena's message can be seen as contradictory if one believes that constituting women as wives mires them in familial oppression which conflicts with or undermines the liberation flowing from the experience of woman as autonomous worker. Two, one can visualise the Sena as spreading a message of female autonomy (woman as worker) in conjunction with a system of familiar cultural iconography that will make this role feasible and appealing to women. Finally, one can ignore the issue of 'female power' and emphasise 'Hindu power' because these rituals are after all Hindu and the Sena espouses Hindu nationalism. The

economic benefits flowing from the Sena's projects strengthen
the appeal of being a 'Hindu' woman in the slums of Bombay

Two other examples of the use of cultural symbols within
the Sena's vocabulary will further highlight the various con
testing interpretations of woman embedded within its political
message. The Rani of Jhansi is used as a model female image
The figure of the Rani is emancipating in that she transcended
the conventional female role by leading troops to battle. How
ever, she led troops not as an independent or legitimate ruler
but as a regent for her infant son whom she adopted as
prospective male heir in order to legitimise her role as the head
of Gwalior state. So once again a multiplicity of interpretation
of woman arises: an independent female warrior and ruler,
mother fighting for her son who defines her political legiti
macy and a *Hindu* woman. Feminists would argue for th
affirmative interpretation. In the same vein the tiger, which i
the symbol of the Sena, represents a dual image of femal
power. The tiger is the 'familiar' of the goddess Shakti c
'power', so in this sense it is a symbol of female strength. Bu
Shakti is the consort of Shiva and ultimately subordinate t
him.[35] This myth makes female power dependent on male wil
Once again one must ask if Shakti's power diminishes becaus
Shiva's masculine will can overpower her. However, it can als
be argued that all interpretations of female power offered
above are legitimate since they do empower the Marathi wome
of Bombay who show their approval by responding to th
Sena's call for action. I believe this multiplicity of meanin
based on familiar symbols and rites gives the Sena's message
flexibility that resonates among the Marathi Hindu women
Women can feel powerful as wives or workers or warriors
They do not have to choose. Indeed they may slip from one rol
to another. It would be presumptuous to hierarchise this powe
according to a feminist perspective by informing Marath
women that any power derived in the home as a wife i
circumscribed or limited. Therefore, they must reject any suc
notion. However, the possibility of long term advantages t
women flowing from female activism under a Hindutva ban
ner is rather slim or, benefits are bought at a great cost.

It is not possible to depict the Shiv Sena as a party that is full
committed to female emancipation. There are no women in th

upper echelons of the Shiv Sena. Women corporators or city council members from the Shiv Sena are elected from 'women only' municipal wards and firmly follow the lead of male advisers. There are no women present as leaders in the Shiv Sena *shakhas* or local party units. Therefore, the entry of women into the public arena under the banner of Hindu fundamentalism has not resulted in an actual female voice in political decision making. If the Sena refused the entry of women into the ranks of leaders, it does not appear that female social activism will ultimately offer any 'real' power for women. Further, even if eventually women do become leaders in the Sena like Uma Bharati and Sadhvi Rithambara of the BJP and VHP, one must question any form of female power or liberation born out of and sustained through hatred and violence.

In this section I have outlined the normative basis of the Sena's political activism through an analysis of the various images of women underlying this party's practices. In the next section I briefly sum up the structural context that enables the Sena's success.

### The structural context

The Sena concentrates on Hindu, Marathi, lower class and caste, women. Its focus on a small community with shared norms and values[36] maximises the appeal of its vision of 'woman' and minimises the possibility of dissent. In contrast, feminists have found that their respect for diversity often makes action difficult as the presence of diverse voices makes consent on an efficient strategy difficult to obtain.

I have already pointed out the manner in which the Shiv Sena provides economic benefits to women, for example, income generation projects, day care, medical help and so on. These benefits are not available from a weak Municipal Corporation that cannot and sometimes will not provide such basic amenities to its populace. Finally, to promote grassroots participation, the Shiv Sena has 221 *shakhas* or local offices located throughout the slums of Bombay. Their mid-rung leaders live and work in the slums enabling daily interaction with women. In contrast, feminist leaders in Bombay come mostly from the middle class, do not live in the slums and have not cultivated multi-faceted mutual relations of trust with these women.

In conclusion, the Shiv Sena, by providing an identity that brings Hindu women together, limiting their focus to a small, homogenous, mass base, providing economic benefits and cultivating a mutual relation of trust with the Marathi women has successfully mobilised women.

## The Shiv Sena and feminism

The Shiv Sena (like the feminists) encourages women to come out and shout slogans which emphasise feminine power. But, unlike the feminists, the Sena is harnessing this power not to challenge patriarchy but to foment communal hatred. Additionally, feminists find that the issues around which they organise protests coincide with Shiv Sena-sponsored issues, for example, obscenity in films. There is a resemblance here to the feminist dilemma in the United States where radical feminists find themselves in the company of the religious right as they agitate against pornography. In both the religious right and the Shiv Sena ideologies the underlying image of woman differs greatly from that of the feminist movement. Despite the differing cultural contexts of their ideologies, both the religious right and the Shiv Sena seek to celebrate woman as wife and mother, and obscenity involving women is seen as denigrating the purity of the woman's role in the family. In contrast, feminists see pornography as embedding women further in the cycle of male domination which also shapes and includes the role of women in the family.

In Bombay during the riots the Shiv Sena successfully provided an identity for women. As Madhusree Datta explains:

> The Shiv Sena managed to give women as a collective an identity. For example, in Bandra (E) the local MLA is Shiv Sena. He is a famous goonda. There are no two ways about it. He has been in jail many a time. Madhukar Sarpotdar was openly carrying arms . . . during riots nobody dared to touch him but after the riots for whatever reason, the army decided to arrest him. At that time thousands of women, at twelve o'clock in the night, at one call came out and slept on the road so the military jeep could not enter . . . . This is a sense of belonging (to) a collectivity[37]

This feeling of belonging to a collectivity or a community enables the women to come out and protest in a violent manner.

The Sena's success turns on the multiplicity of meaning hidden within the cultural symbols it has chosen to emphasise. The multi-faceted identity of Marathi Hindu womanhood which the Sena has created is based on rituals and ceremonies which reinforce a sense of comfort and belonging in a hostile world by drawing on the strengths of everyday life. As yet feminist organisers have not been able to provide an alternative identity which can woo women away in large numbers from the appeal of the Shiv Sena.

In contrast, the construction of 'woman' based on rebellion against the family as theorised by Indian feminists is alienating and requires an abundance of strength and determination to face social censure. The difficulty of enabling women to challenge patriarchy is illustrated by the experience of feminist organisations in Bombay. I spoke to Madhushree Datta and Flavia Agnes of *Majlis* (literally this means gathering,) and Shenaz Shaikh of *Awaz e Nisvan* (The Voice of Freedom). Madhushree Datta is a documentary film maker while Flavia Agnes is a lawyer. They use *Majlis*, (a non-profit feminist organisation) as a forum to promote awareness of female oppression through cultural devices such as plays and films. *Majlis* also provides legal aid to women. *Awaz e Nisvan* is the first organisation which focuses exclusively on Muslim women. It attempts to raise the consciousness of Muslim women by arranging weekly meetings where they speak of their experiences as well as providing legal and social aid.[38]

All three women spoke of the difficulty of organising women to resist male dictates. Even if they enjoy attending the meetings at these organisations, most women will not return if expressly forbidden by a male guardian. These organisations are viewed as a temporary forum for airing grievances and not as providing a permanent means for altering behaviour. I would maintain that the experiences of these two organisations are fairly typical of Bombay feminist groups.

## Implications for alternative female activism

Rather than ending with a critique of the Sena's use of female power, I propose to use this analysis of the Sena's challenge to feminism to raise fundamental questions about successful female mobilisation. Feminists can utilise the Shiv Sena's experiments to help them clarify their vision of a collective identity. Madhusree Datta makes the following observation about the Shiv Sena women:

> So when a woman comes to me, she may get enriched or she might not get enriched but she definitely does not belong. She realises she does not belong. Though she talks of her rights . . . at the very same time it attacks the concept of family, of patriarchy . . . the Shiv Sena does not take away that comfort from them. A lot of women come here for their maintenance rights or divorce rights — but they do not belong to us. But it (i.e. the Shiv Sena) gives them a different kind of belonging. *Now our (i.e. feminist) weakness is we did not realise this desire to belong. We thought of need, of rights (but not of the desire to belong) . . . Rebellion does not make a movement, does not make a craze. Rebellion remains an alienating, isolating factor.*[39] It may give a moral boost to a lot of people but that does not make a movement.[40]

Rebellion is alienating and isolating. Resistance to oppression and exploitation is not enough to bind people together for collective action. Fifty per cent of the population of Bombay and a larger proportion of Shiv Sena supporters live in urban slums choked by sewage, rife with unemployment, and torn apart by criminal violence. Residents of these slums feel they have no roots, no sense of belonging, and no meaningful context for their day to day life. Both women and men are searching for a sense of belonging.

Feminists are attacking the fundamental expression: 'belonging to the family'. The very assumption of the feminist movement is that one does not belong, one should not want to belong to the larger society in its present form. A collective identity must be constructed which provides an alternative to and challenges the conventional myths and symbols of society while simultaneously creating a sense of belonging. Feminists in India have not been successful in forging such an identity yet.

In contrast, the Shiv Sena's message is not alienating. The Shiv Sena does not want to tear down structures; it wants to shore up existing ones. Yet it does so by providing a sense of power to women. The Shiv Sena offers a space in the public sphere for women. Women enjoy this freedom and at the same time are not faced with the alienating battle against the entrenched mores of society.

In these times of extreme cynicism it becomes tempting to end by denying the female ability to affect change or to believe in the fundamentals of a revolutionary identity. Given the horrors perpetuated by women in the Bombay riots, this temptation increases tenfold. But, one ought to overcome temptation.

The success of the Shiv Sena in organising women in Bombay should not discourage feminists or others disturbed by the violence in Bombay. Women do still come to organisations like *Majlis* and *Awaz e Nisvan*. They appreciate a forum in which to discuss or rail against the exploitation they face in the family. As small groups of women communicate in feminist forms perhaps several alternative, feminist, identities will emerge that are not exclusive and driven by hatred but challenge the traditional image of women in society. In addition, feminist leaders must recognise the success of the Shiv Sena's grassroots network. Therefore, feminists should construct direct meaningful relationships by living and working in the slums as the Shiv Sena has done to create the trust necessary for grassroots mobilisation. Indian feminists must reclaim the political space the Shiv Sena has encroached upon to provide a positive alternative to the fundamental message of violence and hatred this organisation is spreading.

### Conclusion

Materialist and/or structural explanations fail to interrogate the role of constructed identity in political mobilisation since they assume identity is immutable and hence of little theoretical interest. By adopting a feminist concern with the construction of woman, I highlighted the Shiv Sena's vision of woman and the implications of this ideal for female mobilisation. But a focus on the creation of identity does not necessarily imply a rejection of material and structural factors. Indeed, the impact of the Sena's image of woman was buttressed by structural factors such as grassroots contact, provision of economic benefits and focus on a homogeneous mass base.

## Notes

1. The research for this paper was made possible by a grant from the Shastri Indo-Canadian Institute.
2. This is a Sanskrit word which loosely translated means 'Hinduness'. However, in India it has become synonymous with militant Hindu nationalism which claims that the only true India is Hindu and minorities (read Muslims) can live in India only if they accept Hindu cultural dominance .
3. The Bharatiya Janata Party or the Indian People's Party, is a national party espousing an ideology of Hindu nationalism.
4. *Times of India*, January 15, 1993
5. A small apartment building.
6. Notice how the Shiv Sena leader makes an explicit dichotomy between 'Us' (Hindu) and 'Them' (Muslim).
7. This observation implies that the Hindu men have become weak like women, (hence the offer of bangles) and have failed to protect Hindu lives.
8. Personal interview, Pramod Navalkar, Shiv Sena leader, April 20, 1993.
9. Teesta Setalvad, 'Giving the Riots a Human Face,' *Telegraph*, April 5, 1993,
10. Ekta, *Report of Communal Riots in Jogeshwari East, December, 1990*, January, 1991.
11. The Shiv Sena terrorises Bombay by extorting protection money from small businessmen, and participating in many criminal activities. The city police do not care to prevent this as they are either involved in such activities or fear Shiv Sena retaliation.
12. See Madhu Kishwar, 'Religion at the Service of Nationalism: An Analysis of Sangh Parivar Politics,' in *Manushi*. no. 76, May-June, 1993. Also, Madhu Kishwar, 'Safety is Indivisible: The Warning from the Bombay Riots,' and Flavia Agnes, 'Behrampada—A Beseiged Basti,' *Manushi*. January-April, 1993; Amrita Chhachhi, 'The State, Religious Fundamentalism and Women: Trends in South Asia', in *Economic and Political Weekly*, March 18, 1989. See Tanika Sarkar, 'Women's Agency Within Authoritarian Communalism: The Rashtrasevika Samiti and Ramjanambhoomi,' in Gyanendra Pandey ed., *Hindus and Others: The Question of Identity in India Today*. New Delhi: Viking Press, 1993.
13. It would be impossible to cite all the work on Indian feminism in all its richness and variety. However, see Maria Mies, *Indian Women and Patriarchy: Conflicts and Dilemmas of Students and Working Women*, Concept Publishing Co. New Delhi, 1980 and *The Lace Makers of Narsapur: Indian Housewives* tious Traditions: The Debate on Sati in Colonial India,' *Cultural Critique*, Fall, 1987 for interesting theoretical work on the construction of 'woman' in India within western and colonial discourses.
14. I realise the notion of 'family' is contested as Indian feminists have protested the application of the model of a western, nuclear family with working father and a home-bound mother to areas of Indian life in the urban slums and villages where women work with men outside the private domain. But, even if this idea of family is rejected, it should be admitted that women still face oppression in the form of abuse, rape and dowry burning (to name a

few) because their role in the domestic arena subjects them to the power of husbands, sons or fathers. Further, even Marxist feminists would argue that the position of women in the domestic arena makes them vulnerable to capitalist exploitation which is linked to patriarchy.

[15] See Ted Robert Gurr, *Why Men Rebel* Princeton University Press, Princeton, N.J., 1970.

[16] I refer to works such as Theda Skocpol, *States and Social Revolution*, New York Cambridge University Press, 1979., Charles Tilly, *From Mobilization to Revolution*, Reading, Mass, Addison-Wesley Publishing Co., 1978., Jeffrey Paige, *Agrarian Revolution: Social Movements and Export Agriculture in the Underdeveloped World*, New York, The Free Press, 1975. Also, in the Indian context see Leslie Calman, *Protest in Democratic India*, Boulder, Westview Press, 1985.

[17] James Scott, *The Moral Economy of the Peasant: Rebellion and Subsistence in Southeast Asia*, New York and London, Yale University Press, 1976.

[18] See Ashis Nandy, *The Intimate Enemy*, New Delhi, Oxford University Press, 1983, and Tapan Raychaudhuri, *Europe Reconsidered*. New Delhi, Oxford University Press, 1988, for two excellent analyses of this reconstruction of Hinduism.

[19] Robin Morgan, *Sisterhood is Powerful: An Anthology of Writings from the Women's Liberation Movement*, New York, Random House, 1970.

[20] Donna Harraway, 'A Manifesto For Cyborgs: Science Technology, and Socialist Feminism in the 1980s,' in Linda J. Nicholson, ed., *Feminism and Postmodernism*, New York and London, Routledge, 1990.

[21] Susan Bordo, 'Feminism, Postmodernism and Gender-Skepticism,' in Linda J. Nicholson ed., *Feminism and Postmodernism*, New York and London, Routledge, 1990.

[22] Atul Kohli, *Democracy and Discontent: India's Growing Crisis of Governability*, New Delhi, Cambridge University Press, 1991. pp. 13-21.

[23] This observation occurred again and again as I interviewed journalists, inhabitants of the slums and even lower level Congress politicians

[24] Darryl D'Monte, 'Fire Down Below,' in Dileep Padgaonkar, ed., *When Bombay Burned*, Bombay, UBS Publishers, 1993. p.109.

[25] One lakh=100,000.

[26] Darryl D'Monte, 'A Grisly Second Round,' op. cit., p.131.

[27] See Rajni Bakshi, *A Long Haul*, Bombay: Build Documentation Center, 1986 and H. van Wesch, *Bombay Textile Strike 1982-83*, Bombay, Oxford University Press, 1992, for two excellent analyses of this strike.

[28] See note 13 for examples of work assuming this perspective.

[29] This acronym denotes a non-political, Hindu organisation: Rashtriya Swamsevak Sangh.

[30] Tanika Sarkar, 'Women's Agency Within Authoritarian Communalism: The Rashtrasevika Samiti and Ramjanambhoomi' in Gyanendra Pandey ed., *Hindus and Others: The Question of Identity in India Today*, New Delhi, Viking, 1993. pg. 43.

[31] *Ibid*. p. 43.

[32] Local offices.

[33] Daycare centres.

[34] Madhusree Datta, personal interview.

[35] This interpretation is common within folk culture. But for a scholarly look at Hindu symbolism, see Alain Danielou, *The Gods of India: Hindu Polytheism*, New York, Inner Traditions International, 1985.

[36] See Mancur Olson, *The Logic of Collective Action*, Cambridge, Harvard University Press, 1971 which argues that small, homogenous, groups are a precondition for successful collective action.

[37] Madhusree Datta, personal interview.

[38] Shenaz Shaikh, Founder of *Awaz E Nisvan*, personal interview, March 21, 1993.

[39] My emphasis.

[40] Madhushree Datta, personal interview.

# The Woman Shiv Sainik
## and her Sister Swayamsevika

TEESTA SETALVAD

The promise of a Hindu *rashtra*, unsullied in its saffron-sprayed glory, has proved an irresistible lure to thousands of women from all corners of the country. This was best illustrated on December 6, 1992 when more than 20,000 *kar sevikas* chanted in frenzy as their lathi-wielding brethren brought the Babri masjid down.

On the ground, in the midst of the violent fallout in Bombay in December 1992 and January 1993, other zealous sisters had exhorted their men—12-year old sons included—to burn and loot Muslim homes and shops, and in several instances, had even brandished sticks themselves.[1]

Over the past decade or so there has been a marked visibility of groups of women Shiv Sainiks who have successfully risen to the defence of their menfolk found guilty of murder, rioting and possessing illegal arms. This militant band of women have rallied with equal vehemence and anger when the Shiv Sena, and its Hindu chauvinist and dictatorial ideology have come under attack.[2] The technique of 'gheraoing' (surrounding) the protagonist, either in protection or aggression, is among those which have been successfully used to settle disputes relating to women, and has been deployed even where local police have been found corrupt or wanting. Nor has the militancy been limited to bands of women Shiv Sainiks. In Ahmedabad middle class Gujarati women unashamedly shed the veneer of respectability and led attacks on Bata shops in July 1992 under the mistaken impression that the chain was owned by a Muslim.

This large-scale mobilisation by various sections of the Hindu right, publicly manifested during inter-communal riots where women have led attacks against other women in the past five years or so, and especially visible in western India, turns on its head an earlier assumption that women, with children, worst victims of any kind of violence, stick together and 'protect' other women. It also signals the success of the Hindutvavadis' wooing of Hindu women. Armed with the godlike images of Durga and Shakti (identified as sources of woman power by sections within the women's movement long before they were hijacked by the Hindutvavadis) and reinforced by the real-life rantings of Sadhvi Rithambara, the newly militant Hindu woman needs little further inspiration.

Maharashtra, a state that has given birth to both the Rashtriya Swayamsevak Sangh (RSS) in 1925 and the Shiv Sena (SS) in 1966, is also at the forefront of the current surge in the popular mobilisation of women by sections of the Hindu right. Among the most articulate and visible sections here are the zealous and fiery bands of BJP women, bolstering support for wider party programmes and the aggressive group of women Shiv Sainiks who formed a ring of defence around male party leaders who were being hauled off by the police for criminal acts such as rioting and possessing illegal arms. In the last round of communal rioting that took the shape of a pogrom against the Muslim community in Bombay in January 1993, women Shiv Sainiks were seen actively preventing the police from rescuing Muslim boys and youth whom fanatical Hindu mobs were about to set aflame. These distinctive branches, the Hindutvavadi women's wings, cultivate a difference from each other in approach, culture and appeal. Through this difference they cater to various sections among Hindu women. But while maintaining this public distinction in tactics and approach, they retain a single-minded similarity of ideology and perspective.

The Shiv Sena's Mahila Aghadi appeals through the inherent militancy of the parent outfit, to perceived notions of thwarted regional aspirations. The VHP's Durga Vahini, with its emphasis on physical martial arts training, has the ten-armed Durga as its symbol. For unmarried women with leadership aspirations this notion of female preachers and teachers dates back to the late nineteenth century in the Hindu revivalist sect, the Arya Samaj.[3]

A series of underground meetings of the Vahini at which *katars* (knives in black sheaths) were distributed and martial arts displays held took place in Bombay over a period of three months in 1992. These successfully mobilised women in preparation for the Babri Masjid demolition on December 6, 1992. The Sadhvi addressed women, who responded with frenzied applause, thus: 'if you are required to draw them out, ensure your *katars* taste blood.'[4]

The RSS *Swayamsevikas* whose separate identity took organisational shape with the establishment of the low-profile women's organisation in 1930, are the political and cultural backbone of this resurgence among large sections of Hindu women. All the BJP's women parliamentarians are today members of the Rashtrasevika Samiti, which has now emerged as a high profile organisation. The BJP's Mahila Morcha, formally launched in 1980, has, they claim, 13 lakh (13,00,000) members.

These carriers of RSS thought have mastered unique methods to transmit the parent organisation's ideology. Through door-to-door whisper and rumour campaigns in normal and relatively peaceful times, they disseminate prejudiced and jaundiced readings of current situations, interlaced with history. During communal outbursts, often engineered by notions of 'avenging of past and present wrongs', these whisper and rumour campaigns take on a positively Machiavellian role. In the first stages they succeed in spreading fear and insecurity among a given community, giving credence to fantastic tales of impending danger and attack. The resultant paranoia, fuelled by gory tales of blood and revenge caused by the 'enemy' are pre-condition enough to justify violent blood-letting from 'their' side.

The most recent evidence, at the time of writing, of these tactics in operation was during the two phases of rioting in Bombay in December 1992 and January 1993. As statistics revealed, the majority of the dead were Muslims. Horrifying accounts of the violence that raged through the city in that period revealed a pre-conceived pattern in December and through the ten days of January 1993—the lives, homes, businesses and establishments of Muslims were singled out for brutal attack.

Extensive interviews with a large cross-section of Hindus throughout this period, however, revealed a diametrically opposed perception of this reality. According to them, it was they, not the minority community, who lived in constant danger of a violent attack.[6] The ludicrous lengths to which this well-orchestrated paranoia drove many Bombayites has frightening implications. One night in the early phase of the January riots, upper middle class residents of Dadar Chowpatty in central Bombay drove their private cars onto the beach, shone their headlights into the sea to ward off an imminent Iranian invasion. In another case, a veteran Marathi film artiste warned her daughter (incidentally married to a Muslim) of 'an impending attack by three lakh Muslims.' A temple bell was rung four times in the course of one night at Worli Koliwada (on the sea coast in central Bombay) accompanied by frenzied warnings, 'they are coming, they are coming.' Hordes of sword-wielding residents, unaccustomed to rioting in the past, were thus emboldened to slash the homes, hands and throats of neighbouring Muslims. Domestic workers doing their rounds each morning in the middle class housing colonies would often carry tales portending imminent danger.

On an everyday basis, the exclusive *shibirs* (camps) run by the Rashtriya Swayamsevika Samitis concentrate their training on small numbers. 'We are not interested in large, public meetings. Groups of 20-30 women who are regularly given "intellectual sessions" where Indian history [the RSS brand] is taught, religious sessions where hymns and prayers are recited, and physical training in yoga, judo, sword and stenguns is imparted. . . this prepares our women to speak in public and take a lead in political affairs.'

But at the heart of the growing appeal of these publicly visible arms of right-wing Hindu organisations was a strategy adopted by them in the early and mid-eighties. Both the BJP's Mahila Morcha (formed in 1980) and the Shiv Sena's Mahila Aghadi that came into existence five years later, did so in response to the success of the autonomous feminist movement. Through successful agitations and media campaigns, this movement, consisting of various fledgling groups all over the country, has put real-life women's issues like rape, dowry, child molestation and wife battering, with whatever limitations, on the nation's consciousness and agenda. A growing awareness among urban, educated middle class women of their rights and status, when faced with an everyday deprivation of both, forced the women's wings of these parties to take cognisance of this need.

Having co-opted the issues that were first raised successfully by the autonomous feminist movement, how did these outfits soon overtake other women's groups in popularity ? Part of the answer lies in the inherent differences of approach between the two. The ideology of women's liberation challenges notions of women's status and domination within the family and in other layers of society, pushing women to not merely ask inconvenient questions, but take painful risks. The ideology of Hindutva, on the other hand, appears more attractive in the short term: it speaks of inconvenient issues only when they are publicly visible blots like dowry murder or rape. But, in its very defence of Hindu tradition and authority, the challenges do not appear too painful to handle. The BJP promises a happily married and fulfilled life, a dignity within the community, with no risks being taken. The struggle towards Hindutva gives women a respectable space within the community, a struggle that even fulfils temporary political aspirations and leadership qualities.

Until about a decade ago, women had been systematically drawn into the RSS ideology since the thirties, but on a low-key basis. It now became important for even Hindutvavadis to give public shape to their mahila wings and, at the very least, pay lip service to burning social issues that exposed conditions for women within the family, and within society. Adept at organisation, the women's outfits of these two wings of the Hindu right far outstripped others in using these as successful tools for mass mobilisation in the early eighties.

Once this mobilisation became successful, however, and the systematic disinformation unleashed by various organs of this ideology began to create bogeys in the public mind, the autonomous women's movement failed—as other sections of the democratic polity had failed—to counter this propaganda.

Particularly obvious was the failure of the women's movement and others to tackle the saffron brigade's systematic attempt to 'demonise' the Muslim community, especially with allegations about polygamy and population growth (related to family planning).[7] In the mid-eighties, especially during the second national women's conference, intense debate had raged within the autonomous feminist movement and socialist feminist groups on women's issues and religious questions, especially those connected to minority rights. The public debate over the Shah Bano case reflected this.

Before this juncture, there had been a broad consensus within the women's movement on the need for a Uniform Civil Code but serious differences arose on the question at this stage, with a significant section arguing for a Gender Equal Family Code. However, the BJP, and other Hindutvavadis, successfully usurped this plank—on the pretext of it being a burning women's question—and set themselves up as its main champions. The women's movement was unable to make any major impact on the terms of the debate.[8]

In keeping with the strong-arm image of the Shiv Sena, its Mahila Aghadi, backed by the parent organisation, adopted a philosophy of rough justice, using brute force to secure a woman maintenance or any other form of legal redress. Sudha Churi, *pramukh* (head) of the Mahila Aghadi, proudly claimed in an interview that it was only because they had the Shiv Sena *shakha* (branch) behind them that all disputes were settled readily. 'If a husband who, say, is unwilling to pay maintenance, is brought to our *shakha* and told to pay, do you seriously think he will refuse ? If we lead a *morcha* to the police station demanding the arrest of a husband and in-laws involved in a dowry death do you think that the police will refuse us ? Come on, we are part of the Shiv Sena.'

In a society where many institutions of the state are close to collapse, the police and state bureaucracy racked by corruption or incapable of providing prompt succour for any common grievance (a case in court takes a decade to settle on an average), the attractiveness of an organisation that offers quick and ready justice, whatever the means applied, enjoys a special appeal. Some years ago, women Shiv Sainiks 'gheraoed' a senior advocate in Thane, north of Bombay, and physically prevented him from appearing on behalf of a temple priest who was allegedly guilty of child murder (sacrifice). Similar tactics were used to prevent another lawyer from appearing for a rapist in a court in north Bombay.

Five years ago, soon after the release of a commercial Hindi film, *Zakhmee Aurat* (wounded/wronged woman) that propagated its own variety of rough justice —castration for men in revenge for rape—enjoyed a disturbing popularity in many slums in Bombay where the scourge of child abuse, molestation and rape had reached frightening proportions, with no signs of justice for the victims.[9]

The experience of an autonomous feminist group, the Women's Centre in Bombay, that was 'outwitted' by these very tactics of the SS Mahila Aghadi, is worth mentioning. For the past decade, this group has been counselling and actively taking up cases of women victims of dowry demands, battering, rape, sexual molestation etc. Some years ago, a woman employed in Saudi Arabia as a domestic help was victimised by her employers and after being bundled back to India, came to the Women's Centre for help in settling the wages that were due to her. With no aid from either the Indian government or the Saudi Arabian Embassy in Bombay, the Centre had to throw up its hands. Some weeks later, the woman came back to inform the Centre that the matter had been settled successfully. Apparently, the Shiv Sena Mahila Aghadi had gone to the employer's house, threatened him with his life, and had recovered her dues.[10]

The BJP's Mahila Morcha has a different approach. While dealing with issues such as dowry burnings, they have agitated for the social boycott of the husband's family. But by and large, after women's issues gave them initial credibility, they shifted their emphasis to the mobilisation of women for a singlehanded purpose, widening the party's political base. This is all part of the struggle for a golden future: 'the protection of Hindu sanskriti and Hindutva.'[11] According to the President of the Morcha, Jaywanti Mehta, women, particularly in western India, 'got truly drawn to the party after Advaniji's rath yatra in 1990.' Today, the mahila wing boasts a string of fiery women leaders. From the agitation against the Bihar Chief Minister Lalloo Prasad Yadav's policies in Bihar to the *teen bigha* (three measures) agitation in West Bengal where 2,000 women recently courted arrest, to the anti-liquor agitation led by Shanta Reddy, secretary of the BJP Mahila Morcha in Andhra Pradesh, the thrust of the activities is wider socio-political issues that help in building a mass base for the BJP. 'What began as a religious purpose with the Ram rath yatra and the Ekta yatra has got successfully converted into a political mission.'[12]

Jaywanti Mehta proudly describes the 'fire that has driven

women in large numbers to join this movement.' Her own background is in the RSS and she has benefitted from its rigorous training. During her two-year tenure as President, Mehta has maintained the tradition of holding *'prashikshan shibirs'* (training camps) on a wide range of issues: legal aid, education, health, consumer rights, etc. All these camps do not merely tackle day-to-day issues that concern women but mould women into articulate political beings. They have a unique feature. Every session begins and ends with brief lectures on the RSS reading of history.

The clarion call that has fired these thousands of Hindu women to come out in defence of Hindu *sanskriti* (culture) and for Hindutva is likened to the second struggle for true Indian Independence: 'Just like at the time of Independence Sarojini Naidu, Aruna Asaf Ali, K. Upadhyaya and others were at the forefront, dynamic women are emerging and joining us,' Mehta asserts. Prominent names like Ila Pant, Prabha Narayan (wife of Shankar Narayan, former Chief Secretary, Andhra Pradesh) and Sushma Swaraj, a former socialist, are listed to prove this claim.

It is when one attempts to grasp the struggle for the defence of Hindu *sanskriti* and Hindutva, as many of these women see it, that one is faced with the insurmountable mental barrier of thorough indoctrination. The current situation is likened to a mass awakening after years of darkness and suppression symbolised by 'Moghul rule and plunder by Muslim rulers during Shivaji's time'. Independence in 1947 is seen as an opportunity thrown away because of the dominance of 'communist' ideas that stifled *'rashtrabhakti'* (patriotism). Now that the wave of Hindutva surges through most Indians (secularists are the worst enemies of this movement) women who have always been enraged at this slur on their country, culture and religion, are taking to the streets.

On the face of it, there is a world of difference in the tactics, approach and appeal of the woman Shiv Sainik and her sister Swayamsevika. But when one looks somewhat deeper, the similarities are striking. At a prosaic, organisational level, after having latched on to the obvious popularity of 'women's' issues, both the SS Mahila Aghadi, and the BJP Mahila Morcha have innovatively used religious and cultural functions to first get women together and then, to promote their ideology. The traditional *haladi kumkum* ceremony enjoyed only by married women, and the Ganapathi and Diwali celebrations are all occasions to come together. Traditional skill and craft competitions are also organised, but at the bottom of this organisation, as Churi puts it, is an *uddesh* (purpose): get women together and propagate our policies and ideas.

Both wings of Hindu fascist ideology concentrate their energies on strengthening their movement through systematic interaction with children, teaching them discipline, giving training and lessons in history. Mothers, wives, daughters, sisters of Hindutva do the home and hearth proud in preparing young minds for the future of the movement.

Something is known about the insidious indoctrination that takes place through the RSS-run Bal Bodha Kathayans (storytelling sessions for children). Short, pithy tales that portray Muslims as the enemy build a deep psychological distrust of them, which is exploited at opportune moments to avenge 'past' wrongs.

The SS Mahila Aghadi's *shibirs* for women and *balwadis* for children also perform this function diligently in their own way. In structure and approach there exists a striking similarity in the parent organisations—the RSS and Shiv Sena—while popular perception has written off the organisation of the SS as more of the hot-headed hoodlum variety.

The commonality in nomenclature of the Shiv Sena *shakha* with the RSS unit of daily organisation is not insignificant. The Sena's adoption of paramilitarism, the disciplined and organisational style of the RSS in the mid-sixties reflected the common background of many senior Maharashtrian leaders with experience in the RSS.[13] The choice of Shivaji, a martial hero as symbol of the organisation, its very name Sena which means army, only enhance the ideology of physical training for war ingrained by the RSS. Like the RSS, the Shiv Sena has never shied away from violence. Since its inception, and especially in recent years, it has flaunted—unchecked—its ability to cause violence and bloodshed, albeit for the protection of 'Hindu' interests.

Early accounts of Shiv Sena *shakhas* that describe the highly charged atmosphere and excitement among the young boys gathered together, have a likeness to the culture prevalent in the RSS *shakhas*. The phenomenon calls to mind the comment made by a member of the Thalburn Hitler Youth:

'without really meaning to, this organisation grew

rapidly. I think most boys joined for the same reasons I did. They were looking for a place where they could get together with other boys in exciting activities. I don't think the political factor was the main reason boys joined . . . we weren't fully conscious of what we were doing but we enjoyed ourselves and felt important.' [14]

For sisters in the Hindutva family too, the war is still on, a post-Medieval, post-Partition war that has one single enemy. This demon was responsible in the past for plundering Bharat mata (Mother India), sullying her forever and in the worst blow of all, dividing the country along communal lines. To rise in defence of this culture and country, these women may join their men in taking on the enemy. The enemy 'within' may only redeem himself by repeated proof of his 'nationalistic' credentials. Or else, today the time is right to avenge all these past wrongs and current failings.

But ironically, both have been forced to pay lip-service to the secular cause and hence in conversations with many women Shiv Sainiks and Swayamsevikas, prominent names of Muslim women who are part of their organisation are proudly bandied about for public consumption. Nafisa Hussain of the BJP has taken up cudgels on behalf of a Uniform Civil Code. Shahnaz Babi (introduced in conversation as film actress, Parveen Babi's cousin) is another name of a leading BJP woman activist.

Inherent problems within their own organisational structures which are anti-woman are conveniently shelved. Bal Thackeray, the SS supremo, has periodically used public platforms to hurl foul sexist abuse at women in public life, simply because their political views differ strongly. When this is discussed with women in the Sena they have nothing to say except to call it an 'unfortunate tendency'. Only a few months ago, former President of the BJP Mahila Morcha, Mridula Sharma, committed an unfortunate *faux pas* when she condoned the practice of dowry and said that in cases of domestic violence 'the woman should learn to adjust.' The immediate uproar led BJP President LK Advani to publicly berate her, hurriedly issue the social charter at the BJP's national convention in Bangalore (June 1993) that contained five paragraphs on the 'upliftment of women and children.'In 1987, another former Mahila Morcha President Vijaye Raje Scindia led bands of women in a protest march against the anti-sati legislation and in 'preservation of past glory and culture.'

Further queries on whether or not any of these women's wings have examined any irregularities or inadequacies in Hindu personal law do not merely put them on the defensive. When unable to explain why they have not raised systematic campaigns about the denial of property rights to lakhs of Hindu women, towards a general adoption law, against female infanticide etc., astonishing notes of anger and vengeance creep in. Far from any genuine concern over women's issues, these women's wings selectively use campaigns and planks of action to further Hindutva's single point ideological plank, baiting of the Muslim.

Nothing better reflects the hollow concern of both the Mahila Morcha and the Mahila Aghadi to genuine issues of concern for women than their spontaneous reactions to the gang-rape, under spotlight, (and possibly videotaped) of 13 Muslim women in Surat in December 1992. A local BJP politician is said to have joined hands with a Congress (I) counterpart to lead the attack. Not only has the BJP taken no action against this local leader, but neither Jaywanti Mehta nor any of the other prominent women leaders of the BJP have pressed for his ouster.

Pressing questions for their reaction to the Surat incident bring out pat responses of 'the anger felt by young Saurashtrians at the pampering of Muslims by the government.'[15] Having said that, angry stories about the similar humiliation of Kashmiri Pandit girls are hurled back. 'What did these socialists, Usha Mehta, Mrinal Gore and Pramila Dandavate do at that time ?'

The Hindutva ideology has been successful in demonising the Muslim community to a large extent in the public consciousness. The utter desensitisation among both men and women of the Hindutva bandwagon against the victimisation and assault of Muslim women reflects a dangerous extension of this ideology. Extensive research of pre and post-partition times reveals how this tendency of avenging your own community through the humiliation and desecration of the 'Other's' women dates back decades. [16] It found reflecion once again in the Surat and Bombay riots. Both violence and vengeance, integral paradigms of this ideology may now justifiably be used against the most 'precious' (for notions of community honour) and vulnerable sections of the enemy community, its women.

## Notes

[1]   Teesta Setalvad,'Women Jump Feet First into the Communal Mainstream,' *The Sunday Observer*, January 3-9, 1993.

[2]   Hundreds of women Shiv Sainiks 'gheraoed' and assaulted lawyer M P Vashi, for challenging the inflammatory mobilisation by Shiv Sena candidates during elections.

[3]   Sucheta Mazumdar, 'For Rama and Hindutva: Women and Right Wing Mobilisation in Contemporary India,' *COSAW Bulletin*, Vol. 8, 1994.

[4]   *Illustrated Weekly of India*, October 1992.

[5]   Interviews held by this author in the course of research and documentation about the riots.

[6]   Extensive interviews with Ammu Abraham, Secretary, Women's Centre, and many other grassroots feminists.

[7]   Ibid.

[8]   The author wrote a column on this subject in the Gujarathi daily *Samkaleen* during the year 1986-87.

[9]   Women's Centre records and through accounts of its Committee members, especially Ammu Abraham.

[10]   Jaywanti Mehta in an interview with Teesta Setalvad.

[11]   Three leading Swayamsevikas (who requeseted anonymity) in an interview with Teesta Setalvad.

[12]   JA Curran, *Militant Hinduism in Indian Politics: A Study of the RSS*, International Secretariat, Institute of Pacific Relations, 1951.

[13]   William Sheridan Allen, *The Nazi Seizure of Power*, Chicago, Quardrangle Books, 1965.

[14]   Jaywanti Mehta in an interview with Teesta Setalvad.

[15]   Ritu Menon and Kamla Bhasin, 'Recovery, Rupture, Resistance: State and the Abduction of Women During Partition,' *Economic and Political Weekly*, WS, April 24, 1993.

# Women, Hindutva and the Politics of Caste in Tamil Nadu

V GEETHA AND T V JAYANTHI

## I

In a seminal article on the 'militantly communal Hindu woman', Tanika Sarkar notes that the appeal of Hindutva for women has to be seen in the context of women's religiosity. Religion, she observes, gives woman 'access to a world of meanings enclosed in epics, allegories or other forms of religious texts that she can interpret and dwell on and thereby transcend her own immediate and closed world of limited experience.'[1] It seems to us that religion not only sustains and enriches the imaginative, inner life of women but also structures their feelings and experience in very specific ways. Observance of pollution and purity rituals, fasts, breaking up calendar time into various festival days and auspicious or inauspicious moments, patterning cuisine to suit these sanctified blocks of time—these and other related practices that are routinely carried out in the traditionally female domains of the household (kitchen, courtyard, pooja room) serve to inscribe into women's lives and onto their bodies marks of religiosity. Therefore any and every foray into the religious world of allegories and miracles is at once regulated and bounded by these practices that are also invariably caste and culture determined.

It is this elaborate, patterned and culture and caste-specific marking of women's lives that is now sought to be displaced and re-produced in realms beyond the household by the activities of the BJP-RSS-VHP combine. In Tamil Nadu, for instance, the VHP, under the aegis of a school network run by the Vishwa Hindu Vidya Kendra has, for some years now, been conducting annual *Vilakku Poojas*: Every year during Navarathri celebrations, 1008 women come together in a lamp-worshipping ritual. These women, as a senior VHP woman leader in the state told us, are not only middle class, upper caste women but 'women from the slums and harijan colonies as well'.[2] The women carry lit lamps in an orderly procession through particular city throughfares to the venue of the ritual where the lamps are consecrated to the Goddess Ambal (a form of Parvathi) who is iconised in the form of a huge sacred lamp. The ceremonial ritual that follows is but a spectacular re-enactment of a household event most upper caste Tamil women are familiar with. However, in the rarefied ambience of the chosen public venue that has been decorated to resemble a temple interior, an otherwise routine though particular practice is endowed with universal significance. Further, the spectacle creates, provisionally at least, an exalted community of the 'truly religous' within which all differences of caste and class cease to matter. Navarathri, a largely upper caste festival, becomes an occasion for all women to remember their origins, their 'Hinduness', if you will. The VHP has in its repertoire several such spectacles, all of which attract women through their ability to mediate certain existential fears and concerns that haunt the Hindu wife throughout her life. The *Saradu Pooja (Saradu-mangalsutra)* is explicitly oriented towards securing the well-being and longevity of the husband and becomes a collective expression of female marital fidelity that will remain steadfast to its 'dharma' even in the face of the husband's infidelity, neglect and desertion. Such publicised family rituals as the *Vilakku Pooja* and *Saradu Pooja* not only help to confirm women in their 'indispensable' roles in the family but also underscore their religiosity that is often deemed to be fundamental in assuring prosperity in the family.[3]

Such an interpellation of women as essentially Hindu religious subjects achieves two purposes: firstly, it persuades women to see themselves as legitimate, equal and valued participants in public and even political demonstrations of Hindu fervour and faith; secondly this erasure of boundaries between home and the world, private and public spaces, religion and politics through ceremonial enactments of familiar household rituals transforms and reinscribes the public Hindu cause as a deeply felt and experienced private wrong that every woman, irrespective of her caste and community origins, will wilfully nurse deep within her heart of hearts. Thus, Hindutva comes to exist not only as an empowering political ideal but also as a soulful, spiritual urge, even a desire, that impels behaviour and action. Middle-class, upper caste women from Triplicane (a Hindu and Muslim neighbourhood in Madras) who squatted on the roads (in 1989) in protest at midnight, braving the night and torrential rain because police had refused permission for their *shilanyas* procession (to celebrate the ceremonial laying of the foundation ston at Ayodhya) to wend through a particular mosque-dotted street, displayed a tenacity and strength of mind that night which surprised even their male mentors. To every woman assembled there — and not all of them had particular links with the Hindutva combine — the *shilanyas* represented a righteous cause which, if thwarted, would cause them great personal hurt.

The transformation of the Hindutva idea into a matter of great personal concern for 'ordinarily religious' Hindu women has been effected chiefly through the informal networking activities of the Rashtra Sevika Samiti and the VHP. For these organisations rely not only on the modality of traditionally acceptable and ironically significant festivals such as the *Vilakku* and *Saradu Poojas* but also utilise legitimate spheres of middle class, upper caste cultural and leisure activity to propagate their notions and concerns. Music and dance associations, *bhajan* societies, societies that patronise men (and sometimes women) of scriptural leaning and even charity organisations and their varied activities are put to good use by Hindutva ideologues who use these forums to establish subtle links between politics, religion and culture and to identify a viable cultural geography that all Hindus may relate to. For women, who constitute a large majority of these societies as members and volunteers, Hindutva becomes an evocative dream landscape that had all along nurtured their aesthetic and cultural sensibilities.[4]

It is however a moot question, and one which this paper will attempt to address, whether the Sangh *parivar's* (the right uses the term 'family' to describe itself) dreams of a Hindu *rashtra* may be sustainable at all in the historically anti-Brahmin, anti-

Sanskrit cultural mileu of Tamil Nadu; and more importantly and of pertinence to our immediate purpose at hand, whether the Hindutva combine will, indeed, succeed in its avowed aim of co-opting all Hindu women in the state to its cause.

## II

The Hindutva cause in Tamil Nadu is, as yet, upheld chiefly by brahmins but vigorous efforts are being made to interest and enthuse other castes as well in the founding of a Hindu *rashtra*. The Hindutva combine seems particularly keen on enlisting the support of territorially dominant caste groups such as the Gounders, Nadars and Thevars and has undertaken specific programmes of action towards this end. At a 'Raising of Hindu Consciousness' conference held in Coimbatore on February 21, 1993 non-brahmin leaders of the Hindu Munnani, an RSS affiliate organisation, were granted pride of place and posters announcing the conference prominently displayed their names rather than those of the local or national leaders. A young BJP activist in Madras city told us that in the Tamil Nadu unit of the BJP, it was practically impossible for brahmin cadres to attain responsible leadership positions in the party. While the veracity of this statement may be disputed, the fact remains that the BJP has seen fit to 'non-brahminise' its ranks as much as its ideological predelictions will allow. The RSS in Tamil Nadu is headed by Rangaswamy Thevar and many of the BJP's district units are peopled with non-brahmins from the dominant castes in the region. A resolution passed by the BJP's Tamil Nadu Executive Committee in February 1992 demanded that a statue of Pon. Muthuramalinga Thevar, Forward Bloc Leader, Congressman and admirer of Subhas Chandra Bose be erected in Madras at a spot where a statue of King George V stands today. The resolution also extolled Muthuramalinga Thevar as a fervent Hindu and a great patriot. It is clear that the Thevars are being wooed in the name of their much revered and long-departed leader who figures as a guardian diety in community rituals and in the name of a Hindu religion, whose interest, the BJP claims, the Thevars have historically defended.[5] The BJP is also attempting to carve out a constituency for itself amongst the Nadars, a powerful and dynamic caste that rose from a near-untouchable status in pre-colonial times to emerge as a socially and economically strong community during the colonial period and after. In their early past, Nadars had displayed certain sanskritising tendencies and the elite among them had taken to sporting a tuft and wearing the sacred thread in the manner of Tamil brahmins. However, when the non-brahmin movement came into its own in the Tamil country, the Nadars became one of its strongest and most convinced supporters, though a section of the community owing allegiance to Kamaraj Nadar, former Chief Minister of Tamil Nadu, professed loyalty to the Congress. Today the BJP, in an attempt to work certain ambivalences in Nadar history to its advantage, has sought to champion the community's interests, claiming that Nadars, many of whom are traders, are being subjected to unfair trade deals by competing Muslim traders in southern Tamil Nadu.[6] The BJP has achieved marginal success in establishing itself as a worthy political contender in Coimbatore district in western Tamil Nadu where a section of the fasitidious and increasingly bourgeois Gounder community have aligned themselves with that party. Further, the proximity of Coimbatore to Kerala has resulted in a seepage of Hindutva ideology from across the Western Ghats.

The Hindutva combine's wooing of the non-brahmin castes may be seen to proceed along two trajectories. While the combine seeks to appeal to a particular caste's perceptions of its own dominance it yet needs to contain an unruly flowering of particular identities for this would work against its underlying objective: the creation of a Hindu *rashtra* bound together by a common Hindu sympathy and subject to a common leadership. Therefore, the Hindutva combine, even as it encourages the growth of dominant caste identities, attempts to construct an overarching political context defined by an apparent castelessness, a context that would co-opt the specialities of a non-brahmin identity or identities and render them irrelevant even while playing upon the principle of difference that underwrites these identities. It is here that the combine's delinking of gender and caste concerns assumes discursive and political significance. Responding to a question on whether the Rashtra Sevika Samiti had caste-specific strategies in mind for mobilising women to its cause, Kamala Motilal, who heads the Samiti in Tamil Nadu, insisted that the Samiti did not recognise caste differences among the women who enlisted in its *shakas*. Likewise, Girija Sheshadri of the VHP, who supervises the latter's network of schools in the state and its women-oriented activities, stated that the Parishad considers women as Hindus, first and foremost, and did not seek to enquire into their caste origins. She pointed at the practice of conducting *Vilakku poojas* as a fitting instance of her organisation's essentially catholic activities that sought to involve all Hindu women, irrespective of their caste, in a common and universally appealing cause. Kamala Motilal, in what seemed, in retrospect, a bizarre parody of feminist notions of sisterhood, explained that women do not internalise notions of caste difference and prejudice as men are wont to do; besides they live their lives in such a way that women of various castes are thrown together in work and contractual relationships that are part of everyday life. This makes for a shared intimacy such that caste ceases to be a determining factor in female relationships. Women, concluded Kamala Motilal, have really no difficulties in seeing themselves as part of a seamless all-Hindu community.

What seems interesting in this context are the strategies of elision that are being consciously advanced by the Sevika Samiti and the VHP in their attempts to 'decastefy' women. The initial strategy, it is clear, consists in refusing to recognise that caste differences do underwrite female relationships. The second strategy, in a subtle gesture of reversal, accepts the markings of caste on women but considers these irrelevant in the name of a shared sisterhood. The third strategy is the most important of all three, for it seeks to universalise and render consensual what are obviously partisan and caste-bound practices, in the name of this proclaimed sisterhood. Thus all Hindu women, as we shall soon see, are sought to be implicated in constructions of female selfhood that would, ultimately, confirm them in their subordinated roles in the family and the caste-community within which the family is located and to which it is firmly bound.[7]

How does the Hindutva combine effect the construction of these new identities? Girija Seshadri explained to us that her schools have a well-orchestrated programme to educate mothers through their children. Thus, children studying in VHP schools are encouraged to practise in their homes the values that are imparted to them in their schools. For instance, says Girija Seshadri, the children who are largely from lower middle-class families are taught notions of cleanliness, worship, charity and patriotism. The children are expected to, and often do, carry these notions home. The implications of this value education are clear enough. Mothers are indirectly initiated into accepting and accommodating themselves to a whole range of ideas and practices that, to quote Girija Seshadri, 'they may not be familiar with, given their lower middle class background'. Once again, she refrained from identifying the castes of these lower middle class families, though it was clear from her half-embarrassed, half-apologetic tone, that they were not upper caste. The ideas and practices the VHP school children communicate to their mothers outline:

- modes of greeting; the appropriate Hindu greeting is *namaste* rather then the familiar Tamil *vanakam*.
- modes of living; the emphasis is on 'discipline' and 'cleanliness'. These notions are central to Tamil brahmin self-perceptions and are often used in an exclusivist sense to define their Other; the unclean, flesh-eating, non-brahmin rabble.
- modes of socialising; the schools attempt to promote 'unisexual' learning. Boys, too for example, take tailoring lessons. Parents are, likewise, encouraged to 'allow' their daughters as much freedom as they would their sons. On the other hand, girls are made aware of their primary responsibility — the upkeep of the family.
- modes of leisure activity; these include learning of a useful craft and the practice of charity. VHP schools organise feeding the poor sessions once every month. Children supply the necessary rice and lentils and on the appointed day mothers are prevailed upon to cook in the school's huge kitchens, especially designed for the purpose.
- modes of religious activity; here, the all-important *Vilakku pooja* serves to bring mothers together. Further, mothers are encouraged to observe the cycle of festivals that have, conventionally, been celebrated by the RSS. *Raksha bandhan* as a means to 'promote healthy relationships between boys and girls and to prevent them from entertaining "base" thoughts about each other,' has been imported into Tamil homes and, according to Girija

Seshadri, met with no resistance.

These modes of living and acting are seen as so many effective catalysts for the evolution of the new Hindu woman; decisive, strong, courageous and yet not lacking in motherly affection and religious piety. This new Hindu woman is projected as the fulcrum of the valiant Hindu community of the future, one where all differences, of caste, class, language and ethnicity will be dissolved. The feminist notion of the empowerment of the female self may be seen to suffer an ironic deflection here: the empowered Hindu woman is to defend caste and community honour rather than struggle against caste and religious dogma; only now caste and community honour are defined to mean an abstract and exclusive 'Hindu' honour. In this context, it would be useful to consider what exactly constitutes female honour and power in Hindutva discourses. Girija Seshadri pointed out that the VHP organises periodic legal camps for women where they are made aware of their rights in the family, workplace and society. Women also debate questions of property rights, marriage norms and the feasibility of divorce in Hindu society during these legal sessions. A VHP activist, based in Madras, was vociferous in her condemnation of violence in the family and said that if the circumstances warrant it, the Parishad's women activists advise the affected woman to leave her marital home. However, Girija Seshadri hastened to point out, the Parishad does not recommend divorce as a solution. Family and home were, after all, 'naturally secure and safe' institutions and women must come to terms with the fact the onus was on the woman to balance her personal life and career with the demands of home and family. Girija Seshadri added that she counselled her teachers to regulate and plan their time, so that their home chores would not suffer on account of their hectic schedule at school: 'Women have it in them to make or ruin a home. If a woman's life is in disarray she has no one but herself to blame. I, personally, have no patience or sympathy for weepy women. There is no point in crying. We have to learn to be strong.'

Like the VHP, the Samiti also attempts to thus empower women but rather than resorting to community networking efforts, the Samiti utilises its *shaka* and *boudhik* sessions for this purpose. It must be pointed out here that, unlike the VHP, the Samiti's activities are not socially and culturally integrated into the life of the local community.[8] The VHP's broad Hindu religious and cultural appeal has won it easy adherents while the Samiti's strict and disciplined notions of patriotism and nationalism have not been able to enthuse the 'ordinarily religious' woman. Of course, like the VHP, the Samiti works in tandem with religious and cultural organisations but it has proved to be a less attractive option for women than the VHP.

It remains to be seen how and through what means the explicitly communal content of the Hindutva combine's political, social and cultural posturings is encoded as a gender issue. Tanika Sarkar has pointed to 'the very careful and significant handling of the baby Ramalala image' in Ayodhya discourses. She observes that Ram as puranic hero is remembered in the shadow of his various losses. He loses his father, mother, his brothers, his kingdom, his wife . . . 'An entire series of deprivations has now been collapsed into the shape of that irresistible human idol — the deprived male infant . . . While the appeal of the homeless baby would be a general one, it would be especially poignant for women.[9] To this image of the hapless baby is juxtaposed another figure: the roving and lustful Muslim marauder. While the call of the infant demands that women assume a protective, yet, heroic role, like Jijibai and the Rani of Jhansi, the image of the malevolent Muslim rapist calls on women to extend their protective instincts to embrace an ever-threatened motherland.

In the Tamil country, where cultural and historical memory does not resonate with the images and sounds of partition and where invocations of medieval Muslim prowess can stir no dormant or residual Hindu pride, the call to defend the motherland — constructed as an extension of an exalted and inviolable female self — from Muslim lust and rapacity are not likely to evoke sympathy or recognition. Neither can the image of the cherubic Ramalala serve as a locus to bring women together in the cause of an abandoned infant. Tamil religious lore is replete with godly infants and no particular pride of place is accorded to Ram in popular religious culture. The Hindutva combine has, therefore, had to modify its ideological message though it never lets its anti-Muslim emphasis lose momentum. A prominent VHP woman activist from Madras displayed, in the course of her conversations with us, a near-palpable hatred for 'those diabolical Muslims', whose fundamental values, religious and moral norms, she insisted, contradicted every known premise of the Hindu religion. When persuaded to explain the violence against women that followed in the wake of the December 6 events she firmly said, 'We train our women to be prepared for anything. They have to learn to face up to things like rape.' She added that not a single Muslim woman was affected in the violence that followed the demolition of the mosque, for 'it was simply not in the Hindu mindset to thus harm or rape women.' In its eagerness to project the Muslims as a perfidious and evil community, the VHP in Tamil Nadu has had to resort to the telling of absurd tales that attest to Muslim conspiracy and cunning. The VHP Hindu monthly in Tamil, *Hindumitran* in its September 1992 issue, referred in one of its news items to the growing practice among women of using 'sticker *bindis*'. It was alleged during the BJP meeting that the adulteration of the traditional *kumkum* in recent times was the reason for the popularity of sticker *bindis*. *Hindumitran*, quoting, significantly enough, a Tamil Sidha healer (the sidha healers are believed to be native to the Tamil country and their art and philosophy of healing has come to be closely identified with indigenous Dravidian traditions) opined that this adulteration of the *kumkum* was the handiwork of Muslim traders who dealt in the substance and who were determined to harm Hindu women by thus rendering impure something that the women were wont to consider sacred![10]

The Hindutva combine exhibits a generalised hatred and paranioa towards all minority faiths and Christianity and Christians have come in for criticism as well.[11] A resolution passed at a VHP Women's conference, organised simultaneously in several districts of Tamil Nadu in September 1992 read thus: 'Christian propaganda pamphlets are distributed in front of Hindu temples and during Hindu public festivals. Further, when the elders and men of the family are away, betrayers of our nation enter Hindu homes, preach Christianity and refuse to leave. They also collect donations by force. Innocent and trustworthy Hindu mothers are thus converted to Christianity and made to participate in anti-national activities. Hence the propagation of Christianity and the flow of funds from foreign lands should immediately be banned.'[12] What is important to note here is that the charge, absurd though it is, suggests dark and insidious motives impel the preachers of the Christian faith. The vulnerable mother-in-the household image is juxtaposed to the fawning and cunning Christian proselytizer. These images, together, invoke ideas of seduction and it is not accidental that one of the VHP's favourite means of discrediting Christianity is to point at the alleged 'lasciviousness' of Christian priests.

### III

Hindutva's anti-Muslim, anti-Christian tirades in Tamil Nadu, however, represent less-than-inspired attempts at a communal use of gender concerns. The VHP's encoding of gender concerns possesses a further and more subtly articulated dimension that is of greater pertinence in the Tamil context. Both Kamala Motilal and Girija Seshadri as well as a local BJP activist in Madras stated clearly that the Hindutva combine's primary objective in Tamil Nadu was to dispel the various 'myths' ostensibly constructed by the non-brahmin/Dravidian movement; especially the 'myth' of a brahmin/non-brahmin divide and the related 'myth' of an Aryan-Sanskrit/Dravidian-Tamil divide that is supposed to underwrite Hindu social and cultural history in the Tamil country and elsewhere. Almost all the Hindutvaites we spoke to were vociferous in their condemnation of the non-brahmin/Dravidian movement and though they were willing to grant E V R Periyar was a great social reformer, were convinced that the movement for which he worked all his life was essentially divisive, destructive and the obverse of Hindu cultural expression, as we have traditionally known it. Sevika Samiti and VHP activists displayed a near-compulsive desire to 'other' the non-brahmin/ Dravidian movement, when prodded to examine its contemporary significance. They constantly played up the corrupt and 'immoral' political practices of the parties that had grown out of the movement, as if to say the imperfect and flawed political substantialisation of the ideals of social justice articulated by the movement negated these ideals themselves.

Historically, Tamil brahmins have constistently opposed, ridiculed and heaped abuse on the non-brahmin movement since its inception in 1916, and unlike a fair section of their counterparts in Maharashtra, have not sought to come to terms with the movement's relentless and oftentimes savage criticisms of brahminism and brahmin hegemony. Earliest brahmin criticisms of the movement have characterised it as the very antithesis of the Congress' struggle for Home Rule.[13] Thus juxtaposed, and considered the dark Other of Congress, the non-brahmin/ Dravidian movement has come to constitute a moment, a focus of dread, anxiety and fear in the imagination of brahmins in the Tamil country. So much so that the latter have come to construct themselves as a ghettoised community, the 'jews' of south India! (This is an ironic gesture on two counts: firstly, privilege is interpreted to mean deprivation and, secondly, Tamil brahmins who, like upper castes elsewhere, claimed descent from Aryans in the early modern period now see themselves as the 'jews').

What is of significance here is the gendering of the terms of discourse that frame brahmin and non-brahmin perceptions of themselves and of each other. In Hindu caste society female honour and caste honour are symbiotically linked entities such that a violation of the former often signifies a ruination of the latter. Often, upper caste hegemony is facilitated in part by the self-ordained rights of the upper caste male to the labour and sexuality of lower caste women, being established through countless everyday events of domination and control. Further, for the patriarchs of the upper castes to retain their positions of dominance, the control of the sexuality of their womenfolk and that of the men from the lower castes also needs to be established firmly. Thus, even as the upper caste men seek to guard the 'honour' and sexuality of their womenfolk jealously, they seek to image men from the lower castes as coarse, vulgar and lustful. Conversely gross fantasies abound in the sexual imagination of men from the subaltern castes about the supposed promiscuity and sexual prowess of the upper caste woman.[14] Punishment of or transgression of custom-established sexual mores is, as may be expected, partisan in caste society. While the women from the lower castes may be seduced, raped or abused at the will and pleasure of upper caste men, the desire of a lower caste male for an upper caste woman is often deemed an act of insolence and is usually dealt with most severely. Hence it is not surprising that in the Tamil context where a brahmin woman's chastity has been considered an index of that community's honour that the brahmin woman becomes an object to be coveted and disliked, one that simultaneously instils desire and hatred. She becomes the means through which time-honoured claims of ritual purity and religious sanctity as proclaimed by the brahmin caste as a whole are shown to be false and hypocritical.[15]

The Hindutva ideologues have attempted to work the problematic politics of caste and sexuality to their advantage. The Tamil brahmin male's antipathy to his political Other, the non-brahmin, has resulted in the latter being perceived as rude, upstartish and of lowly cultural origins. In the imagination and consciousness of brahmin women, the non-brahmin exists as a dark and disruptive intruder whose very presence may contaminate and violate brahmin female selfhood.[16] Hindutva ideologues with their proclaimed mistrust of the politics of non-brahminism/Dravidianism appeal to this barely articulated but pervasively experienced fear and disgust. The horror which Muslim masculinity has come to evoke in the Hindi-speaking regions of the north is, thus, sought to be displaced onto the non-brahmin castes who are, thereby banished to the margins of family and civic life. We are not suggesting here that the Hindutva combine indulges consciously and intentionally in a perverse politics of sexuality or that brahmin women who constitute a large section of the combine's female adherents are aware of this intricate politics in relation to themselves. We have merely attempted to explain and delineate the contours of a region-specific communal and hate compaign that plays upon historical and conventional sexual stereotypes and patterns of socio-sexual behaviour.

Certain questions, however, remain: While this 'othering' of the non-brahmin/Dravidian movement in specifically gendered terms may appeal to certain deep felt anxieties in the pschye of the brahmin woman, it is not likely to strike a chord of hurt or anger in the minds and hearts of women from the non-brahmin castes. Besides, it might interfere with the progress of the other Hindutva objective in Tamil Nadu — the co-option of the dominant non-brahmin castes for the cause of the future Hindu *rashtra*. To transform a particular mode of ideological interpellation so that it might serve to implicate not only the group that has a historical relationship to the ideology in question but society as a whole, ideologies have to be rendered consensual.

To successfully 'other' the non-brahmin/Dravidian movement, then, Hindutva ideologues have to project it as one that is essentially misogynistic, anti-patriotic, threatening to family and civic order and culturally inferior. Thus far we have detailed molecular efforts at constructing upper caste and, more specifically, brahmin hegemony. It now, remains to be seen how such constructive initiatives are integrated with critical strategies that are aimed at undermining and disrupting existing forms of political and social commonsense.

## IV

In contemporary Tamil Nadu, the non-brahmin/Dravidian movement lives not so much in the political practice of the parties that have grown out of it as it does in the historically evolved commonsense of the Tamil people. It was this commonsense that mediated perceptions of Mandal and Masjid in the Tamil country and proved a deterrent to violent and paranoiac reactions as were witnessed elsewhere in the country. Salient aspects of this commonsense include: a critical relationship with brahminical Hinduism; Tamil cultural pride; opposition to Hindi; notions of social justice, particularly in relation to caste determined deprivations. This commonsense has, of course, not remained unchanged. Some of its features have been altered, others re-interpreted but at no time in the past has the non-brahmin legacy suffered such mutations as have come to afflict it at the current historical conjuncture.[7] In fact, it would be no exaggeration to say non-brahmin commensense stands in danger of being fractured, of being split at its heart today.

Recently in the Tamil Nadu State Legislative Assembly while replying to allegations by an opposition party member that the AIADMK was dabbling in religion and attempting to forge an alliance with the BJP, the Chief Minister of Tamil Nadu, Jayalalitha, replied that if her popularity was growing it was because of the steps taken by her to maintain the temples of the state. She also said that she had received a large number of laudatory letters on this account. When her attention was drawn to a speech by E V Ramasamy Periyar where he had attacked Hinduism, she replied that 'It was natural for parties and persons to change their view in tune with the times. Just because EVR whose tradition we follow, broke idols it does not mean we should also do the same.' Referring to the charge that she supported *kar seva* at Ayodhya she replied that there was nothing wrong in calling for a *kar seva* which was only *Thirupani* (service to the God) 'to build a temple'.[18]

Jayalalitha is not alone in her espousal of Hindu religious causes. The Minister of Education in her cabinet, C Aranganayagam, while speaking in Madras on the occasion of the consecration of a school building belonging to the Jaigopal Garodia Hindu Vidyalaya (run by the Vishwa Hindu Vidya Kendra), on August 2, 1992 remarked that he was happy to note the school strove to instil patriotism and pride in the country's heritage in its students. He added that the Chief Minister was, likewise, concerned that children grew up with an awareness of their wonderful cultural past and had planned to include 'patriotism' as a compulsory subject in special schools to be set up in the state in all districts, Aranganayagam refuted charges that he was being false to the Dravidian heritage by thus speaking at a function organised by the VHP. The minister characterised the Parishad as an organisation committed to public service and said he found nothing wrong in thus being asked to speak at an educational institution run by that organisation. Several other ministers, including V R Nedunchezhiyan, one of the founder-members of the DMK have also, at various times, shown themselves to be not too averse to associating with the BJP.[19]

The AIADMK government had, from its earliest days in office, actively encouraged Hindu religious causes and obscurantist religious practices. It set up a corpus of funds, to be collected through donations, for renovation of temples in the state. It also announced a decision to set up an Institute of Vedic Studies. Further, ministers and state machinery have been involved in the conduct of various religious festivals with the Chief Minister herself participating in one of these.[20] Jayalalitha's wooing of the Hindu faithful has rendered her dear to the brahmin community in Tamil Nadu and she has been widely perceived as 'one of us' by the community at large. It is noteworthy that she has done or said nothing to dispel notions as regards her upper caste biases. In fact, it seems that she is engaged in a wilful political task in this respect. For instance, she fielded a number of brahmin candidates in the 1991 elections to the state assembly, a practice that had been consciously rejected by the DMK. It is clear that in her 're-reading' of Periyar, Jayalalitha has deemed it fit to consign to oblivion his relentless campaign against brahmin hegemony. Likewise, she has successfully exiled from the official Tamil political sphere, at least, issues of Tamil nationalism that even a much subdued DMK had raised from time to time.[21]

Jayalalitha represents a historical moment that seems to have brought the non-brahmin/Dravidian movement full circle. For, at the present conjuncture, the movement stands in danger of being parodied even as it is being upheld as a hegemonic and ruling ideology by the AIADMK, the ruling party. In other words, the non-brahmin legacy has been split at its heart, such that its rhetoric of social justice and Tamil nationalism has been displaced and transformed in the ideological pronouncements of AIADMK leaders; while its powerful and historically significant critique of brahminism, caste and Sanskritic cultural hegemony has been consigned to the margins of history by the patent and outright abjuring of these concerns by the ruling party. While the AIADMK is projected as the 'truly' Dravidian party in the present hour, its opponents are sought to be discredited in various ways. Such a re-mapping of the non-brahmin/Dravidian movement's concerns has enabled Jayalalitha to carve out a political constituency for herself where she has come to exist as a gigantic metonym for the movement.

What is noteworthy about this new Dravidianism is that, in a manner characteristic of all latecomers into history, it has sought to re-construct its past. Jayalalitha's propaganda team has, thus, 'produced' a new history of the non-brahmin/Dravidian movement in Tamil Nadu; and appropriately enough, this history, apart from being displayed through posters at AIADMK party conclaves, has been encapsulated in a dance-drama shot on video. Titled 'Dravida Sakthi', the dance-drama plays out the progress of the movement from its earliest days, traces its political successes under E V R Periyar and C N Annadurai and then executes a nimble leap over to the 'golden days of M G Ramachandran'. Karunanidhi's achievements and his party's historical role in sustaining the non-brahmin legacy is, thus, neatly excised from memory. It closes with a paean to Jayalalitha who is shown as a fitting inheritor of a glorious past and whose period in Tamil politics is then shown to be the high point of all that had taken place before. Significantly enough, the dance drama, in the words of its director, Yougisethu, portrays the triumph of a woman who makes her way honourably in a man's world, braving trials, disasters and conspiracies. The dance-drama video is expected to 'tour' Tamil Nadu in a specially designed *rath* (chariot).[22]

It is clear that Jayalalitha has sought to co-opt the non-brahmin/ Dravidian legacy to her own purposes and if her ideological and political predelictions are any indication, she may well be the bearer of the Hindutva message in the state. In distinguishing a 'true' Dravidianism that is clearly identified with her person from a 'false' one that is displaced onto her detractors, particularly the DMK, she has created the conditions for the emergence of a new political ideology in the state; one that will be determined, in the last instance, by Hindutva concerns, but which, meanwhile, will absorb, retain and eventually attempt to reconcile the vestiges of non-brahminism/Dravidianism to Hindutva.[23] At a time when the non-brahmin legacy is under pressure to re-constitute itself the AIADMK's attempts to render the former less problematic for the upper castes might well succeed. For, the persistence of caste riots involving dominant non-brahmin castes and dalits in rural Tamil Nadu has raised the question of the non-brahmin movement's relevance to dalits. While this has forced the issue of dalit liberation onto the political agenda of parties like the Pattel Makkal Katehi (PMK) and other small political groups, it has also produced a contrary effect. That is, instead of broadening the basis of the anti-brahmin, anti-caste struggle, it has led to the emergence of strong and belligerently posed caste identities as well. Since films in Tamil Nadu bear a symbiotic relationship to politics, one may invoke examples from the film world to indicate how this has happened. Over the past two years several films have been made that bear titles attesting to the honour, pride or courage of this or that dominant caste. In almost all of these films, the dominant castes, while they may err now and then, are shown as well-intentioned, charitable and the 'natural' leaders of the countryside. Feudal relationships are portrayed as essentially 'human' ones and women are shown their place in the kitchen or the household in question. Social conflicts are solved by caste elders and exploitation is shown to be an instance of personal greed, cruelty and rapacity. Such defiant statements of caste power that, in an earlier era, had helped to extend the frontiers of civil society and bring within its purview non-brahmin castes now reflect a desire to re-feudalise civic space.

What seems of immediate importance to us in all of this is the nature of Jayalalitha's appeal: her foregrounding of her 'feminine' selfhood in a variety of ways and the dangers such an appeal represents to the intertwined causes of social justice for the subaltern castes and the emancipation of women. It is in this context that we need to enquire into the phenomenon of 'Jayalalitha worship' that is widely prevalent in contemporary Tamil Nadu. For, more than anything else, it is likely that this incipient fascism, a veritable cult of the leader, may herald the arrival of Hindutva and, as the irony of history would have it, in the name of non-brahminism/Dravidianism.

In recent times the Tamil political sphere has come to be informed almost entirely by the cult-like status accorded to Jayalalitha. On the occasion of her birthday in 1993 — it falls on February 24 — the state witnessed a group of women, headed by the Social Welfare Minister, Indirakumari, carrying milk pots as offerings to a local deity. The milk was to be used in the ceremonial bath that is often accorded gods and goddesses in Tamil Nadu's innumerable temples. This time the *abishekam* as it is referred to, was in honour of Jayalalitha and for her wellbeing and prosperity. On the same day several ministers in her cabinet presided over religious functions organised in the city to pray for their Chief Minister and a special *Vilakku pooja* was organised in an important city shrine.

These activities may be viewed as a logical outcome of several modes of Jayalalitha worship that have been going on in the state for many months now. Ever since Jayalalitha assumed office the city has come to be periodically studded with giant sized cut-outs and posters imaging her person. On these posters she is shown smiling or clapping her hands appreciatively; at other times thinking , and in one cut-out she emerges out of a huge rose while a shimmering silvery moon appears behind her as a sort of a halo. In yet another cut-out she is shown standing in front of a lion, much like the Goddess Raja Rajeswari, while another one has Jayalalitha reading a book titled 'Her story'! All cut-outs usually carry dedications in prose and verse and bear the names of party MLAs and members.

Jayalalitha has thus come to dominate the physical as well as the imaginative landscape of Tamil society and her overwhelming visibility has granted her the status of a demi-god; one who is beyond reproach, infinitely capable, benign and generous. Thus it is not surprising that she was recently represented in a poster as the goddess Karumari Amman (a powerful and popular female goddess of Tamil Nadu). Jayalalitha's earliest attempt to inscribe herself in a religious-mythic space may be dated back to the year 1991 when, during the election campaigns that eventually swept her to power, she projected herself as a hapless Draupadi surrounded by evil Kauravas who in this instance were the DMK. (It may be recalled that Jayalalitha was allegedly molested on the floor of the Tamil Nadu Assembly in 1989 when the DMK was in office.) Since then, she has, successfully, inscribed onto herself all travails that women are wont to suffer in a patriarchal society and has managed to render female self-worth as synonymous with her own. Morever the Tamil people's honour, conventionally associated with the Tamil woman's honour, has also come to be defined by Jayalalitha's self-worth. It must be said here that the often vulgar and patently anti-woman metaphors, references and quips in the public speeches and writings of DMK partymen had led to an alienation of the woman voter/citizen from that party. It is significant that these multiple linkages between Jayalalitha, Draupadi, Tamil women and Tamil society were cited as reasons at a VHP women's conference about why Jayalalitha should initiate speedy action in a particular case of custodial rape that occurred in Tamil Nadu in June 1992. The VHP's women's conference in fact moved a resolution on this matter and pointed out that one ought not to forget that 'epic battles between Rama and Ravana and between Pandavas and Kauravas were waged in the past to wipe out the shame that was inflicted on women.'[24] It is evident that Jayalalitha's narcissistic identification of the Tamil people and, indeed, all womanhood, with herself has rendered her a mirror image of her 'subjects'. As the words on one of the posters printed to commemorate her birthday cryptically put it: 'The stern image of the above inset [a reference to the image of a stern faced Jayalalitha in one corner of the poster] has lead to this mirror-image [the reference is to a smiling Jayalalitha] of her citizens.'

Even as Jayalalitha is being constructed thus as a goddess, her cause is being defined as an explicitly feminist one. In an interview she granted to All India Radio, Madras soon after her assumption of office in June 1991, Jayalalitha asserted that one of her primary goals was the strengthening and emancipation of women. When she was allegedly humiliated on the assembly floor Jayalalitha sought to appeal to women and, especially feminists, to bear witness to her 'fate'. Since then, her Draupadi image notwithstanding, she has made much of her interest in women's issues and concerns. This interest found expression in the 'cradle baby' scheme, when, in an attempt to deter and mitigate the incidence of female infanticide in the state, the Tamil Nadu government announced that cradles would be made available at Public Health Centres (PHCs) and other government premises and if parents so desired, they could deposit their unwanted female babies in these cradles, rather than kill them. While this measure has come in for sharp criticism from women's groups in the state, it has been hailed as revolutionary measure in official circles. Much is also made of the Chief Minister's concern about the evils of drunkenness and alcohol-related violence in particular. While official policy on liquor has been soft and attuned to the interests of the liquor lobby, ideologically the thrust has been towards 'eradication of the Drink Evil' and a government-sponsored film in which Jayalalitha herself made a guest appearance was made to educate the people on the horrors of a drunken existence. While liquor-related violence continues as before, this film, that failed to enthuse viewers, has served the AIADMK's propaganda machinery as visible 'proof' of their leader's supreme concern for womankind. Jayalalitha as puranic goddess and as a women's rights activist has, thus, come to represent for her adoring female devotees at least, one who can do no wrong but who stands in imminent danger of being taunted, violated, abused. As watchful guardswomen, Jayalalitha's adoring female mob, carefully assembled from Madras slums, has come to constitute an informal protective squadron, ever ready to avenge any intended or unintended tarnishments of their Lady's name. One person who will vouch for the seriousness of the group's purpose is the Janata Party president Dr Subramaniyam Swamy who was the unfortunate victim of its wrath recently in Madras. Dr Swamy, who has been increasingly critical of alleged corruption in the AIADMK and of the allegedly corrupt practices of Jayalalitha, was attacked in the precincts of the Madras High Court.

In a state that used to pride itself on its rationalism and self respect, ministers, MLAs, party members and the people at large are, at present, engaged in a continuous effort to outdo each other in their praise and profession of loyalties to Jayalalitha. Hyperbole has come to characterise political discourse in the state and one finds fulsome praise heaped on the Chief Minister without the least hint of irony. When the Chief Minister ceases to be a mere political figure and is transformed into the 'Triumphant Devi of a Heroic History', 'The Radiant Lamp of Tamil Nadu', the 'Lion-like Leader', the 'Goddess in the Hearts of Adi-Dravidas' and the 'Spring of History' it will certainly not be too long before she is identified with and comes to stand for Bharat Mata, the ever vulnerable, yet nurturing and essentially courageous Mother of Hindutva discourses. Jayalalitha has already rehearsed her role on a narrower stage and played 'Mother Tamil' before a local audience and might well be catapulted into national glory if she aligns herself with the Hindutva combine.

## V

Before we conclude, we would like to pose a few questions, albeit rhetorically, for the answers to these questions depend on very many crucial variables, not all of which are aspects of the Tamil political, social and cultural universe. Will Hindutva ideologies be able to interpellate women as permanent and consistent Hindu subjects? In Tamil Nadu, as we have shown, Hindutva's consensus building efforts are, yet, at the primary stage and symbolic events such as *Vilakku pooja* may not really be effective catalysts, like say, the Ram temple at Ayodhya which drew together thousands of devout *kar sevikas*. On the other hand, given the increasing Hinduisation of the political sphere in the state and the politicisation of religion — the transformation of the Mahamaham festival into a tele-event whose central player was Jayalalitha is a case in point — it is possible that, with active encouragement from the AIADMK, Hindutva ideas may percolate into the commonsense of the people of Tamil Nadu. But, the mobilisation of women will prove effective only if Hindutvaites succeed in their other objective, the winning over of Sthe dominant non-brahmin castes. Here, again, as we have argued, chances are that, in the present political context, the AIADMK's own re-organisation of the political practice and ideological basis of non-brahminism/Dravidianism may serve the Hindutva combine well. Powerful and belligerent sections of the important dominant castes in the state might well join with the Hindu upper castes, demonstrating, thereby, a will to power in the future Hindu *rashtra*. Jayalalitha's rhetorical non-brahminism, bereft of its power of critique and its sense of history, will, no doubt help to cement the union with Hindutva.

It is painfully clear that one cannot be too complacent about the intentions and objectives of the Hindutva combine. One would do well to recall Brecht's advice to Walter Benjamin: 'what they (Nazis) are planning is nothing small, make no mistake about it. They are planning for 30,000 years ahead. Colossal things. Colossal crimes. They are out to destroy everything . . . That is why we too must think of everything.'

Having said all of this, one must also point out that traditions of resistance to brahmin hegemony are not entirely dormant or inactive in Tamil Nadu. The DMK has made it clear that it takes the communalisation of the body politic to be a very serious issue and seems determined to invoke its own history in the struggles against Hindutva. Likewise, the Dravida Kazhagam and PMK have continuously sought to resist Jayalalitha's efforts at the Hinduising of the political sphere. Women's groups, civil liberties organisations and dalit liberation groups in the state are also organising their resources towards anti-communal work. But it is clear these political tasks alone cannot stem a Hindutva tide, if one were to wash over us tomorrow. It is imperative that we begin speaking to women, with whose life and work we are immediately familiar in a different language; one which cues in on their everyday religiosity and works at transforming it towards more creative endeavours. The task seems immensely difficult, considering that in the Hindu cultural universe, faith and folly co-exist and devotion sometimes leads to destruction.

# Notes

1   Tanika Sarkar, 'The Woman as Communal Subject: Rashtrasevika Samiti and the Ram Janmabhoomi Movement', *Economic and Political Weekly*, August 31, 1991.

2   In conversation with V Geetha and TV Jayanthi. Information about Rashtrasevika Samiti and VHP activities in Tamil Nadu has been put together out of interviews, informal conversations with women from these organisations and with BJP activists in Madras as well as occasional publications of the RSS, BJP and VHP.

3   *Vilakku* (lamp) and *Saradu* (also knows as *thali* and *mangalsutra*) signify auspicious marital status (as we, no doubt, know from our films). *Thali* exists as a veritable transcendental signifier in the Tamil cultural universe. Its power of signification is enormous and a symbol is resonant with such meanings that even a bad and wayward husband partakes of its sanctity and is redeemed on that account. Cinema has, further, granted the *thali* an aura and an invincibility and it figures as almost a character with a life of its own in Tamil films.

4   Writing of the power of ethnic appeal, Stanely J Tambiah, ('The Nation State in Crisis and the Rise of Ethno-Nationalism', *The Thatched Patio*, September/ October 1992) notes that ethnic sentiments are experienced through various socio-cultural practices. These practices comprise 'a whole repertoire of performative devices and vehicles that are taken from public culture and popular religion and are deployed in mass participatory politics; such as processions, borrowing elements from religious pilgrimage, *bhakthi* ecstasy and 'holy war' . . . which glorify one's own kind and demonise the enemy.' It seems to us that the appeal of Hindutva is, likewise, mediated through familiar cultural experiences that are integral to one's sense of the self. In Tamil Nadu such experiences would include Karnatic music and Bharatanatyam dance, *harikathas* etc.

   These cultural events have, at least, in the post-independence period, been associated with the upper castes and it is possible that the image of a Hindutva of the future when associated with such events become tinged with nostalgia and memory.

5   The Thevars have a long history of militancy and caste feuding behind them. Throughout the nineteenth century they were engaged in status wars with upwardly mobile Nadars in southern and south-eastern Tamil Nadu while in the twentieth century they have indulged in reprisals against democratic-minded dalits.

6   For a succint history of Nadars, see Robert Hardgrave, *The Nadars of Tamil Nadu*, Berkeley, 1969.

7   The Hindutva combine's strategies may be seen to be in direct contrast to those advanced by Periyar and Phule. For the latter, the real empowerment and emancipation of women were contingent on the destruction of the caste structure and the re-organisation of the patriarchal family.

8   The VHP's women are in close touch with even members of organisations such as the Lions Club. The club thus serves as a forum for Hindutva concerns and as a valuable source of funds. In September 1992, when some

of us attempted to undertake a pre-emptive anti-communal programme on the eve of Ganesh Chathurthi, we found, to our confusion and embarrassment, that we had with us a woman from the Lions Club who told us that when a *shilanyas* procession had been organised the previous year it had had a peaceful passage. The point is that she had been a part of that procession and now on behalf of the Lions Club unit she represented, had joined us in our preparations for an anti-communal march. To her, the *shilanyas* procession was a mere 'religious' event and she obviously did not or would not see it as a politically and communally volatile act. Nor did she seem to be aware of the relationship between the *shilanyas* and the subsequent incidences of communal violence in Tamil Nadu.

9   Tanika Sarkar, ibid.

10   *Hindumitran,* September 1992.

11   The Hindutva combine's successes in Kanyakumari district of southern Tamil Nadu must be, at least partially, attributed to the ubiquity of Christian fundamentalist propaganda in the area.

12   *Hindumitran,* September 1992.

13   V Geetha and SV Rajadurai, work in progress.

14   It is significant that assertions of non-brahmin identity in Tamil Nadu have, in some instances, produced gross fantasies about the sexuality of brahmin women. CN Annadurai's fictional and dramatic writings may be profitably read to this end. The neglected and passionate young wife of an old brahmin priest is a figure that appears and re-appears in fictional and cinematic representations of brahmin life. Two such films, *Savitri* and *Ithu Namma Aallu* (This is our Girl) created considerable controversy in the state and an outraged brahmin community even went to court over this issue.

15   It is important to note that for brahmin men the honour of their womenfolk is the most significant index of their superior status. In the course of the reform debates that raged in Madras over the Post-Puberty Marriage Bill — the bill was introduced in the Madras Legislative Council in 1915 — the orthodox among the brahmins argued that raising the age of marriage for brahmin women would either increase the number of spinsters in the community or encourage licentious behaviour amongst women. Whereupon many non-brahmins among whom pre-puberty marriages were rare, indignantly wondered whether their daughters were any the less chaste for having married late!

16   Those of us who have grown up in a brahmin household in Madras carry memories of voices that used to drop to a whisper while uttering the word *shudra* or *paraya;* of faces that twisted into a grimace while referring to the 'low-caste' origins of many a DMK leader. In most brahmin households, children grow up thinking of all non-brahmins as crude, coarse and vulgar and it is an article of faith with most brahmin women that all the terrible things that are likely to happen to women take place 'out there' and not in good, brahmin homes. While helping victims of domestic violence regain their confidence and self-worth some of us have had the experience of listening to painfully defensive stories that usually ended with, 'How could this happen in a brahmin household?'.

17   V Geetha and SV Rajadurai, 'Neo-Brahminism: An International Fallacy?',

*Economic and Political Weekly*, January 16-23, 1993.

[18] *The Hindu* March 20, 1993.

[19] Ibid.

[20] Jayalalitha was the Chief guest at the Mahamakam festival in February 1992 which is celebrated once in 12 years, and is marked by thousands of people taking ritual dips in the famous Mahamakam tank in Kumbakonam. She was welcomed with religious honours accorded to *mutt-heads* and *sanyasins*. She was seated on an auspicious and specially chosen site. In full view of thousands of people who had gathered in Kumbakonam for the festival and to catch a glimpse of their Chief Minister, and a state-wide television audience, she was given a ceremonial ritual bath. (This practice of drenching with water/milk/honey is usually only carried out on deities and idols in a temple.)

[21] V Geetha and SV Rajadurai, 'Off with their Heads: Suppression of Dissent in Tamil Nadu, *Economic and Political Weekly*, June 6, 1992.

[22] *Dinamani* February 24, 1993.

[23] At the Hindu Munnani conference in Coimbatore, BJP leader Govindacharya observed that the Dravidian ethos was an integral part of Hindutva and could not be considered as representing a contradictory and oppositional civilisational principle. Predictably, the AIADMK has not refuted him.

[24] *Hindumitran*, September, 1992.

# Resisting Women

## ZAKIA PATHAK and SASWATI SENGUPTA

This essay has a history. It will explain how two texts — a diary of the anti-Mandal agitation in Delhi University kept by a woman student-activist and the audio-cassette of the *Mahaloya*, a hymn-cum-recital celebrating the goddess Durga — came to inhabit one story.

The diarist is an upper caste, middle class woman from Bengal, studying at Miranda House, an undergraduate college for women affiliated to Delhi University. The diary came into our hands towards the close of 1990, when the agitation was disintegrating. It ends on a note of contained disillusion.

For some time we had been interested in the myth of the Hindu goddess Durga, embodiment of militant energy which is glorified: goddess as warrior. And particularly its textualisation in the *Mahaloya* cassette since it is so popular in Delhi.

Suddenly it seemed urgent to bring the two texts together, to raid the myth in the interests of contemporary feminist politics. In other times, this may not have suggested itself to us. But today, the rabid religious revivalism promoted by Hindu extremist organisations and exploited for electoral gain makes it imperative for dissenters to enter that discourse and counter it.

A recent study of the operations of these organisations describes the rhetorical strategies they employ to homogenise the Hindus into a votebank.[1] All complex conceptualisation is avoided. The authors found the bookshop attached to the central office of the Bharatiya Janata Party devoid of ideological litera-

ture. They describe the style of the senior leader of the Rashtriya
Swayam Sevak Sangh whom they interviewed as quiet, deploy-
ing parables. 'There was a striking absence of reference to any
basic text.'[2] These organisations have appropriated the goddess
Durga, evidently in a move to match the warrior god Ram. The
Vishwa Hindu Parishad has named its women's wing the Durga
Vahini (army). Of the six festivals adopted by the Rashtriya
Swayam Sevak Sangh the Navaratri festival, which is centred on
the worship of Durga, is one.

The reading together of these two discrete texts, diary and
myth, is thus a happenstance constituted by a moment of history. It is a reading which is at the same time an intervention.
The Durga myth as it is disseminated in rightist readings pro-
duces the 'true woman' of Hindu tradition. Mythic narrative is
licensed to mix the 'real' with the 'imaginary'. Rational discourse keeps the two orders of telling separate. So that when it
suppresses the involvement of the subject in the production of
knowledge as *the* reality it is complicit with the operations of the
former. Thus secular and religious discourses collaborate to
engender the subject. The subsidiary myths and stereotypes
spawned by this co-habitation exert compelling power over
women in the Academy, neuterising female militancy to secure
consent for patriarchal politics.

The diary, which we scrutinise in section I, is written as an
'objective' account of the agitation. The discourse of objectivity
is institutionalised in the Academy and interpellates a unitary
subject. We argue that in the act of writing itself, this subject
fractures. Four loose sheets, enclosed in the diary, abruptly in-
terrupt its narrative and instal a resisting subject. Can this resistance be productively directed under mythical sanction? Activists
must be wary of rightist readings of the Durga myth which
masquerade as the right reading. We find that the *Mahaloya* as it
is popularly received promotes a patriarchal ideology. Section II
visibilises the narrative strategies by which female militancy is
neutralised: it is first disempowered in order that it can be
worshipped. Our reading recuperates an Other Durga.

# I

On August 7, 1990 the Government of India under Prime Minister

V P Singh published a notification announcing their intention to implement the recommendations of the Mandal Commission Report (MCR) of 1979. The Commission had been appointed to consider measures towards positive discrimination for the OBCs, backward classes other than the scheduled castes and tribes; for the latter quotas in education and employment are already operative. The MCR recommends a quota of 27 per cent for the OBCs.

The notification unleashed a student agitation in Delhi University against the MCR. Since quotas for the OBCs are already operative in the southern states, agitation against the report was located largely in the northern states; and as the national capital and seat of the Government of India, Delhi was the focus of the agitation. Delhi University students formed the core of the agitation because political parties preferred to remain silent on the issue for reasons of electoral arithmetic, the OBCs comprising a sizeable votebank.

A large number of women students participated in the agitation including our students at Miranda House. As we observed their solidarity, it became a matter of some concern to us how they would experience gender discrimated behaviour. The guiding slogan of the anti-Mandalites was: 'Mandal *ka* proposal Merit *ka* disposal' (the MCR will finish off merit). Merit for them represented an absolute principle of universal applicability in education and employment. As 'objective' criterion, it interpellated a unitary subject undifferentiated by gender, class or caste. Would this subject remain intact through their experience as activists in a political movement? Or would it disintegrate into contending subjectivities? Would they recognise the gendered stereotypes that produced their own behaviour and that of their male colleagues? Would these feed into each other to position them as the 'true woman' of Hindu tradition? Or would they implode?

It was midway through the agitation that we came to know through a colleague of ours that one of our students was keeping a diary.* We decided to scrutinise it for its textualisation of a gendered subject and its negotiations with other subjects.

The diary is scanty, about 5,000 words. It begins on August 7,

---

* We thank Sharmila Purkayastha for bringing the diary to our attention. Our gratitude to Lily Chakravarty for allowing us to use it.

and stops at September 11. Entries are not made regularly. It is written on the kind of notebook that students use for classnotes and tutorial essays. Clearly it was started on a sudden impulse. A word about our location vis-a-vis the diary. We do not give it representative status, as establishing an itinerary of perceptions for all women students who participated in the agitation. But we do valorise the diary as a genre for women's speech: as the fragment that is of cognitive value in its interrogation of official discourse.

First person narrative taken with the interior monologue is a favoured genre and form of writing for women. It offers opportunity for expression to those historically excluded from public discourse. It sanctions discontinuity, freeing speech from demands of conceptualisation and systematisation made on rational discourse. The diary is held together by the ritual unity of the autobiographical 'I'. As such, the student's diary would be a promising text for our inquiry. Because the diary is 'spontaneous', it visibilises 'provided subjectivities'.[3] Because it is private, not accountable to authority, it can indulge a resisting, transgressive self.

Genres are sets of expectations.[4] The diary of our student frustrated them. It is cast on the model of the official diary; it refuses the generic conventions of the private diary. Emotional commitment is absent. Official time dictates the framework of dates. It begins on August 7, when the notification was published by the Government of India and stops at September 11 with the hearing of the writ petitions against the MCR by the Supreme Court. The past tense—the tense of authority: the events seem to tell themselves[5] —is invariantly used. The style is bare. Figurative language is at a minimum. Modifiers are scarce. Definite/indefinite articles and verbs are sometimes omitted making for a laconicity that is a feature of official reporting. The occasional phrase is from officialese, for example 'anti-social elements', 'untoward incidents'.

> *August 8.* Demonstration started in campus—near Jai Jawan—condemning the government for its action, especially V P Singh.

> *August 10.* First demonstration at Boat Club.

*August 11.* More demonstrations in the campus. Some classes suspended.

*August 13.* The hostellers stop the day-scholars from entering the college in order to boycott the classes totally and make them attend a rally at 11 am. At Kranti Chowk, degrees and marksheets were burnt to show their futility. [*Kranti* means revolution; it was the name given to the *chowk*— the intersection in the campus—where the students used to hold their meetings.]

*August 14.* A torchlight demonstration was taken out in the evening around 7 o'clock. It went around Kamalanagar and surrounding areas and ended at the Vice-Chancellor's residence where the students *gheraoed* [surrounded] the house and submitted a memorandum asking the VC to come up with a statement. Though TV cameras and reporters and photographers were to be seen working furiously, no significant mention was in the newspapers.

The suppression of emotional time, the editing out of emotional commitment and response belong to a male ethic where the expression of feeling is officially perceived as a weakness. 'Rational' discourse is arguably male discourse. Why did the diarist model her diary on gendered, rational discourse? Clearly she was positioned in her 'choice' as a student of the University. The Academy institutionalises rational discourse; *ipso facto* establishes its 'objectivity'; and accords it epistemological status. Objectivism gives 'reality' an ontological status; the truth is available independent of the subject or of language. 'While the University provides an open space for all sorts of disagreement and challenge, and indeed encourages scepticism and quests into new territories of thought and knowledge essential for the life of the mind, it is intrinsically bound to standards of scholarship based on cognitive rationality.'[6] Reason is perceived as value-neutral and free, and opposed to emotion. Since it has been historically perceived as 'natural' to men, the diarist's choice of rational/objectivist discourse is a tacit admission that feeling *is* a weakness which women suffer from and it must be repressed. It is gendered history that has produced her 'choice'.

But all discourse is dialogic; in ways beyond its conscious control it articulates emotions as it engages with other voices, other subjects. The narrative practices of the diary disperse the unitary subject into a sub-text where gendered and class subjectivities position the diarist and set up resistances.

> *August 16.* A rally was taken round the campus. The response seemed quite good. The rally went round the whole university area . . . shouting slogans all the while.

The slogans are then reproduced, occupying as many as twelve lines on the page, and are given both in English and Hindi. This is neither direct nor free indirect speech: it is an enactment. The controlled narrative voice is displaced by a collective one which sustains the fiction of objective reporting at the same time as it allows an enactment of the politicised subject. The exuberance of the slogans is exorbitant: the subject of tradition is flouted. Middle class women still find it difficult to walk the streets of the city along with men, shouting slogans. Class positioning is deeply implicated in gendering discourses, which work through subsidiary myths: 'A woman's place is the home.' ' Silence is an excellent thing in a woman.'

The entry of August 18 is also marked by the excitement of political participation.

> *August 18.* A fund collection drive was undertaken simultaneously at Connaught Place, Chandni Chowk and South Extension. The students did *any* kind of work to collect money. Donations from 50p to Rs. 50 were taken. Several groups of students were engaged in enlightening the public on the nature of the agitation. People *actually* stopped, listened, sympathised and gave money *freely*. (emphasis added.)

Politicisation is accompanied by a need to enter public discourse. The newspapers had reported that in many cases money was extorted from helpless passers-by. The modifiers in the last sentence are evidently rebutting this charge. The entry also glows with the sense of student-solidarity, with an enlightened public supporting them against Authority.

The diary is informed by a polemic of Us and Them. The Them is only separated out by way of the constituents of authority: the government, the police, the government controlled media, the Vice-Chancellor; and the Us remains homogenised—except for the initial distinction between hostellers and day-scholars—over several entries. We have traced articulations of class and gendered positions which threaten the unitary subject. It is not threatened by caste positions. In the entry of August 18 above, 'any kind of work' obviously refers to the shoe-polishing ostentatiously performed by the men students on the streets, to bring home the condition they would be reduced to, if the MCR were to be implemented. Since shoemaking and polishing is ascriptively the work of the lowest castes, the diarist's failure to note the implication of caste in socio-economic backwardness—specifically the concern of the MCR — reflects the upper caste formation of the anti-Mandal students.

Linguistic practices are complicit in sustaining the fiction of the unitary subject. 'A rally was organised . . . .' 'A decision was taken . . . .' Construction of sentences in the passive voice represses the agent of the action. Who decided? Who organised? It is common knowledge that decisions of the general body of students were taken after lengthy discussion lasting well into the evening/night when women could not be present.* Did the women resent this? Does the passive voice allow their resentment at marginalisation to remain unexpressed? The entry of September 3 will say: 'after 25 days of the movement one does not know its manifesto . . . even if it has been chalked out, one is not aware of it.'

The entry of August 24 is longer than most and critically different. Dissension is recorded for the first time. The entry foregrounds 'organizational lapses' and 'untoward incidents'. But it refrains from making them connect.

> *August 24.*   The decision was taken yesterday that the agitators would go to parliament and form a human chain to plead their cause. The papers announced it. Thus the police had prepared themselves in advance by applying Section 144 around the parliament and forming barricades at strategic points so that a continuous human

---

*This was a problem with the Teachers Association too until it was resolved at a stormy meeting some years ago: the time of voting was fixed at a reasonable hour and announced in advance.

chain could not be formed. The demonstration remained peaceful but tear-gassing and *lathi*-charge started the moment the students tried to cross the barricades. There was brutal *lathi*-charge all round which left many injured. Several girls from the hostel too got injured.

- The shock came when the incident was reported in the TV news. It was diluted to an unbelievable extent.

- This rally put to the forefront the organisational lapses. There was no co-ordination between the IIT Indian Institute of Technology group, the south campus and the north campus groups of Delhi University. Several untoward incidents also took place because of some south campus guys and anti-social plants in the rally. This probably puts to the forefront the state our democracy is in.

Both the lapses and the incidents are percieved as violations of democratic norms. But while the former are dwelt on in subsequent entries, there is a studied silence about the latter.

The 'organisational lapses' signal a crisis in the discourse of the Academy. The cognitive rationality of the University requires its scholars 'to constantly examine and re-examine. . . above all to know that knowledge is always open to change and modification'.[7] The diary entries of August 25, 27, 28 are filled with anguish and dismay at the dogmatism of the anti-Mandal students who are intolerant of opinions opposed to their own, even from speakers invited by them to address their meetings, such as Swami Agnivesh and Rajmohan Gandhi. 'A farce because of total lack of decorum'; 'everyone hurling questions at each other'; 'rowdy', 'the debate had to end abruptly'. 'He was interrupted so many times in the course of a single sentence that he had to leave the mike.' The speeches at the Boat Club on September 4 when students and farmers made common cause are dismissed angrily as 'histrionics'. The operation of power politics is recognised! It is least concerned with rational debate or the OBCs. The 'movement' has been hijacked. Violence erupts. Women students are confined to the hostel. 'We are all under house arrest so to speak' (September 7).

The 'untoward incidents' are not specified. It is only familiarity with officialese and its evasions that enables their being read as sexual harassment. 'Anti social plants' can also be sourced to this. The recourse to officialese is a strategy to keep the community together in a sense of solidarity; but it is also the subject-effect of social gendering ('A woman should remain silent about the body'), and of the gendered rational discourse of the Academy ('such incidents are of marginal importance', emotions are out of place.) The diary strains against the discourse of objectivity and its rationale that true knowledge is independent of the subject. It cannot bring to crisis the sexed subject of rightist discourse.

It is abandoned. Four loose sheets, enclosed in the diary, return to August 24, and break open the silence. They are reproduced below in full.

> On 23rd night in the GBM [General Body Meeting] I came to know that there was a rally (to parliament) the next day with the intention of forming a human chain. The foremost aim was to show the solidarity of the students (mainly) antimandalites. Since the parliament was in session, to make an impact a crowd was required. Gunjan thus requested & appealed to the girls to join the rally.
>
> I decided to be a part of it since I was taking part actively in the agitation at that time. Most of my friends, and their friends too decided to go. The girls were scared but I did *force* the fear out of at least a few people's minds. We left about 9.30 the next morning for Kranti Chowk where the buses would be waiting.
>
> The response was good. About 55-60 of us went to Kranti Chowk around 10 o'clock; from there we were transported by bus to some road near the Parliament. A crowd had already assembled in a line. The moment we got down, the guys there made us go to a water tanker to wet our hankies and *dupattas*. I was frankly quite bewildered but they explained that it would be very necessary in case tear gas shells were fired. We obeyed them. Almost everybody had a *dupatta* [veil/scarf] irrespective of what they were wearing. Lots of us were not in *salwar*-suits. The day was very hot and the *dupatta* was for keeping the head comparatively cool mainly.
>
> Next we formed a chain and started moving towards the parliament building. In the meantime lots of other

people had joined us—people from IIT [Indian Institute of Technology], South Campus, Delhi University etc. The crowd had really swelled. We had hardly moved a few paces than we encountered a police barricade. They just had a rope to make the barricade though the police and women police were armed. I along with a lot of others was still under the illusion that the police were actively supporting us since in the University campus they seemed quite supportive. I was not scared of the police as such. After some slogan shouting in the road near the barricade the decision was taken to try & approach Parliament through some other road. So the chain now moved on. We were standing in one file in the middle of the road. The movement was very slow. Whenever we saw water taps we wet our *dupattas* since the temperature was rising quite steadily.

Roads were inevitably getting blocked because people formed groups to chat or just sit down. There was one police jeep around with one driver and two more officials in it. They were trying to clear the road. All of a sudden the jeep braked sharply and moved back with such speed that several guys would definitely have come under its wheels had they not jumped or rolled out of its way. But that's what the police wanted, I suppose! This incident horrified me to a degree.

Finally the chain started moving again. Suddenly we were given a certain amount of salt each. I was surprised but then somebody told me that the salt helps to clear the throat if one inhales tear-gas. At this time JMC (Jesus and Mary College) girls were performing a street-play. I could not see it since there was a huge crowd around. Then we reached a dead end. At this point I could see the Parliament House but I heard that since early morning police had imposed Section 144 in the area and also put up barricades. So all of us (around 10,000 people) sat down on the road and the pavement to wait and decide the next step. It was 2.30 p.m. now. It was the first time I looked at my watch after 9.30 a.m. There was general chaos while we (girls) were sitting quietly on one side of the pavement. A few South campus guys too were sitting near us. The chaos really started when the AMCF [Anti-Mandal Commission Forum] workers bought some fruits and distributed them in lieu of lunch. Some people just went mad trying to get hold of those few apples and bananas. This was presumably the lunch time in the various offices like PTI [Press Trust of India], Red Cross, etc. A lot of officers tried doing some charity—towards girls only. They wanted to give money or buy some fruits. We refused politely but firmly. After some time they got the message, I suppose, since they moved off and just stood aside to watch the great *'hangama'* [show].

The central committee members by now had come to the decision that just waiting there would not be of any use so the only recourse was to try and break/cross the police barricade. Several students went forward and then all hell broke loose. Everybody was running and trying to save one's skin. There were police everywhere firing tear-gas shells and charging ahead with *lathis*, [canes] rifles etc. and hitting whoever came in the way—whether boy or girl. There were no women police anywhere. There were lots of girls who had been sitting around me but had run inside one of the buildings to save themselves. I thought I could survive staying where I was. Moreover my room-mate (whom I had half coaxed and half bullied into going) was stuck now since people were running and jumping over us. So the three of us (my room-mate, Jyotsna and me) just put our heads down and tried to save ourselves. There was a proper stampede going on. Suddenly one guy who was himself running from the police just stood over us and this stopped people from coming over us. A policemen came and hit him hard quite a few times. We started screaming at the policeman and this brought him to his senses. He stopped to look at us for a moment and this gave us a chance to run and the guy too. We ran inside a building too but the acrid fumes of the tear-gas were everywhere. I covered my eyes and nose with the wet *dupatta* but one can't help but breathe. This was making me feel very sick. There was a chap at the back of this building (Red Cross Building) and a lot of girls as well as guys were

already there. Everybody had their eyes half-closed almost since the fumes were still there from the tear-gas
shells. There was a lot of misbehaviour on the part of
guys at this time. They tried pinching the girls while
giving them salt, tried to kiss some while supplying wet
hankies. Some chap offered me a hanky. I evaded him
since I could see a tap. While we were trying to recover
from the burning sensation in the eyes and also skin
(face and hands) guys came running in several times.
They were being chased by the police.

Several girls from the hostel had got hurt. They were
taken inside a makeshift shade and massaged. One girl
was quite serious and had to be sent to the hospital.
Suddenly there was chaos again. The police came to the
back shade chasing some guys. They were armed and
were using their _lathis_ indiscriminately; whether the guys
were moving or not they were being beaten. All the girls
created an uproar and begged the police to get out. They
refused and said they wanted to get hold of the guys.
Finally the police went out and we made the guys go off
as well. Never once did we (girls) get out of the building
campus after this.

The next shock came when I saw some mounted police
come in to chase the guys out. They had _lathis_ too and
were using them. At this point several officials from the
Red Cross also got hurt since they had come out to have
a better look at the show. The police this time were
determined to scatter the mob totally. Several guys who
got beaten up tried to throw stones at the police which
agitated the police all the more. We restrained the guys
and made them get out by a side gate. The police were
ready to beat us also but gave us a certain amount of
time to get out and run. By this time a lot of guys too had
broken beer-bottles, iron rods, stones etc, in their hands
and were using them to get even with the police. They
climbed on top of buildings and threw things at the
police and us too from there. Several girls tried getting
hold of one guy but it was impossible. He seemed bent
upon throwing stones. When somebody asked him which
college he belonged to, he just snarled some answer

which sounded like 'none'. This made us all suspect some foul play because this had been a student's rally and guys who came unarmed, suddenly how did they get broken bottles, brickbats, stones and iron rods?

A few girls got hit on the head and arms because of the brickbats being hurled but we managed to get out on to the main road through another building, and stood there on the pavement since the police at this time were after the lives of the few guys who were around. The people on the road were finding this to be a lot of fun and actually were laughing.

A final shock was still to come. The DCP (District Commissioner of Police) arrived running with several other policemen, on the scene. The first thing she said on seeing us standing by the side of the road was 'Bastards! *Maron Salon ko* [kill the bastards]. You've ruined my career!' Then she too ran after some guys herself.

I felt so enraged that I could have throttled her with my bare hands, I could hardly decide whether throttling her would give me more pleasure or tearing her with my nails. I'm sure everybody else was thinking of the same.

By this time the crowd had dispersed. Our girls were the only ones who formed a group. We then moved towards the bus stop to catch regular DTCs (Delhi Transport Corporation) buses back to the hostel if we could not get an empty one [arranged by the AMCF]. On the way I saw several police vans with guys who had been arrested in them. Most of their shirts were torn and some had wounds too.

We sat at the bus stop for some time till some guys arranged for a bus. Finally we arrived at the hostel about 5.30 p.m. The final straw was the report in the Doordarshan (TV) news (bulletin) which TV reported— no doubt—but from government's point of view totally. This was evident in the shots they showed and the report of the casualties.

It will at once be evident that the mode of rhetoric here is radically different : this is the genre of the private diary. The first person singular takes over. An early sentence qualifies the verb

with an auxiliary of force. 'I did *force* the fear out. . .' Sentences
are constructed in the active voice. The first person plural is
differentiated: 'We, the girls. . .' proper names occasionally occur. A colloquial style replaces the style of official reportage:
'They got the message.'

The diary was distorted communication. Its reticence on sexual
harassment is here exploded. Emotions are given in the raw: 'I
could have throttled her.' The loose sheets rupture the discourse
of objectivity and its porous knowledge and violently install a
resisting subject.

The street is a gendered space. Increased participation by
women in political demonstrations is contesting orthodox notions of the street but most middle class women still hesitate to
join them and are inhibited in their behaviour there. The diarist
had 'half-coaxed and half bullied' her room-mate into joining.
Significantly the word 'street' does not occur in the diary; it is
always 'the road'. Thus the street is a site where the myths of
rightist discourse ('A woman's place is the home') and their
contestations by feminist discourse are both available, producing different meanings and mediating practices.

Rightist discourse about women is operative through patriarchal stereotypes of the Good Woman which dictate codes of
dress and speech. A woman must be covered ('A woman is
defined by her body'). The diary had made no mention of the
*dupatta* or veil. The loose sheets note that all women were wearing them irrespective of dress ensemble. The *dupatta* is part of a
particular ensemble of dress—the *Shalwar-Khameez* (shirt and
long pants). The loose sheets specifically state that it was worn
by almost everybody 'irrespective of what [dress ensemble] they
were wearing.' Clearly this signals; the diarist attributes its use
to the heat—'mainly'. The modifier suggests there may have
been other—conservative—reasons. Speech codes assign women
to a linguistic space demarcated from that of street language. It
is arguable that the diarist's fury at the police officer's language
is doubly produced: not only by its violation of the reason and
restraint associated with authority but also of the speech code
for women which forbids abuse. The diarist is also positioned by
myths about women's nature. ('A woman is not aggressive by
nature, she keeps the peace'). The women students are shown to
protect their male colleagues from their own aggressive nature:

'we made the guys go off as well' and from the police—'all the girls created an uproar and begged them to get out'.

The relationship with the police demonstrates how the stereo-type of woman as essentially peace-loving positioned both men and women. 'They were ready to beat us also but they gave us a certain amount of time to get out and run'. The diary entry of the same day recalls that 'the guys were court arrested but the girls were allowed to go peacefully.' 'There was general chaos while we (girls) were sitting quietly on one side of the pavement.' 'Several guys who got beaten up tried to throw stones at the police which agitated the police all the more. We restrained the guys and made them get out of a side gate.' Policemen were evidently compelled into some kind of dialogue with the women, who used their gendered status to protect their male colleagues '. . . they were being beaten. We begged the police to get out. . . they refused and said they wanted to get hold of the guys. Finally the police went off and we made the guys go off as well.' But there is a sense of power that permeates this paragraph and it seems to issue from the successful translation of the stereotype from the private space to the public domain. Women prefer to remain in tradition even while resisting it.

How did the diarist then *experience* the gendered discrimina-tion in the agitation? Universities seldom have direct educa-tional, professional violence exercised against them. The violence to which they are exposed is more of a hegemonic nature, realised through gendering discourses which process social myths and spawn stereotypes. The diarist joined the agitation because it seemed to promise equality, therefore unity, with men, and liberation from repressive social practices. Indications that women were welcomed for reasons of political expediency — 'Since the parliament was in session, to make an impact a crowd was required'—are not heeded for their implications. Experience of direct violence—'misbehaviour' 'girls from the hostel too got injured'—brings the realisation that breaking out of gender ste-reotypes and espousing political activism deprives them of the armour of tradition. 'We never got out of the building campus after that.' Sexual harassment, 'eve-teasing', is now experienced as sexual terrorism. Its perpetrators merge with the police.

Political movements — of the left and the right — are decep-tive in the promise they seem initially to make for the emancipation of women. At the most they offer a temporary advance. They are riddled with contradictions of class, caste and gender. The fracturing of the unitary subject complicates any simple polemic of Us/Them. Student solidarity is threatened by male misbehaviour, itself produced by cultural stereotypes of the woman-on-the-street. Gender solidarity is rudely shocked by the policewoman who puts her career first: 'Bastards. You've ruined my career.' Police, supportive on the campus—'So I was not afraid of them'—were brutal outside. The general public once seen as supportive—'people actually stopped, listened and sympathised'—are now experienced as a lunch-hour office crowd greatly amused at the *'hangama'* and the 'show'; the presence of girls in the agitation provokes them into 'doing some charity—to the girls only. They wanted to offer money or buy some fruits. We refused politely but firmly. They got the message.'

'Experience is already always an interpretation *and* in need of interpretation'[8] As teachers engaged in furthering the feminist project we interpret the diarist's disillusionment in positive terms. The diary had closed on a note of despair:

> *September 04.* There is nothing concrete going on . . . Where will it lead? . . . When will there be an end to all this?

The loose sheets end on a note of anger: with the diarist weighing the rewards of two forms of pleasure: 'throttling' the officer or 'tearing her with my nails'. The translation of despair into anger has potential for social change. Agency for social change can come about only when the alienated self perceives its alienation in terms other than those of personal psychology, individual weakness. The diarist experiences collective anger. 'I'm sure everyone else was thinking the same.' Alienation is recognised, however dimly, as structurally caused.

We do not claim that the resisting woman is the authentic female subject, the loose sheets the authentic female voice. Rather we have argued that resistance is discursively produced, not lodged in a self. At any moment, as we have shown, there are a number of discourses and subject positions available to a woman. How did it come about that the diarist 'chose' the discourse that positioned her? Wendy Holloway suggests a notion of 'invest-ment' which leads out of the impasse of determinism and agency.

'. . .When the forces propelling people's actions have not been theorised as reducing to biology or society, they have been seen as a product of rational decision making.' [9] The notion of investment is proposed as a productive meeting of paradigms. Holloway draws on Lacanian theory to explain 'the somewhat anarchic character of desire: desire as a motive force or process is common to all signification . . . . Significations are a product of a person's history and what is expressed or suppressed in signification is made possible by the availability and hegemony of discourses.' The diarist's choice of rational objective discourse is compelled by the hegemony it enjoys in the Academy. But it is a hermeneutics of suspicion. It comes as no surprise to be told after we completed this essay, that she has all along been maintaining a private diary. At the same time she assured us, that the diary she gave us was never meant for public viewing!

The 'movement' petered out. In January 1991, the anti-Mandal students, unwilling to sacrifice an academic year and jeopardise their own future, settled down to preparing for the forthcoming university examination. The diarist 'chooses' to end her narrative with the Supreme Court hearings of the petitions against the MCR. This narrative closure suspends the promise of collective anger. It represents an uneasy capitulation to a male ethic which perceives problems centring on gender discrimination as of marginal importance. Indeed, as we have been made to note, to study gender discrimination as a major concern in an account of a movement for social justice is to be frivolous! Over and over again this sanctinimous ethic has operated to fragment the history of power and divide the dispossessed. Is it any wonder that the diarist fails signally to relate to the other socially dispossessed?

## II

Sociologists of religion describe the relation of myth and reality as of two kinds: the systemic and the critical.[10] According to the systemic orientation, myth can exist outside religious structures so that the sacred and profane exist in a single realm of discourse; the University and the Judiciary mediate this relationship. The critical orientation holds that myth is removed from reality and objectified; myths exist as fragments in the mind and can, at moments of crisis, motivate choice.

This essay argues implicitly for a systemic approach. The myth of Durga is everywhere. In high art and on calendars and commercial films, in scholarly writings and in jokes. The subsidiary myths circulating in the culture may be said to process it. Among the institutions which disseminate the myth is All-India Radio, controlled by the Government of India in its Ministry of Information and Broadcasting. Through its annual broadcast on the eve of the Durga puja festival, AIR acts as a multiplier bringing this textualisation of the myth, known as the *Mahaloya*, into countless Bengali homes.

The story of the broadcast is interesting.* The hymn-cum-recital in praise of the goddess has been recited in Bengali homes for decades. In the late twenties, the Calcutta station of AIR decided to broadcast the recital. At the auspicious hour of four in the morning, it was performed in their studios before an audience of 200 persons. The script was written by Bani Kumar, Pankaj Mallick was music director and Birendra Bhadra recited it. The broadcast was very popular and so repeated every year. Then, in 1958, torrential rains flooded the city and AIR transport, grounded all over it, was not available to pick up the artists from their homes and bring them to the studios. In desperation the police were approached; they gallantly agreed to put their vans at the disposal of AIR for the purpose. The programme went on the air on time. But AIR's troubles were not quite over; the artists were squeamish about returning to their homes in these vans (Black Marias) in broad daylight since they were used to transport criminals! Eventually, in the fifties, when high quality long lasting tapes were manufactured, the *Mahaloya* was recorded on audiocassette and became available in the market. It is now widely played at Bengali gatherings at the start of the festival. How does the *Mahaloya* process the Durga myth?

### III

The most important and popular festival of the Bengali Hindu is Durga Puja. This deification of female energy as the militant mother within the culture is at odds with the lived reality of most Bengali women. What is the Durga myth then: a fierce

---

* Our thanks to P C Chatterji, retired Director General of All India Radio, for the story.`

polemic against the prejudice that woman's essential nature is passive, her fulfilment lies in fecundity and therefore she is in need of male protection and guidance? Or is it an opiate whose main office is anodyne as it displaces woman's energy and suffering onto a consolatory myth? Does it empower woman or does it simply offer a temporary release after which she is more immovably situated in a patriarchal structure? We examine an audiotext *Mahisasuramardini* popularly referred to as the *Mahaloya* for its representation of the militant goddess.

It is necessary to recall at this point that Hinduism is not a religion with a founder or an ecclesiastical organisation with sects branching off and taking positions in relation to the teachings of the founder. It exists instead as a mosaic of cults, sects and deities and the juxtaposing of these are often from social needs.[11] Hindu deities are therefore constituted through plurally authored, multiply motivated myths which must be read not only as alterations and reinterpretations but also as appropriations and contestations. Durga is also constituted through variant myths. *Mahisasuramardini* mediates, arbitrates and even suppresses certain versions among the available pastiche of Durga myths and attempts to emerge as a totalising narrative which renders its material as coherent, continuous and unified. We argue that the militant goddess as produced by the text and received/decoded by the popular culture is in effect an ideologically motivated, patriarchal representation of female miltiancy. We are not reconstructing an intended meaning which may have preceded the creative process. Instead, we attend to the signifying surface of the text and visibilise the narrative strategies in order to dismantle its patriarchal politics.

Serene, richly feminine in attire, flanked by her four children, Ganesh, Lakshmi, Saraswati and Kartik, Mahisasuramardini—Durga's most popular reincarnation in Bengal—is iconographically represented in her domestic role as the wife of Shiv and mother of several divine children.[12] Yet she rides a lion. Literally. Her ten arms wield martial weapons, most prominent of which is a *kharag* or a broadsword. Thrusting a trident into the chest of the demon Mahisasura who has half emerged in a human form from the carcass of a slain buffalo lying at her feet the goddess is hypostatised at the moment of a violent act. She embodies Shakti or energy. But energy which is a natural force is made meaningful as an ordered system of norms and interdicts within culture. As a wife the energy is procreative, confined within the private space while the warrior's energy is a militant one legitimately erupting in the public space.

Wife. Private space. Energy Procreative.
Warrior. Public Space. Energy Militant.

The terms here need attending to for these are the terms of difference operating in society through which submission to phallocentricity is effected. If icons represent what are believed to be the essential features of a deity then what does Mahisasuramardini's popular oleograph signify? How do her worshippers decipher this symbol of socially recognised contradictions? How do they know her story?

*Mahaloya* literally means 'great dwelling'. In the Hindu religious calender it refers to the *amavasya* (the 14th night of the dark phase of the moon when it is darkest) immediately before Durga Puja. Since 1950 however the word has gradually also come to mean the special annual broadcast by All India Radio at four in the morning of this day for most urban Bengalis. This hour-long broadcast is titled *Mahisasuramardini*. It comprises of a Bengali narration which breaks into Sanskrit now and then and songs sung in Bengali and Sanskrit which we shall call hymns, as these are formal invocations of the goddess, so as to distinguish them from the Bengali songs. The Bengali narration is in a male voice while the songs and the hymns, at times solo, at times a chorus, use both male and female voices. The icon of the goddess Mahisasuramardini described earlier, is installed for the annual religious festival five days from the broadcast. Produced initially by All India Radio, today the text is also available in the form of a two-cassette pack, marketed by HMV, one of the leading recording companies in India as well as the T-series company usually associated with audio piracy. The text accepted and by implication endorsed by the state—All India Radio is a government controlled medium—as well as the dominating commercial bourgeoisie, is popular and readily available, more likely to be found in an urban Bengali household than any canonised religious text about the goddess. This popular text is therefore instrumental in disseminating knowledge of the goddess—the divine meaning and purpose behind her existence. We shall call the text of the broadcast *Mahaloya* from now as this is how it is known popularly.

We begin our analysis of the popular perception of Mahisasuramardini as mobilised by this text by first presenting an excerpt from *Mahaloya* that narrates the birth of this militant goddess and its account of how she is empowered to fight and defeat the demon Mahisasura and so acquire the appellation Mahisasuramardini, literally she who slays the buffalo demon. We then visibilise the narrative strategies and so deconstruct this representation of female miltiancy as patriarchally motivated. Finally we present another reading of the text which counters the first.

Transcribed below is the section which narrates the story of Mahisasuramardini's genesis from *Mahaloya*. Allowing for cultural and language differences, we have tried to remain faithful to the Bengali original. The voice of the narration is male and its language, Bengali.

> ... In the darkness with Vishnu immersed in meditative sleep the gods lost their right to heaven to Mahisasura. Defeated, dejected they sought Bramha's protection. But it was Bramha whose boon made Mahisasura invincible. Following his advice the gods then placed their case before Shiv and Vishnu. Hearing the plight of the gods and the demon's tyranny Vishnu frowned and Shiv turned red with anger. Enraged, Vishnu's body emanated a powerful glow as did the bodies of Bramha and the other gods. This mass of energy gradually congealed and took the form of a beautiful goddess who then announced her identity : ...

What follows is a hymn in Sanskrit, sung by a woman ( given on the following page). This it then followed by the Bengali narration, again in the male voice, translated as below:

> This beautiful Mahashakti created from the collective energy of the gods had fair skin, dark eyes, red lips ...

After this account of the goddess' birth follows the story of her empowerment, as an epic catalogue of the gifts that the gods bring her is narrated in Bengali. Most of these gifts are the martial weapons that the popular icon wields like the trident

अहं     रुद्रेभिर्वसुभिश्चराम्यहमादित्यैरुत      विश्वदेवैः ।
अहं मित्रावरुणोभा बिभर्म्यहमिन्द्राग्नी अहमश्विनोभा ॥१॥
अहं सोममाहनसं बिभर्म्यहं त्वष्टारमुत पूषणं भगम् ।
अहं दधामि द्रविणं हविष्मते सुप्राव्ये यजमानाय सुन्वते ॥२॥
अहं राष्ट्री सङ्गमनी वसूनां चिकितुषी प्रथमा यज्ञियानाम् ।
तां मा देवा व्यदधुः पुरुत्रा भूरिस्थात्रां भूर्यावेशयन्तीम् ॥३॥
मया सो अन्नमत्ति यो विपश्यति यः प्राणिति य ई शृणोत्युक्तम् ।
अमन्तवो मां त उपक्षियन्ति श्रुधि श्रुत श्रद्धिवं ते वदामि ॥४॥
अहमेव स्वयमिदं वदामि जुष्टं देवेभिरुत मानुषेभिः ।
यं कामये तं तमुग्रं कृणोमि तं ब्रह्माणं तमृषिं तं सुमेधाम् ॥५॥
अहं रुद्राय धनुरा तनोमि ब्रह्मद्विषे शरवे हन्तवा उ ।
अहं जनाय समदं कृणोम्यहं द्यावापृथिवी आ विवेश ॥६॥
अहं सुवे पितरमस्य मूर्धन् मम योनिरप्स्वन्तः समुद्रे ।
ततो वि तिष्ठे भुवनानु विश्वोतामूं द्यां वर्ष्मणोप स्पृशामि ॥७॥
अहमेव वात इव प्र वाम्यारभमाणा भुवनानि विश्वा ।
परो दिवा पर एना पृथिव्यैतावती महिना सं बभूव ॥८॥

**\*\*\***

(*shankar*), the sword (*kaal deva*), the bow and the arrow (*surya*)
the discus (*vishnu*) and the lion (*himalya*) which carries her to the
battlefield. And so the demon is defeated and the goddess celebrated as a figure of restitution in the right cause. The middle
class Bengali listeners of the *Mahaloya* we spoke to in Delhi said
unanimously that the deification of female militancy in the form
of Mashisasuramardini proved that Hinduism—as practised in
Bengal at any rate—accomodates feminism as it recognises militant female energy and allows it to erupt in the public space
during states of Emergency.

What is it that allows the *Mahaloya* to be read this way? It
uses, as we have said, two languages, Sanskrit and Bengali, two
modes, narration and songs, and voices, male as well as female.
The meaning of Shakti that is popularly realised depends precisely on this apparently polyphonic but univocal structure. The
meaning making process is always resident in a specific historical moment of powered relations and so the goddess' representation is crafted out of the relation between the two languages,
two modes and the voices. The narrative component in any
ritual attempts to rearticulate values and goals in a culturally
meaningful structure. In this instance it is the sequential plot of
the Bengali narration which becomes the intelligible whole gov-

erning the succession of songs and hymns. This Bengali narration, unlike the songs and the hymns, is in a male voice and within the dominant brahminical-patriarchal tradition a male guru is indispensable for an interpretation of the specialist scriptures. Finally, the use of Sanskrit which is the language of the Hindu scriptures helps locate the text within quasi-religious discourse even as the access to Sanskrit remains the Bengali language.[13] Meaning is thus confined to the domain of this narration in vernacular.

The narrative of the goddess' birth by the Bengali male voice constructs a beginning for militant female energy. The moment of beginning is of political importance as through articulations of beginnings basic statements are made about our relationships with nature and our perceptions of the source of power in the universe. Indeed nature—the ontological reality—is available epistemologically only through cultural narratives which construct nature as prediscursive, prior to culture, a politically neutral surface. Our knowledge of the 'nature' of female militancy is thus a cultural concept constructed through narratives such as the *Mahaloya*. According to the Bengali male narration, in the beginning were the gods who collectively create and empower female militancy. The primordial energy of the universe is thus specifically male and it has the power of fertility as well. The Bengali narration's counter factual myth of male procreativity defines the female sex role as secondary and dependent. It acknowledges militant female energy and allows it to claim the public space for the restitution of the right cause. Woman's aggressive potential is recognised but the controlling creative force that empowers her and sets the agenda is unequivocally the privilege of the male who prescribes the particular context in which it is allowed articulation. She is created by them, does their bidding and is praised and applauded. This celebration of female militancy must have serious consequences in determining the woman's role as a social agent. Her militancy is mobilised and allowed eruption only where it is patriarchally controlled. Exaltation of militant female energy is thus not the same as emancipation.

The Bengali narration does not deny female power. The goddess is addressed as Mahamaya Sanatani (permanence manifested in time), Niyati (fate), Mahashakti (energy) and

Prakriti (nature). But such invocations are immediately followed by a reminder that she is also Narayani (wife/shakti of Narayan) Bramhani (wife/shakti of Bramha) and Maheshwari (wife/shakti of Maheswar). Students of comparative religion and cultural anthropology recognise that the name is a regulative principle which casts its bearer in a definite mould forcing the bearer so to say to conform to the ideal qualities expressed by the appellation, in this case that of the wife whose sexuality is ultimately controlled and confined by the husband.[14] Thus defined, the female form is powerful as Shakti and procreative as Prakriti but she is not autonomous. In a number of Hindu myths male deities are identified in terms of their wives but such names are absent from this narrative. Moreover in this case the wife is not even a complementary existence. The Bengali narration states that she is created by her husband.

According to certain readings God was female, representing life in the form of the Earth Mother in certain agricultural communities in India.[15] Terracotta figurines of the Mother Goddess have been excavated from Mohenjodaro in the Indus valley and from Buxar in the Ganges valley in the northeast. The Shakti cult of female power is traced back to this time. The Aryan view of women was radically different. Their pantheon was predominantly male and their family patriarchal. The acquiring of wives by the Indo Aryan male gods can be read as the coercion of the Mother Goddess in the Vedic Hindu pantheon. This recognition was necessitated by the influence of the Tantric and Saktic movements which had been gaining momentum outside orthodox Vedic Hinduism for many centuries. Myths are thus processed through cultural stereotypes and the attempts to historicise the divine is to recognise that the sacred writ is socially constituted.

Our first reading locates a constructed beginning for militant female energy. But there is another beginning and it is contestatory. In a short article of two pages published in a Bengali perodical *Bartoman* Pragati Roy mentions a startling fact.[16] The 125th Sukta, Xth Mandala of the *Rig Veda* challenges the dominant phallocentric world view of the text. Composed by a woman—Baakrishi—in itself unusual for the *Rig Veda* is largely a male composition, the hymn declares female energy to be the autonomous force of the world. This is the same hymn, reproduced on page 291, left untranslated by the male commentator of the Mahaloya.

> I am Devi, I am Shakti. I am the God of the world.
> I have borne Mitra and Varuna, Indra and Agni
> and the twin Ashwini Kumars too.
> Somadeva — destroyer of the God's enemy
> Twasta, Pusha and Baug are my creation.
> I am the worshipped.
> I provide the means to worship.
> I have created the world. And Human Society. And its riches.
> I am knowledge. I manifest knowledge.
> I am worshipped by the Gods.
> I feed the world and grant divination.
> The sky who is called the father
> I am mother to him
> I am spread over the world, the sky and the ocean.
> I move through the world as wind. As freely.
> I manifest myself as the world. It's my own glory.

This hymn constructs another beginning in which the original creative impulse, autonomous agency and speech is claimed for the female. The implicating force of this hymn is demobilised in the first reading of the *Mahaloya* through the twin strategies of being made available only in Sanskrit and its position within the order of telling which, in effect, becomes the order of occurrence as sequence signifies causality. The hymn constructs another beginning for female militancy. A beginning which is subjected to primordial molestation by the naturalising patriarchal discourse of male autonomy and female subordination of the Bengali male voice in the *Mahaloya*. The hymn, a choric presentation in Sanskrit, is left untranslated. It is preceded by the patriarchal story in Bengali of the goddess' creation and followed by a reminder in Bengali again that she is the collective creation of the gods. Recuperated, it implodes within the coherent structure of the *Mahaloya* which now appears as fraught and politically intransigent as the struggle between the dominant and dominated.

It is now possible to say that the *Mahaloya* encodes the act of subjugating female energy which is necessary for the triumph of patriarchy. But the subjugation and supression is not complete.

Traces remain which can deconstruct the apparently seamless patriarchal narrative once we are made aware that ideology masquerading as coherence and plenitude is actually full of contradictions which can be located in any text.

The songs and the hymns which were marginalised in the first reading as merely providing relief and the occasional recourse to Sanskrit can no longer be seen as reconciliatory. The songs, unlike the Bengali narration, do not have a telos. They are non sequential, yet by repeating words and phrases they form associations which iconise the goddess:

> (1) Words like *sharat* (Autumn harvest season in Bengal), *bhor* (dawn), *aalo* (light), *nabo/nobin* (new), *shudha* (nectar) and Vasundhara (Mother Earth) make clear the goddess' close association with the fertility of vegetation and rejuvenation.

> (2) Words like Doshoprohoronodharini (martial goddess with ten arms, Bahubaladharini (many armed martial goddess), Ripudalabarini (she who destroys the enemy), Asurabinasini (she who destroys the demons), Raktobijashini (she who destroys Raktobij) foreground the goddess' militant nature.

> (3) *Brahmo* (knowledge), *dhan* (riches), *sangeet* (music), *dhyan* (thought process), *shidhi* (salvation), *roop* (Beauty), *josho* (Fame) and *joy* (victory) are recognised as the goddess' domain.

> (4) Throughout the songs and the hymns the goddess is invoked as the autonomous mother and not the wife.

The 'image' of Shakti thus crafted is one of self sufficient autonomy. Procreative but neither secondary nor dependent. A restituting force capable of destruction if her order is threatened. She is not submissive or subordinated to a male deity. She creates and maintains the world and fights without male directions and support against male demons and she always wins. This representation of the female thus challenges the *Dharmashastras* where the woman is incapable of handling her own affairs and socially inconsequential without relationships with men.[17]

By locating in the *Mahaloya* the struggle between patrinomy and maternal authority we deconstruct 'natural' assumptions about female nature. Our purpose has not been to rescue the text from patriarchy and restore it to the distraught mother but to prove that knowledge of female nature is textual representation and therefore constituted in history which allows intervention and the possibility of change.

### In concluding

An opposition has been constructed between the 'elite theory' of the Academy and the 'real world' of action for social change. That opposition needs to be problematised if it is to be retained. As the introductory section of this essay told it, it was our constitution as historical subjects in the 'real world' post-Hindutva that plotted two discrete texts, diary and myth, into a single story. The story narrates how 'real experience' is produced.

Stories are notoriously difficult to end; endings are open or arbitrary. We end ours with the liturgy of our faith in theory. Without feminist theory, we could not have got started on our story. It taught us to valorise women's speech. Our diffidence in giving so slight a document as a student's diary so much importance was matched by that of the diarist, expressed as nervous amusement at the serious uses to which we were putting it. We would not have had the temerity to give it evidential status had it not been for the subaltern theory of the fragment. We also learnt that the usefulness of a document to the researcher is enhanced when the document focusses on concerns of secondary importance to the researcher. How else could we have withstood intimidation by the left-inspired culture of political correctness and approached the diary of an anti-Mandalite with sympathetic concern for the production and negotiations of a gendered subject? Deconstructive theory showed us that texts are put together. Narrative theory helped us to take our texts apart. Discourse theory freed us from the tyranny of 'reality' by refusing it ontological status; enabling us to prise open the collaboration of power and knowledge in the readings of the Hindu right and its patriarchal practices.

Liturgy means public worship; in its Greek derivation: a gratuitous performance ! So be it.

## Notes

Section I of this essay was written by Zakia Pathak, Section II by Saswati Sengupta. Each gained from the other's criticism: the pronoun 'we' in these sections is by way of thanksgiving. To Sharada Nair and Lola Chatterjee, for their insightful comments and scholarly assistance, our grateful thanks. To Sharmila Purkayastha, for her enthusiastic involvement from start to finish, our warm appreciation. To Shankar Pathak and Debasish Chatterji, for all manner of sustenance, the other side of acknowledgment.

1   Tapan Basu et al, *Khaki Shorts and Saffron Flags, A Critique of the Hindu Right* (Tracts for the Times 1) New Delhi, Orient Longman, 1993.

2   Ibid, p. 38.

3   I borrow this phrase from Valerie Walkerdine in Sidonie Smith, *Subjectivity, Identity and the Body*, Indiana University Press, 1993, p. 4.

4   Jonathan Culler, 'Literary Competence,'in Jane Tompkins, ed., *Reader Response Criticism*, Baltimore, Johns Hopkins University Press, 1980, p. 116.

5   Emile Benveniste, in Hayden White, 'The value of Narrativity in the Representation of Reality', in WJT Mitchell, ed., *On Narrative*, London and Chicago, University of Chicago Press, 1980, 1981 p. 3. Benveniste is distinguishing *histoire* and *discours*, the involvement of the subject. In the former 'Truly there is no longer a narrator. The events are chronologically recorded as they appear on the horizon of the story. Mere no one speaks. The events seem to tell themselves.'

6   Brigitte Berger, 'Multiculturalism and the Modern University.' Special Issue, No 4, Fall 1993, Boston University Press, p. 521.

7   Brigitte Berger, Ibid.

8   Joan Scott, 'Experience,'in Judith Butler and Joan Scott, eds.,*Feminists Theorise the Political*, New York, Routledge, 1992, p. 37.

9   Wendy Holloway, 'Gender Difference and the Production of Subjectivity,' in Helen Crowley and Susan Himmelweit, eds., *Knowing Women*, Oxford, Polity Press in association with the Open University, 1992, pp. 250-57.

10  Richard K. Fenn, 'The Sociology of Religion: A Critical Survey,' in Tom Bottomore, ed., *Sociology, the State of the Art*, London, Sage, 1992, pp. 101-27.

11  Romila Thapar, 'Communalism and the Historical Legacy,' in K N Pannikar, ed., *Communalism in India: History, Politics and Culture*, Delhi, Manohar, p. 23.

12  In Bengal, married daughters customarily return to the natal home during Durga Puja and quite often Durga herself is cast in the role of returning daughter during the festival.

13  Aijaz Ahmed, 'Fascism and National Culture,' *Social Scientist*, Vol 21, Nos 3 & 4, March/April 1993, p. 34. The power of Sanskrit in high brahminism's homogenisation of population in belief systems is described. See also, Thomas B. Coburn 'Experiencing the Goddess: Notes on a Text, Gender and Society,' *Manushi, A Journal About Women and Society*, No. 80, New Delhi, Manushi Trust, 1994, pp. 2-10. Coburn argues that Vedic recitation in Sanskrit has never been widely understood by those who hear it.

[14] J Gonda, *Notes on Names and the Name of God in Ancient India,* North Holland Publishing Company, London/Amsterdam, 1970, p. 47.

[15] Romila Thapar, *A History of India,* Harmondsworth, Penguin, 1966, p. 103; Joanna Liddle and Rama Joshi, *Daughters of Indpendence: Gender, Caste and Class in India,* Delhi, Kali for Women, 1986, pp. 51-69; David Kinsley, *Hindu Goddesses: Visions of the Divine Feminine in the Hindu Religious Tradition,* Delhi, Motilal Banarsidass, 1986, pp. 98-115.

[16] The hymn read in isolation, e.g. in the *Bartoman,* does not have anything like its effect in the *Mahaloya.* Decontextualised there in the popular reading by virtue of its language, Sanskrit, its meaning explodes only when the Sanskrit translation is made accessible.

[17] For instance, *Manu Dharma Shastra,* 5: 147-49, 9: 14-17.

# Report of the Women's Delegation to Bhopal, Ahmedabad and Surat

AIDWA, CWDS, MDS, NFIW

A joint delegation of four national women's organisations, the All India Democratic Women's Association (AIDWA), the Centre for Women's Development Studies (CWDS), the Mahila Dakshata Samiti (MDS) and the National Federation of Indian Women (NFIW) visited some of  worst riot affected areas in Bhopal, Ahmedabad and Surat from February 16 to 19 1993. The delegation consisted of Susheela Gopalan, MP, and Brinda Karat from AIDWA, Vina Mazumdar from CWDS, Primila Loomba from NFIW and Husna Subhani from MDS and was accompanied by two members of Media Storm (a Delhi based women's media collective) Ranjani Mazumdar and Shikha Jhingan, who videotaped some of the interviews. All the preliminary work for the visit was done by the local units of the organisations who are working in these areas.

The primary purpose of the visit was to obtain, through direct conversations with women riot victims and their children, some understanding of their perception of the communal violence and its impact on their lives; and to assess the effectiveness of official measures for their relief and rehabilitation, especially of families which are now headed by women. The visit was planned as a part of the ongoing struggle against communalism.

The delegation met close to 500 riot-hit women of both communities, with a ratio of 4:1 (minority:majority). Many of the discussions were conducted in groups. In some discussions riot-affected women of both communities participated. However

most were held community-wise because of the different locations. *None of the women we met were members of any women's
organisation except a few in Ahmedabad who were members of SEWA.*

### General findings

#### Attacks on women

Women of both communities have been deeply affected. The
articulation of their feelings by widows or mothers who have
lost their sons/husbands was in the common language of grief,
whether they were Hindu or Muslim. The insecurity, the fear is
also common. However there is a qualitative difference in the
nature of attacks. The women of the majority community who
we met spoke of their family members being stabbed or killed by
bomb blasts. In residential areas where there was arson and loot,
the women categorically stated that they were not targeted or
physically attacked. There was one case of such an attack reported to us in Bhopal where two members of a family were
reportedly raped although we could not meet the victims.

Attacks on women, including sexual atrocities—stripping, rape
and burning, verbal abuse etc.,—took place more on women
from the minority community. In Bhopal, in two areas of the old
city, the women told us that the mobs shouting 'Bajrang Bali Ki
Jai', many of them in police uniform, surrounded the area. They
first asked the women and girl children to leave, demanding that
they hand over the males in the family including children. When
women refused they were physically assaulted, a few were
stripped, at least two were raped. In Ahmedabad where we
found the deepest communal polarisation, filthy sexist slogans
were written on the half-burnt walls of a few minority community houses. Women in a camp in the city recalled that they were
surrounded by a group of men who unzipped their trousers and
made obscene gestures. The women were rescued by the police.

*The delegation is in no doubt that whereas there may certainly be
unreported instances of sexual attacks on women of the majority community in these cities, the brunt of such atrocities was borne by women
of the minority community, the worst of such cases being in Surat. We
feel it is important to emphasise this point because we found a concerted
and deliberate attempt in all three cities to ignore or whitewash this
reality or 'balance' it by saying 'it happened on both sides'.*

## Women's reactions

In both Bhopal and Surat which have not witnessed communal violence before, the women were categorical in their condemnation of the violence and seemed totally bewildered about what had happened. In group discussions they kept asserting that there had never been any animosity, 'our children play together' they said. In Bhopal, a woman from the majority community whose husband and son were killed when they were returning from the shop they owned some distance away, said, 'We had no enemies. They used that road every day. I never ever felt any fear, but now I do.'

In all group discussions we asked women what had caused the riots. Usually there was a silence to begin with and then one of them would burst out 'that mandir-masjid issue . . .' 'It is all for "kursi", what have we got to do with it?' When asked what should be done, most women said 'anything to stop the violence'. But what? we asked. In four or five meetings including two in majority community areas they said 'build a hospital or dharmashala so that both communities can use it.' We found many instances both in Bhopal and Surat where women of different communities had saved each other.

In Ahmedabad we found a much deeper communal divide, symbolised by the main road in Bapu Nagar, an area of recurring riots which is referred to as the 'Hindustan-Pakistan' border. In many slum areas there had been virtually an exchange of population over the last eight years which have seen four major riots. Here many women of both communities spoke in the language of the fundamentalists of their respective communities. The most graphic example of the overriding distrust and suspicion of each other was when the delegation visited Shahpur, a mixed neighbourhood where seven children and two women of one family of Muslims had been trapped inside a house and burnt to death. About 50 yards away there is a colony of the majority community. The women here refused at first to discuss the incident, saying that none of them was present that day. However later they said, 'It is the Muslims who burnt the house thinking it belonged to Hindus because it was sold by the Hindu owners only two months ago. . . .' In fact the house was sold two years ago, and in any case the leader of the mob, a local BJP man, was identified and later arrested (some said he was arrested on different charges not related to this case but we could not verify this.) However, the women showed little sympathy for the victims.

Again, in Ahmedabad we met a group of Muslim women who said they will now teach their children to prepare to sacrifice their lives for Islam. In many areas, when we spoke to women of the majority community about the atrocities on women of the minority community, their reactions were rather sceptical. Most said they were unaware of any such thing. This could be partially true because the main source of information for the women seemed to be the fabrications put out by the 'rumour mill' but it could also point to a growing trend of a process of deeper communal division.

*We found no evidence of direct participation of women in the violence.* In Ahmedabad we were told of a woman, Saira Bano, daughter of Haji Bano who was apparently involved in 17 stabbing cases and is now in custody. We were unable to get any details. In Vijay Nagar, Surat, the minority community victims said that women also had thrown petrol bombs and acid bottles on them from the rooftops. However this seems unlikely because, according to their own statements, later verified by our visit to the area, most of the women of the majority community had been evacuated from the area before the violence started.

*Although it is not possible to generalise, the delegation found ample evidence of feelings of solidarity and harmony between women of the two communities and examples of courage in saving each other. However it would be suicidal for the women's movement to ignore the increasing influence of communal thinking among women which was also apparent in many of the discussions the delegation held.*

### Relief and rehabilitation

*Women who have been the most affected in the riots expressed the feeling, in all the three cities, that their needs are the least listened to.* Everywhere we heard the same refrain, 'officials come but they do not speak to us... they spoke to my son/father/husband... they do not listen to our problems, they say you are (illiterate) women what do you know ...' Many widowed women of the minority community are in the 'iddat' period and so do not meet people. *Secondly, relief itself had become a cause for further exploita-*

*tion, corruption, poisonous propaganda, with each side claiming that 'the other' had got more relief. . . 'The government gave their camps relief not ours'.*

As far as government measures were concerned we found that most of the widows we met in Bhopal had received the full compensation of Rs 220,000 partly in cash, partly in bonds. Their information about the bonds was however, very vague. In Ahmedabad and Surat the situation was bad. A cash payment of Rs 60,000 had been made but there were discrepancies in the remaining amount to be given in bonds. *Nobody knew either the exact amount due to them or which Government bonds they were to receive.* In not a single case have the bonds been given. *Moreover, in all three cities these payments have been given to only those whose husband's bodies have been identified.* Women who have been the most traumatised with their husband's or son's bodies burned beyond recognition have not received any compensation as there is no 'direct proof' of their husbands/sons being killed. The women have not even been told what 'proof' is required to get the compensation and therefore many of them are entirely dependent on relief handouts.

*Compensation cases are apparently being settled by some relatives of the women/community leaders and concerned officials. Most of the women are only partially informed of what has been given, none of them has signed a receipt,and the majority do not have clear ideas of the procedures involved.* In one widow's case, the compensation has been used by her adult son who does not live with her, to acquire an additional autorickshaw. The mother continues to stay in the relief camp run by a religious group, with her smaller children. Many cases of compensation to widows and mothers are held up because the bodies of their dead husbands and sons could not be identified to the satisfaction of the required procedure.

We met women in Bhopal who were also victims of the Carbide explosion and are thus doubly burdened. In Ahmedabad we met women who had barely recovered from the communal riots of 1989 only to be targeted again. We saw no evidence that the government was taking any special care in such cases. On the contrary in Bhopal we were told that all the sewing centres where the gas victims were employed have been closed. In Ahmedabad the women who had been victims two or three times said not a single official had visited their camp, and no 'survey' has taken place. Earlier, a highly competent social activist had informed us of the 'virtually foolproof' survey system of the District Administration.

Although forms for employment have been filled by many of the women who now have the full responsibility of the household, none had much hope that either they or a member of their family would be employed. All the women said that the officials avoid giving any firm answers. We raised this question with the officials in Bhopal. Their answer was revealing: 'Most of the women are illiterate and we do not have such posts. According to official figures, of the 138 families identified, only 21 persons are in employable age. Of them, only 8 have the required educational qualifications.' In other words, in official eyes the women who need employment most are neither eligible nor qualified — so much for the Prime Minister's declaration that all widows or one of their dependents who want employment would be provided jobs.

Scores of the women we met were self-employed or doing home-based work. All this has been destroyed in the riots. Tailors who lost clients' materials in the burning of their homes said not only was no one prepared to give them work but many were demanding a refund of the value of the material given. In Surat several of the minority community victims were from families which had invested lakhs of rupees in small units (powerlooms, dyeing, leather, garments etc.) and workshops in their residential premises, all of which has been destroyed.

Official assertions that needs and claims are being assessed are questioned by many victims, who say surveys, if done, were very perfunctory, and *assessment was limited to house damage only*. The maximum paid for house repair is Rs 5,000 going down to Rs 500. In many areas surveys for have still not been done. Compensation claims of lakhs for the income generating property destroyed are not even being processed.

### The role of government , police and communal organisations

There was nothing, 'spontaneous' about the riots. In most areas they were planned, motivated attacks on the minority community. The delegation saw evidence of Hindu houses and shops being marked with signs like 'This is a Hindu house', "This is Ram's shop' 'Jai Shri Ram' etc., in areas of mixed population where only Muslim houses were burnt. In Surat in many such areas the women and children of the majority community were 'evacuated' before the violence began, indicating the planning that went into the whole event.

. The role of the BJP-VHP Bajrang Dal combine was clear in the statements of the women 'They made us shout Jai Shri Ram'. 'They came shouting Bajrang Bali Ki Jai', 'They were all wearing Kesari [saffron] scarves' etc. In some cases in Bhopal and Ahmedabad the women named men who led the attacks. Most, however said they were attacked by 'outsiders whom we do not recognise'. But the slogans were the same everywhere. A young scheduled caste woman in Vijay Nagar in Surat who had hidden six people in her home, said she heard the mobs shouting 'Jai Shri Ram', '*Musalmano ko kato maro*' (kill the Muslims).

In two areas in Surat and one area in Bhopal we were told the BJP men had threatened Hindu families who tried to save Muslims that the 'same fate will befall you'. In one area in Surat many Muslim women had escaped the killings and destruction of their houses only because their 'Hindu *behnen*' (sisters) sheltered and later helped them to escape in saris, with bindis and *mangalsutras*. It was impossible to get an interview with the brave humanitarians. We did manage to hear a few whispers — 'it was a collective decision of many of us'. But as a large crowd pushed their way into the room, the women went silent. Several men became very vocal and offered information — which did not tally with what the Muslim women had told us earlier. Clear hints not to talk were given by an elderly gentleman and women clammed up. Clearly they were too scared of the consequences to even admit to an act of courage which saved members of 'the other side'. It was the campaign of hate for the last few years launched by the BJP combine that led to a situation where the mob committed acts of the most savage violence. The vocal patriarch, who had treated us to a great deal of sentimental nostalgia about his excellent relations with Muslims, (but he had not visited, even once, the bulldozed rubble just behind his house that had till a few weeks back been a secure Muslim mohalla) informed us in the end that 'everyone is BJP here'.

We also found ample evidence of the existence of fundamentalist Muslim groups particularly in Ahmedabad though their organisation and network cannot be compared in their reach, to the communalists of the majority community. In all the three cities the evening of the 6th of December was marked by celebration (*jashna manaya*) in some areas, on the destruction of the mosque. In Bhopal women reported that victory processions were taken out. On the 7th morning in all three cities, the call of the Babri Masjid Action Committee (BMAC) for a protest *bandh* saw groups of aggressive Muslim youth trying to forcibly shut down shops, leading to clashes, arson, loot and stray stabbing incidents by Hindus. Within a short time of the attacks a massive 'retaliation' started.

The ongoing process of criminalisation of politics provides an added dimension to increasing communal violence. Many criminal elements are reported to be working closely with communal organisations. Several names were mentioned to us —of persons with notorious criminal records, who were also leading men in politics and who were 'close to the CM' (Chief Minister), and so on.

The police in Bhopal, Ahmedabad and Surat were reported as being either nonresponsive, absent, mute spectators or actively conniving with the criminals. There was indiscriminate firing in many places. In one area, Allah Nagar, (Ahmedabad) the delegation was told of four cases where women were shot by the police. Two were killed. We met the other two survivors.

The worst atrocities in Surat took place from the afternoon of the 8th till the 9th, but the police did not intervene till the morning of the 9th when some victims were evacuated to safety. In Bhopal, according to many of our informants, it was a 'joint operation' by the Bajrang Dal and the police, or men in police uniforms. Everywhere we were told that a big section of the attackers were in 'uniform', but armed with swords, acid bottles, 'desi' guns, knives etc.,— not 'traditional' police weapons. These 'joint' gangs shot to kill and we saw scores of homes where doors and windows were scarred with bullet marks. It was only when the government was dismissed and the army called in that these men were not seen on the streets.

The delegation asked the Chief Secretary about action contemplated or taken against public officials for dereliction of duty. We were told that a judicial enquiry was on, and affected persons should submit affidavits to the Commission. According to the women, many of those against whom there was prima facie evidence had not been arrested.

### Planned rumours and the role of the media

As in most riot situations rumours were rife, particularly in majority community areas: 'They are coming', 'be prepared'. All of this created panic and insecurity. In two places stories were floated (prior to the attacks on women) that there had been mass rapes of Hindu women. In Bhopal, a local paper printed a story that 80 Hindu women had been raped. Another report said that inmates of a working women's hostel had been attacked and raped. The delegation visited the hostel, met the Warden and the residents who categorically condemned the story. They said they had sent a written denial to the paper concerned, but it was printed as a small item tucked away 'where few would read it'. In Surat, before the attack on Vijayanagar there was a similar rumour that 'scores of Hindu women were attacked'. A Muslim woman teacher told the delegation that in a peace committee meeting in her area on the morning of the 7th the Muslim members were told the story: 'This is what your people have done... everyone is angry.' Some time later, the area was attacked. In Ahmedabad before the second round of rioting in January, some papers highlighted an exceedingly inflammatory story of a Hindu family who had to flee Pakistan and come to Rajkot. The interview spoke of mass rapes of Hindu women, concerted attacks on Hindus all over Pakistan etc.

Circulating rumours of rapes of women seemed to be a common feature in the plan to inflame passions on the understanding that the *izzat* of the community is linked to that of its women. It is diabolical that totally fabricated reports of attacks on women were used as a reason and later justification for the worst atrocities on women themselves. Some of the local papers in all these cities highlighted all the attacks on Hindus, many in exaggerated forms, while the reality of the massive suffering of the minority community was underplayed. The impact of this type of biased reporting was to further inflame passions. *No action has been taken against any of those responsible for publishing such inflammatory reports.*

### Conclusion and recommendations

Despite the variations demonstrated in different neighbourhoods the women's accounts — unprompted and unrelated as they were — provide insights into some highly significant common patterns, that may provide a basis for future action by all anti-communal forces, including the state, the media and the women's movement. These are listed below.

## A. *Evidence of planning and long term aims in use of rumour-patterns in looting/arson and targeting of attacks*

Rumour was used subtly, not only to incite, but also to encourage terror, so that some people would flee their homes and resistance from either group would be less. In Bhopal, some of the fleeing was even brought on by officially sponsored evacuation in a few areas. This was followed by arson and looting of the evacuated homes.

Strangely enough, while TV sets and other consumer goods were looted — scooters, sewing machines, etc.,—items related to the family's livelihood, for example fabrics in home-based tailoring shops, yarn/looms in home-based workshops which were stored and kept were targeted for destruction, not looting. Compensation may assist the victims to obtain a new machine, but goods received from the customers cannot be replaced, so the chances of losing one's regular market become high. For the yarn makers and weavers of Surat, the Mahajans who provided the initial raw material, now destroyed, will place no further orders until there is full compensation for the loss of goods and potential markets.

This targeted attack on the livelihood of the victims suggests two aims: a) to promote a climate of hopelessness/despair encouraging them to quit the job and/or the place; and b) to enable someone else to occupy the vacant physical/economic space.

While the delegation came across ample evidence of despair and bewilderment, we were not able to gather enough information on the full extent of actual of future displacement of families/households/individuals.

Displacements have also been caused by death, disablement of one or more of adult members, and destruction of homes. Many were reported as having gone away to relatives, or to villages.

## Recommendation 1

We strongly urge collection of more authentic/reliable data on the households/individuals affected by such displacement, especially women and children to establish their present status, security and rehabilitation.

We are convinced that without this basic exercise, the wider objectives of relief and rehabilitation measures to restore public confidence in the credibility of the community and the state, and to defeat the strategies of the communal organisations (aided, often unthinkingly, by rumour mongers and irresponsible sections of the media) will not be achieved.

Since public confidence in the government machinery is particularly low at present, we recommend that these exercises be conducted by credible, independent research organisations, assisted by the state machinery.

Where judicial enquiry has been ordered — as in Bhopal — such investigations provide an invaluable assistance to the commissions. But the procedures of a judicial enquiry per se cannot obtain the kind of detailed information that we are advocating. On the other hand, a judicial enquiry that is carried out without the support of such dependable investigation could achieve results which are quite the opposite of what is required.

## B. *The role of the neighbourhood community*

This represents one of the most contradictory and confusing elements. On the one side we have vehement statements from the women of the shelter, succour and support they received from the neighbours belonging to the other community—*especially from the women*. They talk about established relationships, participation in each others' festivals, being schoolmates and playmates. At Bhopal the solidarity with the one woman who had saved them is so strong that they stand together to tell us: 'we want neither the Mosque nor the Mandir—build a hospital or an educational institution there — so that all can benefit.' At Ahmedabad, many women, victims of bullet wounds and other injuries, lost husbands or children and were *convinced* that this would not have happened if their erstwhile Hindu neighbours—mainly scheduled castes — had not been moved out of their area.

Yet in the same city—where apparently over the last few

years of riots, some amount of communal relocation of populations has taken place—we found very disturbing evidence of
growing alienation, polarisation, suspicion, and lack of communication between the groups. This provided ripe ground for
planted rumours to flourish, for example, on difference in the
compensation paid by the government to members of different
communities. Such religious separations also encourage *separate
relief arrangements*, for example by NGOs whose assistance is
apparently available only to members of their own community.
The women perceived the housing societies as at least partially
responsible for the increasing distance and suspicion between
the communities. Since the housing societies are now a fairly
common model adopted for urban developers in many growing
cities we feel it is imperative to investigate their potential for, not
actual contribution (even if unintended) to, aggravating communal and caste divisions.

**Recommendation 2**

We, therefore, recommend a careful investigation by an independent organisation, of the real role played by the housing
societies and other factors in promoting such dangerous reor-
dering of populations, and the techniques being used to widen
communication gaps between them.

### C. *Need for new model peace committees/ community organisations*

Mohalla-based peace committees, wherever they exist, are the
monopoly of men. The Chief Secretary, MP government, informed the delegation that they have decided to experiment
with *mohalla* committees drawn from both communities (a welcome move, however belated). But the administration has not
thought of calling on women to serve on these committees.

While our information on this matter is inadequate, the impression we got from the women's own perception was that the
neighbourhood leadership is that of the old style community with
leaders being patriarchal, authoritarian, and drawing legitimacy
from traditional sources which no longer command much influence in today's political scenario, and which are also susceptible
domination by anti-democratic, communal forces. While we did
find some small pockets where the assurance of security given by

such groups remained effective, in many other cases such assurances proved to be utterly meaningless. We also learnt of successful intimidation of neighbours who had tried to save people.

In the backdrop of the growing urban conglomerations and the utter failure of the local administration to manage crisis situations, a wider, more informed discussion needs to be initiated on the need for decentralisation and far wider people's participation at the grassroot level.

## Recommendation 3

In our opinion, such mechanisms (mohalla/ward committees) if they are to be meaningful in today's context must be genuinely representative of the neighbourhood, and they must be visible and accountable. The participation of women, youth, as well as various communities on such bodies would be thus far more constructive.

## D. *Communication, rehabilitation, and administration of justice: special problems of women.*

Whether as victims of undeserved tragedies, or as humane neighbours, the women shared the fate of being second class citizens. *They are not informed of their rights or responsibilities as recipients of compensation, as surviving members of families which have lost their male heads, or as responsible citizens in restoring normalcy.*

The government performs its responsibility of communication through gazette notification and newspapers, and expects all concerned parties to know what they are expected to do. Not one of the nearly 100 women that we met in different mohallas in Bhopal was aware that a judicial enquiry had been constituted, that affected individuals/groups were supposed to file affidavits before the judge by a certain date; or that pending the judicial enquiry, no action would be intiated by the government against any erring officials. Some of the women we met in Bhopal had, during the destruction of their homes, lost their pass books for their regular remittances as victims of the gas disaster. They were not aware that the government was issuing duplicate pass books in such cases.

We appreciated the offer of the Additional Chief Secretary, MP, that if someone brought such cases to him, he would see to it that they were attended to by the concerned officials. But this is no solution to such a major problem. Where women, especially uneducated or illiterate women are the most concerned, or affected group, an effective system of communication has to be instituted.

## Recommendation 4

Pending more permanent arrangements, senior government officials, flanked by the multiple concerned agencies whose cooperation is necessary to complete 'processing' of a case, must hold special meetings with women affected by the riots and explain to them in clear terms the procedures necessary, and give them names of the officers they must reach and so on.

Local women's organisations, educational institutions, and individuals whose secular and humanitarian credentials are beyond dispute can help in making these efforts successful and in restoring public confidence, in empowering and reassuring the women who are now in despair; and in identifying potential leaders from among them for inclusion in the mohalla committees that we recommend. They do exist: we were able to spot several even during our short visit.

## E. *Traumatised children: need for special care*

Children who are witnesses to and victims of acts of violence against themselves, their families, neighbours and friends require very special care according to specialists. We found no evidence of such arrangements in any one of these three cities. One misguided relative is even teaching a little toddler to repeat like a catechism how his parents had been attacked, killed, by whom, etc.

The studies that we have suggested, should provide adequate data to consider and design specialised training to those responsible for caring for such children, be they relatives, or neighbours or philanthropic organisations.

We would like to insist that it is a common responsibility for our society to supplement mere physical care in the case of these children with some specialised attention to assist their recovery instead of leaving their future to accident or chance, which seldom plays a benign role in such cases.

## F. *Need for political education: recommendation to women's organisations*

Women's vulnerability and powerlessness have been enhanced by their lack of political education, consciousness, and participation. Particularly in the context of Ahmedabad which has several committed women's organisations, the danger of this neglect needs to be underscored. We hesitate to generalise on this issue, but our limited interviews did show that even the most committed work among vulnerable sections of women is not capable of enabling such women to liberate themselves from the pressures of divisive identity politics, without a conscious direction to confront this type of politics which is so inimical to women's rights and the movement for equality.

## G. *Punishment of criminals*

As far as punishing of culprits, including the involved public servants, is concerned, the women have no expectation of obtaining justice. Given the present dismal record in this regard, the delegation shares this perception. However as responsible citizens we strongly urge the government to expedite the due process of law in all such cases instead of obstructing it, if it is to win back its credibility in the eyes of the women of this nation.

Detailed reports on each of the cities visited, follow.

## BHOPAL

The joint team of national women's organisations visited Bhopal on 16 February 1993. Our specific aim was to meet with and interview women in the worst affected areas of Bhopal and record their experiences, sufferings and perceptions of the disaster that befell them in the post-demolition communal frenzy that engulfed their city for well over ten days.

The areas visited were: Kainchi Chola (Old Bhopal), Kainchi Chola New Block, Ammunagar, Indiranagar, Rajiv Nagar, Tila Jamalpur, Ward II, Acharya Narender Dev Nagar and the Working Women's Hostel situated in the posh colony surrounding the Circuit House. Some areas were mixed, some largely Muslim and others mainly Hindu. The team met and spoke to well over 150 women, Hindus and Muslims, in groups, individually, in the family, in their houses, and on the streets; about 50 were interviewed in detail.

The suffering of women in a period of senseless communal violence, arson, loot and terror is often disposed of in one sentence: that women and children are the worst victims. What barbarities they witnessed, how deep were the wounds inflicted on them, what role they played in their moments of agony, remains unexpressed. The team was keen to record women's testimonies regarding what they actually experienced, their present situation and reactions to what had happened, and to assess their overall situation and needs.

Some aspects of the communal holocaust that swept through many parts of Bhopal—a city that had never experienced communal riots before, not even during the partition — came through clearly in our interviews with the women.

* The demolition of Babri Masjid was received by a section of the minority community with a deep sense of shock and humiliation. Ateeranbi of Kainchi Chola kept repeating 'What have we done to see these dark days?' The communal divide that the Ayodhya tragedy caused was expressed by Wahi Dabi and others 'We have lived in peace with Hindus, but the mohalla people themselves started the attack.'

* The news of vandalism in Ayodhya arrived in Bhopal when the memory was of the demolition that the BJP government had carried out was still fresh: bulldozers had been used to raze hutments to the ground and nearly 20,000 people (mostly poor and belonging to the minority community—among them many gas victims who were just beginning their life anew) had been displaced.

* The loss suffered by the majority community by way of arson and loot was mainly on December 7, and lives were lost through stabbings. Saroj Kumari's husband Santosh was stabbed while returning home. Theirs was a court marriage and she expressed fears that her mother-in-law, who had not approved of her son's marriage with Saroj, would not allow her to keep the compensation received. Haridevi's husband Radha Kishan, son Dev Anand and his uncle Mohandas were killed at Indiranagar at 11.00 a.m. as they were returning home after closing their shop. A crowd of about 50 men had attacked them.

* The minority community as a whole was subjected to

double danger—first at the hands of the Bajrang Dal and RSS, and then at the hands of the police, the two often acting in collusion. In some areas the women we spoke to said the two were indistinguishable. 'They were all wearing police uniforms', and were led by a policeman named Shyam, whose house, adorned with a huge BJP election symbol, was pointed out to us. Zetoonbi's husband was sleeping when Shyam brought four 'policemen' into the house and shot him. Because of the curfew the body lay in the house for three days. She has preserved the bloodstained quilt within which the body lay wrapped during those days. Rehana Sultan, a widow, said, 'They came and killed my son, Anees. I cannot say whether they were policemen or those men in police uniform.' Rafiqua bi's husband Abdul Aziz was asked to come to the police station, and he never returned. She has no idea of his whereabouts, or if his is one of the many unidentified bodies that were burnt. In Indiranagar women also complained that the police was asking the attackers to loot.

They pointed out the rooftops where 'those men in police uniforms' had collected and from where they pelted stones, threw petrol bombs, shouting and abusing all the while, and the police force just stood by.

* Women in some areas were subjected to sexual assault. At Acharya Narendra Dev Nagar women were tortured, molested, raped and then burnt to death. Shakila's jhuggi was burnt, when she ran out she was stoned, then caught, stripped naked and raped, but, said Anwar Jahan, 'Shakila jumped into the fire to save herself the shame.' Roshan was stripped and raped but has gone away to Bihar. Afsana Khatun, eight months pregnant, was burnt with acid, stripped and attacked with swords. Seventy five year old Rehmatbi's feet were chopped off and her son done to death before her eyes. *They refused to disclose any details of the attacks on young women who were living there for fear of ostracism or reprisal that they might face.*

* It was also at Acharya Narendra Dev Nagar that we met Kamlesh Sharma, who had given protection to 40 members of the minority community, hiding them in her house, despite threats to her family, earning the former's eternal gratitude. It was the Muslim women who called her in to meet us and the solidarity between all of them forged during the period of terror

was the one heart warming, positive memory that we brought back from Bhopal.

* In all the areas that the team visited, except Kainchi Chola (old Bhopal), the general perception was that armed, well organised bands of attackers came from outside and did not belong to the area.

* Rumours were spread systematically to fuel the fires of hate and revenge. To check on the rumour that had even made its way to the print media, that the girls in the working women's hostel had been kidnapped, raped and detained in a mosque, the team visited the hostel, and interviewed the warden and the girls. They all categorically denied that any such incident had taken place. The warden said that since the hostel was located in an elite area where high government officials resided, the security was tight and life normal and secure. The girls said they had walked around the area even during curfew. In this hostel too, the young residents, like the women in Acharya Narendra Dev Nagar, roundly declared their objection to building either a mandir or a masjid at Ayodhya. Their views were expressed in identical language with the uneducated women of AND Nagar; 'build a hospital, a college or something that *all groups* can use'.

* In the areas where large scale arson and loot had taken place, the sum of Rs 5,000 dispensed as compensation was totally inadequate. Many women sew clothes to earn a living. Along with their belongings the cloth received from the customers was also burnt. They are losing customers because they cannot make good the losses suffered by those whose cloth too was burnt.

Women whose husbands or sons were killed and then burnt have not received any compensation, for their dead are declared as 'missing' persons and there is no proof that they actually died in the riots.

* In many cases when fires broke out people rushed out of their houses to put out the fire but police arrested them or shot at them.

* The problem of economic rehabilitation of women who have not, till now, been engaged in any earning activity is apparently not being addressed at all. The Prime Minister had announced that either a woman or man from such households would be provided employment. But the delegation's discussion with the Chief Secretary and the Additional Chief Secretary revealed the

hollowness of such promises. Out of 138 households who came within this category, only 21 members were said to belong to the 'employable' age group. Only eight out of them fulfilled the required educational qualification for government employment.

\* On enquiring into the conduct of errant or biased public servants, the two officials informed the delegation that with the appointment of a judicial enquiry, the matter had become 'subjudice'. The Commission had already notified dates for submission of affidavits by all affected parties. No special methods had been initiated to ensure that such communications reached the affected women, especially the poor and uneducated ones.

\* The Additional Chief Secretary also informed us that joint peace committees (of the two communities) were being formed in all mohallas. To our question whether they contained any women, he was rather nonplussed, 'We did not consider women as a separate sectoral interest, but this can certainly be considered.'

It is clear that despite all that is known about women's illiteracy, lack of information and other handicaps, and the fact that their vulnerability is always a central issue in communal riots, no thought had been given to dealing with them directly. While we appreciated the Additional Chief Secretary's offer that individual cases referred to him would be passed on to concerned officials for expeditious dealing, it was painful to realise that despite the frequency of public disorders, and riots in particular, the governmental system was still so ill-equipped and insensitive to the special needs of women victims of such crises.

## AHMEDABAD

In Ahmedabad on February 17, the team visited Gomatipur, Shastri Nagar, Bapu Nagar, Aman Chowk Camp, Jihwarnagar, Sah Alam, Millat Nagar, Shahpur and Allah Nagar. Both Hindu and Muslim women collected in much larger groups in Ahmedabad and the team was able to meet about 175 women. The number of women interviewed exceeded 50.

\* Ahmedabad has experienced riots repeatedly in the last decade. The communal divide is much deeper than in many other places. Over the years communities have been relocated and ghettoised. Haji Gaffar Ki Chali earlier had a mixed population but harijans moved out and now it is entirely a Muslim mohalla (area). Bapu Nagar has two very distinct areas where the two communities face each other with a road in between referred to locally as the Hindustan-Pakistan border.

The relocation of population along religious/communal/caste lines posed a whole range of questions. Who decided on this; was it a deliberate policy, or accidental? Many of the Muslim women we met were vehement in their rejection and condemnation of this measure. Halima Bi, who lost her mechanic husband — killed by a boy from the neighbourhood whom she knew — was vehement that their present plight was a direct consequence of the fact that harijans had moved out from the mohalla five years ago. 'They were our neighbours and friends. Many of us did the same work. The Society [housing society] moved them out. After that the Hindus started attacking us. Now we do not speak to the Hindus.'

Another was equally vehement: 'I grew up among, and with harijans in the village, and after I came here. I played with them, we celebrated all festivals together, Why were we separated and left isolated? The Society has disrupted our lives — and left us unprotected.'

This mysterious malignant influence — of the Society — which separated and relocated people over the last few years, turned out to be that of housing societies. The one referred to by the women we have quoted is the Santosh Nagar society. For a working/lower middle class neighbourhood, this building complex is strongly fortified and enclosed by high iron railings and gates, with a police camp across the road.

We do not know how many such societies there are, how they are financed, whether they have mushroomed only to make a profit out of people's craving to *own* a house, however cramped, or whether they only represent the standard, much advocated self-financing solution for urban housing shortages familiar to urban development specialists. The fact remains that in both Ahmedabad and Surat women riot victims spoke of these housing societies as being responsible for causing isolation, suspicion and hostility between different communities. The most classic (and tragic) case is possibly that of Bapu Nagar, now divided into several isolated and hostile groups, living within a stone's throw of each other.

Though a mixed locality, Bapu Nagar is the worst affected area of the city and deeply polarised. Mukta Behn spoke about the death of her son, Nanu, who was shot in Arban Nagar. Nilima Birendra Roy said she lived in constant fear of stoning from across the road. She could not sleep at night as she lived alone, and fearsome noises disturbed her. She was, however, even more disturbed by reports that 'those people' (i.e. the Muslims) 'had received far more'. She was obviously referring to compensation. But had she lost anyone or anything to qualify for compensation? No. Her two daughters are married and do not live with her. She had spotted a Bengali in the delegation and hoped for more sympathy from her, instead of difficult questions. Kamla Behn, a social worker of the area demanded that police should force bolt the doors that opened towards their side of the area.

* Many of the women gathered there perceived the notorious liquor dealer and Mafia lord, Latif, who was allegedly close to the Chief Minister as the real mischief-maker in the city. Repeated mention by different groups of these high profile political bosses who are also known to be criminals raised another question in our minds. Stereotypes are known to contribute greatly to racial, ethnic, cultural and religious tensions in other parts of the world. Has something similar been happening here? Have these high profile criminal characters come to symbolise a stereotype of 'the other' community, especially as they are politically powerful and generally believed to be invulnerable?

* Among the minority community, feelings of insecurity still prevail. In some areas people have not returned to their homes. Women who had collected at the Aman Chowk Camp, which is in the process of being dismantled, had come from Bapunagar, Jumma Dhobi ki Chal, Indira Garib Nagar, Arban Nagar, Sanjay Nagar etc., and they have not gone back to their homes, either because the homes are burnt, empty or unsafe. Many of the inmates are veterans of former riots. Mumtaz, whose age we can only guess at (as she has obviously aged before her time) is a broken woman: she lost one son (a rickshaw puller) in 1985, another in 1987 and her husband, a mill worker, in 1993. Her home was burnt twice, after looting. She is in fact homeless. There is another son, who does not live with her. He has, however, been very efficient in collecting the Rs 20,000, paid by the government as compensation, on his mother's behalf, and investing it promptly in buying a second autorickshaw. No one

from the government has of course talked to Mumtaz herself — she was in mourning for the *iddat* period.

Rabeya Bibi, an *agarbatti* worker, and a member of SEWA, is clear, consistent and articulate in her testimony. Her husband was killed in the 1985 riots. She herself was 'cut up' and her right arm was burnt by acid. She spent a year in hospital recovering, while several other women neighbours nursed her baby. She is still reasonably young and supports five children. Police came to her jhuggi on 8 January, asking her to vacate her home—'We can't protect you'. A woman Police Inspector (Rabeya knows the name) said, 'We don't want Muslims here, why don't you go away? After all wasn't that why the country was divided?'

Rabeya also told us that no 'survey' had been done in the camp and pointed out the other women who had lost everything, but who were helping to look after her own children. In an unemotional voice she said that the crowds attacking their colony were accompanied by policemen and Bajrang Dal activists.

We collected several such stories from 20 other women at the camp. Government assistance to this camp has now stopped. A Muslim philanthropic group  continues to run it, as they realise the women are not able to go home.

\* Complaints about inaction and partisan behaviour of the police were widespread. In Gomatipur, Mumtaz Bibi, who lay on a charpoy, unable to move, said she was shot by the police when she tried to bring in her children when disturbances broke out. Zarina, aged 25, who is left with the burden of bringing up five children (one her own and four of her husband's from his first wife) said the police caught her husband and killed him before her own eyes. Abida Bibi said that when the stoning started she and her children were watching television. She tried to send the children to safety to her brother's house but police entered and started shooting. They even shot into the house. A wounded man, Wahid, fell in the doorway. She tried to pick him up, just then a bullet pierced through her leg. Women of Gomatipur and Shastrinagar named BJP leader Bansi Maharaj and his nephew Dinesh as organisers of the attacks. The nexus between the communalists and social criminals was emphasised again and again by the women.

\* The team did not come across any cases of rape in any of the areas it visited in Ahmedabad. However, there were shocking tales of extremely obscene behaviour of the crowds that attacked and came shouting 'Bajrang Bali ki Jai'. They made indecent and sexually suggestive gestures and as Nadira Bibi said *'Nangi galian bolte the'* (they were shouting obscenities). Some opened their trousers/shorts and shouted to the women to come out.

\* In Ahmedabad riots are referred to as *'toofan'* (storm). When storms become endemic, they may destroy more than houses and people. They may even erode or weaken years of constructive committed work by dedicated people who believe in a cause.

Ahmedabad, during the last two decades, has been one of the critical centres of the women's movement, and the birthplace of the most famous organisation of poor, informal sector working women, whose dynamism and empowerment has inspired hundreds of others—not only in India, but abroad. The city also has a large number of committed women's organisations, some with hoary traditions of social service to all in distress—irrespective of community conventions, or religion/caste norms.

In such a city polarisation of even relief operations by separate groups left us shocked and bewildered. Our information is very limited, and we had no opportunity for dialogue with these sister organisations whose work has been the source of great pride and inspiration for many of us.

In one of the worst incidents, in Shahpur—a mixed neighbourhood—nine members of the same family (assembled for a wedding), seven of them children, were trapped inside a burning house, and killed. Women from some neighbouring houses (one of them said she worked for a women's organisation) first professed total ignorance about the event. Later one of them said that the house had been burnt by Muslims, mistaking it for a Hindu house. She also admitted that no one from their own households had gone to offer condolences afterwards. She herself was too preoccupied with her sick husband.

A number of young women were standing by. Their silence was more eloquent than the older woman's prolonged effort to justify her own inaction.

A few other houses were also burnt in the same neighbourhood—including one where the ill-fated wedding was to take place, and the one next door, which belonged to the local BJP leader. Fortunately no one was killed in these. However, the members of five harijan households left the neighbourhood out of fear, for which no other explanation was forthcoming.

There are other complicating factors. Some Muslim members of Shahpur own an explosives factory, where the majority of workers are harijans. Apparently, an accident in that factory some time earlier had contributed to the widening gap between the two communities. Perhaps the growing prosperity of a few Muslim households — from garment exports and other trades— also contributed to the division. It is possible that the camaraderie of poor harijans and Muslims, looked back on with such nostalgia by many, has been disappearing in the vortex of economically upward mobility and competition for socio-political status and power. But the issue that women's organisations must face —especially all those who work for the empowerment of the marginalised — is about their own role in preparing their members to withstand the *toofan* and its contributory forces.

### SURAT

The delegation visited Surat on 18 February.

### *Vijay Nagar II: night of terror*

We met Jamila bi, eight months pregnant, in the Haji A M Lockhart and Dr A M Mulla Sarvajanik Hospital. She had witnessed the killing of her husband and four children. Her body bore the ugly marks of violence. She was found unconscious on the morning of the 8th and brought to the hospital, her mind a blank. She could not even remember her name. As we moved out of her room, she tried to follow us with a bundle of clothes on her head. 'Where are you going Jamila?' '*Kahinbhi*' (wherever . . .) she answered.

Anwari Begum (19 years) who died in the same hospital a week earlier had come from Assam only a few months ago, and was married to an Imam in Vijay Nagar II. Anwari told people in the hospital that her husband was hanged from the fan, then cut into pieces and burnt. She was dragged out from an inside room, stripped and raped, also burnt and left for dead. She was brought to the hospital with 80 per cent burns.

The delegation met 15 women from Vijay Nagar II and eight children. This is a predominantly middle class/lower middle class neighbourhood with Muslim houses surrounded on all sides by the majority community. In the middle there is a big open field with a deep pit on one side for sewage repairs. We were told that many burnt bodies were thrown into the pit and covered up. Most of the houses have at least two stories, some have more.

The area was attacked by big mobs of 'outsiders' identified by the women. The electricity was cut off. But some time in the evening, from a multistoried building in a neighbouring area, big flashlights were put on. All the women referred to these as 'focus' lights. We asked whether they knew about a videotape being used. They all said they had only heard about it later. At the time they did not know. In fact nobody we met could confirm the report.

The official count of those killed in Vijay Nagar II is 38. There was no break-up available of men, women and children. However, we were told that the police had 150 photographs of unidentified bodies, many burnt beyond recognition, including one of a woman with two children clinging to her.

When the delegation visited Vijay Nagar II, there was not a single Muslim woman there. We met them in other areas. Hafiza bi has lost her two sons, two daughters-in-law, a granddaughter and grandson. She was unable to speak, her voice choked, her eyes filled with never-ending tears. The surviving daughter-in-law, Asiya, told us:

> We heard there was trouble in the city on the 7th. Our neighbouring colony people came and told us 'don't worry, nothing will happen here'. We decided not to leave. At that time the whole family was there—three brothers (including my husband) their wives, myself and all our children. Then we heard that 300-400 men from Varacha Road had come and were outside the colony. We were very scared. But again our neighbours came and said nothing would happen. We spent the night in fear. The next morning a group of people from the neighbouring colony came and said to our people: take down the loud speaker from the masjid, because people from outside may see it and attack. At about 10 a.m, a young man (Muslim) came in a Maruti car to take

his sister away. He was driving away fast. At the edge of the colony he was stopped and his car searched, nothing was found. But a little distance away the car was attacked. I do not know what happened to them. My husband Zakaria, brother-in-law Yahya and a friend Vasudev who lived near us went to the neighbouring colonies to find out the position. They came back with assurances. The atmosphere was very tense. We were scared but the children were hungry so we had to cook and feed them. In the afternoon our colony was attacked. There was shouting and heavy stoning. We all went up to my sister-in-law's room on the 4th storey. There were people running here and there. We heard screaming. It was dark, the electricity had been cut. We could smell things burning. So we decided to somehow try and escape. We all ran across the field to a big empty building. Many women, children and men were running, trying to escape. Some men caught me and tore off my clothes. They stripped me. I started screaming and fighting and somehow I escaped. My sister-in-law Zarina and Mumtaz were caught. My neice Noor Jahan, only 14 years old, was also caught. *They could not escape. They were stopped and raped, then burnt to death. The children saw it.* A girl called Y gave me her dupatta to cover myself. But later she was also caught, and raped. . .my brothers-in-law, Yahya, Suleman and also Mukhtar were killed and burnt . . .only my husband escaped . . .

Two children, a boy and girl, had hidden in a corner of the open field and escaped attention. Zarina's daughters (12, 7 and 5 years) were witnesses to their parents' death. 'They caught my mother, my brother fell to the ground ...my little sister was clinging to her. They hit her with a sword and she fell to the ground bleeding . . . they took my mother's clothes off and threw her on the ground . . .she was screaming, somebody took me away.' The 12-year old girl was also stopped.

I started screaming and crying please let me go, let me go. . . A man took pity on me. He said go quickly, run away. I ran to a house (Hindu). The lady saw me and started crying. She said what have they done to you .. .

don't worry now you are safe. She gave me clothes and food and the next day I left with the police.

Zahida Bano said that her mother, her sister, her father and brother were all dragged outside. Zahida hid herself in a small toilet at the back of the house with her two younger siblings. After a few hours she heard a scratching at the door and heard a faint voice. It was her half-conscious, bleeding mother who had been hacked and left for dead by her attackers. Zahida pulled her in, covered her and hid her under the charpoy. Three times a mob came raging into the house, but in the darkness they missed her. Later the mob came outside and poured kerosene and set the house on fire. Zahida says she started screaming for help, when 'some Hindus' came and found her, the children and her injured mother and took them away to a house in a neighbouring area.

A group of five women, five men and eight children took shelter in a tiny kitchen. The baby kept screaming till the de-spairing parents locked her up in a refrigerator (the electricity was off) for three hours.

These are only a few samples of the horror stories that we heard. Many of the women said that they had seen police jeeps in the area, but nowhere did the police intervene. It was only after the worst was over that the police took the survivors out of the area. There was only one case where a woman expressed her gratitude to the police for having saved her child and bringing him to the camp, where they all moved later.

The case of Vijaynagar symbolises many issues that disturbed us deeply. Careful planning of the carnage was evident. Non-Muslim houses had been marked with bold letters and slogans 'Jai Sri Ram', 'Hindu no Makan'. The women said some persons came to check ration cards a day or two earler—that was un-doubtedly when the identification was done. Hindu families were 'evacuated' on the 7th—most of the women we met in the evening blandly told us they were 'away'. One exception was Shanta Behn, a harijan woman who sheltered several fleeing women. Her husband was away and she paid no heed to the terror tactics of the rampaging mobs: 'anyone who shelters will suffer the same fate'. Finally, she gave the women saris to escape in. All the saris had been returned, she told us. The housing society work was evident here too. Some complexes had the crescent and the star, others had a Ganesh, Lakshmi or Shiva etched on the frontage of houses. We found most of the tenants in the houses owned by Muslims were Hindus. In one house the women said they had all been 'away' during those days and could tell us nothing. However, the desire to talk was strong — and one middle-aged woman, very anxious to tell us about her ailments (blood pressure, aches and pains) inadvertently let slip that she had sent for her daughter and son-in-law to come and occupy one of the other apartments in the same house which was now 'vacant'. We could not help wondering if this had been done with the owner's consent, or was this the beginning of a takeover ? Since when had it been vacant anyway?

## A different kind of fear

The terrorising of members of the majority community who wanted to or did give shelter to riot-victims was found in another area in Surat. The delegation met 14 middle class Muslim women of Katar Gaon Masjid Mohalla, where 35 Muslim houses —surrounded by the houses of the majority—were burnt, bulldozed and reduced to rubble. On the 7th evening this area was surrounded by armed mobs. The people rushed out, some separately, some in groups. Many doors were locked to them. But some gave them shelter. One of the women, an elderly widow, disclosed to the delegation in detail how 'Hindu sisters' had kept some of them for over 24 hours and given them 'saris and bindis and *magalsutras*' so that they could escape. 'Later when we went to return the clothes, they were scared. They said, don't come back because we have been threatened.'

The delegation decided to visit the area. The first building we saw was a Youth Club office with a huge lotus painted on the front door and BJP slogans on the walls. Just a hundred yards away were the destroyed Muslim homes. We were told by the young men at the 'Club', all quite belligerent, that no such incident of 'help' had taken place and we would not be able to find even a single such woman. We went into the area on our own and were directed to Gandhi Chowk. We met some women who were very helpful and said yes, many people took shelter in this area. Just as we were beginning to get the details, an elderly man rushed in along with four or five young men, and denied that any such help had been given. They also refused to let us videotape the discussion. 'Yes some people came, what could we do? We sent some to a mandir which is under construction, it has no walls. After half an hour, we went and told them "What is the use of your staying here as you are unprotected and if they see you, there are no stairs even for you to come down".'

This statement contradicted the Muslim women's account— that the '*behnen*' had thought of the mandir, but had discarded the idea as unsafe. Then one of the men also said, 'A man who gave shelter was killed in Phulysara.' The five women who had initially agreed to talk to us sat silent throughout this discussion. Our statements about the feeling of gratitude expressed by the victims who had been sheltered brought forth some sparks of emotion—a slight smile, a few glowing eyes, but no voice. By this time another woman had walked in and had sat down next to them. After listening to the conversation she said, 'I am a BJP worker.' Immediately all the men said, 'We are all BJP here.' We asked, 'Does that make you ashamed that you saved Muslims?' 'It was not us,' the elderly man said, 'It was the compounder a few homes away and . . . in that area.' We did not have the time to go look for 'the compounder' but we did conclude that this was a different kind of fear, the fear of being punished for saving the other', punished like the man in Phulysara.

One important point made by the Muslim women in the morning and the reluctant men in the evening was that the police did not come to the area till the 10th, that is, three days after the mob had burned and looted the 35 homes.

The delegation met a group of women residents of Triveni Nagar. They said that the propaganda for the municipal corporation election (scheduled for January) was on. In early December a group of BJP men had come to their homes and after giving them 'slips', warned them against taking 'slips' from the Congress. These same men came on the 8th of December and assured the Muslims that no harm would come to them. Ahmedi Begum said:

> On the 9th I saw with my own eyes the same men leading a group who were shouting slogans and who started heavy stone throwing. The UP Muslims were

killed. The BJP men came and took away a Marathi Hindu family who lived next door. Half an hour later they burnt our homes. I ran out from the back door and escaped. My three year old son was so scared he did not utter a word for weeks. Even now he cries at night in his sleep . . .

We met other groups of women from Nanpura, Hidayatnagar and Rajiv Nagar. In Nanpura, which is an area dominated by families involved in the fishing trade, locally known as 'Maachi Jaat' there had been no trouble in decades. Members of the two communities met and peace was maintained. Then, on January 17, a young man of the Maachi community was killed by a group of Muslim youth. After his funeral procession, the mobs attacked the Muslim area. Five people were killed including a woman, Setun Bibi, who was burned to death.

Surat has had no history of riots since 1927. The incidents started on 7 December when a group of Muslims reportedly led by a Mr Pardewala of the Dalit Muslim Suraksha Sangh tried to enforce the bandh call given by the Babri Masjid Action Committee. There were some clashes. A popular Saurashtrian police officer was badly injured. Rumours were also floated about the rape of Saurashtrian women. This seemed to be a design to make a section of the community active participants in the carnage and devastation that followed.

# Interviews with Women

## S ANITHA, MANISHA, VASUDHA, KAVITHA

While working on a research paper on 'Women and the BJP-RSS-VHP' we met prominent members of the women's wings of these organisations and put a number of questions to them. As students it was easier for us to elicit frank and often unguarded responses. Mridula Sinha (Secretary General of the Mahila Morcha of the BJP) was extremely cautious due to the furore that her earlier remarks on dowry had caused. Asha Sharma of the Rashtriya Sevika Samiti, though seemingly liberal on issues of property and education for women, came up with startling remarks on sati. However, we had a very fruitful and uninhibited five hour session with Krishna Sharma (women's wing, VHP); often we had to check ourselves from reacting to the definite note of aggression that dominated the conversation.

## MRIDULA SINHA
Secretary General, BJP Mahila Morcha

Q. *In earlier statements you were reported to have endorsed dowry - could you elaborate?*

A. The press has misrepresented my position. The Mahila Morcha of the BJP has always agitated against dowry deaths and early marriage and has encouraged women's education. In ancient India women were accorded great respect. It was Muslim invasion that restricted women to the domestic role.

Q.  *What role do you see for a woman, in the family?*

A.  She is mainly responsible for child rearing. She should, if need be, take up three-four hour jobs (like teaching) so that she can devote enough time to her family. It is her adjustment that can keep the family united.

## ASHA SHARMA
Rashtriya Sevika Samiti

Q.  *What are the activities of the Rashtriya Sevika Samiti?*

A.  Its activities are geared towards fostering nationalism as well as developing talent. The former is done through poetry, songs and biographies of great women like Rani Lakshmibai, Ahilyabai Holkar . . .

Q. *Do you also include Razia Sultan?*

A.  . . . and the latter, through poetry and songs. We set up special camps for the physical training of women where, among other things, we teach them driving and shooting.

Q. *What is your stand on women's education?*

A.  We encourage women's education; as an educated mother she will be better equipped to inculcate the right values in her children—the values of nationalism and pride in Indian culture. We are against the concept of a 'modern woman' as she epitomises selfishness.

We teach women to give first priority to the family—a career should be taken up only in case of financial need and should be subject to the approval of the family. There is a natural division of labour—women, being more sensitive, should take care of children. Everything else is secondary.

Q.  *Should the men not share the burden of home making?*

A.  They are not equipped for this task. Only a woman has the sensitivity to keep the family together.

Q. *What are your views on sati?*

A.  Sati is derived from the word *satitva* which means 'purity of mind and the body' and the willingness of a woman to give supreme sacrifice to save this purity—as in the case of self immolation during the partition riots.

We draw our lesson from Sita who remained pure even in Lanka, brought up her children in spite of Rama's abandonment and refused the offer of a second *agni pariksha* [trial by fire].

*Q. Do you endorse Roop Kanwar's sati?*

A.  That was not a voluntary sati. This is why we encourage physical training of women.

*Q.  How do you see the mobilisation of women in the demolition of the Babri Masjid?*

A.  What masjid? There was no masjid there. It was a symbol of humiliation which was removed to safeguard the self respect of the Hindus. As far as women are concerned, they have always come forward in times of crisis.

KRISHNA SHARMA
Women's Wing, Vishwa Hindu Parishad

*Q. What is the role of the schools run by the VHP?*

A.  During the children's formative years, we concentrate on Dharmic [religious] studies — Gayatri *mantra*, Hanuman *chaleesa*, etc. This is followed by regular formal education.

A sense of community is imbibed by celebrating festivals like Holi, Shivaji Jayanti and Maharana Pratap Jayanti. We also encourage our students to follow purely Indian culture.

*Q. What do you mean by 'purely Indian culture'?*

A.  The culture that has prevailed since aeons—the way of life that is followed by the majority. Hindu dharma is not just Hindu religion; it assimilates the larger Indian consciousness.

*Q.  Is your school open to girls?*

A. Yes, we encourage women to study.

*Q.  Do you follow the same pattern of education for boys and girls?*

A.  We also teach women to demand less—when women demand more, it leads their menfolk to corruption. A man may be satisfied with two sets of clothes but women will desire a dozen saris. Overall, we have a similar pattern of education. Women, sants and politicians make a nation—but it is women who give birth to sants and politicians. Ram's greatness was because of Sita, Kaushalya and Kaikei. Ram took Kaikei into confidence and requested her to ask for the two boons so that he could go in to exile to destroy Ravan. It was Kaikei's sacrifice that enabled Ram to accomplish his mission. A happy life is not possible unless women compromise and are willing to sacrifice.

*Q.  Why can't men sacrifice or compromise?*

A.  They can, but it comes more easily to women because they are more emotional. This is what happened in Vedic times.

[At this point she asked our names to find out which community we belonged to. After this she launched into an anti-Muslim tirade and held the Muslim invasion responsible for the deteriorating condition of women.]

... In Kashmir, there is parading of naked (Hindu) women [she was unable to substantiate this with factual information].

If a girl who has been raped commits suicide, will her brother not take revenge? Hindus must make sure that they are feared by others. We have to prove our mettle. If they rape 10-15 of our women, we must also rape a few to show them that we are no less.

Muslims have four wives and can even marry within their own family. When they cannot look upon their own cousins with respect, how will they respect other women? It is because of this that women were forced to kill themselves at the time of the partition.

*Q.  If a family can afford only one child's education, whom should it choose, the girl or the boy child?*

A.  It is important that both get basic education but as it is the man who must earn and support his family (while the woman manages the household), his education is more important. This division of labour is natural. [We were told that if a gun and a doll are placed before two children the male child will pick up the gun while the female will opt for the doll].

Q. *If a girl who is being married off by her family against her wishes, seeks help from the women's wing of the VHP, what advice will you give her?*

A. Though every woman wants to get married, she does not say so due to her cultural conditioning. Every father wishes to see his daughter married and hence be assured of social security.

Q. *What would you suggest in case she wishes to pursue her education?*

A. After marriage she will have many responsibilities in her new home. It is not advisable for her to bring disquiet by refusing to compromise. If ordained by her fate, her husband will permit her to study.

Q. *A girl may wish to marry a person her parents do not approve of . . .*

A. We try and explain to her that her parents have lived longer; they know what is best for her. We oppose a marriage only if there is a wide age gap between the bride and the groom. Earlier on, the child bride and groom grew up together, so there was no question of incompatibility. Late marriage leads to adjustment problems. However, in today's context, it [child marriage] is no longer legally acceptable.

Q. *What advice would you give to a victim of wife beating?*

A. Don't parents admonish their children for misbehaviour? Just as a child must adjust to his/her parents, so must a wife act keeping in mind her husband's moods and must avoid irritating him. Only this can keep the family together.

Q. *In spite of all adjustment, if the beating continues, how should the wife react, 'to keep the family together'?*

A. Ideally, if she learns to stifle her screams, the matter will remain within the four walls of the house. Otherwise every house will become a 'Mahabharat'. However, it she is persistently beaten for no particular reason, then she can take up the matter with her kith and kin (*biradari*); legal action should remain the last resort.

The family you are born into and the family you are married into are predestined. Just as you cannot change your parents you, also, cannot change your husband.

Q.  *But the legal system permits divorce. How do you react to that?*

A.  If a woman seeks divorce, we advise her to try to adjust, since a woman cannot remain single, when she remarries, she will face similar problems in her new home. Divorce, therefore, will not change her situation. Conciliation would be a better option, both for the woman and her children. Divorce can be considered only if every other option fails. Moreover, with deseases like AIDS monogamy is advisable for women.

Q.  *But there are preventive measures . . .*

A.  They are not foolproof. Moreover an Indian woman can attain true happiness only with one man.

Q.  *What are your views on polyandry?*

A.  Though it could be justified earlier as the sex ratio favoured women, times have changed. However, a man may remarry if he does not have any children by his first wife, provided she agrees.

Q.  *Can a woman remarry in a similar situation?*

A.  No, society will not allow it—neither will the man's ego permit it.

Q.  *In case a man remarries after an extramarital affair, what course of action would you suggest for the first wife?*

A.  Admittedly, it is a difficult situation for her, but she should try to accept it for the sake of the children, more so, if she is not financially independent.

All these problems arise because of westernisation. Even the West reveres Indian family life, but we are forgetting our roles as *janmatris* and *nirmatris*.

In the joint family system, the couple's interaction was limited and the attraction remained alive for years after the marriage. Now, with the western concept of honeymoon and nuclear family they grow weary of each other in no time, leading to various problems.

In the West, women don't hesitate to drag their own husbands to the court with allegations of rape.

Q. *What else can a victim of conjugal rape do?*

A. If a couple are married, how can you call it rape—this concept is alien to our culture. In any case, if a woman is physically and mentally strong, she can assert herself.

# Notes on Contributors

KUMKUM ROY is a historian who teaches at Satyawati College, Delhi University. She is currently a Commonwealth scholar based at the School of Oriental and African Studies, London.

PURSHOTTAM AGARWAL teaches Hindi at Jawaharlal Nehru University, Delhi. He has been involved in anti-communal work for many years.

URVASHI BUTALIA is a publisher, teacher and activist, involved in women's publishing and research and activism on gender issues.

TANIKA SARKAR is a historian who teaches at St Stephen's College, Delhi University. She is author of several books and articles on issues relating to gender and history.

RATNA KAPUR is an advocate, researcher and visiting faculty at the National Law School of India University, Bangalore.

BRENDA COSSMAN is Associate Professor at Osgoode Hall Law School, York University, Canada.

VASANTH KANNABIRAN is a poet, activist and researcher, involved particularly in exploring issues relating to violence and communalism. She works with Asmita Resource Centre for Women, Hyderabad.

KALPANA KANNABIRAN is a sociologist, activist and researcher. She works with Asmita Resource Centre for Women, Hyderabad.

V GEETHA is a writer and translator who writes on political and cultural matters pertaining to contemporary Tamil society. She works with Snehdi: Forum for Women, a support group for women victims of domestic violence.

T V JAYANTHI works in a private computer firm and is with Snehdi: Forum for Women, a support group for women victims of domestic violence.

AMRITA BASU is Professor of Political Science and Women's and Gender Studies at Amherst College, Massachussetts. She has written and published widely on women and is currently writing a book on Hindu nationalism in India.

SIKATA BANERJEE is with the Department of Political Science, University of Washington at Seattle.

TEESTA SETALVAD is a journalist and activist who has been deeply involved in anti-communal work in Bombay. She is also co-editor of a monthly newsmagazine, *Communalism Combat*.

ZAKIA PATHAK has taught in the Department of English at Miranda House, Delhi University. She has also been in professional social work, and has published widely on gender in journals and newspapers at home and abroad.

SASWATI SENGUPTA teaches English at Miranda House, Delhi University.

FLAVIA AGNES is a lawyer and activist. She has been involved in the women's movement for over two decades and has written and published widely on issues related to it.

S ANITHA is a student of political science at Jawaharlal Nehru University Delhi, MANISHA, VASUDHA and KAVITHA are students at a south Delhi college.

THE ALL INDIA DEMOCRATIC WOMEN'S ASSOCIATION is affiliated to the Communist Party of India (Marxist), the CENTRE FOR WOMEN'S DEVELOPMENT STUDIES is a research institute in Delhi, the MAHILA DAKSHATA SAMITI is affiliated to the JANATA PARTY and the NATIONAL FEDERATION OF INDIAN WOMEN is the women's wing of the Communist Party of India.

# Index

Abraham, Ammu 244n.6
Adoption 146
Advani, L.K. 242
Aggarwal, Purushottam 6, 29, 75
Agnes, Flavia 7, 136, 227
Rangnekar, Ahilya 151
Ahmed, Aijaz 60
Ambedkar B.R. 45
Anti-Mandal agitation 270, 280
Asaf Ali, Aruna 240
*Awaz e Nisvan* 227, 229
Ayodhya 190, 207, 247, 259, 265, 301
    *see also* Babri Masjid; December 6
    1992; Ramjanmabhoomi

Babri Masjid 12, 77, 136, 141-42, 147-
    48, 163, 169-70, 189, 209, *see also*
    December 6 1992;
    Ramjanmabhoomi
Bachetta, Paola 80n.16
Banerjee, Sikata 7, 216
Bano, Shah 83,101-02, 142, 151, 238
    *see* Divorce
Basu, Amrita 7, 158
Bharati, Uma 7, 33, 53, 97, 147, 151,
    158-79, 193, 225
Bhasin, Kamla 80n.1
BJP (Bharatiya Janata Party) 35, 85,
    89, 92, 95, 97-102, 104, 134, and
    *passim*
Buddhists 44
Butalia, Urvashi 1, 38, 58

Chandra, Sudhir 33
Chhachhi, Amrita 103, 105, 113n.6
Chikalia, Deepika 174
Chinmayanand, Swami 33
Chipko Movement 159
Churi, Sudha 238, 241
Communalism, 32, 60, 88, 137, 150,
    151, 158, 171, 180n.1, 198, 204,
    226, 300, 302, 317, 319; and
    impact on women, 121; and the
    Hindu right, 84; and violence,
    77, 198, 216, 306, 308, 314, 316,
    323; the internal enemy 44, 46;
    religious fundamentalism and,
    170-71,176
Cossman, Brenda 8, 82

Dalits 123, 133, 261
Das, Veena 80n.1
Datta, Madhusree 226
December 6, 1992 5, 233, 235, 254 *see
    also* Ayodhya; Babri Masjid
Desai, A.R. 126; Ramjanmabhoomi
Deshpande, G.P. 33, 34
Divorce 142, 145, 155n.16, 208, 212,
    334
Dowry 208, 212, 236, 238-39, 329
Dravidianism 255-56, 258, 260-62,
    266
Durga 270-71, 287, 290
Durga Vahini (VHP) 151, 161, 169,
    196, 234-35, 253, 267n.8,

Feminism 218, 224-27, 236-37, 239, 253, 284-85

Gandhi, Indira 175
Gandhi, M.K. (Mahatma) 133, 170, 175
Garg, Mohini 173
Geetha, V. 9, 245
Golwalkar, M.S. 96, 185, 187, 188-89, 197, 202-03, 206
Godbole, S.T. 41

Hedgewar, Keshav Baliram 183, 185, 203
Hindu rashtra 84-85, 91-92, 141, 161, 167, 171, 198, 201, 212, 223, 236
Hindu right 84-85, 86, 90, 92, 96, 102, 106-07, 110-12, 252 *see also* Hindutva
Hindu nationalism 158, 164, 169-70, 174-76, 178, 223
Hindu man: lust and cowardice of 204; virtue and misplaced chivalry of 38, 47-48, 50, 254; passivity 38, 42; politics of case 248
Hindutva 1, 3, 4, 10, 21, 27, 34, 41, 82, 83, 96, 102, 105, 107-108, 110, 111, 113n.3, 117n.42, 159, 160, 169, 181 190 and *passim*; and patriotism, 45; anti-Christian element of, 254-55; anti-Muslim element of, 255; women and, 181, 205, 245-47
Hindu woman 59, 75, 79, 84, 97, 102, 104-08,140, 163, 185, 187, 219, 224, 227, 234, 271
Holkar, Ahilyabai 330
Husain, Nafisa 242

Jain, J.K. 192
Jayalalitha 258-62, 265-66, 269n.70; and Draupadi 263, 264
Jayanthi, T.V. 9, 245
Jhabvala, Ruth Prawer 123
Jhansi, Rani 193, 224, 253
Jijabai 253

Josh, Bhagwan 37, 43
Joshi, M.M. 171

Kakar, Sudhir 36
Kannabiran, Vasanth 121
Kannabiran, Kalpana 121
Kanwar, Roop, 83, 104, 168, 330 *see* Sati
Kapur, Ratna 8, 82
Katyar, Vinay 33, 41
Keer, Dhananjaya 43
Kelkar, Lakshmibai 183, 186, 203, 204
Kidwai, Anis 62
Kohli, Atul 220
Kumar, Radha 3
Kunzru, Pandit Hriday Nath 72

Lakshmibai, Rani 330
Law 83, 86, 87, 104, 112
Lesbianism 99

Mahabharat 72-73
*Mahaloya* 270-71, 287, 290-91
Mahila Morcha (BJP) 97, 98, 103-05, 146-47, 161, 169, 171-73, 235-36, 240, 329
Mahila Aghadi (Women Shiv Sainiks) 233-34, 236, 238-41, 243
*Majlis* 227,229
Malkani, K.R. 173
*Manusmrti* 11 14, 16-27
Mass violence 122, 124, 138, 181, 198, 220, 217, 322;   *see also* riots; feminisation of, 217-32
MCR (Mandal Commission Report) 272, 276, 286
Mehta, Jaywanti 239, 240, 243
Menon, Ritu 80n.1
Morgan, Robin 219
Motilal, Kamla 249-50, 255
Myths 163, 283, 286, 288, 292

Nadars 248, 267 n.5
Naidu, Sarojini 240
Narayan, Prabha 240
Nasreen, Tasleema 134

Padmini 36, 55n.2, 62, 67
Pant, Ila 240
Partition the 58, 60-61,78,136, 253
Patel, Kamlaben 61
Pathak, Zakia 8, 270
Pawar, Sharad 221
Periyar, E.V.R. 258, 260, 267n.7

Raje, Vasundhara 167
Ramaswamy, Sumati 75
Ramayan 72-73
Ramjanmabhoomi 7, 97, 159, 173,
    182, 189, 190-91, 209, 211, 213,
    *see also* December 6, 1992; Babri
    Masjid; Ayodhya
Rape: 30-31, 43, 59, 74, 124, 133, 151,
    165, 166, 204, 236, 256,263, 300,
    332, 335 and morality 32, 52; and
    taboos, 29, 59; and sexual assault,
    138, 284, 315; as a political act,
    31, 39, 79, 307; as a weapon, 54,
    179; conjugal, 335;implicit
    approval of, 31, 39; of minorities,
    122, 179, 315, 322; outrage
    against, 166, 239
Riots 301, 317, 321, 328;
    Ahmedabad, 302-03, 317, 321;
    Bhopal; 190, 306, 313-14;
    Bhagalpur, 77-78, 79; Bombay,
    30 77, 79, 130, 131, 136, 153, 216,
    233-34, 79, 130, 131, 136, 153,
    216, 233-34; compensation, 303,
    304, 316, 319; Surat,30-31, 77-79,
    190, 300-03, 305-06, 322, 328;
    victims of 299
Rithambara, Sadhvi 7, 33, 53, 151,
    158-59, 161-67, 170, 173, 176, 179,
    188, 193-94, 225, 234
Roy, Kumkum 6, 10, 75
RSS (Rashtriya Swayamsevak
    Sangh) 1, 12, 59, 80, 85, 89, 90, 91,
    and *passim*

Sahgal, Damyanti 62
Samiti (Rashtra Sevika Samiti) 147,
    161, 184-86, 188, 196-207, and
    *passim*

Samrat, Ashok 44
Sarabhai, Mridula 62
Saraswati, Dayanand 34
Sarkar, Tanika 1, 132, 181, 222, 245
Sati 104, 120n.70, 168, 207, 212, 242,
    330. *See also* Kanwar, Roop
Savarkar, Vir 33, 35, 39, 40, 42, 45,
    49, 52, 185
Savitri 55n.3
Scindia, Vijayaraje 7, 97, 143, 158-59,
    161-62, 164, 167, 169-71,
Secularism 82, 84, 86-92, 95, 108-10,
    114n.12, 116n.24,
Sengupta, Saswati 8, 270
Seshadri, Girija 250-52, 255
Seshadri, H.V. 96
Setalvad, Teesta 7, 233
Sexuality 26, 29-30, 44, 103, 146,
    268n.14,15 and the Hindu
    woman 60, 256, 293; Draupadi's
    39, 54, 55, 263; in the Hindu-
    Muslim relationship 35, 37, 185,
    191; Sociology of   49
Shaikh, Shenaz 227
Sharma, Krishna 329
Sharma, Asha 329
Shiv Sena 140-41, 155n.12, 216, 218,
    220, 222-30, 230n.11
Shivaji 50, 51
Singh, V.P. 175, 272
Singh, Bhagat 193
Sita 55n.3, 67, 72, 106, 174, 191, 208,
    213, 332
Sinha, Mridula 98, 146, 172, 242, 329
Swaraj, Sushma 240

Thackeray, Bal 242
Thapar, Romila 130
The internal enemy 44, 46
Tamil Nadu, castes in 255, 256, 257,
    258, 260, 261, 262, 266, 268 n.16
Thevars 248, 267 n.5 Grounders, 248;
    Nadars 248, 267n.S

Uniform Civil Code 141, 146, 153,
    155n.14, 172, 176, 238, 242;
    obscenity, and 141

Upadhyaya, K. 240

Vajpayee, A.B. 171, 173
*Vedas* 11, 13-14, 18, 25
VHP (Vishwa Hindu Parishad) 3, 76,
    77, 113n.5, 160, 173, 192, and
    *passim*
Vivekananda 38

Women: abducted, 63-65, 73-74, 76;
    and literacy, 99; and equality, 82-
    84, 92-95, 101, 108, 110; as

symbols, 38, 49; 130, 295; as
workers, 223; as warriors, 289; as
wives, 223, 252, 289; and
celibacy, 161; and destitution, 59;
martyrdom of, 195; of minority
groups, 122, 123, 302; rehabilitation 63, 309, 311, 316; repatria-
tion of 71, 78; stereotype of the
good, 283; violence against, 77,
149, 150, 164-65, 173, 300, 333 *see
also* rape; widows 59, 302